W9-BYN-925

About the Underground Guide Series

Welcome to the underground!

Are you tired of all the fluff—books that tell you what you already know, ones that assume you're an idiot and treat you accordingly, or dwell on the trivial while completely ignoring the tough parts?

Good. You're in the right place.

Series Editor Woody Leonhard and Addison-Wesley bring you the Underground Guides—serious books that tackle the tough questions head-on but still manage to keep a sense of humor (not to mention a sense of perspective!). Every page is chock full of ideas you can put to use right away. We'll tell you what works and what doesn't—no bull, no pulled punches. We don't kowtow to the gods of the industry, we won't waste your time or your money, and we *will* treat you like the intelligent computer user we know you are.

Each Underground Guide is written by somebody who's been there—a working stiff who's suffered through the problems you're up against right now—and lived to tell about it. You're going to strike a rich vein of hard truth in these pages, and come away with a wealth of information you can put to use all day, every day.

So come along as we go spelunking where no book has gone before. Mind your head, and don't step in anything squishy. There will be lots of unexpected twists and turns . . . and maybe a laugh or two along the way.

The Underground Guide Series

Woody Leonhard, Series Editor

The Underground Guide to

Windows™ 95

Slightly

Askew

Advice

from a

Windows

Wizard

Scot Finnie

Series Editor Woody Leonhard

ADDISON-WESLEY PUBLISHING COMPANY

Reading, Massachusetts • Menlo Park, California • New York • Don Mills, Ontario
Harlow, England • Amsterdam • Bonn • Sydney • Singapore • Tokyo
Madrid • San Juan • Paris • Seoul • Milan • Mexico City • Taipei

Many of the designations used by manufacturers and sellers to distinguish their products are claimed as trademarks. Where those designations appear in this book, and Addison-Wesley was aware of a trademark claim, the designations have been printed in initial capital letters or all capital letters.

The author and publisher have taken care in preparation of this book, but make no expressed or implied warranty of any kind and assume no responsibility for errors or omissions. No liability is assumed for incidental or consequential damages in connection with or arising out of the use of the information or programs contained herein.

Library of Congress Cataloging-in-Publication Data

Finnie, Scot.
  The underground guide to Windows 95 : slightly askew advice from a
Windows wizard / Scot Finnie.
    p.   cm. — (Underground guide series)
  Includes index.
  ISBN 0-201-40652-7
  1. Microsoft Windows (Computer file) 2. Operating systems
(Computers)   I. Title. II. Series.
QA76.76.O63F565   1996
005.4'469—dc20   95-54161
                                                  CIP

Sponsoring Editor: Kathleen Tibbetts
Project Manager: Sarah Weaver
Production Coordinator: Erin Sweeney
Cover design: Jean Seal
Text design: Kenneth L. Wilson, Wilson Graphics & Design
Set in 10 point Palatino by Pre-Press Company, Inc.

1 2 3 4 5 6 7 8 9 -MA- 0099989796
First printing, March 1996

Addison-Wesley books are available for bulk purchases by corporations, institutions, and other organizations. For more information please contact the Corporate, Government, and Special Sales Department at (800) 238-9682.

Find us on the World-Wide Web at:
http://www.aw.com/devpress/

Dedication

To the memory of my good friend, colleague, and partner in Windows crime, Dale Lewallen. There's stuff in here that sprang from his incredibly agile mind. Windows 95 is about half of what we dreamed about many a late night as we feverishly planned the future of computing. But Dale would have liked it nonetheless. I miss you, man.

To Cyndy, who stuck by me through two of the longest years of my life (and hers) during the research and writing of this book.

To the many folks who helped me along the way, especially Addison-Wesley Series Editor and amazing guy, Woody Leonhard, and Addison-Wesley book editor extraordinaire, Kathleen Tibbetts. Thanks also to Scott Arpajian, Paul Bonner, Ed Bott, Jackie Gavron, Preston Gralla, Yael Li-Ron, Jim Louderback, Ed Passarella, Greg Pastrick, Enrique Salem, Gina Smith, Erin Sweeney, Wendy Taylor, John Teddy, Sarah Weaver, and my tech editor, Eileen Wharmby.

Most of all, this book is dedicated to my son Brian, whom I love dearly, and to Dale's daughter Kira. I suspect they may some day regard Windows 95 in passing and wonder what all the fuss was about.

Contents

Foreword

What, *another* Windows 95 book?

Well, this one is different.

In this Underground Guide, Windows maven Scot Finnie explains what's *really* going on in Win 95. From the Start button to the Control Panel, from the Registry to the dial-up "connectoids," Scot brings you real-world tips and advice that could only come from somebody who's plunged into the depths of Windows 95. Where other Windows 95 books start sounding like the script to a "Stupid PC Pet Tricks" episode, Scot heaps on mounds of nitty gritty know-how, the likes of which you won't find anywhere else.

Based on the actual, shipping Windows 95 (as opposed to early beta test versions, which drove almost every other book you see on the shelves), this Underground Guide gives you the straight story on what works, what doesn't, which tricks pay off big time, and which aren't worth your time. Scot will steer you around the land mines, take you through the major attractions, and save you hours and hours of frustration along the way.

Think of *The Underground Guide to Windows 95* as the real Windows 95 User's Manual, via the School of Hard Knocks.

Woody Leonhard
Series Hack

Author's Note

It's in your hands, and there has to be a reason. I can tell you this much: You don't have to brand yourself a "dummy," be a certified (certifiable?) Windows wizard, or in any way label yourself to make this book your armchair advisor. *The Underground Guide to Windows 95* was written for people, not demographics.

It was also written entirely from the "shipping" version of Microsoft® Windows 95™, unlike many other Win 95 books, which were written from buggy pre-release code so they could sprout up on store shelves around the time the operating system did.

I don't pull punches. There are great things and silly things about Windows 95. I tell you about both: how to take advantage of the good stuff and how to mix in a little wizardry to bypass what's a tad confused.

Windows 95 is a better place to be once you get to the other side of the installation, figure out how things work, and finish monkeying around with the doodads. This book gets you through all that with a minimum of head scratching and hair pulling. Maybe you're beyond that already and what you really want is to make this thing work for you—instead of vice versa. Great, because that's what this book does best.

Buying and reading a book like this one is a little like stopping at a gas station to ask for directions. Maybe you don't want to do it. But you've got to admit, it's usually the shortest distance between two points. Give me a little time, and I'll show you how to master Windows 95.

Decided? I thought so. You're about to become a Windows 95 expert. And have a little fun doing it. Next thing you know, I'll be buying *your* book.

Scot Finnie
Cambridge, Massachusetts

1 First Things First

The last thing one discovers in composing a work is what to put first.

Blaise Pascal
Pensées, 1670

When I was a teenager, long before personal computers were even a gleam in some electronic engineer's eye, I began my apprenticeship for this whole computing thing with a pile of second-hand metric tools, my girlfriend's garage, three or four 1950s and early 1960s vintage VW Beetles, and a very special spiral-bound book called *How to Keep Your Volkswagen Alive*, by John Muir.

Muir's book was steeped in 60s vernacular and culture. He pretty much expected everyone reading the book to have at least shoulder-length hair, and he was forever telling us to tie it back whenever we were about to undertake some operation like pressing one end of a wooden stick to one side of an ear and the other end to the engine block while the motor was running to listen for potentially ominous sounds. You couldn't learn Muir's tricks in auto shop, let me tell you. His book became my bible. I read it over and over again. And I fixed up a lot of Volkswagens. Later I even worked as a mechanic for a while.

Somewhere along the way, though, I hung up the box-end wrenches, the Go-Jo, and even Muir's book in favor of the first Norton Utilities and the DOS manual. Thing is, it really wasn't much different in the early days of PCs. The big difference seemed to be that you didn't have to scrub up afterwards. Windows 95, however, is a whole different kettle of fish. Unlike the cars of the 1990s, it's designed to put many of its controls and adjustments right in users' hands. You don't need special tools to make it go. All you need is a little knowledge and the willingness to stick your hands in now and then.

I hung up my tools for Norton Utilities and the DOS manual.

You know what? That's a very satisfying experience. Most of us are held hostage by the specialists in our lives. The experts. They have us over a barrel. The doctors, lawyers, auto mechanics, plumbers, and so on, because they have knowledge we don't have. That isn't a bad thing. But every now and then, it's a good feeling to do it yourself. In fact, the entire personal computer revolution was

1

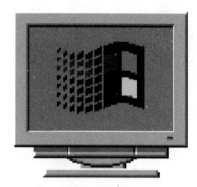

Figure 1.1 Unwarranted Microsoft art: This is your PC on Windows 95

based on this idea—that one person, and one machine, could do great things together.

There's nothing wrong with just diving in and trying something.

OK, so we're past the revolution stage. I guess you can read that gleam in my eyes. The point is, it's very satisfying to take control of your PC. The biggest problem with computers is that they tend to belittle us, if we let them. They make us feel humble because of the misperception that they're infallible and that anything that goes wrong is something we did. The fact is, the opposite is usually true. Anything that can go wrong with a PC, usually does—and through no fault of yours or mine. Read this book with an open mind, with the sense that you can make it happen, that a little knowledge goes a long way, and that there's nothing wrong with just diving in and trying something. Because that's really all it takes to master Windows 95.

Get Oriented

First things first. The point of this chapter is to get you properly oriented to this book and to Windows 95. And to demystify the hype on both sides of the aisle surrounding the operating system.

I'll start with some of the customs I've adopted to explain stuff. Windows 95 is filled with multilevel menus and dialogs. You know, open this, then click that button, and then open the next thing. To save time and cut down on wordiness, I adopted a convention of slashes (/) to separate commands in a string. The types of commands between the slashes in a phrase like

```
Open First This / Next That / Then the Other Thing
```

can vary quite a bit. They may pertain to menu items, tabs, folders, buttons, or selections in a dialog. But don't let that throw you. It really doesn't matter how Microsoft chose to present choices at each step. What matters is that the words between the slashes precisely match the labels you'll find on things at each turning point. And they do.

Buzzwords are the bane of any computer book. I've worked pretty hard to eliminate them when I could and point them out to you when I couldn't. Since acronyms are a fact of life—and since the help you get from Microsoft in documents, online, or other sources will very likely be seasoned with them—I've left them in and just explained them on first mention. To a certain extent, verbal shorthand like *OS* (for operating system) and *app* (for application) help to make the repetition of these terms easier to read.

There are two recurring symbols in this book: the Wand and the Bug, both shown in Figure 1.2. I hope they are self-explanatory. The Wand probably is. It denotes a tip or shortcut that you're definitely going to want to know about. Rather than leave those nuggets buried within the rest of the text, I pulled them out so that you could find 'em easier. The Bug is a bit less specific. It's a warning about something. That something could be a bug in Windows 95. It could be an annoying feature that might as well be a bug. It could be a limitation of the operating system. Or it could just be something that deserves a little . . . uh, negative attention.

Figure 1.2   The *Underground Guide's* Wand and Bug symbols

How This Book Is Organized

There really is a sense of order here. Promise. The first four chapters cover the stuff that anyone who uses Windows 95 is going to bump into sooner or later. Chapter 5 aims to up the ante on the first four chapters. Chapters 6–8 cover mobile computing, getting connected to the Internet, and networking, respectively. More than likely, at least one of those chapters will help you do something extra with Windows 95 that you want to do. The last chapter applies to everyone, while the Appendix is, I hope, similarly useful to all.

The Truth about Win 95 System Requirements

What do you need to run Windows 95? Well, there's hardware and software. There's also Microsoft's version of this story, and then there's mine.

Add New
Hardware

According to Microsoft, Windows 95 will run on a 386DX or better PC with 4MB of RAM, a plain-vanilla VGA video card and display, 35–40MB of free storage space on the hard drive, either a 1.44MB 3½-inch floppy drive or CD drive, and a mouse.

Get real. Win 95 bogs down on a 486DX/33. The real minimum system requirements are a 486DX2/50 CPU with no less than 8MB of RAM, a SuperVGA video card with, at the very least, 512K of VRAM and matching 14-inch or larger display, at least 60MB of free hard disk space, either a 1.44MB 3½-inch floppy drive or CD drive, and a mouse. Even with this configuration, though, you're going to be limping.

The truth about the RAM question is just this: Windows 95 runs a bit faster on lesser CPU PCs than the old Windows did. But it runs applications slower. And that's not a good trade-off. Even in 8MB of RAM, with all the stuff Win 95 loads into *protected* (over 1MB) memory, and the fact that its task-switching interface will tempt you to run more apps simultaneously, and because it's designed to run both 16-bit (Windows 3.*x*) and 32-bit (Windows NT and Windows 95) applications—you're going to run out of RAM fast. Windows 95 is a far more complex OS than the old Windows. Keep that in mind. As the complexity travels up the scale, the demands of your hardware also increase. So, don't skimp on RAM.

How to smile when you start your Win 95 PC

If you want to smile when you start your Win 95 PC, you should be able to say all these things (or better) about it: It has at least a 486DX4/100 CPU (Pentium 75 or higher preferred), 16MB of RAM, a 520MB or larger hard drive, 16-bit sound card, at least a double-speed CD drive, local-bus SuperVGA card with at least 1MB of VRAM and a graphics accelerator, a 15-inch or larger display capable of supporting 1024 × 768-pixel resolution, a 1.44MB 3½-inch floppy drive, and a mouse. If you're buying a new PC, add these things to the consideration list: A Plug and Play BIOS, Enhanced IDE or SCSI disk controller (preferably on PCI local bus), 2MB of RAM on the video card, at least a 17-inch display, flash BIOS, and a Windows 95–compatible keyboard.

Three Flavors of Win 95

Windows 95 comes in three flavors. This can be confusing, but let's straighten it out. By far the most popular, and the one you should absolutely get if you have a CD drive, is the Upgrade CD version. On the box in the fine print beside the barcode you should see "Update Windows 95 (CDROM)." This version presupposes that you have DOS 3.2 or better installed on your PC. It will also upgrade Windows 3.0 or better. The point is, you don't have to have Windows installed already to "upgrade" to Windows 95. Your hard drive just has to be able to boot to a DOS command prompt. If you think the DOS on your PC is older than DOS 3.2, trust me, you're going to have to upgrade your hardware anyway. But, to find out, boot to the DOS prompt, type VER on the command line, and press Enter. DOS will respond with its version number.

The second flavor is the floppy disk–based Upgrade version. It has the same requirements of the existing OS on your PC and costs the same $89 or so on the street as the Upgrade CD version. There's a very big difference, though. A whole lot of the extras and niceties have been left off the floppy version. If you can possibly swing the CD version, do (and see Chapter 6, "The Mobile Win 95," for pointers on how to do that).

The third flavor is tougher to find and costs twice as much as the other two. It's also floppy disk-based. But it is very different from the second flavor in that it's the full installation version, designed to be used on a PC that doesn't have DOS 3.2 or better already installed on it. Forget this. It's both cheaper and easier in the long run to buy the CD Upgrade version and the latest version of DOS 6.*x* if you don't have DOS on your PC. Just install DOS 6 and then use the Windows 95 CD to upgrade.

Version Control

What version of Windows 95 do you have? Microsoft has publicly said that it will issue regular updates of Windows 95 (on something like a quarterly basis) to fix bugs and probably to add tweaks and drivers and stuff like that. This book was written from the 4.00.950 version of Windows 95, the first one Microsoft released to stores around the world.

System

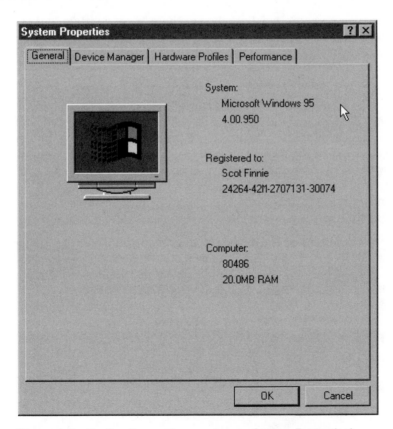

Figure 1.3 Finding the version number on System Properties' General tab

To find out what version you've got, open the Control Panel (Start/ Settings/Control Panel) and double-click the System icon. When System opens, it'll read "System Properties" in the title bar, and you'll be looking at the four-tab dialog shown in Figure 1.3 (tabs are those labels along the top that you can click to change the contents of the screen). General is the tab that's on top, with its contents visible, when you first open System. And it's the right one to check for your version. In the upper right corner, under the heading System, you'll see

```
Microsoft Windows 95
4.00.950
```

If the number on the second line is different than the one shown here, you have a newer version of the operating system. Rejoice. Because that means that, with luck, there're at least a couple hundred fewer little bugs you might encounter on future dark nights.

Microsoft has released some "bug fix" updates to Windows 95. For the most part they're aimed at network installations, but there are one or two that are generally useful. Plus who knows what else they'll fix next week. If you have Internet access, you can download them from Microsoft's Web site at this Internet address (URL):

```
http://www.microsoft.com/windows/software/updates.htm.
```

Speaking of bugs, want to be a Win 95 insider? Well, then you have to know how to execute the official Windows 95 animated credit-screen Easter Egg, which is shown in Figure 1.4. An Easter Egg is something a programmer inserts in the code of the product that hackers like us go searching for. Hence the name. Anyway, this giant Easter Egg with names flying against the insidious blue-sky background set to music is something you'll want to do, well . . . once. Here's how.

Right-click anywhere on the desktop background color. From the popup menu, choose New/Folder. You're going to rename this folder three times in a row. Make sure you type the folder names exactly as I've shown them below. Rename the "New Folder" folder by typing

```
and now, the moment you've all been waiting for
```

Press Enter. Now Press F2 and type

```
we proudly present for your viewing pleasure
```

Press Enter. Now Press F2 and type

```
The Microsoft Windows 95 Product Team!
```

Press Enter. You didn't forget the exclamation point, did you? To launch the Easter Egg, just double-click the folder.

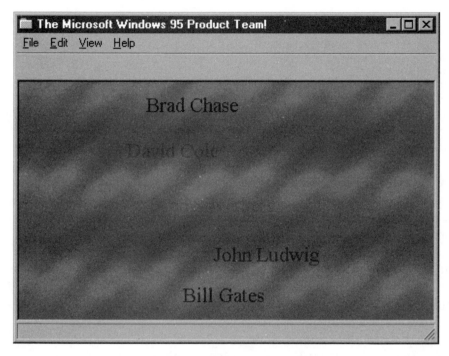

Figure 1.4 The official Win 95 credit-screen Easter Egg

What Drive, What Folder?

Please note that this book makes an assumption throughout, based on the Win 95 Setup default, that you have or will install Win 95 on your C: drive in the C:\WINDOWS directory (or folder). It is possible, and in fact is preferable in some instances, to install Windows 95 in a folder with a different name or on a different hard drive. If that's the case for you, just substitute the drive letter and/or name of your Win 95 main folder for any instances in this book where I refer to C:\WINDOWS or the Windows folder.

HEADS UP!

> No illusion is more crucial than the illusion that great success and huge money buy you immunity from the common ills of mankind, such as cars that won't start.
>
> Larry McMurtry
> Danny Deck, in *Some Can Whistle*, 1989

If you're brand new to Windows 95 at this moment (you won't be for long, don't worry), touch down right here and now, OK? This part is like a Quick Start card for the completely new and uncorrupted. Even if you've been using

This part is a Quick Start for the new and uncorrupted.

Win 95 for a while, this stuff may be illuminating, especially if you used the old Windows.

Installation

Setup

Installing Win 95 is way different than installing any other mainstream PC operating system. The closest cousin to it would be OS/2 Warp's installation. Among other things, Windows 95 runs a hardware detection sequence that tries very hard to identify most of the hardware components in your PC. Once it identifies a specific manufacture and model of hardware, it installs a Windows 95 driver for it using the default interrupt request and input/output range settings for the card. If the settings on your cards and other hardware were changed when your PC was manufactured or if stuff was added later that conflicted and so had to be changed, you could be in for some trouble.

Now, if you have fully Plug and Play hardware (PnP), Windows 95 can change the settings automatically if they conflict. But it's unlikely that each and every hardware component in your PC is PnP compatible. If purchased recently, you hopefully have a PnP BIOS. But the ideal of Plug and Play—to make a Windows 95 that is completely automatic in both its hardware detection and configuration—is still a long way away.

The installation departs from what you might expect in other ways. There are a lot of options to choose from. One of them you should be aware of is Save System Files, snapped for you in Figure 1.5. This little euphemism means: Make it possible to completely uninstall Windows 95 and return me back to my previous Windows installation. For first-time installs, I highly recommend choosing "yes" on this screen. There are times when being able to revert to your previous Windows installation, make changes there, and then reinstall Windows 95 can be a real advantage.

Startup and Shut Down

Shut Down...

Even the terms have changed—for the better. I'm talking about launching and exiting Windows. Here's the deal. When you turn on your Windows 95 PC, you're not going to stop at a DOS prompt first and type WIN to launch Windows. Windows 95 starts its graphical self by default. By and large, that's a good thing because it saves memory—believe it or not. That's because Windows 95 loads *virtual device drivers* (VxDs) for most hardware up in high memory, amidst all those megabytes we've got that most of us could never make much use of under the old DOS and Windows. As a result, it makes sense to get there as fast as you can when you turn on your PC and to not even load the *real-mode* DOS .SYS and .EXE file drivers (most of which Windows 95 disables). If you always start in Windows 95 and spend very little time in DOS, you're not going to need the

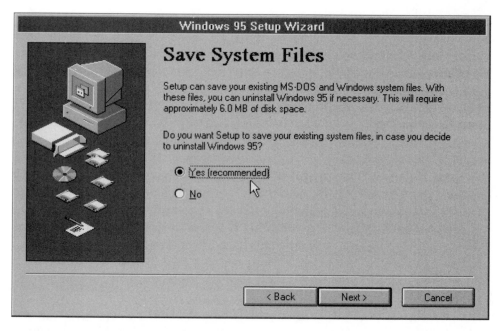

Figure 1.5 Setup's Save System Files option

real-mode drivers. And they're just taking up memory. The VxDs are also much faster than the real-mode drivers.

Exiting Windows 95 is quite a bit different, too. There's some stuff you need to understand. Depending on system configuration, you have three to five Shut Down options. You bring up the screen shown in Figure 1.6 by clicking the Start button and choosing the first option on the Start Menu, which is, not surprisingly, labeled "Shut Down."

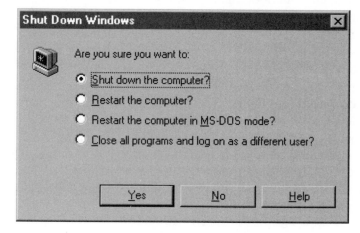

Figure 1.6 The Shut Down Windows dialog

Shut Down is just what it sounds like: preparing to turn off the PC.

The most common options in the Shut Down Windows dialog are "Shut down the computer," "Restart the computer," "Restart the computer in MS-DOS mode," and "Close all programs and log on as a different user." Because it's simply explained, I'll start with the last one first, and get it out of the way. "Close all programs and log on as a different user" will appear only if you're on a network. Its whole reason for being is to make it easier for people to share a PC. "Shut down the computer" is just what it sounds like. It prepares the computer to be turned off. When Windows 95 has finished getting things in order in preparation for you to hit the off button, you'll see a black screen with jumbo yellow-orange characters that read: "It's now safe to turn off your computer." Do yourself a big favor and don't turn off the PC before you see this screen.

Restart is like pressing Ctrl-Alt-Delete, or hitting Reset.

"Restart the computer" is the same idea as pressing Ctrl-Alt-Delete or hitting the Reset button. The slang term for this is *warm booting*. It can be useful when you make a system configuration change. Its chief advantage is that it's faster than a *cold boot*, i.e., the kind for which you turn off the power. The difference between cold booting and warm booting is pretty esoteric. Suffice it to say, if you're planning to turn off your PC, choose "Shut down the computer." Also choose it if you're having any problem whatsoever with your PC and are hoping that exiting and restarting will help. If you're in a hurry, you plan to keep working, and you've just made a configuration change or something, choose "Restart the computer."

If after you choose "Shut down the computer" you get to the "It's now safe . . ." screen and realize that you don't want or need to sit through a cold reboot, you can just press Ctrl-Alt-Delete to force a warm reboot.

The Lowdown on DOS

DOS hasn't disappeared from underneath Windows 95.

A lot of people get confused about the Shut Down option "Restart the computer in MS-DOS mode." Understand this: Despite Microsoft hype to the contrary, DOS hasn't disappeared from underneath Windows 95. Microsoft doesn't really want you to know that underneath Win 95 there's a new DOS—DOS 7. DOS is far more tightly integrated into Windows than it ever was. Microsoft says they've placed some pieces of the DOS kernel into the Windows 95 code. Effectively, they've *virtualized* some aspects of DOS, that is, made it a part of Windows 95.

MS-DOS Prompt

Anyway, when you choose the Shut Down option, you're exiting Windows to the DOS command line. Before you happily run off with that knowledge, however, note these important caveats. Unless you want to run a DOS application that absolutely must wrest control from Windows (and if you do, see the next wand tip), odds are you're better off *shelling out* to DOS, that is, opening a DOS window from within Windows. To do that, click the Start button, choose the Programs menu item, and then choose the MS-DOS Prompt entry on the Programs menu. A window will open on your screen that is DOS within Windows. Now, if you used the old Windows, you're probably rolling your eyes right now. The process of shelling out to DOS under Windows 3.*x* was notoriously unstable, slow, and resource intensive. Moreover, many programs refused to run shelled to DOS. There was really no point to shelling out, except for a quick nip out to create a directory or something.

So why should you run a DOS window under Win 95? Well, for one thing, when you exit to DOS, you're going to have to load those real-mode drivers. By contrast, when you open a DOS window, all the VxDs that Windows 95 loads are still in effect. That's true of a lot of other services, too: networking, long filename support in DOS, and memory management (which is the biggie).

When you open a DOS window, VxDs are still in effect.

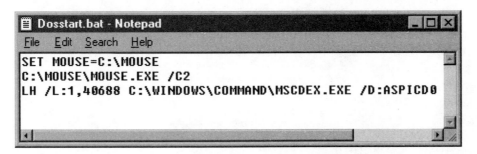

Figure 1.7   The DOSSTART.BAT file, which lives in the Windows 95 folder

There's an easy way to load any such drivers that might have been in your AU-TOEXEC.BAT **file before you upgraded to Win 95. Check out the** DOSSTART.BAT **file in your Windows folder (it looks something like Figure 1.7). Windows runs this file when you choose the restart in MS-DOS mode option. You can edit the file to your heart's content. For example, for newer DOS games, you might want to add your real-mode mouse driver in** DOSSTART.BAT.

But for any .SYS **device drivers meant to load in DOS's** CONFIG.SYS **file, you have a wholly different path. You can adjust some** CONFIG.SYS **and** AU-TOEXEC.BAT **settings for MS-DOS mode from the Properties screen of any individual DOS program. To do that, right-click the DOS program in a Windows folder. Choose Properties from the popup menu. Click the Program tab on the five-tab Properties screen. Then click the Advanced button. The result is the Advanced Program Settings screen (check Figure 1.8). By clicking the check box beside the MS-DOS mode line, you'll enable automatic entry into MS-DOS mode (the same as "Restart the computer in MS-DOS mode" on the Shut Down screen) any time the program is launched from Windows. Behind the Configuration button, there's a dialog that lets you add other lines that'll load into memory when you restart.**

Notice that the top line of the Advanced Program Settings dialog has an entry described as "Prevent MS-DOS-based programs from detecting Windows." This is very useful for forcing programs designed around Windows 3.*x*'s shelled DOS limitations. Many DOS programs were purposely written not to run in a DOS window from the old Windows in order to prevent performance erosion and out-of-memory errors.

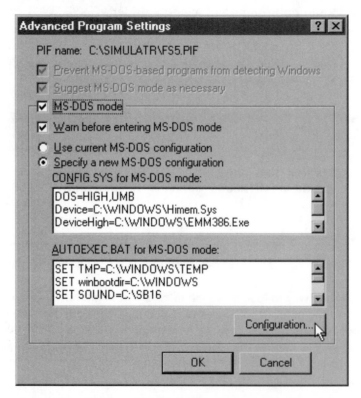

Figure 1.8   Advanced Program Settings for any DOS program

If you choose "Restart the computer in MS-DOS mode," do not, I mean DO NOT, launch Windows thereafter by typing win. This is especially true if you've modified the DOSSTART.BAT file, because you'll end up running unneeded real-mode drivers underneath the VxDs. This will have an impact on system resources and could affect performance. You may encounter other difficulties, as well. You have to retrain yourself to Ctrl-Alt-Delete or hit the Reset button to get into Windows once you've exited to the command line. Or, type exit from the DOS command line to return to Windows.

Shelling out to DOS is a much better experience under Windows 95 than it ever was in previous Windows versions. Let me put it this way. You can install a program like Microsoft's Flight Simulator 5.0 from a Win 95 DOS window.

Windows 95 doesn't extend the degree of control over shelled DOS programs that OS/2 does. But the amount of control is a whole lot better than anything Microsoft has ever provided before. In addition to the pointers given in the previous wand tip, you've got full control of memory settings (I show 'em to you in Figure 1.9), as well as a lot of behavior and appearance modifications. They're all located in the Program, Font, Memory, Screen, and Misc tabs on the properties screen for each DOS program.

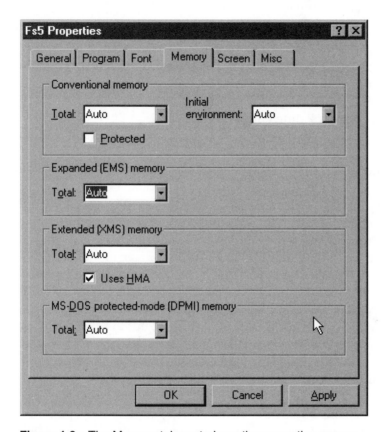

Figure 1.9   The Memory tab controls on the properties screen for every DOS program

Here's some cool stuff about running DOS from a DOS window under Win 95.

1. Open a graphical folder display of any directory from within a DOS window by typing `start` **followed by the pathname of that directory. To open the current directory as a Win 95 folder, type** `start.` **(Include the period.)**

2. Start Windows-based programs from the DOS command line in a DOS window. Just type the name of the program. For example, to start Notepad, type `notepad` **from any directory in a DOS window.**

3. When run from a DOS window, DOS 7 adds some useful directory shortcuts that can be used within commands like CD **(change directory):**

> **. . = moves to parent directory (one level back)**
>
> **. . . = moves to grandparent directory (two levels back)**
>
> **. . . . = moves to great grandparent directory (three levels back)**

Windows App Controls

You're in for a surprise running 16-bit apps under Win 95.

The first time you run your tried-and-true 16-bit Windows apps under Windows 95, you're going to be in for a bit of a surprise. They look a little different than under the old Windows. And some of the window controls and knobs have been shuffled around. Even Calendar, Clock, and other stuff that doesn't come with Windows 95 (but will still be available if you upgraded a previous Windows installation) will look different.

That's because the title bars and certain other things of Windows are controlled by Windows, not by the applications. Windows 95 brings a new deal, and it automatically retrofits all pre-existing programs whose developers didn't monkey too much with their title bars.

The Underbar, Window, and X-buttons

Chief among the differences is the addition of the three gray buttons on the right side of the title bar. And gone are those cryptic up, down, and up-and-down triangle arrows from the old Windows. The one on the left, which I've dubbed the "Underbar," is the Minimize button. (The bar image in the icon represents a task button on Taskbar.) When you click the Underbar button, the program or folder window collapses into its task button on Taskbar. Click the Taskbar "task button," and the program window opens again. The point of minimizing is to get the darn thing out of your face when you're not using it, but to keep it running in idle and ready at hand so that it'll come back in a flash when you want it. (For more on minimizing and Taskbar, see Chapter 3, "The Desktop Interface.")

Window button showing normal size option

The middle button controls window size. It actually toggles between two states. The icon represents a window with the darker top line meant to evoke a title bar. When this button is showing a single large window on its face, clicking it will maximize the window to the full size of the screen. When the button is showing two windows, one atop the other, the window is currently maximized and when you click the button, its size will return to "normal" size. Normal is a bit weird on this deal. A better way to think of it is as the Custom size because this is the window mode in which you can drag the corners and edges of the window to resize it, as well as drag it around by its title bar to reposition it.

The last button—the "X-button," a.k.a. the Close button—gives us something new: one-click closes of open windows. Oh, you long-time Windows users can still double-click the icon that appears all the way to the left of the title bar of any window to close it. The X-button is just a click faster—once you get your muscles to remember it's there. From now on, *remember:* In the new Microsoftese, X means close or delete.

.INI Files

`.INI` files are text-based program initialization files. There was a bonanza of them to be found in the Windows directories of previous Windows versions. Windows installed a bunch of them, as did many applications and even hardware devices. If you're completely new to Windows, you can skip this right now and move on to the next section. This little bit of warning is for crusty Windows diehards like me who are going to freak the first time they go to adjust something in `SYSTEM.INI` or `WIN.INI` after installing Windows 95. Heads up: `.INI` files are a thing of the past. You'll still find the vestiges of `SYSTEM.INI` and `WIN.INI` in your Windows folder, but they're there only as repositories for stuff placed in them by installing older Windows programs.

So where's the stuff that was in there? Meet System Registry, the new database of all things configurable, controllable, and tweakable in Windows 95. For more on this guy, see Chapter 4, "Files, Folders, Exploring," and Chapter 5, "Customize It."

Heads Up: `.INI` **files really are a thing of the past.**

ONBOARD HELP AND ANSWERS

> To get it right, be born with luck or else make it. *Never* give up. Get the knack of getting people to help you and also pitch in yourself. A little money helps, but what *really* gets it right is to *never*—I repeat—*never* under any conditions face the facts.
>
> Ruth Gordon
> *Myself Among Others*, 1970

There's more than immediately meets the eye in Win 95 that can help you figure things out or get out of a jam. The online Help system (not really "online," but a local program Windows installs on your hard drive) presents over 350 topics by Contents, Index, and searches to words or phrases you enter. The Find view is shown in Figure 1.10.

 Help

You'll find Help on the Start Menu. Use it. It's the first operating system Help that's not really just a lot of bits and bytes taking up space. Among its finer points are mini-Wizards for some topics, like getting connected to the Internet or hardware conflict troubleshooting, that actually lead you through the process of getting properly configured or out of trouble.

In the "practically lame" department is something you may come across if you do a Custom Setup of Windows 95 called the Online User's Guide. According to Setup, you'll chew up 7.8MB of disk space if you select the Online User's

Guide. Pretty much all it does is install 10 .AVI **animations that show some Windows 95 basics. It's a pretty steep storage price to pay for some gimmicky moving pictures. I'd skip this option.**

TIPS.TXT **and** FAQ.TXT **are little treasure troves of tips.**

What often gets overlooked are the more than 20 readme-type text files on various subjects installed in your Windows folder. In particular, the TIPS.TXT and FAQ.TXT files offer a lot of useful information. I strongly recommend you print and read them. And don't forget the other files. (For a list of all of Win 95's readmes with a brief description of what each covers, see the Appendix.)

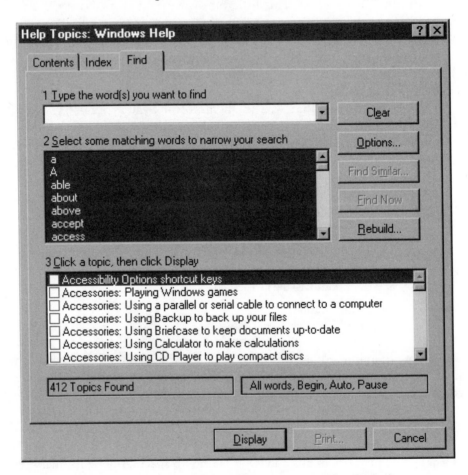

Figure 1.10   The main Windows 95 Help screen, showing the Find tab

Windows 95 CD owners: You've got the full text of the Windows 95 Resource Kit on your CD. This thing provides over 1,000 additional topics mostly aimed at figuring out tough nuts and helping you customize Windows 95. It looks just like the main Win 95 Help; take a look at Figure 1.11. Don't overlook it. There's

no automatic installation for the Resource Kit, but installing it is easy enough. Insert the Windows 95 CD in the drive. When Microsoft's AutoRun feature opens the CD's main menu (or you open the CD drive window in My Computer), choose "Browse This CD." Double-click the Admin folder. In the new Admin folder window, double-click the Reskit folder. In that folder window, double-click the Helpfile folder. With the right mouse button, click and drag the `WIN95RK.HLP` file out of this folder and drop it on your desktop. On the subsequent popup menu, choose Create New Shortcut(s). Now click the new icon once to select it and then press the F2 key. Type `Win 95 Resource Kit` and press the Enter key. Finally, using the left mouse button, drag and drop the icon directly onto the Start button. You'll find the Resource Kit listed on your Start Menu (check out Chapter 3, "The Desktop Interface," for more on Start). When you choose it from Start, it'll open up on your screen—looking very much like the regular Help screen—as long as you've inserted the Windows 95 CD in the drive.

Figure 1.11   The Windows 95 Resource Kit on the Win 95 CD

The Welcome Box

The first thing you see when you enter Windows 95 successfully for the first time is the Welcome to Windows 95 screen shown in Figure 1.12. If you're really new to Windows, you might want to install the Tour option. Or, better yet, if you've got the CD version of Win 95, open My Computer and double-click your CD drive icon to launch the Tour from the disc. The Tour is a rudimentary animated interactive tutorial that covers Starting a Program, Exploring Your Disk, Finding a File, Switching Windows, and Using Help. If you've used Windows in the past, then you might get a leg up by pressing the What's New button, which details some of the basic differences between Windows 3.*x* and Win 95.

The other helpful deal on the Welcome screen are the tips that appear in its main window. You can cycle through them with the Next Tip button. And if you don't turn off the Welcome screen, you'll see a different Win 95 tip every time you start the operating system. The Product Catalog button is a sales pitch for Microsoft. You might find the stuff under its "Programs Designed for Windows 95" selection useful. But keep in mind that its information is circa August 1995. The Online Registration button is covered in Chapter 2, "Up and Running." Bottom line on this button: Despite all the hype surrounding Microsoft's online registration, I recommend using it.

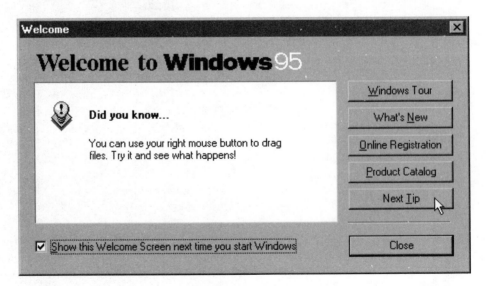

Figure 1.12   The Welcome screen for Windows 95

Welcome

If you're like me, you find facing the Welcome screen every time Win 95 starts a tiresome experience. So get rid of it. Uncheck the box beside the description: "Show this Welcome Screen next time you start Windows." If you want to get it back after that, double-click My Computer. Then double-click your C: drive (or whatever drive Windows is installed on). Find the Windows folder in your open drive folder and double-click it. Scroll to almost the end of your Windows folder and look for the file labeled "Welcome." Double-click it.

AutoRun and the Windows 95 CD

It might be a little disconcerting the first time you encounter this: Whenever you insert an AutoRun-compatible CD into a drive on a machine where Windows 95 is already running, there'll be a pause, then the CD's "busy" light will flicker, you'll hear a snatch of music, and suddenly a large blue box will open on your screen, something like the one in Figure 1.13. Down the right side of this screen are buttons for the Tour, Microsoft Exposition (the hard-sell part of the Product Catalog on the Welcome screen), Hover!, Cool Video Clips, Browse This CD, and Add/Remove Software.

Figure 1.13 The Windows 95 CD-ROM AutoRun menu screen

This bit of magic isn't really all that magical. There's a file in the root directory of the CD called AUTORUN.INF. It points to the AUTORUN.EXE file in the CD's AutoRun folder, like the lines displayed in Figure 1.14. Any time you insert a CD, this AutoRun stuff is like AUTOEXEC.BAT for a CD. It launches automatically.

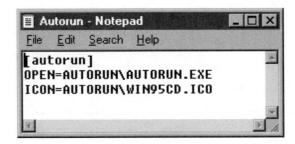

Figure 1.14   The AUTORUN.INF text file viewed in Notepad

Most of the options on the Windows 95 AutoRun menu screen are straightforward. Hover! is a 3D bumper car game. Cool Video Clips is designed to show off Win 95's multimedia capabilities; it offers a bunch of movie trailers and stuff like that. The two most useful options are on the bottom. Browse This CD opens a folder window of the CD, as if it were in My Computer (which, by the way, it is). Add/Remove Software summons your Add/Remove Programs control panel program, which you use to install stuff from the CD. Finally, if the AutoRun screen pops up in your face when you don't want it to—which it does sometimes—just click its X-button.

THE CONTROL PANEL AND ACCESSORIES

The basic tool for the manipulation of reality is the manipulation of words. If you can control the meaning of words, you can control the people who must use the words.

Philip K. Dick
I Hope I Shall Arrive Soon, 1986

Control Panel

I'm not going to spend a lot of time detailing the workings of all the Control Panel tools and Accessories programs that come in Windows 95. There's a whole lot of this stuff, and for the most part, it's pretty darn self-explanatory. Some of the control panels and applets are explained in depth in other chapters, wherever using them wisely is important to doing something else or where I thought it might be useful to point them out. Suffice it to say that the main thing you need to know is that the Control Panel is found hanging two levels off the Start Menu: Start/Settings/Control Panel. When you select this menu item, you get the folder shown in Figure 1.15. Meanwhile, most of the Windows 95 applets dangle off the Start/Programs/Accessories submenu, that is, in menus that spring off Accessories.

What I am going to do is give you an overview. If you used any of the previous versions of Windows, the Control Panel will look familiar, but it really isn't.

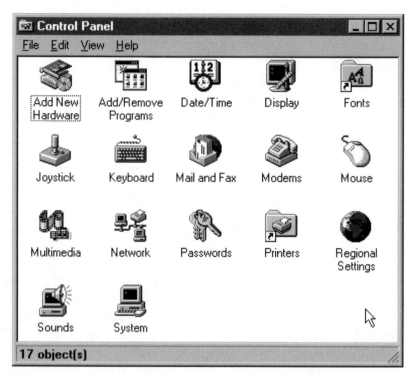

Figure 1.15 The Control Panel folder for a typical Win 95 installation

Virtually nothing about it is the same, except for some of the settings it offers. To start with, nearly every control panel program is a properties sheet. I get into this in more detail later, so don't worry about it. Besides, the distinction is more important to Microsoft, I think, than to anyone using the operating system. If you think of properties sheets as electronic forms, you get pretty close to what they're about. You get check boxes, radio buttons, sliders, scroll boxes, and the like. And you get to place your order with Windows 95 for how you'd like stuff to work.

> **Virtually nothing about Control Panel is the same as the old Windows.**

Some of the control panels returning for an encore from Microsoft operating systems of yore, dressed in disguise, are Date/Time, Keyboard, Mouse, Network, Printers, Regional Settings, and Sounds. Completely new control panels include Accessibility, Add New Hardware, Add/Remove Programs, Display, Fonts, Joystick, Mail and Fax, Modems, Multimedia (well, this was sorta there before), and System. Depending on the options you chose during installation, and your system configuration, you may see several others.

Many control panels pull double duty as the properties screens for specific things in Windows 95 (see Table 1.1). You get to properties screens by right-clicking the object and choosing Properties from the popup menu.

Table 1.1 Control Panels That Are Also the Properties Screens for Win 95 Things

Control Panel	Same as
System	Properties for My Computer
Network	Properties for Network Neighborhood
Mail and Fax	Properties for Inbox
Display	Properties for the Desktop
Printers	Double-clicking Printers in My Computer

Applets

Accessories

Here's where things get a bit more complicated. Win 95's Setup is complex enough that there are literally four main tracks with three main options. If you choose to customize the installation, you're faced with lots and lots of choices about whether to install literally dozens of features, functions, and applets. For a complete overview of the CD Setup options, check out the Appendix.

For those who are coming at this with previous Windows experience, some of the applets that made the cut are Calculator, Character Map, Clipboard Viewer, ClipBook Viewer (Windows for Workgroups), File Manager, Hearts, Media Player, Minesweeper, Passwords (WFW), Netwatcher (WFW), Notepad, Packager, Paint (Paintbrush), Program Manager, Solitaire (big surprise), and Task Manager.

Say bye-bye to At Work Fax (WFW, replaced by Microsoft Fax with Exchange), Calendar, Cardfile, Clock, Dr. Watson, Microsoft Mail (WFW), PIFEdit (integrated into DOS program properties), Recorder, Remote Access (WFW, replaced by Dial-Up Networking), Print Manager (integrated), Schedule+ (WFW), Terminal (replaced by HyperTerminal), and Write (replaced by WordPad). *Note:* If you upgrade a previous installation, much of this stuff will still be around; it just hasn't been updated for Windows 95. In a few cases, it also won't be useful any longer—if it ever was.

Some of the new applets and tools include Backup, CD Player, Direct Cable Connection, Disk Defragmenter, FreeCell, Briefcase, Phone Dialer, ScanDisk, System Policy Editor, and System Registry Editor (major revision of the REGEDIT.EXE Registry Editor).

Where is this stuff? At first glance, it may seem that many of the applets I list as being in Windows 95 really aren't. Oddly, some of these items—such as the Clipboard Viewer—are available only after setup, by adding them from the Windows tab of the Add/Remove Programs control panel. Others, like System Policy Editor, are installable from the Apptools folder on the Windows 95 CD. Still others, like System Registry Editor and Packager, are installed in the Windows folder, but Setup doesn't create icons for them. Finally, some tools, like WordPad, are installed by some installation tracks and not others. You can add them separately with Add/Remove Programs.

Beyond this introduction, there's no really good way to provide an overview. So instead I'm going to call out a few of the better programs included with Windows 95 (but not necessarily installed on your machine).

WordPad. There are bigger all-new extra programs in Windows 95, like Inbox and the Microsoft Network. But under the heading "Applets," WordPad is probably the biggest. Win 95's Write replacement is slow. It also doesn't support multiple open documents, which is really annoying. But one thing it does do is handle files much larger than what chokes Notepad. Even better, it can open and save documents in Microsoft Word 6.0 for Windows format, as well as Rich Text Format and regular Text. You'll find it in Start/Programs/Accessories.

WordPad

HyperTerminal. I cover this guy in Chapter 8, "Connections," but it's worth mentioning now because, finally, Windows has a truly useful basic communications package. You'll find it in Start/Programs/Accessories.

HyperTerminal

ScanDisk. This one's covered in Chapter 4, "Files, Folders, Exploring." It's a Windows disk diagnostics and repair utility that supports long filenames. It's fast, efficient, and reliable. You should be running this thing about once a week. You'll find it in Start/Programs/Accessories/System Tools. There's also a DOS 7 version of ScanDisk, which you'll find tucked into the Command folder inside your Windows folder.

ScanDisk

Disk Defragmenter. Want Windows to run faster? Run Disk Defragmenter once a month. This utility reunites all the various patches of your data files, kinda like putting the Scarecrow back together. That makes your drive run faster. Check out Chapter 4, "Files, Folders, Exploring." Disk Defragmenter is on the System Tools menu beside ScanDisk.

Disk
Defragmenter

System Registry Editor. This little gem is your best partner in crime for making Windows 95 a more hospitable place to be. You'll locate it as the REGEDIT.EXE file in your Windows folder. But before you start monkeying around with it on your own, read through the precautions in Chapter 5, "Customize It."

System
Registry Editor

Briefcase. If you've got more than one PC and you work with the same data on both, Briefcase is a very useful tool. It makes the job of synchronizing the data files on two or more PCs much easier. Check out Chapter 4, "Files, Folders, Exploring," for how to use it and some important caveats. You add a New Briefcase to your desktop by right-clicking the desktop and choosing New/Briefcase from the popup menu.

My Briefcase

TOUGH QUESTIONS, STRAIGHT ANSWERS

> Truth is tough. It will not break, like a bubble, at a touch; nay, you may kick it about all day like a football, and it will be round and full at evening.

> Oliver Wendell Holmes, Sr.
> *The Professor at the Breakfast Table,* 1860

Seeing can be tough at times, since we're stuck taking Microsoft's word on some things.

Ready for a little demystification? Both Microsoft and its critics like to shroud their arguments about what's good or bad about Windows 95 in a lot of hype, marketing terminology, and operating system techno-babble. Those of us who try to follow this stuff have been sucked into a vortex of terminology like *thunk layer, Ring 0, preemptive multitasking* and *multithreading, virtualized,* and a bunch of other stuff I won't trouble you with. So here's a little straight talk, as I see it. And seeing can be a bit difficult at times, since for some things we're stuck taking Microsoft's word—or not. Some of this is informed opinion.

Where's DOS, and What's Different about It?

As I said earlier, DOS is alive and well and living underneath Windows 95. If, for example, you use the MSD (Microsoft Diagnostic) tool that shipped with the last versions of DOS, Windows, and some Microsoft applications to gather information about Windows 95, you'll find that it reports the version of DOS running under Windows 95 as DOS 7. Check out Figure 1.16.

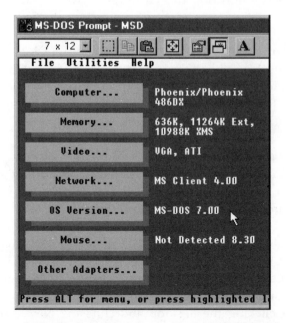

Figure 1.16   Don't let 'em tell you there's no DOS in Win 95

Speaking of MSD, Microsoft ships MSD.EXE **v. 2.13 dated 7/11/95 (like all the Windows 95 files) on the CD version of Win 95. It's in the** \Other\Msd **folder on the CD. Just copy it off the CD to your** \Windows\Command **folder. It runs better from the DOS command line in MS-DOS mode.**

Now this doesn't prove a whole lot, actually. Microsoft claims that it's taken a segment of the DOS kernel (core code) and virtualized it (repackaged it in Windows' memory). And it would appear they have done this. But that's not enough to proclaim that DOS is dead, long live Windows 95. Bottom line: DOS is very much still a part of Windows 95. (This is less true of Windows NT, by the way, but that's a whole different book.)

The distinction is somewhat academic, in any case. Windows 95 is very clearly a transitional OS for Microsoft. There'll surely be a Windows 96 and/or 97. After that, we're probably facing a merger of Windows NT and Windows 95, with a lot of refinement to the core code (we can hope), as well as a refined interface. Part of that new interface, as I see it, will be the merging of applications (like Office) with the OS. Microsoft-trained apps will be modules that essentially plug into the programming interface of the operating system, rather than being wholly separate entities that reside atop the OS. (I'll probably be eating these words in a few years. . . .)

Part of some future Windows interface will be the merging of Office with the OS.

Anyway, on to the "what's different about it" part. There are a lot of things that are different about DOS, really. I'm not going to detail them all. But some things you should know. The Windows 95 upgrade kills off a lot of files from your previous DOS installation and replaces most of them with DOS 7 versions. In fact, one installation tip you'll read about in Chapter 2, "Up and Running," is to make a backup copy of your DOS directory before you install, especially if you're a DOS-head and plan to dual boot between the old and the new. (See Chapter 2, page 44, for an explanation of dual booting.)

Like SYSTEM.INI and WIN.INI, CONFIG.SYS and AUTOEXEC.BAT are essentially vestigial under Windows 95. You can run the operating system without either (unless Windows 95 lacks virtual device drivers for any of your hardware). Even so, you'll want to run Win 95 with DOS's initialization files to control things like environment variables and the path statement. And the Windows 95 installation just comments out a lot of things, leaving CONFIG.SYS and AUTOEXEC.BAT otherwise intact. For peace of mind, leave it that way, if for no other reason than that some pre-Windows 95 DOS and Windows may expect to find either or both of these files. (In fact, at least one Windows 95 tool—the Emergency Recovery Utility—expects to find them.)

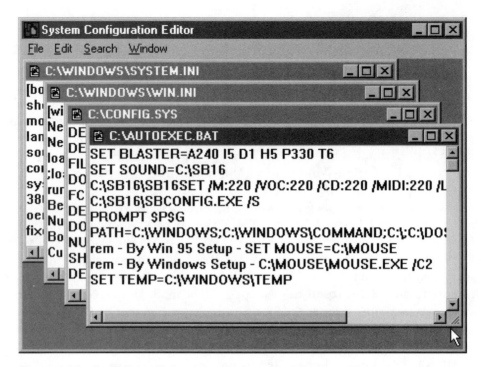

Figure 1.17   SysEdit is still there, but you're not going to need it much

The oldest Windows tip in the book is a little program called SysEdit, the one shown in Figure 1.17. It's a handy program that gives you edit and search access to CONFIG.SYS, AUTOEXEC.BAT, SYSTEM.INI, and WIN.INI (as well as some other files that may not be applicable to your Win 95 installation). Since the introduction of Windows 3.0, Microsoft has quietly included the text-editing System Configuration Editor (its formal name) in the C:\WINDOWS\SYSTEM directory. Translated into Win 95ese, that's the System folder inside the Windows folder. The filename is SYSEDIT.EXE. To create an icon for it, right-click the Start button and choose Open from the popup menu. Then double-click the Programs folder to open it. Right-click the Programs folder background and choose New/Shortcut from the popup menu. Click the browse button, double-click the Windows folder, and then double-click the System folder. In the Filename field, type sysedit.exe and press Enter. Click the Next button and type SysEdit in the Select a Name field. Then click the Finish button. Close down the folders, and you'll find SysEdit on the bottom portion of the Programs submenu.

Does Figure 1.18 look awfully familiar? Since .INI **files, and even** CONFIG.SYS **and** AUTOEXEC.BAT**, don't have the importance under Windows 95 they once had, Microsoft delivered a new little program, very similar in operation to SysEdit, called Log Viewer. What does it do? Well, it gathers up all the many**

**numerous Win 95 log text files, showing the dates when they were last
changed. These files report problems Windows 95 encountered and can be
useful in helping you to troubleshoot. You'll find it on the Windows 95 CD in the
`\Other\Misc\Logview` folder. The `LOGVIEW.EXE` file is the only thing
in there. Copy it into your Windows folder and create a shortcut for it as
described for SysEdit in the preceding paragraph.**

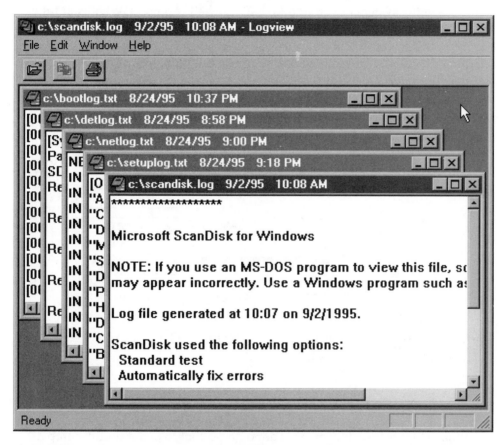

Figure 1.18   Log Viewer looks a lot like SysEdit, but it rounds up Win 95's log files

What's the Real Story about Win 95's Architecture?

Win 95's architecture is based on Windows 3.1's. Rather than being an all-new operating system, Win 95 is a major upgrade of the previous Windows. Most of the
core code—or kernel—of the newer operating system is a 32-bit code that is more
robust than the 16-bit-only previous DOS and Windows. Win 95 provides full
support for 32-bit applications—the ones written specifically for Windows NT
and Windows 95. But it also provides backwards compatibility and support for
16-bit applications written for Windows 3.*x*. Therein lies the big problem.

**Rather than be-
ing an all-new
OS, Win 95 is a
major upgrade
of Win 3.1.**

What isn't fully 32 bit are parts of the graphics engine, interface controls, and even parts of core code.

To quote a Microsoft technical document: "The design of Windows 95 deploys 32-bit code wherever it significantly improves performance without sacrificing application compatibility. Existing 16-bit code is retained where it is required to maintain compatibility, or where 32-bit code would increase memory requirements without significantly improving performance." Input/output, device drivers, networking, the file system, memory management, and scheduling portions of the operating system are all 32 bit. That's all well and good. What isn't fully 32 bit, though, are parts of the graphics engine, interface controls, and even parts of the kernel. Check out the following little chart supplied by Microsoft in an early version of its Reviewer's Guide (see Figure 1.19). Maybe the gist of it will help you get your mind around this.

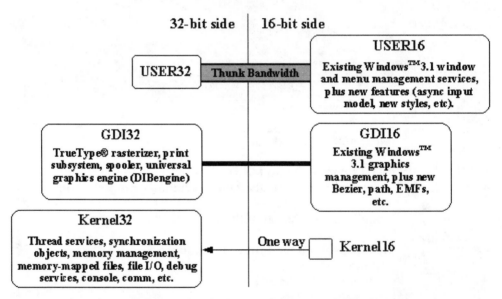

Figure 1.19   Stuff that's 32-bit and stuff that isn't—more isn't than should be

Think of 32-bit code as a wider pipe the program is running through.

What 32-bit purists like me find annoying is that to maintain full compatibility with 16-bit apps, Microsoft chose to put a crimp in the style of 32-bit apps, thereby cutting into the robustness of the environment for managing multiple 32-bit apps. From my viewpoint, that's a good part of why I want 32-bit power in my OS. The truth is, though, the compromise may make sense, for two reasons. First, while 32-bit code is more powerful (think of it as a wider pipe the program is running through), it also requires more memory. Second, there's a huge installed base of 16-bit Winapps out there. Microsoft figured that if it showed a preference for 32-bit apps, a lot of corporations, in particular, might have said, no way. That's just another reason why Windows 95 is a stepping-stone for Microsoft. As soon as Windows 95 apps are more prevalent—and an 8MB of RAM minimum requirement on paper (16MB in practice) is something the market can bear—Win 97, or whatever, will come out and, we can hope, without this intermixture of 16-bit and 32-bit code. This will also make that future Windows version more reliable. And that is a good segue to the next section.

What about Application Reliability?

Application reliability is what it comes down to, after all. And the reliability of Windows 95, and the reliability of applications running on it, are almost the same thing. "Out of Memory" errors are by no means a thing of the past under Windows 95. Neither are what were known under the old Windows as GPFs (General Protection Faults). But both of these maladies happen less frequently.

If you were running only Windows 95 applications, theoretically your likelihood of encountering a program crash would be much lower than if you were running Win-16 apps under Win 95 or the old Windows. Each Win-16 program self-determines when and if it will yield itself to the operating system, thereby allowing it to direct CPU resources to other operations. An uncooperative Win-16 app can hog system resources all day and other apps will just be SOL. That's the kind of thing that can cause crashes.

Under Windows 95, Win-32 apps run in a protected area of memory and can be safely *preempted* by the operating system—that is, temporarily put on hold—so that the OS can allow other programs CPU time. The thing is, because Win 95 was designed to cope also with Win-16 apps, it has to allow some regular stopping points; otherwise it might tend to crash those apps. But that slows everything down. It can also affect reliability, since the intersection of this handling of 16-bit and 32-bit code is kind of a dicey proposition. We'll all be a lot better off when we dump our 16-bit apps and get an operating system that's designed specifically for 32-bit apps.

> **Forced compatibility for 16-bit apps slows everything down.**

There are four different types of apps you might run under Windows 95. Win-16 apps, like Word 6.0 for Windows, are probably the most common. Most 16-bit Winapps run just fine under Windows 95. My experience has been that, from a reliability perspective, if they launch without a hitch, they'll be at least as reliable as they were under Windows 3.*x*. Some Win-16 apps have either major or minor incompatibilities, though. Some things Win-16 apps can't take advantage of under Windows 95 are automatic uninstall, long filenames, improved common dialogs, and multithreaded operations (I'll get to this in a minute). The other 16-bit app type is DOS apps, which I talked about earlier in the chapter. Again, my experience has been that they're more reliable under Windows 95, although you may have to jink around, tweaking their properties or running them in MS-DOS mode to get them to work properly.

There are actually three different Microsoft Win-32 specs in vogue these days. They've gone through various naming conventions, and I'm not going to try to keep up with those. The first one was the Windows NT Win32 spec. Not long after NT shipped, Microsoft created some .DLL files for Windows 3.1 that allowed it to run 32-bit applications specifically written to use these .DLLs—the second Win32 spec. And then came the Windows 95 Win32 spec. Supposedly, the Win 95 spec is a large subset of the NT Win32 spec. Ugh! Here's the deal. Some Windows NT apps are supposed to run under Windows 95, but I wouldn't count on it. Fully compliant Windows 95 apps are supposed to run under Windows NT. But, again, for other reasons, I wouldn't count on it.

I've found Win 95 apps a trifle wanting in the Reliability Department.

Your best bet is to purchase Windows 95 apps. How reliable are they? On paper, very reliable. But using myself as a test universe—mostly with Microsoft Windows 95 apps—I've found them a trifle wanting in the Reliability Department. I'm not really sure why, so I'm not going to hazard a guess. All I can say is that, like most things, maybe it'll take a while to get the kinks out. One thing worth noting is that Windows 95 apps are a pleasure to use. They're designed to take full advantage of Win 95's many good points. On my desktop, that translates into a marked productivity boost.

What Are Preemptive Multitasking and Multithreading?

You know, when General Motors markets cars, they tend to do it by selling you the future. *Buy GM cars now because they'll all be safer in the future. Yessiree, they'll all have daytime running lights.* The truth is, only a few of GM's models currently offer this safety feature—small headlights that switch on whenever the engine runs in order to improve your car's visibility to other motorists.

Microsoft is doing the same thing. While Windows 95 supports preemptive multitasking and multithreading, the truth is, Microsoft and our apps aren't taking full advantage of them.

Preemptive multitasking is more a feature of the operating system than of applications (although the applications must support it). It's the ability of the OS to serve as a traffic cop regarding multiple running programs, holding off some in favor of others, giving every one a turn. Play nice with the other apps, now, OK? To a considerable extent, the favoritism that Windows 95 must play with 16-bit apps greatly curtails its 32-bit multitasking power.

Multithreaded operations are more a *potential* feature of 32-bit applications (although the OS can make use of it, too). Within a single 32-bit application, multiple operations—or threads—can occur simultaneously under Windows 95. That's true of Windows NT and OS/2 Warp, as well. If you want a good example of where this might be useful, consider what happens in just about any word processor when you print a long document. Maybe it's "printing in background," but that's a background that tends to intrude in a big way on the performance of the foreground—if you know what I mean.

The kicker is, application developers have to completely rewrite specific modules of their applications for Windows 95 in order to take advantage of multithreading. Most didn't do that for their first versions of Windows 95 applications. In fact, you're more likely to see those kind of benefits from Win 95 apps that you've never heard of before.

These two buzzwordy capabilities amount to walking and chewing bubble gum at the same time, with a dash of "octopus procedures" to describe the potential of multithreading. Some day, it'll all be second nature for Windows programs. Right now, it's still just the future. And the future isn't now.

What's Plug and Play?

The next chapter gets into the effects of Plug and Play—and how to deal with them—in a big way. It covers setting up and running Windows 95 for the first time. So maybe this is a good place to explain this mother of all Windows 95 marketing hype.

Don't get me wrong. The goal of PnP is a worthy one indeed. I've been playing with PCs longer than I'd care to admit. Long enough so that dealing with hardware interrupt requests and input/output range conflicts has become something I don't have to think all that much about. But you know, this inherently annoying aspect of Intel-based PCs bites everyone sooner or later. Recently, I wound up spending three hours messing around with a CD drive in one of my PCs. You see, I had installed a new hard drive and disk controller a couple of weeks earlier. Everything seemed to be fine, but then my CD drive began having intermittent problems. Not all the time, just once in a while. Then, while I was trying to change the jumpers on my CD interface card, I inadvertently tore the wire that lets my CD drive play audio CDs (using Win 95's CD Player program). I had to order a new one for $18. Sure, I figured it out. But, man, what a pain in the butt.

This is the kind of stuff that PnP is supposed to put out of business. If Windows 95 (and its successors) are wildly successful. If PnP doesn't cause PC manufacturers major headaches. If hardware makers hear it from us that we want PnP. If it doesn't cost too much. If we're all willing to buy brand-new PCs once all the other ifs are satisfied. If all these things come to pass, the reality is that Plug and Play could be a major boon some time before the end of this century. Don't hold your breath.

Plug and Play is supposed to make each hardware device that matters on your PC reveal its name, rank, and serial number (almost literally) to Windows 95, whereupon the operating system will automatically install the correct driver for it. Moreover, the fullest definition of Plug and Play involves Win 95's intervention in hardware conflicts. For that, every single piece of memory-addressed hardware in your PC must be a PnP device. These devices can also reveal the settings of their software-configurable jumpers to Windows 95. So, in an ideal world (or, in this case, PC), whenever Windows 95 detected a conflict between two hardware devices, it would reconfigure one of them automatically. For all this to work, not only do all the components have to be PnP compatible, but the PC itself also must have a PnP BIOS.

At this writing, I haven't come across a single newly manufactured PC that meets all these criteria. Most are shipping with Plug and Play BIOSs, but that's the least expensive part of the equation. If you're in the market for a new PC, definitely ask the manufacturer whether the components and the BIOS are PnP compatible. Don't get a PC that doesn't have a PnP BIOS.

Plug and pray?   That's the bad news. The good news is that Windows 95 isn't without partial improvements on this score. People joke about "Plug and Pray," but what's really going on is a variation on Plug and Tell. During the Windows 95 Setup, your PC gets a thorough workout (as shown in Figure 1.20). Win 95 bangs on it to see what'll shake loose and to figure out just what's in there. This takes several minutes of your time, and you wouldn't want to go through it each time you start Windows. But what it's doing is building a database about your hardware. The database holds the default hardware settings, as well as common variations of those settings specific to your devices. If your PC was conflict-free going into the install, Windows 95 will set up correctly. Even if you have hardware conflicts, Win 95 will do its darnedest to make things work. And once you start it successfully, you'll be able to see exactly what devices are in conflict (Start/Settings/Control Panel/System/Device Manager).

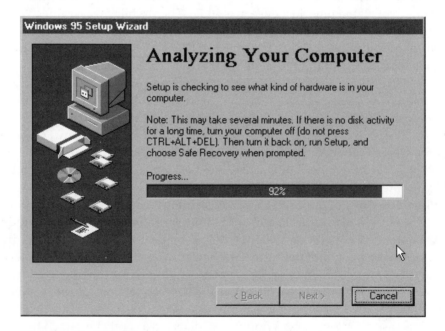

Figure 1.20   Win 95's Setup banging on your PC's hardware

It ain't perfect, but it's better than the old way. And now I'm going to sell you the future a bit. Because if Microsoft hadn't done this—another stepping-stone—we'd never get to the promised land of no worries when it comes to hardware configuration. We're not there yet, but we're on the right track.

*   *   *

A quick road map for the impatient (and who isn't?): Between here and the beginning of the real guts of this book, which starts with Chapter 3, "The Desktop Interface," is a little piece of work called "Up and Running" (Chapter 2). It's about installation. You say you've already installed Win 95, so you don't need this? Listen, everyone needs that chapter. Heck, I need it. Even if you skip it now, make a mental note to go back and check it some time. Hey, I didn't make it Chapter 2 for nothing, OK?

2 Up and Running

But their determination to banish fools foundered
ultimately in the installation of absolute idiots.

       Basil Bunting (1900–1985)
       The Spoils

Stop. Look. Read this. Initial setup is probably the hardest part of Windows 95. Even if you've already installed the operating system, you may be experiencing difficulties that could be traced to installation. This chapter isn't only for folks who are just now cracking the shrink-wrap on the blue-sky box. It's for everyone.

It's quite possible that you're working with Windows 95 unaware that Setup failed in some way or that you missed an opportunity to install a utility, doodad, or feature you could really use. You could be paying the price of missed functionality or shoddy performance—without knowing it. It happens all the time. And if you haven't installed yet, there's a wealth of stuff in this chapter that'll save you time and aggravation.

Most people who install Windows 95, as opposed to buying a new machine **Most people** with Win 95 already set up, do it as an upgrade of a pre-existing Windows instal- **upgrade.** lation. I'll get into the nuances of and some variations on the upgrade installation a few pages beyond. Right now, it's overview time. For anyone who's ever installed a previous version of DOS or Windows, the Win 95 Setup can be a real eye-opener. At the top level, this is how it differs from installations of previous Microsoft operating systems:

1. Setup can upgrade both DOS and Windows at the same time.

2. There's an extensive hardware detection and configuration phase.

3. Win 95 has a broad feature set, with many more optional components.

4. Setup fully upgrades any supported, pre-existing network configuration.

5. It sets up the Exchange Inbox "universal" mailbox, if selected.

6. It creates a Windows 95 floppy boot disk, at your option.

Figure 2.1   Screen art you could do without

7. It provides safe recovery for setup failure and verification of installed components.

8. You can register your copy of Win 95 online.

9. It launches the Win 95 tour optionally on first startup (CD only).

10. An uninstall option lets you revert to an upgraded DOS and Win 3.1*x* installation.

Wild and Woolly

Win 95 Setup is a complex, chaotic place. Microsoft designed it so that you could just close your eyes and click OK. But don't. Getting the most out of this operating system starts right here.

The types of installs this book covers

There are limits to what this book can cover. So these are the disclaimers. I'm focusing on the CD upgrade installation only. There are two main types of upgrade installations: The DOS-and-Win 3.*x* upgrade and DOS-only upgrade. The second type is sometimes—somewhat erroneously—called a "clean installation." A truly clean installation is when you install Windows 95 using the $209.95 suggested price, floppy-based, full version of Windows 95. It boots from the first floppy and formats your drive as if the drive had never been formatted before. If you opt for this one, you'll probably get into no end of trouble. Unless you're installing on a Linux box or something, you don't need it. If you've got a CD drive and DOS installed on your system, get the $89 street price CD Upgrade version of Windows 95. If you don't have a CD drive, check out Chapter 6, "The Mobile Win 95," for tips on dealing with your lack of a CD before you buy the floppy upgrade version of Windows 95. (In fact, Notebook users, turn to the setup instructions in Chapter 6 before you do anything else.)

Windows95 (D:)

Why am I pushing the CD version? It's not just a convenience thing, although that's reason enough. Microsoft left a lot of stuff off the floppy upgrade disks. Some of the things the CD offers that are MIA on the floppies are QuickView and WordView, file filters that let you see files without having to open their applications; the Windows 95 Resource Kit in the form of a Help application; the System Policy Editor (see Chapter 5, "Customize It"); all the DOS 6.22 versions of the files that Win 95's Setup deletes from your hard drive; useful utilities, such as Log Viewer, a new version of Microsoft Diagnostics (MSD), and several others; script files that support installation of a SLIP connection to the Internet (see Chapter 7, "Get on the Net"); and a stack of NetWare-oriented networking tools and troubleshooters. Trust me. You want the CD version. If you don't have a CD drive, maybe it's time to consider an upgrade.

INSTALLATION DECISION TREE

> I shall be telling this with a sigh
> Somewhere ages and ages hence:
> Two roads diverged in a wood, and I—
> I took the one less travelled by,
> And that has made all the difference.
>
> Robert Frost (1874–1963)
> *The Road Not Taken*

This part's about forks in the road. The upgrade installation CD presumes you have DOS 3.2 or newer already installed on your hard disk (and DOS 5.*x* or newer if you plan to dual boot with a pre-existing version of Windows). At minimum, it will upgrade your DOS installation to DOS 7. If you have any version of Windows 3.*x* already installed, it also can upgrade that installation. This second fork is the road more often travelled, since it requires markedly less post-installation messing around. Which one should you choose?

You may have read magazine columns where computer-expert purists were chastising anyone even considering a Windows upgrade installation. I can sympathize with that point of view. The old Windows was a major pack rat. It sucked up configuration and program files from every passing application like a suburban raccoon plundering trash cans. Trouble is, it wasn't until about 1993 when some major application providers—and then only some—started taking to heart the slings and arrows the computer trade press was firing about how *every* application should have a full uninstall routine like the one in Microsoft Plus! (see Figure 2.2). That way, when you decided you no longer needed an app, you could have it automatically remove all its many tentacles in your Windows installation. Microsoft deserves some praise for helping lead the charge in this area. Symantec was also an early convert. Even so, Win 95's uninstall feature nearly didn't happen. I and others were arguing with Microsoft execs on this point online as far back as fall, 1994. We were told it was impossible to include the feature. I'm very glad they proved themselves wrong.

The old Windows was a major pack rat.

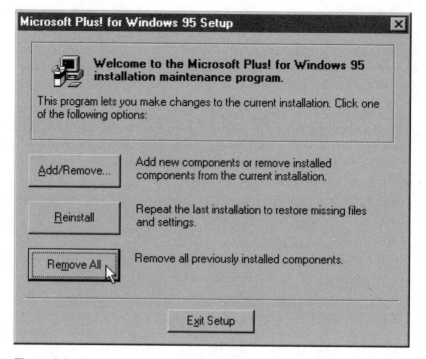

Figure 2.2 Example of removing an entire application, Microsoft Plus!

Anyway, the overwhelming odds are that your previous Windows 3.*x* installation is riddled with crap you don't need. It's the nature of the environment. So it's only natural for pundits to advocate that you take this chance to make a clean break by choosing the DOS-only upgrade. And I agree wholeheartedly—in principle. As you've probably guessed, though, there's a serious "but" coming.

Pros and Cons

Rather than prejudice you with an opinion before you see the facts, take a look at Tables 2.1 and 2.2, where I've set out the pros and cons of these two installation strategies. Make up your own mind, and then I'll give you some advice. *Note:* If you don't have Windows installed on your PC (or if you do but you almost never run Windows applications) and if your hardware is pretty standard, then by all means perform the DOS-only upgrade because you're not going to miss much.

I've weighed the pros and cons over and over, and here's my considered opinion: Unless you're the technically intrepid sort and you're pretty sure that the

Table 2.1 The DOS-and-Win 3.*x* Windows 95 Upgrade

Pros	Cons
This is the surest route to a swift, successful setup and first startup of Windows 95.	Your Windows folder and subfolders will still contain most of the junk they've probably been accumulating for years.
Most of your Windows 3.*x* program installations will run fine as is.	Uses some disk space the DOS-only upgrade wouldn't need.
Your Windows 3.*x* program group boxes will be converted, you'll retain some Windows 3.*x* applets not found in Win 95, and you'll preserve some of your environmental settings.	Temporarily requires more disk space during setup.

SUMMARY: This choice does little to help you clean out the deposits of junk, but it greatly eases and speeds setup and your migration to Windows 95.

Table 2.2 The DOS-only Windows 95 Upgrade

Pros	Cons
This creates a "clean" installation of the Windows folder and subfolders.	Setup and first startup may still go OK, especially if you have plain-vanilla hardware. But things are much more likely to go wrong.
You'll save some disk space over the Win 3.*x* upgrade.	You must reinstall *all* your Windows 3.*x* applications after the Win 95 setup.
It requires less disk space during installation.	You'll lose your Windows 3.*x* program groups, some Windows applets, and configurational settings.

SUMMARY: Expect a tougher setup, and put aside some serious time to mess with stuff afterward. But it's your best chance to clean up your Windows installation.

hardware components in your PC are relatively standard (neither completely on the cutting edge nor so ancient that they've fallen off the charts), go with the Windows 3.*x* upgrade. If you have a multimedia notebook PC, go with the Windows 3.*x* upgrade. If you have any sort of portable PC that has PCMCIA (PC Card) slots and you use them regularly, pick the Windows 3.*x* upgrade. If you bought your PC within the last year or so and haven't installed many applications, go with the Windows 3.*x* upgrade. If the whole idea of installing Windows 95 sets you on edge, go with the Windows 3.*x* upgrade. If you're installing on a Windows machine configured as a network client, do the Windows 3.*x* upgrade. In short, go with the Windows 3.*x* upgrade unless you're one of the purists or a purist wannabe. I don't mean that derogatorily. Some of my best friends are purists. Honest.

THE PARANOID'S PREP FOR THE WINDOWS 3.*X* UPGRADE

> I envy paranoids; they actually feel people are paying attention to them.
>
> Susan Sontag
> *Time Out,* August 19, 1992

If you don't have 40–60MB free disk space, forget Win 95.

Know this before we get started. The Windows 3.*x* upgrade *temporarily* requires somewhere between 40 and 60MB of free disk space. Let me be blunt. If you don't have that much free disk space, you don't have any business installing Windows 95 anyway. Setup needs this much space because you're going to launch it from within Windows (except Windows 3.0 users, who must do it from the DOS prompt). And since Windows 3.1*x* will be running, Setup can't install some Windows components because that would crash the running operating system. Instead, it installs this stuff into a temporary directory that it deletes the first time it starts up.

So clear away some MBs, get the CD out (you *are* installing from a CD, right?), and start paying attention. Like most things, there's a right way and a whole lotta wrong ways to do this. And we're going to make at least an attempt to get rid of some of the junk in your Windows directory. Get us the best of both worlds, if we can.

Microsoft cheaped out on the CD packaging. It put the CD in a flimsy cardboard jacket instead of a plastic jewel case—in other words, something that might actually protect it. Make no mistake: CDs are very definitely not indestructible. The bottom side (the one without the label) is the more vulnerable side. Don't touch that side, don't put an unprotected CD down on that side, and don't put anything on top of that side. In short, put the CD back in the jewel case when it's not in your CD drive. On the back of Microsoft's flimsy cardboard "protector" there's an orange sticker, labeled "CD Key," that has a number on it. You need this number deal to install the operating system.

First things first though. Scrounge a jewel case from somewhere. No other single app is as important as Windows 95, so leave another CD exposed to the elements if you have to. In the jewel case is a plastic seat that the CD sits on. Pull it out and remove any other garbage that might be behind it. Then cut out Microsoft's chintzy cardboard flap sporting the CD Key sticker and stuff that guy under the seat so that the key number is showing on the back. Put the plastic seat back in, and you've now got a proper home for your Win 95 CD. The kind Microsoft should have provided.

Weed Your Old Windows Installation

This is a whole lot easier said than done, but we're going to make a pass at it anyway. As noted earlier in the chapter, some apps have uninstall routines. Are there programs on your system that you don't use much, or at all? If so, check their docs for how to gracefully uninstall them. Some programs that don't have uninstall routines at least tell you in the manual or a readme file what files to delete if you want to uninstall them. You can't just delete their main program directories. Well, with some programs—usually newer, simpler ones—you can. But those aren't messing with your Windows installation, anyway.

Newer, simpler apps probably aren't messing with your old Win installation.

The stuff that's most likely got its hooks in your Windows installation are mondo business apps, software for hardware like sound cards (but don't mess with them unless it's hardware you've removed), utilities, communication programs, and anything with a database. These aren't hard-and-fast rules, and I'm generalizing. But it's a starting point.

Once you've uninstalled or otherwise removed all the apps you can, along with their insidious files, the next step is to scrutinize your `C:\WINDOWS` and `C:\WINDOWS\SYSTEM` directories. Use File Manager to do this. Start by creating a directory below each of those two directories called `\WEED`. When you're making guesses about stuff to remove, it's better not to delete but to move. That way if you get an error while launching Windows 3.*x* or an application that tells you "Can't find X file," you can move it back from the `WEED` directory. Scrutinize the `.INI` files in your Windows directory first. I guarantee you're going to find `.INI` files for programs that are no longer on your PC. Their filenames will give you a clue, but if you're not sure what they belong to, use Notepad to open them up and scan their contents. Every program that creates an `.INI` file in the Windows directory should be required by law to identify itself in the first line of the `.INI` file. The penalty should be . . . well, something really bad. Unfortunately, almost none do this. But scroll around. You'll usually find something—like a pathname to the program directory—that identifies it.

File Manager

Unfortunately, `.INI` files are just the tip of the iceberg. There are also surely `.DLL`s, `.HLP`s, `.TXT`s, `.CFG`s, `.DAT`s, `.EXE`s, and many other file extension types in your `C:\WINDOWS` and `C:\WINDOWS\SYSTEM` directories that didn't originally get placed there by Windows. Do your best to identify them. I wish I could help more with this. Remember, don't delete them; move them into the appropriate `WEED` directory. Later on, when you're sure that everything is working properly (much later), you can kill these `WEED` directories.

`.INI` files are just the tip of the iceberg.

Now, there also are a whole lot of files that Microsoft installed with Windows 3.*x* that you aren't going to need. Virtually any file with a `.TXT` extension is probably a file that'll be outdated as soon as you install Windows 95. You don't need the Windows 3.*x* Tutorial or its Help file. If you have Windows for Workgroups, you can kill off Schedule+ and MS Mail and their `.HLP` and `.DLL` files. Any file that ends in .000, .001, .002, and so on, can die. Unless you're particularly fond of

Get rid of old Windows junk.

a Win 3.1 sound, wallpaper, or screen saver, you can kill off .WAV, .BMP, and .SCR files. Help files are some of the biggest ones in there, so pay particular attention to them. Win 95 will install new Help files for all the programs it installs. Be a lot more careful in the C:\WINDOWS\SYSTEM directory. Unless you're pretty sure, gauging by its filename, that you no longer need a particular file, chances are you do need it.

The last part of the weeding process is to check out SYSTEM.INI and WIN.INI using SysEdit (the SYSEDIT.EXE file in Windows' SYSTEM directory) or any text editor. The first of these configuration files is much harder to deal with, since installing apps sometimes place stuff under the [386Enhanced] heading and don't usually identify themselves. That's where the worst damage is done. And that stuff usually gets installed as files in your Windows installation, too. But it's a tough one. Make sure to look for filenames in SYSTEM.INI you may have moved into a WEED directory. Place a semicolon before any such lines in SYSTEM.INI.

You may find settings for hardware no longer installed on your PC. Delete that stuff.

Definitely scroll through SYSTEM.INI. You may find settings for hardware no longer installed on your system. Delete that stuff. WIN.INI is a bit easier to contend with, since it often has section entries (in brackets) for specific applications. If there are entries specifically for programs you've removed, delete their entire sections and headings. Check out the Load= line at the top of WIN.INI. This is stuff that launches every time you start Windows. Do you need this stuff? If you're not sure what it is, leave it. But if you know it's something you don't need, take it out. Same thing with Run=.

To save yourself major headaches with Windows 95 File Types later on, I strongly recommend that you take a close look at WIN.INI's [Extensions] section. Each line under this section is a pointer that references a specific three-character file extension with a specific program and its path on your hard drive. Are the paths correct? Are there file extensions listed there that you don't use? Are there program names that you don't use? Are there older versions of programs listed? Go over this with a fine-tooth comb and make changes now, before you upgrade over this WIN.INI file, because this section of WIN.INI gets read right into the System Registry during Setup.

Restart Windows to check your work.

Next step is to exit and restart Windows. If you get any error messages while Windows is loading, write down the filenames and their locations and keep trying to load the operating environment by pressing Ignore or OK. If you hang or crash, reboot and look in one of your WEED directories for the file or files mentioned. Move it (them) back to the appropriate Windows directory. If you were particularly aggressive about removing files, you're almost sure to have moved something that Windows really needs or *thinks* it needs. You may have to attempt to start Windows and make corrections a few times before you're successful. It's possible that you placed a semicolon before a line in SYSTEM.INI that Windows really needs. So don't forget to check there (using DOS's Edit text editor).

OK, you've weeded Windows and it loads correctly. Now it's time to try your apps. Launch each one in turn. If you're going to encounter problems, they'll probably happen while the program is loading. But some applications have separate program modules that could be affected. It's your choice how thoroughly you check this out. You can always reinstall these programs later. But, at the very least, load all of your important apps. Follow the same procedure for fixing any errors you encounter that you did for Windows.

There's an optional couple of steps that I recommend at this point. First, reinstall Windows 3.1. (If you've got Windows 3.0 installed and you can borrow Windows 3.1 disks from a friend, this is an especially good idea.) Doing this can help if your Windows installation hasn't been damaged in some way, either during the weed process or from something else long ago. If you do this, choose Custom install and opt to install as little additional stuff as you're comfortable with. Windows is probably going to reinstall some stuff that you just deleted from your `C:\WINDOWS` directory. So take a quick peek afterward, especially at those Help files.

Preparing DOS

The worst of the preparation is over. But there's still some stuff to do. Back in SysEdit or the text editor of your choice, take a hard look at your `CONFIG.SYS` and `AUTOEXEC.BAT` files. Are there device drivers and TSRs loading in there that you don't need any longer? Is there a line that loads anti-virus stuff? Be ruthless about this weeding process. Removing extraneous lines, especially `LOAD=` or `LH=` lines in `AUTOEXEC.BAT` can make a big difference to the success of your Windows 95 install. Comment out (with the `REM` statement) or delete any lines you don't need. Reboot and make sure things are working correctly. Once they are, run DOS's Memmaker utility to optimize your memory management settings.

> **Be ruthless about the weeding process. It's a whole lot easier now than later.**

Next, create a `C:\CONFIGS` directory. Copy these files into it:

- `CONFIG.SYS`
- `AUTOEXEC.BAT`
- `SYSTEM.INI`
- `WIN.INI`
- Any others (like `PROTOCOL.INI`) that might apply to your installation

In the `C:\CONFIGS` directory, create a new DOS directory. Copy all the files from your `C:\DOS` directory to `C:\CONFIGS\DOS`. Use the DOS Attrib utility to attribute the `C:\CONFIGS\DOS` directory as read-only. The command looks like this:

```
ATTRIB +R C:\CONFIGS\DOS
```

Why back up your DOS files? Because Windows 95 deletes a whole bunch of them when it installs. It looks around your drive pretty carefully for where these files might exist. Taking this precaution isn't absolutely necessary, but I recommend it, especially if you plan to set up Windows 95 so that you can boot to either your old Windows or Windows 95, known as *dual booting.* There's a full explanation of how to set that up later in this chapter. (And check the Appendix for the list of DOS files that Win 95's Setup deletes.) *Warning:* If you want to dual boot and you're not upgrading from DOS 6.22 or you're not installing from a CD, definitely back up your DOS directory and make it read-only.

Prep for Dual Booting

A dual-boot configuration lets you go back and forth between booting your machine under Windows 95 and an older version of Windows. If you're interested in setting up such a configuration, there are two very different strategies to consider. Either way, you'll have to make room on your drive for two complete Windows installations in separate directories, one for the old and one for the new. *Note:* You have to be upgrading from DOS 5.*x* or newer to set up dual boot.

The first strategy is to install Windows 95 into a different directory than your previous Windows installation, such as C:\WIN95—a decision you make on one of the early Win 95 Setup screens. By doing that, you won't be performing an upgrade installation of Windows 95, though. Instead, you'll be making a DOS-only upgrade. The second strategy is to copy your entire Windows 3.*x* installation to a new directory called something like C:\WIN31 before you install and then to set up some batch files that help you make the back and forth switch.

If you've got the drive space to burn, I recommend picking one of the two methods and setting up dual boot. (For more on the dual-boot decision, see the "Setting Up Windows Dual Boot" section on page 78.) My general recommendation to all but the most technically proficient users is to make a copy of your Windows 3.*x* installation in another directory before installing. The time to create that backup version of old Windows is now, by the way. You can do it with File Manager, or you can do it from the DOS command line in the root directory by typing

```
XCOPY /S C:\WINDOWS C:\WIN31
```

For Performance' Sake

Speed thrills. If you want things to go a bit faster, run DOS's ScanDisk from the DOS prompt at this point to check for and fix any disk errors. Then run a third-party disk defragmenting utility, such as Symantec's Norton SpeedDisk (in Norton Utilities), if you've got one. You don't have to do this. In fact, Windows 95 has its own disk defragger, and you can run it after Setup. But this is the purist's way to do things.

OK, that's it. It's time to run the Windows 95 Setup. Skip down to the "Setup: A 12-Step Program" section.

THE PARANOID'S PREP FOR THE DOS-ONLY UPGRADE

Even a paranoid can have enemies.

Henry Kissinger
Time, January 24, 1977

So you're going to do the DOS-only upgrade, huh? Well, OK. I'll play along. But first, I've got a warning for you: I strongly advise that you rename your existing Windows directory (if you have one) to `C:\WIN31` and hang on to it for a while. I'm talking weeks or even months. In fact, if you've got the disk space, I'd put off deleting the copied directory until you're absolutely sure you're not going to need it. If you don't have the disk space or don't want to part with it, then my advice is to perform the Windows 3.*x* upgrade instead. Mark my words.

Preparing for the DOS-only upgrade is easier than for the Win 3.*x* upgrade. Maybe I should have added that to the pros and cons list, but the good thing about writing a book is that you get to decide these things and lead people down a garden path and stuff.

The Prep Work

First thing to do is create a `C:\CONFIGS` directory. If you've got old Windows on your PC, make copies of `CONFIG.SYS` and `AUTOEXEC.BAT` to that directory. Rename them in the process to `CONFIG.W31` and `AUTOEXEC.W31`. If you're DOS only, name them `CONFIG.FUL` and `AUTOEXEC.FUL`.

Next, edit the root directory versions of `CONFIG.SYS` and `AUTOEXEC.BAT` with your favorite text editor (or DOS's Edit program). You're looking for any lines that load files in the `C:\WINDOWS` directory. In many cases, any such files— like `HIMEM.SYS`, `EMM386.EXE`, `MSCDEX.EXE`, and `SMARTDRV.EXE`—can also be found in your DOS directory. (But check the dates on these files; the ones in your Windows directory could be newer. If so, copy them to your DOS directory first.) Although unlikely, there could also be non-DOS programs loading from your Windows directory that you need and so should place somewhere else. If so, copy them to a new location and edit the pertinent lines that load them in `CONFIG.SYS` or `AUTOEXEC.BAT` with the new pathnames. Finally, comment out (with REM and a character space) any unnecessary TSRs, anti-virus utilities, and anything you don't really need. Be ruthless about this. Bare-bones `CONFIG.SYS` and `AUTOEXEC.BAT` files are one way to ensure a successful Windows 95 install.

Change or remove references to your Windows directory.

Reboot your PC to DOS and make sure it's working properly. When you're sure it is, run DOS's Memmaker utility to optimize your memory management settings. Once that's done, copy these newer versions of CONFIG.SYS and AUTOEXEC.BAT to the CONFIGS directory. Then create a DOS directory in the CONFIGS directory. Copy all the files from your C:\DOS directory to C:\CONFIGS\DOS. Use the DOS Attrib utility to attribute the C:\CONFIGS\DOS directory as read-only using this command:

```
ATTRIB +R C:\CONFIGS\DOS
```

Windows 95 deletes a whole bunch of DOS files when it installs. Making the directory read-only keeps it from also doing that in your backup DOS directory. It's pretty darn assiduous about hunting down DOS files wherever they are. This step isn't absolutely necessary, but I recommend it.

Now's the time to rename your Windows directory to something else. Use this command from the DOS prompt in your root directory:

```
MOVE C:\WINDOWS C:\WIN31
```

To feather-edge your preparation, run DOS's ScanDisk to check for and fix any disk errors. Then run a third-party disk defragmenting utility like Symantec's Norton SpeedDisk from the Norton Utilities. You don't have to do this. In fact, Windows 95 has its own disk defragger, and you can run it after setup. But it's the purist's way to do things.

Get your hardware docs and setup disks ready. Finally, track down your original hardware driver installation disks for items like your soundcard, CD drive, network card, whatever. You may need them. After setup, don't forget to reinstall all your Windows applications. For some of them, you may be able to just copy their .INI files from your saved old Windows installation into Win 95's Windows folder. You can also resurrect your .GRP files. Do this by copying them to your Windows folder and following the wand tip under the "If You Performed a Clean Install" heading in Chapter 3, "The Desktop Interface."

That's it. It's time to run the Windows 95 Setup.

SETUP: A 12-STEP PROGRAM

> Habit is habit, and not to be flung out of the window by any man, but coaxed downstairs a step at a time.
>
> Mark Twain
> *Pudd'nhead Wilson*, 1894

If you've done your prep work, this should be the easy part. The thing that'll get you—maybe—is if you've got weird hardware that Windows 95 doesn't support. And believe me, the supported hardware list is quite long. Odds are, you're going to be OK.

Even so, I've got one PC that has a hard-disk controller that's a little strange. It was extremely fast under Windows for Workgroups, though, so I guess I can't blame the manufacturer. Anyway, this controller has a daughter card that fits into the adjacent card slot. Man, does that controller give Windows 95 fits because it's like there are two disk controllers in the machine.

A weird-hardware story

Sound fatal? It wasn't. Windows 95 doesn't have its own driver for this wacky card, but it can run the card from its real-mode DOS drivers. So Setup went fine. I just contacted the manufacturer to obtain a new driver for Windows 95, since real-mode drivers aren't as fast as Win 95 VxDs. It's a worst-case scenario anyway. Win 95 can also opt to load generic VxDs for many types of hardware. This is helpful if it encounters a device it doesn't specifically support.

One thing to know, though, is that upgrading from a Windows installation makes this nonstandard hardware trip easier, since weird hardware probably also has drivers running out of SYSTEM.INI. So because the old Windows needed help to work with the hardware, the new Windows can take advantage of that added information to make the right Setup decisions.

Upgrading Windows is easier.

This is one reason why everything that follows in this chapter presumes you're performing a Windows 3.*x* upgrade. Well, that and the fact that the vast majority of us doing our own installs are doing so over a Windows installation. Even so, 98 percent of what I'm going to tell you applies to all the various ways you can install the OS.

Square One

This is about hardware detection, remember? So plug everything in, turn everything on, and make sure it's all working. That includes external peripherals like printers, external modems, CD drives, tape backup devices, whatever. If you've got a PCMCIA slot, insert the PC card or cards you use most often.

Turn on, plug in, setup

It's not the end of the world if you forget something. In my home network environment, I share an external modem with several PCs via a switch box. And I've performed so many installs of Windows 95 that sometimes I forget to turn the modem switch box to the right setting for a given PC when I'm installing to it. Later on, that requires a hardware detection step that takes about 30 seconds, which is no big deal. But with something like an external CD, the detection redux is a lot more annoying. Might as well get it all done in the first pass.

Special hardware requires special steps. I have a high-end video card in one machine that will take the Windows 95 installation only if I use Windows 3.*x*'s SETUP.EXE routine and change the video settings to plain VGA 640 × 480 with 256 colors. The problem crops up as an error message followed by an abort of Win 95 Setup, by the way. Once Windows 95 installs, I can then use its tools for changing the video card driver, adjusting resolution, and increasing color depth. No two Win 95 installations are the same, but where there's a will (and a bit of thought), there's a way.

No two Setup experiences are the same.

Stuff You'll Need

**Be prepared:
It's not just for
Boy Scouts.**

If you're sitting down to do the deed, there's a few things you might need. Your Win 95 CD (or floppies), naturally. The orange CD Key sticker that came with your CD. Your name (I think you have that, right?). A blank floppy, or one whose data you don't mind kissing goodbye. And, of course, this book.

If you're on a network, you'll need your computer's workstation name (you can give it any name you want, but your MIS folk might have a conniption about that) and a workgroup name for domain-type networks like Windows NT.

Inbox

If you're installing the Exchange Mail Inbox and you have a dial-up Internet account, you're going to want the name and/or IP address of your access provider's server, the phone number you use to dial it, your user name, and your password. If you have a network connection to the Internet, then you'll need your server's IP address. Of course, you don't have to configure this stuff during setup if you don't want to. But if you've got this information at your fingertips, it's much easier to configure now.

Step 1.   DOS-only and Windows 3.0 users: Boot to the DOS prompt and install from there. Everyone else, run Windows and choose File/Run. Find the SETUP.EXE file on your install disc and run it. Command line folk, just log to the install drive, type setup, and press Enter.

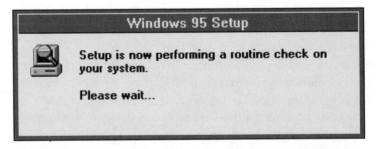

Figure 2.3   You might hang here; it's the first sticking point

Barely even to the first tee and already hit a sand trap? PCs that are low on conventional memory sometimes trip on the very first of Setup's tricks: the scan of your hard disk to make sure there are no disk errors (see Figure 2.3). The on-screen instructions handle this pretty well, but sometimes things freeze before you get to that point. Here's what you do. Reboot your PC. Run scandisk /all from the command line. Once back into Windows 3.*x*, rerun Setup with the /IS switch added to the Setup line, like this: setup /is. That defeats Setup's disk scan step. By the way, this problem isn't caused only by lack of memory. In my experience, PCs that have older standard IDE disk drives with addressing schemes that break the 528MB partition barrier are also affected. And so may drives that have been compressed with non-Microsoft compression tools.

Step 2. You'll breeze through a few screens where Setup is preparing the Setup Wizard and Microsoft will be busy showing you its software license and stuff. Start paying attention when you get to the screen that says "Collecting information about your computer." When you get to the Choose Directory screen, pick C:\WINDOWS (unless you're setting up dual boot without an upgrade of your existing Windows installation). Setup will go off and do its thing for a couple of screens, preparing your Windows directory and such.

Come back to Earth when the Save System Files screen shows up (see Figure 2.4). This deal creates a backup of your system files for your pre-existing DOS or DOS and Windows installation. Definitely say yes to this one. Although the dialog says doing it will add about 6MB to the Windows 95 installation, figure a bit more than that. Save System Files places two files in your root directory: W95UNDO.DAT and W95UNDO.INI. A quick check of two machines that Save System Files was used on showed one using 13MB and the other 10MB for the privilege. I still think it's worthwhile.

Say "yes" to Save System Files.

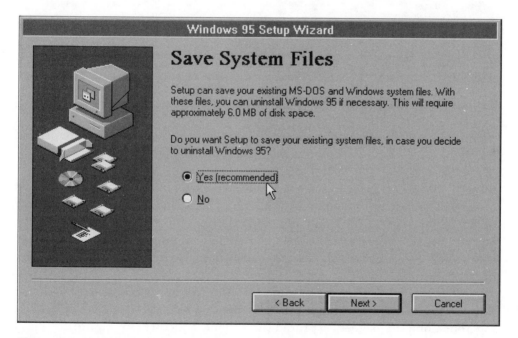

Figure 2.4   Setup's Save System Files screen: Just say yes

Step 3. Choose your primary Win 95 Setup track on the screen that looks like Figure 2.5, the Setup Options screen. I always pick Custom, since I know what I want, and that isn't in any of the tracks. If you're not sure, I recommend choosing whichever one of the other three setup tracks—Typical, Portable, or Compact—

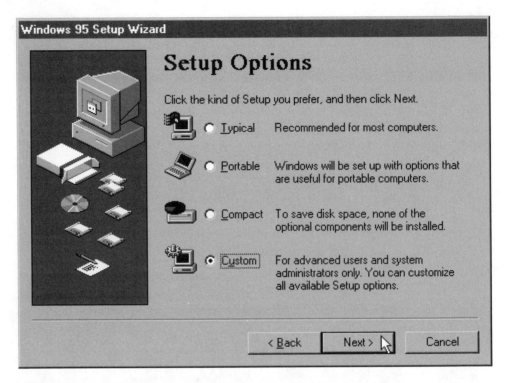

Figure 2.5 Setup Options is an attempt to make option choices for you

sounds like it makes the best sense for you. But later on, when I tell you to make a selection on the Windows Components screen, take my advice, OK?

Step 4. The next two Setup screens ask for two bits of information that you have to enter. The first is User Information. You have to enter your name (or some name) on this screen. The Company field is optional. The next screen (shown in Figure 2.6) asks for your CD Key. Recall that's the number on the orange sticker that was on the back of the cheesy cardboard "protector" your CD came in. Punch in that baby now.

Step 5. If something is going to get hairy, this is where it'll happen. The Analyzing Your Computer screen, captured (with some difficulty) for Figure 2.7, kicks off the within-an-inch-of-its-life hardware detection. On the first of the two screens, where it asks you whether it's OK to check out your system, say yes. One of the little peccadilloes about Setup is that you think clicking OK will launch detection. Not so. The next screen makes you click the Finish button to actually launch it. I think this is because on some PCs, you'll see an intervening screen asking about detecting specific devices that Windows 95 isn't quite sure you have. But anyway, this is annoying if you've walked away after clicking the first OK.

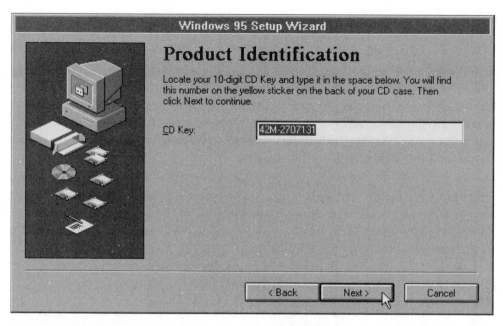

Figure 2.6   Plug in the number on your orange CD Key sticker

Figure 2.7   The major hardware detection thing in motion

Hardware detection is the second Setup sticking point.

Hardware detection takes a while, so this is a good time to go get coffee or something. It's also the second point in the setup process where a snag might occur. Check out the Setup Troubleshooting section a little further on in the chapter if your computer is having a bad day. A quick tip: If Setup hangs at this point, wait at least three minutes without any disk activity before you give up. If after that nothing's happening, try pressing F3 to exit Setup rather than rebooting. If you have to reboot, first try a warm reboot by pressing Ctrl-Alt-Delete. Your last resort is to turn off your PC. See the "Licking Setup Problems" section later in this chapter for more help.

Step 6.   Got through detection OK? Well, take a deep breath and pat yourself on the back. What's next is the decision-making part about the optional components you want installed. Get Connected, which looks like Figure 2.8, is the first screen you'll face. It offers the Microsoft Network (MSN), Microsoft Mail, and Microsoft Fax options. The choices you make on Get Connected actually add some things you might not expect them to. For example, when you choose MSN, you're also choosing to add the WordPad word processing tool. But, no, Microsoft isn't loading down your disk just for the heck of it. There are good reasons for the additions

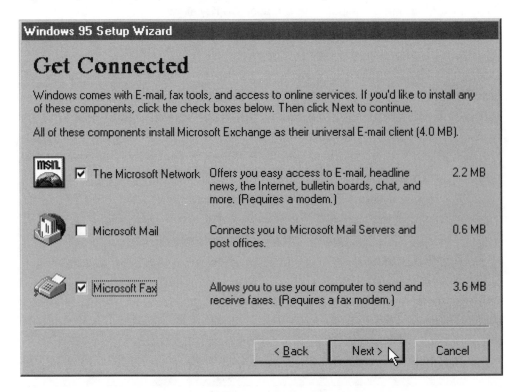

Figure 2.8   The Get Connected screen gives you, um, connection options

Setup makes based on your choices. In fact, Microsoft has gone to great pains to cut down on the extra stuff that gets installed with Win 95 options.

Anyway, if you're looking for a guiding hand at this point, I personally think the Microsoft Network is worth exploring. But if you know you're never going to use it, don't bother installing it. I'd skip Microsoft Mail. Microsoft Fax is a tough call. If you want to send and receive electronic faxes, install it. As a network fax tool, though, it bites.

Step 7.   If you see the screen in Figure 2.9 called Windows Components next, don't just breeze on by it. This is your last chance in Setup to customize your installation, and I recommend you take it. You can always leave everything as it is if you don't want to make choices. Or even click the Back button to change a setting on an earlier Setup screen. For example, you could go back and renege on the decision to fool with a "Custom" install track if it's all just too much to deal with. Anyway, to give yourself the chance to review optional components, click the "Show me the list of components so I can choose" radio button. *Note:* If you chose Custom on the Setup Options screen, then you won't see the Windows Components screen.

This is your last chance to customize your installation in Setup.

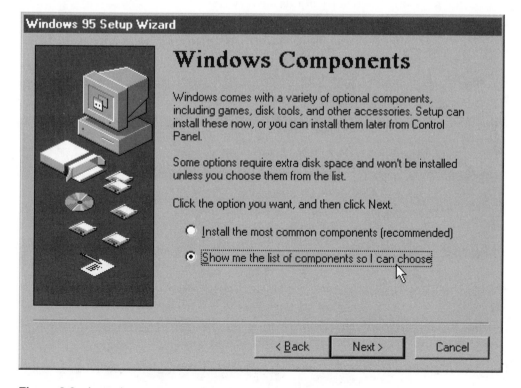

Figure 2.9   Last chance to control the installation options yourself

Step 8.   Select Components is where it all happens. The decisions you make on this screen will have a big impact on many of the handy-dandy stuff I tell you about in later chapters. Now's the time to turn to the first couple of pages of the Appendix and take a look at the table that shows Win 95's four Setup tracks. It also details my recommended installation tracks to help you see the trees through the forest. You can follow my recommendations even if you picked one of the other tracks.

Select Components has more levels than appear at first blush. You click on each heading on the main screen. If there are settings below the heading, the Details button will light up. When you click that button, you'll get a sublisting of options, such as the Accessories sublisting shown in Figure 2.10. Turn something on (set it to be installed) by putting a check in its box. Turn something off by clearing its check box. It's easy, really, but kind of annoying because of the many choices you're confronted with.

You can always rehabilitate your Win 95 installation later.

If the whole thing makes you want to throw that lightweight Win 95 manual across the room, just go with whatever track you picked. You can add individual options or completely rehabilitate your Win 95 installation any time you want to later on. You do that from the Windows tab of the Add/Remove Programs control panel program. Microsoft got this all very right.

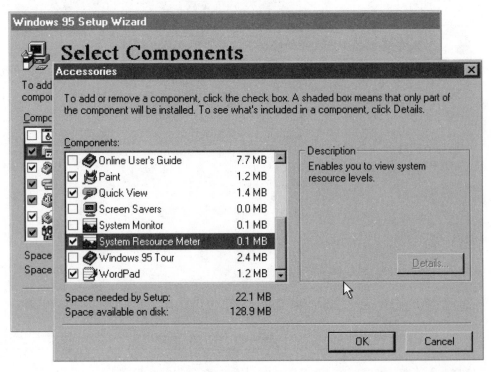

Figure 2.10   The Select Components screen showing the Accessories sublisting

Step 9.　Skip down to Step 10 if the machine you're installing on is *not* running on a network. Network folks, you'll see two successive screens, one that shows the network components that are about to be installed and another that lets you plug in your workstation and workgroup names. You can bypass the network components screen if you want, but this is a good time to add, for example, the TCP/IP networking protocol for connecting to the Internet. (It also can be done later, though.) On the Identification screen, plug in your computer's name. This can be anything you want it to be and doesn't have to be your network user name. If you're on a Microsoft network, such as NT, you'll also need a workgroup name.

Step 10.　Go over the Computer Settings screen carefully. This is one of the first indications of how well Setup's hardware detection did. In particular, look at the two video-oriented entries. Your video card model should be correctly identified. And more than likely, Windows 95 will not have been able to identify your monitor, so save yourself a bit of trouble by giving it that information now.

Did Setup correctly identify your video card?

　　Scroll down to the Monitor listing as shown in Figure 2.11 and double-click it (or press the Change button). Find your monitor's manufacturer in the scroll box on the left. When you click your manufacturer's name, you'll see all the supported monitors on the right. Double-click the one that matches your monitor's model name. If you don't find your specific model, scroll to the top of the Manufacturers box, choose "Standard monitor types," and select Standard VGA or the generic display type that most closely matches your display.

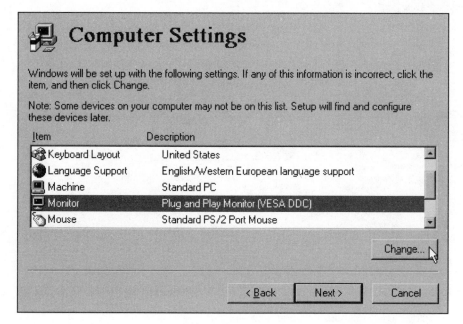

Figure 2.11　Make a tweak or two on Computer Settings to save aggravation

Step 11.   The last decision you have to make is whether to create a Windows 95 Startup Disk. You have to make only one of these, and it's easiest to make during Setup. You'll need a 3½-inch floppy disk that contains no data that you don't mind parting with. The process will add about five minutes to Setup. In the absolute worst-case scenario, you might need this disk if your installation goes south on your first startup. Odds are, you won't need it. But you definitely need a startup disk. You might as well make it now. This is one corner you shouldn't cut.

Step 12.   The last two screens, Start Copying Files and Finishing Setup, that "checkered flag" shown in Figure 2.12, come roughly 15 minutes apart (depending on how fast your hard disk is and the options you chose). All you have to do is click OK on each of these screens. Not much to it.

If you've made it this far without any problems, skip the next part on setup problems and touch back down on the "Running Win 95 for the First Time" section. One thing to know is that Setup really isn't complete yet. In many ways, some of the gorier stuff happens with the initial startup of Windows 95. And there's still some Setup-oriented stuff you've got to do once it successfully loads for the first time.

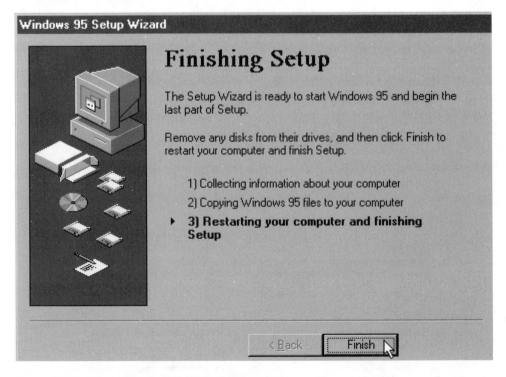

Figure 2.12   The Finishing Setup screen—phew!

LICKING SETUP PROBLEMS

The only way to win is to fight on the side of your adversaries.

Francis Picabia
Who Knows: Poems and Aphorisms, 1950

When Win 95's Setup goes wrong, you're in better shape than you might think to extricate yourself from the dilemma. Generally speaking, when Setup messes up it either freezes or goes into an endless loop. If the problem occurs during the hardware detection phase, don't be too quick about deciding that Setup has frozen. Wait at least three minutes beyond the point of the last hard-disk activity before doing anything.

When you're sure something's wrong, first try pressing the F3 key to exit Setup. If that doesn't work, your only recourse is to reboot. Try a warm reboot first by pressing Ctrl-Alt-Delete. If that doesn't work, go for the full effect and power down your PC. Wait 10 seconds, and then turn it back on.

Windows 95 has a built-in setup feature called Safe Recovery. Give this thing a chance to work before you try anything else. Safe Recovery may launch on its own when you reboot. If it doesn't, boot to the command line and run Setup again. Choose the Safe Recovery option to recover the failed installation. If this was a hardware detection problem, Safe Recovery will automatically skip the portion of the detection that caused the problem. A problem could happen because you have strange hardware or because you've been living with a hardware configuration conflict you were unaware of. But your best bet at this point is to just skip configuring this hardware and work on it after you successfully start up Windows 95.

Make Setup skip problem hardware.

If you encounter an error with either Setup or first-time startup, you can get more information from three log files that Windows 95 creates, which are all in your root directory. `DETLOG.TXT` is the hardware detection log; `SETUPLOG.TXT` keeps track of Setup events; and `BOOTLOG.TXT` records startup steps. You can open any of these files in a text editor, such as DOS's Edit. But they're long and complex. To search them all for error messages, use Edit to create a file called `CHEKLOGS.BAT`. Enter the following lines, which are supplied by Microsoft, into this file exactly as they appear. Then save the file to your boot drive's root directory. Type `cheklogs` on the DOS command line from the root directory, and you'll get a screen report on successes and errors.

```
@echo off
echo "Entries found in Setuplog.txt" >> log.txt
find /i /n "installtype" setuplog.txt >> log.txt
find /i /n "installdir" setuplog.txt >> log.txt
find /i /n "detection" setuplog.txt >> log.txt
find /i /n "runningapp" setuplog.txt >> log.txt
```

```
find /i /n "rootfilesrenamed" setuplog.txt >> log.txt
find /i /n "error" setuplog.txt >> log.txt
find /i /n "failed" setuplog.txt >> log.txt
echo "Entries found in BOOTLOG.TXT" >> log.txt
find /i /n "fail" bootlog.txt >> log.txt
find /i /n "error" bootlog.txt >> log.txt
find /i /n "dynamic load success" bootlog.txt >> log.txt
find /i /n "initcomplete success" bootlog.txt >> log.txt
echo "Entries found in DETLOG.TXT" >> log.txt
find /i /n "avoidmem" detlog.txt >> log.txt
find /i /n "detected" detlog.txt >> log.txt
find /i /n "error" detlog.txt >> log.txt
cls
type log.txt | more
```

Manual detection disabling

If Safe Recovery isn't helping you out and you've tried several times to install, you can follow a manual process for disabling detection of problem devices. Check out DETLOG.TXT (or use the batch file in the nearby wand tip) for information about what device or devices are in trouble. Then run Setup again. When you get to the Analyzing Your Computer screen, opt for "No, I want to specify hardware devices to detect." Clear the check box or boxes beside your problem hardware. Later you can configure this hardware manually. What's more likely, though, is that you'll have to track down which piece of hardware is causing contention on your system. That problem isn't Win 95's fault, by the way. It's one you were probably unaware you were living with.

If you breezed through the detection phase and your problems cropped up during file copying or at the end of install, rerun Setup from the command line and choose Safe Recovery. Try the Verify option. If the Safe Recovery screen doesn't appear, you'll probably get the "Run Setup Again?" screen, shown in Figure 2.13, with the choice to "Restore Windows files that are changed or corrupted." This provides the same sort of setup verification. Choose that option.

CD drive conflicts are among the toughest setup problems to resolve.

If you receive error messages that Setup is unable to find specific files on the CD during file copying phase, suspect a problem with the hardware configuration of your CD drive's controller card. You've probably got an input/output range conflict with another device. The input/output range—sometimes called "I/O Address," "memory address," or "port address"—is the specific block in memory your CD controller (or other device) gets all to its own. You may need to reconfigure your hardware using the setup utilities that came with it or even adjust jumper switches on the controller card. This kind of problem isn't unusual on PCs where a multimedia upgrade kit was added after manufacture. I hope you don't run into this, but if you do, don't panic. Just get out the manual for the hardware and take it step by step. If you get stuck, call the hardware company's tech support number and get help.

Figure 2.13 The Run Setup Again screen with the Restore option checked

RUNNING WIN 95 FOR THE FIRST TIME

> Now here, you see, it takes all the running you can do, to keep in the same place. If you want to get somewhere else, you must run at least twice as fast as that!
>
> Lewis Carroll
> The Red Queen, in *Through the Looking-Glass*, 1872

Your first startup of Windows 95 can be anything from treading through a mine-field of disasters to a smooth, seamless deal that takes about 10 minutes. In the early going, you'll see lots of DOS text screens and the ugly Windows 95 blue-sky screen (which hides DOS goings-on). It may even go back and forth between the two. Win 95 will pause for a while—"Configuring Windows 95 for the first time"—so just relax. As with Setup, I'll deal with potential problems further along. I like to think positive.

At some point, while your hard drive is churning and Windows 95 labors to construct its installation, you'll see the GUI (graphical user interface) kick in. This is a colored background with a mouse pointer and Microsoft's extremely ugly blue-and-black Setup wallpaper with pieces of hardware floating around in it. (Whatever possessed them to use this?) As the first-time startup nears its conclusion, you'll see the desktop and a box showing a list of tasks that Windows 95 is carrying out. The list of things Windows 95 sets up at this point varies depending on your Setup choices. However, you'll probably see the Control Panel, Programs on the Start Menu, Windows Help, MS-DOS Program Settings, Time Zone, and Microsoft Exchange (if you opted to install it).

Most of this part goes off on auto pilot, as long as Setup was fully successful.

Most of this stuff goes off without any need for human intervention. But you do have to pick a time zone on the Date/Time Properties screen (see Figure 2.14). Microsoft shows its Pacific-time-zone bias by making that region the default one for U.S. installations. Just drag the highlight bar to your part of the world and click OK to be done with it. Remember all that IP address stuff I said you might need? You'll need it for the configuration screens of the optional Exchange module. And if you installed the fax stuff, you'll need your fax number, too. The process is self-explanatory, though. Once through this gate, Windows 95 will restart, and you'll have successfully completed Microsoft's end of the whole Win 95 getting-going thing.

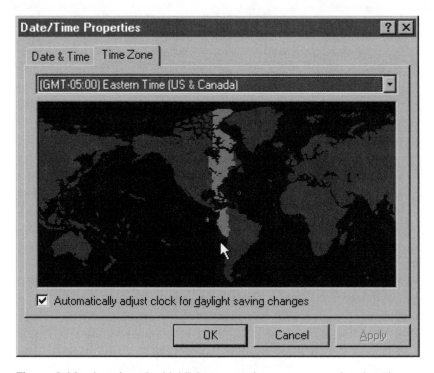

Figure 2.14 Just drag the highlight to your time zone on regional settings

Don't do the online registration—yet.

The Welcome screen displayed in Figure 2.15 is the first thing you'll see after Windows grinds your hard drive around and restarts. This is a good time to take the Windows Tour (CD folks) if you like that sort of thing. I explained Welcome in Chapter 1. What you need to know about it at this point is, don't do the online

Figure 2.15   This deal could well wear out its welcome

registration—yet. Do it later, once you're sure stuff is working. In fact, just close the Welcome screen for the moment. It'll reappear the next time Windows starts, and every time thereafter until you clear the check box beside the show-this-deal-in-future line that appears at the bottom. (*Note:* You won't see this line on the first startup.)

Check Out How Hardware Detection Fared

This is important, OK? Before you do anything else, follow these steps. Right-click My Computer and choose Properties from the popup menu, as I'm doing in Figure 2.16. This opens the System Properties dialog.

System

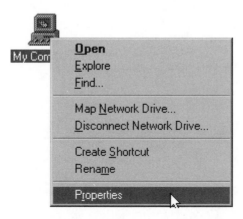

Figure 2.16   Next step: How to open System Properties and the Device Manager

Device Manager is your report card on the hardware detection process.

You've got two main chores in this dialog. The first is to click the Device Manager tab. The Device Manager is a report card on the hardware detection process. For a passing grade, you're looking for nothing unusual. And by unusual I mean entries on Device Manager that have either of two ominous-looking icons—a yellow exclamation point or a red circle with a slash through it. The first icon means the device is installed but turned off. The second, and more likely one, means there's something wrong with the device and it's not working.

There's a lot going on in Device Manager, so I'll step back and explain how this thing works. At the top of Device Manager is "Computer." All the lines below that top line represent "device types," like CD-ROM controllers, as category headings. Your actual devices—things like a specific brand and model of CD-ROM controller—are contained within each device type heading. And there may be more than one device listed under a device type heading. For example, you're apt to find at least two devices under the disk drive device types: your floppy drive and your hard drive.

Device Manager automatically opens, or expands, device types that are hosed.

You'll know at a glance that everything is copacetic in Device Manager if none of the device types is expanded, showing their devices, as shown in Figure 2.17. Device Manager automatically opens device types that are hosed. That way you don't have to go clicking and hunting around to check everything. To see the

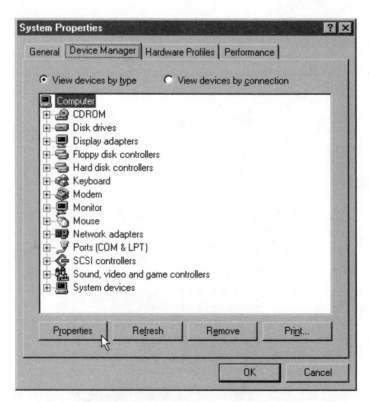

Figure 2.17   Device Manager will look like this when Setup goes well

specific devices listed under a device type, such as "Disk drives," click the plus sign beside its icon. The plus turns into a minus sign, and all detected devices for the class appear below and to the right, like the expanded disk drives shown in Figure 2.18. To close the device type, just click the minus sign.

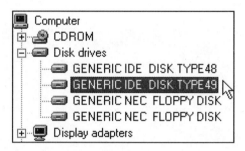

Figure 2.18 Device Manager's expanded hierarchical device structure

If, as you open Device Manager, you see an expanded device type with either a red or yellow icon next to one of its devices, there's a problem with that piece of hardware. The problem might be in Win 95's driver for the hardware, or it could be a conflict with the hardware settings. The settings may be physical switches on the card inside your PC, or they may be controlled by a utility program that came with your hardware. If you've got Plug and Play hardware, you'll be able to make adjustments from within Device Manager. But that's pretty unlikely unless your PC is brand spanking new.

Before you spend a lot of time poking around in Windows 95—customizing stuff and setting it up the way you like it—you should get to the bottom of any and all hardware conflicts you find in Device Manager. You might have to reinstall Win 95, or even uninstall it, to get things fixed. So it's best to nip this in the bud first. Read the next paragraph, which deals with the Performance tab, before you do anything else. It might help.

The Hardware Conflict Troubleshooter is perhaps the single best Help Wizard. To launch it, choose Start/Help. On the Contents tab, double-click the Troubleshooting topic. Then double-click the "If you have a hardware conflict" entry. That brings up the Hardware Conflict Troubleshooter start page. To launch the process, click the button beside "Start the Hardware Conflict Troubleshooter." Follow the instructions from there. The Hardware Conflict Troubleshooter is a great place to start. Although it can't solve every hardware conflict problem, if nothing else, it plants the procedure in your mind.

Regardless of what you found under Device Manager, the next thing to do is click System Properties' Performance tab, which will open the dialog shown in

Figure 2.19. The sentence you want to find will show up about halfway down the screen, if things have gone well. It'll read: "Your system is configured for optimal performance." If you find it, you're golden. There's stuff on the Performance tab that someday you might want to explore, but I wouldn't mess with it now. When you get a hankering to figure this out, turn to Chapter 9, "Living With It."

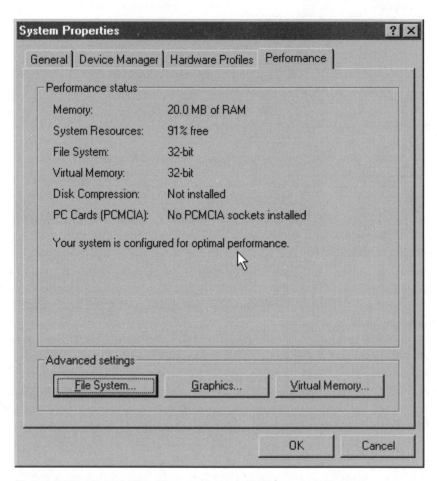

Figure 2.19   Golden! The clean and green Performance tab

If your PC isn't configured for optimal performance, you're probably facing a box with warning messages in the middle part of the Performance tab that look something like Figure 2.20. The most common type of problem reported in the box is when, for whatever reason, Windows 95 wasn't able to load a virtual device driver for some piece of hardware and may instead be using a far slower real-mode DOS driver. This may dovetail with any problems you found under the Device Manager tab. And since by clicking the Details button for any warning line

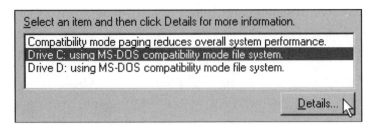

Figure 2.20   An example of warning messages on the
Performance tab

you may find a way to fix the problem, it's a good idea to check this out. Even if
there isn't some automatic way to fix the problem, Windows 95 will give you
some additional info on Details that may help you figure out a solution.

Your PC aced the Device Manager and Performance tab checks? Man, do I
have some good news for you: Windows 95 is safely and correctly installed on
your PC. Finally. You're moving into the post-installation tweaks phase. But scan
this next part anyway on solving startup problems, particularly the stuff about
Windows 95 boot options and the F8 key. And if you ran into a snag, stick around
and pore over this next part.

**If your PC aced
things up until
now, man do I
have good
news.**

LICKING INITIAL STARTUP PROBLEMS

> Everybody's a mad scientist, and life is their lab. We're all trying to experi-
> ment to find a way to live, to solve problems, to fend off madness and chaos.
>
> David Cronenberg
> *Cronenberg On Cronenberg,* 1992

If you crashed or hung the first time Windows went a-launching after Setup,
there's built-in stuff that may solve the problem automatically as well as steps
you can take on your own.

The first thing to try is restarting. But you probably did that. Your next best
step is to try Safe Mode. Before I get into that, let me tell you about one flavor of
startup problem where Safe Mode probably isn't indicated. If you're getting error
messages about specific damaged or missing files or a VxD error, you'll want to
run Setup again, enter Safe Recovery if possible, and Verify or Restore the setup.

For everyone else, here's the deal about Safe Mode. It's the alter ego of Windows 95, a subspecies. Its whole reason for being is to serve as a sort of default,
plain-vanilla installation with hardware settings defaulted to generic drivers in
their simplest forms. So it's not too bright and not too fast. And a lot of things
don't work. It was designed to circumvent a wide variety of problems that users
might encounter. Safe Mode is your best fallback when you get in trouble with
Windows 95. And it never hurts to try it.

The F8 key and Safe Mode

Now sometimes, you'll be pulled into Safe Mode automatically. Other times, it can be really useful to direct Windows 95 to enter Safe Mode. To do that, restart the computer. Keep an eye on things as the PC is coming back up. Just before or during the time when you see the DOS text line: "Starting Windows 95. . .," press the F8 key. Table 2.3 explains the startup options that then become available. Note that the Safe Mode I've been referring to is the one listed as #3 in the table.

Table 2.3   The Seven Startup Options That F8 Provides

Startup Option	Description
1. Normal	Starts Windows, loading all normal startup files and Registry values.
2. Logged (BOOTLOG.TXT)	Runs normal system startup and creates a startup log file named BOOTLOG.TXT.
3. Safe Mode	Starts Windows, bypassing startup files and using only basic system drivers and environment settings.
4. Safe Mode with Network Support	Same as #3, but adds basic networking functionality.
5. Step-by-Step Confirmation	Starts Windows, confirming startup files line by line.
6. Command Prompt Only	Starts the DOS operating system only.
7. Safe Mode Command Prompt Only	The very simplest startup. Starts the DOS operating system only, bypassing the startup files.

Read this wand tip. It piggybacks the one in the "Onboard Help and Answers" section of Chapter 1 about the Windows 95 Resource Kit, which is available as an extensive Help file on the Windows 95 CD. There's excellent setup and startup troubleshooting information in the Resource Kit Help file. In particular, check under "General Troubleshooting" in the Windows 95 Reference section. And don't pass up the "Troubleshooting Specific Setup Errors" and "Startup Errors" sections under the Setup Technical Discussion part of the Installation section. Look around; it's not organized all that well. But it's jam-packed with useful info. I realize this might be something of a Catch-22 if you're having serious trouble starting up Windows 95, but chances are, the answers are in these files. If you have to, take your CD to someone else whose PC has Win 95 installed. There's far more information there for solving problems than I could possibly cram in here.

While you're at it, check out the Windows Startup Troubleshooter. It's basic, but it gives you step-by-step instructions. Choose Start/Help, double-click Troubleshooting, and then double-click "If you have trouble starting Windows."

Early Startup Snags

Some installations are so messed up, they never really get out of the gate on startup. If that happens to you, you'll be really glad you took my advice and created a startup disk during Setup. This disk lets you boot from your floppy disk as a last resort.

Is it hardware or software?

Keep this in mind. There are two main types of problems that mess up Windows 95: software driver conflicts and hardware conflicts. Sometimes they're intertwined. But if you've got a really thorny problem, suspect hardware. To determine whether hardware or software is stalling the computer, press F8 on restart and choose Safe Mode Command Prompt Only from the menu. If you get to the command line OK, your problem is more likely with a device driver or TSR than with hardware.

If that's the case, restart and choose the Step-by-Step Confirmation Startup Option. Odds are, you'll hang while you're doing this. But *where* you hang is all-important. When you know it's a specific command being launched out of CONFIG.SYS or AUTOEXEC.BAT, then you can reboot to the floppy and use DOS's Edit program to comment out that line by placing a REM and character space at the beginning of the line. Sometimes it's something that's launching out of System Registry. If you can't resolve a Registry problem, your best bet is to run Setup again and let Safe Recovery try to fix the problem.

If you've got a driver problem, it could be because Windows 95 doesn't have a standard driver that matches your less-than-mainstream hardware. Both floppy and CD owners have a useful Hardware Compatibility List Help file and several folders of drivers at their disposal. Check out the HCL Help file first. You'll find it in the Drivers folder on the CD. Just double-click the HCL95.HLP file you find there to launch the program. Even better, you can get many of the latest hardware drivers from Microsoft's Web site. If you have access to the Web, plug this URL into your browser:

http://www.microsoft.com/windows/software/drivers/drivers.htm

It shows a long list of new drivers, and you can download any of them just by clicking its link.

Late Startup Woes

If your startup problem occurred later on in the startup process, then restart, hold down F8, and pick number 3—Safe Mode—from the Startup Options screen. If this gets you in, it's still very possible that the problem is hardware-based, not driver-based. But at this point, you're going to have problems with drivers because of the problems with hardware. If you can't get into Safe Mode, which has the funny test-screen look of Figure 2.21, and you've already retried Setup's Safe Recovery, you more than likely have a serious hardware conflict on your system.

Safe Mode is both amazing and annoying.

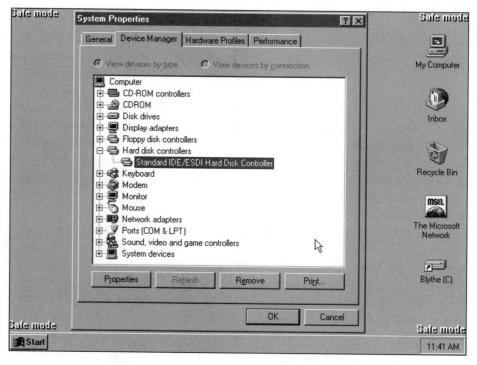

Figure 2.21   Safe Mode is a strange alter ego of Windows 95

Believe me, you won't be the first PC user to discover this the hard way. If you don't think you can fix this yourself, get help. The good news is, your PC will probably run much better when you get it fixed. It's like a car that has crossed spark plug wires.

Chances are, though, Safe Mode got you in there. Repeat the steps I described earlier in the chapter about checking the Device Manager and Performance tabs. You're probably going to find problems on one or both of these screens. First check out the Performance tab for simple fixes. Your real work, however, will likely be done in Device Manager.

Start by looking for multiple installations of a single device under a device type. Nothing messes up Win 95 faster than to have two driver lines installed, for example, for the same hard disk. Remove them both. If you find devices being called out by the red slashed-circle icons, remove them. One of the frustrating things about Safe Mode is that you can't make changes to most of the settings of any of these devices (as you can when you're normally launched into Windows 95). Your only real recourse is to turn them on or turn them off and remove them. In most situations, your best bet is to remove them. Excise the root of the problem. Then close System Properties and restart Windows 95 to see if it'll work. If not, you'll probably have to run Setup again. You may also have to run Setup again if you removed a device that's crucial to running your PC and you don't have a real-mode driver fallback loading from CONFIG.SYS. If this is a device that originally ran from a DEVICE= line in CONFIG.SYS, you might want to place the line back in there (since Win 95 probably removed it). That'll get you going, after a fashion.

Down and Dirty Device Manager

Add New Hardware

If entering and exiting Safe Mode, and whatever you might have done there, turned the trick and Windows 95 booted normally, don't rest on your laurels. Win 95 may have started up normally, but it's probably limping. Get back in there and check the Device Manager and Performance tabs. See what you can see. And if you've got no new problems in Device Manager, run hardware detection again. You do that by launching the Add New Hardware control panel and letting Windows 95 search for all "new" devices, as shown in Figure 2.22. In this case, they're not new devices; they're devices whose drivers you removed. If this delivers more devices with red-slashed circles, you've probably got a hardware conflict.

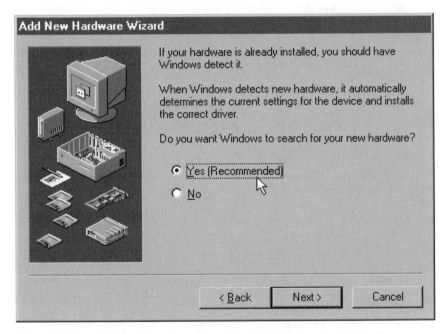

Figure 2.22 The Add New Hardware control panel about to launch detection

But note that you're already ahead of the game: You know what device or devices have a problem. You can use Device Manager to check for a conflict with any device by clicking on it, clicking Properties, choosing the Resources tab, and looking in the window with the heading "Conflicting device list." Windows 95 will let you set the input/output range and interrupt request settings (when normally started; they're not accessible in Safe Mode) on many of the devices from the Resources tab. And that can sometimes be useful, especially if you're making settings adjustments to your hardware with jumpers on the card or via a card's setup utility. But unless your hardware is Plug and Play compatible, making such a settings change solely in Device Manager changes just Win 95's driver configuration. Your hardware will blithely go on trying to work under the previous settings. And you'll have made things worse. But you can see that someday, when you have all PnP hardware, things are going to be much easier.

So, stick with the program. Use Device Manager as an analyzer. Make changes physically to your hardware to get rid of conflicts. Then, and only then, make adjustments to settings on the Resources tabs of devices, as it looks like I'm about to do in Figure 2.23. Or you can remove the devices and redetect them with Add New Hardware.

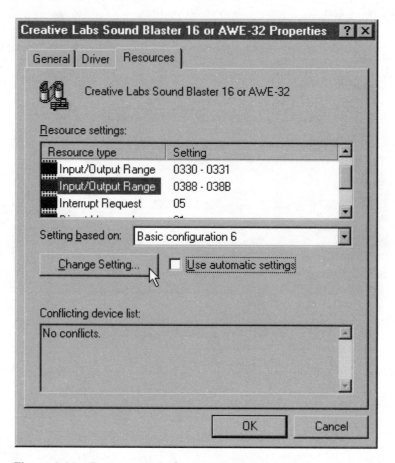

Figure 2.23   Resources tab for a sound blaster card

Device Manager has some other views that can be useful. Select the topmost entry—Computer—and then click the Properties button. What you get is the Computer Properties screen, shown in Figure 2.24, which offers four main views of your whole computer: Interrupt requests (IRQ), Input/output ranges, Direct memory address, and Memory addressing. Check it out.

Getting properties for Device Manager's "Computer" entry doesn't jump out at you, but try it.

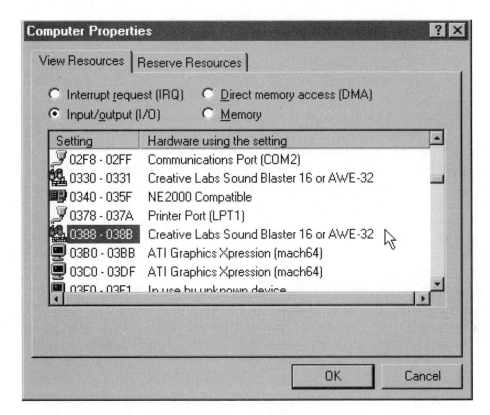

Figure 2.24   Computer Properties screen showing all input/output ranges

This can be useful when you have, say, an interrupt request conflict and need to find an IRQ not being used by any other device in your PC. You'd shift the IRQ setting of one of the conflicting devices to the unused IRQ, and then either change the setting manually in Device Manager or use the Add/Remove Programs control panel to redetect it.

POST-INSTALLATION TWEAKS

tweak (twēk) *verb, transitive*
tweaked, tweak·ing, tweaks
1. To pinch, pluck, or twist sharply.
2. To adjust; fine-tune.
noun
A sharp, twisting pinch.
[Probably variant of dialectal *twick*, from Middle English *twikken*, from Old English *twiccian*.]
— **tweak'y** *adjective*

> *The American Heritage Dictionary of the English Language*
> Houghton Mifflin Company, Third Edition, 1992

Control Panel

**One-stop
screen controls**

Display

OK, almost done. A few tweaks and things. And the big explanation of how to set up dual booting with your previous version of DOS and Windows. Once you get Windows 95 installed properly, go forth and mess with the Display control panel. The fastest way to do that is to right-click the desktop and choose Properties from the popup menu.

It slices, it dices. Think of Display as a merging of the old Windows Setup's Display controls with its Control Panel applets for Color and Desktop. Under Win 95, this whole thing is vastly improved. Also, you don't have to exit it and run a separate DOS program to make adjustments. The Display dialog offers four tabs: Background (which handles desktop pattern and wallpaper), Screen Saver, Appearance (which does what Colors did), and Settings (which handles video drivers and display resolutions—essentially the Setup part of the equation.)

The real cool stuff happens on Display Properties Settings dialog, which is shown in Figure 2.25. You can increase the screen resolution (or Desktop area) from this tab without having to swap Windows disks in and out or even restarting Windows. But before you try that, do the post-installation tweak. Click the Change Display Type button and make sure the Adapter Type (or video card) and Monitor Type selections match your hardware. Windows 95 will probably be in the ballpark on the video card, but it may have selected a video adapter that has the same chip as your card's but that is a different model. So check that out. Win 95 doesn't detect monitors at all unless they're Plug and Play devices. So poke around behind the Change button for the Monitor Type. If you can't find it, choose something from "Standard monitor types." I'd pick the SuperVGA setting that supports your monitor's maximum screen resolution. Most 14-inch displays support at least 800 × 600-pixel resolution and just about any monitor 15 inches or bigger can support at least 1024 × 768-pixel resolution. You should go for the largest resolution your monitor supports. (If you're not sure what that is, check the docs.)

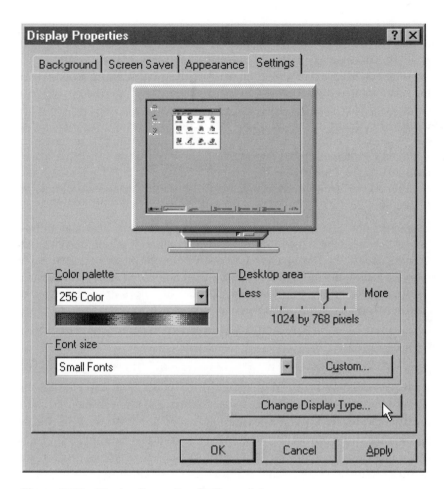

Figure 2.25 Display Properties Settings dialog

Got that done? OK, check this out. Back on the Display Properties Settings tab, move the slider under the heading Desktop area to More (if available) to increase the screen resolution. Click Apply. Then click OK on the subsequent confirmation dialog. You'll get a question dialog asking whether you'd like to keep the new settings. If you click No or don't do anything for 15 seconds, Windows goes back to your original resolution. If you click Yes, you'll be working at the new higher res, and without having to restart. It works going from higher to lower res, too. Unfortunately, Display Properties can only change resolution on the fly; it can't change the number of simultaneous colors displayed (a.k.a. "color depth"). This color depth deal is what they're talking about under the "Color palette" heading.

On-the-fly resolution changes

It's easy to become a bit fooled by some of the stuff going on when you make resolution changes in Display Properties Settings. Any time you make a color depth change—smaller or larger—Windows will prompt for a restart. Your resolution limit and your maximum number of displayed colors are each a function of the same thing: Video RAM. If you try to max out your resolution, say to 1024 × 768 pixels, Windows may prompt you to restart because you don't have enough video memory to both boost resolution and retain your original color depth. So, Win 95 automatically reduces your color depth. (It'd be better if you saw a dialog explaining this instead of a prompt to restart.) By raising the resolution bar, especially jumping two notches, you'll probably have to restart. You don't have to restart if you don't want to. But your changes won't take effect until you do.

Confused? Think of it this way. Your video card is much more likely to be able to handle low resolution (640 × 480) and a large amount of colors (16- or 32-bit) or vice versa (1024 × 768 by 256 colors) than both high resolution and a large number of colors. If you boost resolution beyond your video card's capacity at the current color depth, you'll see the number of colors drop under the color palette heading before you click Apply or OK.

Fontarama

You can scale the size of most fonts Windows displays on the Appearance tab.

Stop squinting at the screen. In Windows 95, desktop, dialog, and menu fonts are adjustable. On Display Properties Appearance screen, you can change the typefaces and font sizes of several Windows constructs, like message boxes, menu items, active and inactive title bar captions, and buttons. For some of these items, notably the desktop, your ability to change the font has been turned off. But you can also scale the size of most fonts that Windows displays, either larger or smaller, on Desktop Properties Settings screen. Click Custom in the Font size area and either use the drop-down Scale box or click and drag the ruler to scale to finer percentage increments. Take a look at Figure 2.26.

Fonts

There's also a Fonts control panel. Microsoft released a nifty little Windows utility in 1992 called Font Assistant. Among other things, it took care of adding and removing TrueType fonts from your Windows installation and displaying them as they print to help you make typeface decisions. The question always was, why did they charge extra for something that should have been built into Windows to begin with?

Well, we don't quite have that now either. When you open the Fonts control panel, something like Font Assistant Very Lite steps up to the mound to help out. You can install new fonts, delete them, sort them, and even review what they look like with the File/Open command (see Figure 2.27). It's a little disappointing, though. During the early betas of Windows 95, the Fonts control panel was a much better little font utility. It's one of the things that got shaved down, I guess in the name of performance because it was kind of slow, especially when you

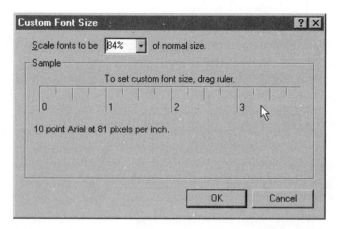

Figure 2.26 Custom Windows font sizes, drag ruler to adjust

chose to show the fonts displayed in their natural form all on one screen. Something you can't do in the shipping version of Windows 95. Oh, well.

If you give fonts half a chance, before you know it they'll own your Windows installation. Font-related dialogs and drop-downs start taking forever to open and Windows takes longer to load. How many of them do you really use anyway? Use Win 95's Fonts control panel to zap all the ugly ones now and then.

Fonts have a way of multiplying.

Figure 2.27 What you get when you open a font in the font folder

Printer Setup

Printers

Pick Printers from Start's Settings submenu (or double-click the Printers folder in My Computer or the Control Panel), and you'll get a folder window showing icons for any printers that are currently set up on your system. When you double-click a printer icon, what pops up is something very akin to the old Print Manager. It lets you manage print jobs. Don't forget the right mouse button, though. Click with it on any printer icon, and you've found the quickest route to changing stuff, like Set As Default and Properties. The first one is an important convenience feature, and the second offers all the custom controls for your printer.

Add Printer

The hands-down best part of the Printers folder, though, is Add Printer. Just double-click this button and answer the questions. It's a certified Microsoft Wizard that takes over the job of setting up a new printer. What it doesn't do is keep you from having to toss all the socks out of your socks drawer as you hunt down your Windows disc (or disks). You'll still probably have to stick in one or the other to load the drivers. Add Printer does give you a list of printer models to choose from and asks useful leading questions instead of making you play a guessing game. The Boyz from Redmond probably figured you'd rather not have 9,437 printer drivers automatically loaded on your hard drive—the price we'd all have to pay to skip the disk swapping. I'll go along with that.

Program Note: If you print to a network printer, don't use the Add Printer Wizard. Instead use Network Neighborhood to locate the printer on the network, right-click its icon, and choose Install from the popup menu. This procedure is explained more fully in Chapter 8, "Connections." You won't even need your Win 95 disc for this trip, since Windows 95 copies the printer drivers from the network server. Pretty neat. (*Note:* some DOS and a few Windows apps expect a "captured" printer port. See Chapter 8 for more on that.)

If you've got multiple printers set up in the Printers folder, it's a good idea to decide which printer you print to most of the time and make it the default printer. You do that by right-clicking its icon and choosing Default from the popup menu.

This "default printer" deal is a very nice improvement in Windows 95. You don't have to go back and change print settings in your apps whenever you change the default printer. As long as your apps are set to print to the default printer, you just make the change once—in the Printers folder.

Modem Mania

Modems

The first time you go to use your external modem, you may find that Windows 95 says you don't have a modem installed. Don't freak. It's just that you probably forgot to turn on your modem during Win 95's setup. Happens all the time. And because it's such a common occurrence, Microsoft gave us a little standalone detection tool in the Control Panel to take care of it. This is painless. Turn on your modem, open the Modems control panel, and click the Add button. Win 95 takes it from there. All you need is your Setup disc or disks. (For more on what's behind all the buttons in Modem Properties, check out Chapter 8, "Connections.")

Online Registration

People who like to think Microsoft is intrinsically evil beat up on the Boyz a lot just before Windows 95 shipped. They said that the online registration deal in Windows 95 was a snoop that ferreted out private information about your PC and sent it electronically to Microsoft, where it would be used for nefarious purposes by the software giant to help it rule the world.

Welcome

Balderdash. The truth is that Microsoft's Registration Wizard does collect some information about your PC, but it's very basic information about the devices, CPU, memory, and the like. Their nefarious purpose? To save themselves some money on tech support when you call them with problems. Oh, I don't think I'd put it past them to analyze the data to see what the average Windows 95 user's RAM and CPU type are. And they'll use that for marketing and future product development purposes, no doubt. But that's really a good thing. That way they won't build a Windows 97 that uses too little or too much of your hardware.

The thing is, the information the Registration Wizard collects doesn't wing its way to Microsoft automatically. The Registration screen, featured in Figure 2.28, shows you what info the wizard has collected. You can't move beyond that screen without specifically choosing to either send the data to Microsoft or not. Your privacy is about as protected as it could be. The only question is, do you want the tech support people to have all the information they can get when you call them? Or would you prefer to work under the slightly paranoid misapprehension that Microsoft is trying to find out more about you than it should? Well, I chose the second option. I didn't send them my information. But I really don't think there's anything wrong with sending it. It might even save your bacon on some dark night.

Your privacy is about as protected as it could possibly be.

Anyway, now that you've got everything humming on your Windows 95 installation, it's a good time to register. I'd advise registering, whether you let the Reg Wizard send your PC underwear or not. To launch the Wizard, you click the Online Registration button on the Welcome screen. You can restart to bring that up, or you can double-click the `WELCOME.EXE` (it'll probably appear as just `Welcome`) icon in your Windows folder. It's an online form. You fill in your name, address, and stuff. I'd skip the phone number; I mean, who knows who they might rent the list to? When you're done, the call takes only about a minute or so.

Adding Win 95 Options after Install

When you decide to explore some of the many other doodads Microsoft ships, but doesn't install by default, on the Windows 95 disc or disks, the process is pretty darn easy. It works exactly the same as I described under Step 8 in the "Setup: A

Add/Remove Programs

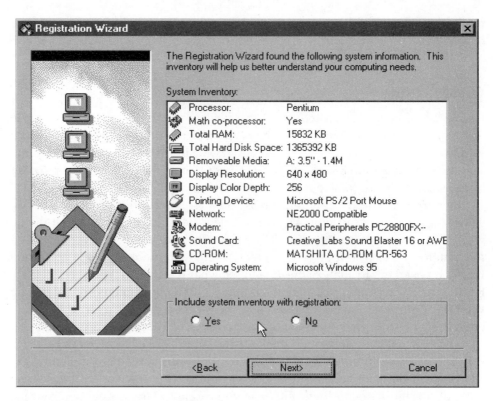

Figure 2.28   Registration Wizard's collected info: You have to click Yes or No

12-Step Program" section. But you don't run Setup again, thank gawd. Instead, open the Add/Remove Programs control panel and click the Windows Setup tab. That gives you the dialog shown in Figure 2.29. All the choices are laid out there before you. The hardest part is sticking the disc in the caddy.

SETTING UP WINDOWS DUAL BOOT

Boot between two versions of Windows, but store them both on your hard disk.

As long as you either kept a copy of your old Windows installation in a separate directory or installed Windows 95 into a directory other than `C:\WINDOWS` (where your previous version of Windows exists), there's a pretty easy way to set up Win 95 to run either Windows 95 or your previous version of DOS and Windows. And to switch back and forth between the two with relative ease.

The one major penalty you'll pay for this convenience is the need to keep on your hard drive two entire Windows installations, both the old and the new. But if you have the extra MBs, it's a great fallback while you're getting used to the new operating system.

There's also a lesser caveat. Since Windows 95 automatically replaces some of your DOS utilities with new versions designed to work with Win 95, when you boot to your previous installation, you won't have access to some of these special-

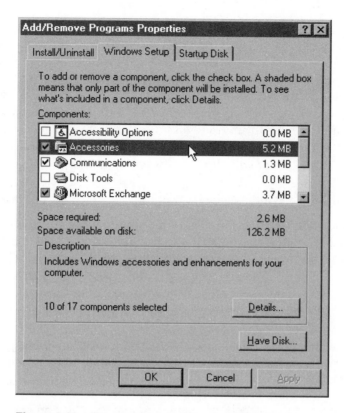

Figure 2.29 The Add/Remove Programs Windows
Setup tab

ized utilities. That won't affect system operation, but it can be annoying. Most of the deleted utilities are available in Win 95's C:\WINDOWS\COMMAND directory. But you'll get Incorrect DOS Version errors with some of them if you try to run them when dual-booted back to old DOSland. That's why earlier in this chapter I suggested you make a backup of your DOS directory. (Also as noted earlier, if you upgraded from DOS 6.22 with a Win 95 CD, you could copy the deleted DOS files from the \Other\OldMSDOS folder on the CD.) If you use my backed-up DOS directory method, once you successfully boot to your old DOS you can edit all references to your DOS directory in CONFIG.SYS and AUTOEXEC.BAT to the path location of your backed-up DOS directory.

Sorting Out the Two Methods

The two methods of setting up dual boot have different trade-offs. By installing Windows 95 into a different directory than your pre-existing version of Windows, you'll greatly simplify your ease of dual booting, at the expense of having to reinstall all of your applications because you won't have performed a Windows upgrade.

By creating a Windows 3.*x* backup directory, however, you have to rename your Windows directory (which can mess with long filenames, although not in a way that creates serious problems) each time you switch between Windows versions and you'll have to take some extra steps to boot your old version of Windows. I detail those steps on the next several pages. There are two main advantages of making a backup copy of your Windows 3.*x* installation and then performing a Windows 3.*x* upgrade on your Windows directory. First, you can perform an upgrade install. Second, you can configure dual boot any time you want to. Maybe you never will. But you always have the option to do so.

Dual Boot without a Windows 3.x Upgrade

To set up dual boot the Microsoft way, without upgrading your pre-existing Windows installation, follow these steps. Install Windows, choosing a different directory to install it to instead of `C:\WINDOWS`. Probably a newly created `C:\WIN95` directory. After Setup, follow Step 1 under the "Dual Boot with a Windows 3.*x* Upgrade" heading a few paragraphs below. Thereafter, whenever you want to go back to the old Windows, follow Step 3 under the same heading.

Is it too late for you? Did you already install Windows 95, upgrading your previous Windows installation without making a backup? And now you wish you could dual boot? As long as you have a boot floppy disk from your previous version of DOS, there is a way. It isn't pretty, but here's what you do. Make copies of the `IO.SYS`**,** `MSDOS.SYS`**, and** `COMMAND.COM` **files on your DOS boot disk, naming them** `IO.DOS`**,** `MSDOS.DOS`**, and** `COMMAND.DOS`**. You'll need to use the DOS Attrib command to set the attributes so that you can rename these files. After you've renamed them, copy them to the root drive of your PC. You'll also need** `CONFIG.DOS` **and** `AUTOEXEC.DOS` **files that at least approximate the** `CONFIG.SYS` **and** `AUTOEXEC.BAT` **files that were on your drive before you installed Windows 95. Maybe you kept backups? (I did.) After all that's done, follow Steps 1 and 3 under the next heading. When you get to the DOS prompt of your previous version of DOS, you can reinstall your old version of Windows to a different directory.**

Dual Boot with a Windows 3.x Upgrade

How often will you boot the old Windows really? This method is for the "not too often" answer.

This method places the burden on the back end, making it a bit tougher to dual boot. But if you follow my advice closely, it becomes something like a five-minute operation, tops. And it'll probably take you half an hour to set up. Here are the steps.

Step 1. Configure BootMulti in **MSDOS.SYS.**

Double-click My Computer. Inside that window, double-click the icon for your C: hard drive to open its folder window. Choose View/Options/View. Click the radio button beside "Show all files" and click OK. Now, find the MSDOS.SYS file icon in the C: folder window. Click it with the right mouse button and choose "Properties." In the Attributes area, click off the check marks beside "Read-only" and "Hidden" and click OK.

Next, right-click the MSDOS.SYS icon again and choose "Open With...". Scroll down the list of applications until you find the Notepad entry and double-click it. You should see an open document with some line entries at the top. Under the [Options] section heading, type this line:

```
BootMulti=1
```

Don't change anything else. Save the file and exit Notepad. One last thing. You'll find the MOVE.EXE file icon in the Command folder inside Win 95's Windows folder. Copy that file to the root directory of your hard drive.

Step 2. Prepare the Directories.

Choose Start/Shutdown/Restart the computer in MS-DOS mode. This is not your old version of DOS, but the new version that comes with Windows 95. Make the command prompt display C:\> by typing CD \ and pressing Enter. Rename your Win 95 and old Windows directories by typing the following two lines exactly as they appear (assuming your Windows 95 installation is installed in the C:\WINDOWS directory and you copied your original Windows installation to a directory named C:\WIN31). Press Enter after each line.

```
move c:\windows c:\win95
move c:\win31 c:\windows
```

Step 3. Go Back in Time.

Press Ctrl-Alt-Delete to reboot your PC. Press the F8 key when you see the words "Starting Windows 95..." in the left corner of the screen. Because of the change you made to MSDOS.SYS, there'll be an eighth option on the Windows 95 Startup Options screen: "Previous version of MS-DOS." Pick that one and your system will reboot to your old version of DOS. You'll also be ready to launch right into the old Windows. Your nostalgic trip will last until the next time you restart the computer.

Your nostalgic trip will last until the next time you reboot the PC.

Step 4. Return to Win 95.

Remember, you can't just reboot to Win 95 with this particular method of dual booting. If you try to just reboot without pressing F8 and choosing "Previous version of MS-DOS," Win 95 will try to launch itself in your old Windows directory. You get lots of interesting error messages that way. Instead, exit Windows and get the DOS prompt pointed at your root directory again. Then reverse your renaming of the directories with these lines:

```
move c:\windows c:\win31
move c:\win95 c:\windows
```

Turn 'em into batch files to speed things up a bit.
Now press Ctrl-Alt-Delete to reboot. Windows 95 will load automatically. I made two little batch files of the two sets of lines I've shown you, one called TOWIN95.BAT (the second one) and the other called TOWIN31.BAT. I just run them instead of mucking around with the MOVE commands.

Other MSDOS.SYS Adjustments

BootMulti=1 isn't the only adjustment that Microsoft provided for. See Table 2.4 for a list of the other ones, along with descriptions. This might come in handy.

Table 2.4   MSDOS.SYS [Options] Section Settings

Setting	Purpose
BootDelay=<Seconds> Default: 2	Sets the amount of time the "Starting Windows" message remains on the screen before Windows 95 continues to boot.
BootFailSafe= Default: 0	A setting of 1 forces your computer to boot in Safe Mode.
BootGUI= Default: 1	A setting of 1 forces the loading of the GUI interface. A setting of 0 disables the GUI.
BootMenu= Default: 0	A setting of 1 enables the Startup Menu. If the setting is 0, then in order to invoke the Startup Menu you must press the F8 key when "Starting Windows 95" appears.
BootMenuDefault= Default: 1 if system is running correctly; 4 if system hung previously.	Sets the default menu item for startup.
BootMenuDelay= Default: 30	Sets the number of seconds your system will pause on the Startup Menu. If the number of seconds counts down to 0 without intervention, the BootMenuDefault is activated.
LOGO=0	Kills the animated blue-sky startup logo screen.

*   *   *

Well, folks, it's off to the races. The next three chapters are where things get really interesting. The book jacket promises tips and tricks and ways to make Win 95 your own (no, I don't write that stuff). They're in there. Don't stop now.

3 The Desktop Interface

A molehill man is a pseudo-busy executive who comes to work at 9 AM and finds a molehill on his desk. He has until 5 PM to make this molehill into a mountain. An accomplished molehill man will often have his mountain finished before lunch.

Fred Allen
Treadmill to Oblivion, 1954

I'm going to get into a big harangue in a minute about user interfaces for PCs. It's one of my favorite subjects (I know, get a life), and since this is my book, you get the benefit of my . . . ahem . . . wisdom. Before I go any further, though, you need to know what this chapter is about.

It's about the desktop, right? Well, if you ask me, "The Desktop Interface" is a pretty crummy name for a chapter. It might have been worse, though. I could have called it something like "The Win 95 GUI" (that's "graphical user interface" in something that approximates English). Anyway, what you're going to find in here is just about everything you need to know about all the major controls and doodads you see on the Windows 95 desktop: Start, Taskbar, My Computer, Recycle Bin—all that rot. So hang in there. This is some of my best stuff.

Old Interfaces Never Die

In 1987 I bought a Macintosh. I'd been using IBM-compatible PCs for many years, so at first I felt like a traitor. Forbidden fruit and all that. Then, for a while, I felt like I'd purchased a very expensive toy computer. But after six months, I wasn't using any other computer—and I'd even convinced my company to purchase several Macs. My Mac days were something of a detour, though, since I came back to the PC for professional reasons in 1989. But the experience taught this computer journalist something very important.

Macs are cool. They were *way* ahead of their time in the 1980s. Apple Computer was ingenious about harnessing the best technology of the day, but just way stupid about attacking the marketplace with its creation. Apple knew how to

Figure 3.1   Completely uncalled-for thumbnail view of the Win 95 desktop

reach users (something today's computer companies, Microsoft included, could take some heavy lessons on). Steve Jobs and crew just didn't know how to play nice with the other computer companies. Under its original visionaries, Apple was asleep at the business-model switch, living in dreamland, planning to rule the world with a better mousetrap. All its successive leaders have had more than one eye on the bottom line, focusing far too firmly on this quarter's P&L statements. You can't make a revolution a reality that way.

It should be the classic B-school case study.   Apple's saga should be the classic textbook case study that every Harvard Business School student is forced to read over and over and over again. The best technology in the world does not money make if you jealously hoard it and don't spread it around enough to make it take seed elsewhere.

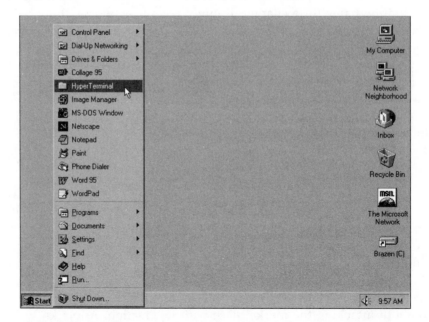

Figure 3.2   The Mac-evocative Windows 95 desktop, with the Open Start Menu showing

In 1995, more than 10 years after the Mac first shipped—an eon in computer years—Microsoft finally made good on its own dream to transform the Intel-architected PC platform into something very like a Macintosh, circa 1989 (see Figure 3.2). Make no mistake. Redmond wanted to do this very badly. Microsoft is the single largest third-party Macintosh application developer. Has been almost from the get-go. Next to Apple, Microsoft probably knows more about the Macintosh than any other company.

Bill Gates was quoted after the launch of Windows 95 as saying it didn't compete with the Macintosh, that in fact Microsoft doesn't even rank the Mac on the list of Win 95's direct competitors. I admire the man's chutzpah (and his marketing genius), but that's a load of bunk. Truth is, Win 95 landed square on the Mac's back. In doing so, Microsoft upped the technical ante on the Mac in only a handful of ways (while continuing to lag behind in many others). Something like 75 percent of those improvements make up the bits and pieces of this chapter. Win 95 is no Mac, but it's enough of one to make this boy's Mac collect serious dust. Besides, Windows is where the software is.

> **Bottom line: Windows is where the software is.**

SO WHAT THE HECK'S A DESKTOP INTERFACE?

Colors, like features, follow the changes of the emotions.

Pablo Picasso
"Conversation avec Picasso," in *Cahiers d'Art*, 1935

Desktop

The desktop interface is probably the single best feature of Windows 95. But unless you've dabbled with others like it, bending your mind around how to use the desktop and graphical interface might not be as stand-up-and-shout obvious as Microsoft's programming gurus and marketing "flaks" would have you believe. Still, as the Campbell's soup commercial put it, "It's in there." And the inside dope I'll dish up will show you just exactly how to master Windows 95.

So, what the heck's a desktop? Good question. In the proverbial nutshell, a desktop is the operating system equivalent of the humble desk blotter. It's the spot where the light shines on your desk. It's the focus around which you store the instruments of business—pens, paper, phone, inbox, outbox, calculator, stapler, white-out, and so on. It's where the important memos, letters, and documents get piled. And, if you're like me, it's where you usually wind up eating lunch because you were goofing off on the Web all morning.

Instead of the office gewgaws you've got flanking your desk blotter, though, I'm talking software tools—word processor, spreadsheet, email programs, online software, presentation package, utilities, and whatever stuff you've always used on your PC but could never quite get to fast enough. I'm also talking about documents and data and all that stuff you've got labeled with personalized crypto-names on your hard drive as well as the stuff people email to you, the stuff you find on network drives, and the stuff you copy or download from, say, CompuServe or the Internet.

Desktop form and function

Once you figure out how the Windows 95 desktop works, the whole idea is pretty much analogous to that shiny worn spot on the center of your gray metal office desk. I don't mean you're going to eat your lunch there. But, as a center of activity on the PC, it's darn near the same thing. It's just a whole lot different from the way you've used PCs in the past. And it takes some getting used to. If you've gotten used to other ways of doing things for lots of years, you may never tumble to this new way. That's OK, too. Win 95 has more than one way to make you comfortable. But try the desktop out first. You just might like it.

What's the real advantage, anyway? The basic premise behind Win 95 is that, like the top of your office desk, you're supposed to be able to focus on the documents, letters, memos, and marketing garbage that comes your way instead of having to reload the stapler every time you want to get something done. And that's about what it's been like working with applications we've had to load and unload 14 times a day—email, word processors, spreadsheets, and so on—just to process the electronic junk people pass us. All the smart people have been insisting on hard copy for years. It's faster to scan. But it fells trees quicker than a July firestorm, and it's completely unconnected to any other data you might have.

Unless you've already used an OS that works like this one, your first reaction might be something like, "Ugh, another graphical time waster that'll rob my PC of system resources." Well, I'm not going to lie to you. The desktop and new graphical controls do take a slice out of memory and chew up some CPU cycles here and there. But, on balance, I'd say they're system resources very well spent.

The Document Launchpad

Brazen (C)
A desktop icon

The icon is very definitely the basic tool of Windows 95. That's been true of every forward-thinking user interface conceived since a bunch of radical scientists rigged people up to instruments at some research park in Palo Alto in the sixties. People hate to read. An icon is a little idea picture—a pictogram—that somehow enters our consciousness without our having to think about it. And, big surprise, Windows 95 has 'em. You can mount icons on the desktop, or just about anywhere you want to put them, and then double-click—just as you might expect—to launch a program, access a hard drive, or check out volumes on the resident local area network.

But yea, verily, brothers and sisters, this is more of a nuisance than it's worth, at least when it comes to launching programs. Why? Because once you launch the app, you still have to monkey around inside it to find the *file* you need up on your screen before you can begin actually getting something done with this overgrown transistor radio. And, where the heck is that blasted file anyhow? Who can tell with these pesky filenames? Is that last week's or this week's version of your client presentation? Don't look at me; I don't have a clue.

The bigger deal is being able to place your *files* on the desktop (or elsewhere). I'm talking about data of all sorts. You know, the stuff you created last Thursday? Or the memo your boss composed FYI? Your income tax return? Your assistant put it together for the meeting that started 10 minutes ago? It's the key to everything? Your expense report? That way-important football-pool entry form? That stuff you use over and over, need it now, where is it? Plop it right on your desktop. Double-click it—the object **is** the thing—and you're home. Now you're saving time. As I was writing this book using Win 95, I started by mounting all the chapters on my desktop. Hey, this Windows 95 thing is pretty cool. Know what? I always know where stuff is. My computer is far more organized than the rest of my life. (Of course, I'm kind of a mess.)

Then again, maybe you don't want to have a bunch of stuff cluttering your desktop. Just because it's an icon doesn't mean it has to be draped all over your desk. There are other places to put icons—more out of your face, but still near at hand. (By the time I finished this book, I had put those chapters elsewhere, but I'll get to that a bit later.)

Plop data file objects right on your desktop . . . the really important ones, anyway.

Control Is Everything

One last thing about the desktop. It's also the dashboard that houses all of Win 95's controls and settings. That includes the controls and settings for shutting down Windows, telling your PC what time it is, adjusting your speaker volume, redecorating the screen, accessing disk drives, specifying how files will look in directory windows, configuring a printer, checking on a print job, finding out how much remaining battery power your notebook has, accessing the Control Panel, switching from one running application to another, undoing that last operation, and undeleting the last file you blew away. To name a few.

Somewhere within the four corners of the desktop all these controls and a lot more are waiting for you to discover them. And there's far more than one way to grab on to this stuff. This is a very good thing. I'll begin with the essentials.

One set of controls you need to know about right off are the ones that control desktop icons, including their arrangement and spacing. Although these controls are related, they are in different places.

To sort the icons on the desktop, right-click anywhere on the desktop background and choose Arrange Icons from the popup menu (see Figure 3.3). Hanging from that menu is a submenu that lets you sort the order in which icons appear by Name, Type, Size, and Date. These controls are borrowed from the folder sort controls, which are explained in more detail in Chapter 4, "Files, Folders, Exploring." When these four sorts are used on the desktop, they have little effect on the order of the default desktop icons.

The Auto Arrange option, however, has a noticeable effect. There's an invisible grid under the desktop. It controls the spacing of icons placed there—if you want it to. When Auto Arrange is turned on, all desktop objects snap to the

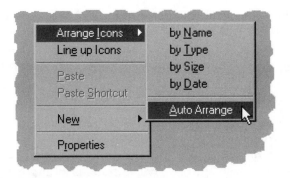

Figure 3.3   Right-click anywhere on the desktop to arrange its icons

An invisible grid beneath the desktop controls icon position and spacing. invisible underlying grid. (When it's on, there's a check mark before the Auto Arrange menu item on the Arrange Icons submenu.) In snapping to the grid, the icons flow contiguously from the upper left corner of the screen downward in columns that march from left to right across the screen. You may have only a few desktop icons, though, in which case you'll probably see only one column.

Microsoft: It would be very nice if users had the option to change the starting point of the flow of icons on the desktop. Many people prefer to have their icons flow from the upper right corner. That way, app windows could be opened on the left side of the screen, where many people prefer them, thereby leaving space for the desktop icons on the right.

So, anyway, with Auto Arrange switched on, icons snap to the invisible desktop grid, all of 'em right next to each other. And you can't move them just anywhere (although you can rearrange their order by dragging and dropping). With Auto Arrange turned off, desktop icons will stay wherever you place them. You can snap them to the nearest grid point—without forcing them to be contiguous—by choosing the Line up Icons command beneath the Arrange Icons menu item. This straightens them up, while leaving 'em free to be moved around.

The other set of desktop icon controls is found in the Display Properties dialog. You find them on Display Properties (shown in Figure 3.4). To get there, right-click the desktop and choose Properties from the popup menu. Once in the Display control panel, click the Appearance tab. Then press the down arrow to the right of the Item field. You'll find two entries in the drop-down scroll box for icon spacing: Icon Spacing (Vertical) and Icon Spacing (Horizontal). Beside the Item field is the Size box. When you select either vertical or horizontal icon spacing, the number you choose in the Size box adjusts how closely together Windows arranges icons when you turn on Auto Arrange or select Line up Icons. If you make the number too small, the icons will overlap one another. If you make the number too big, you may force your desktop icons into more than one column. This will make them harder to see when you have app windows open.

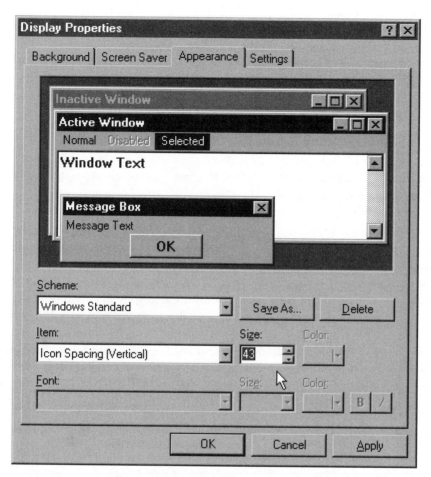

Figure 3.4 Adjusting vertical icon spacing in Display Properties

When working on the desktop settings, focus on the Icon Spacing (Vertical) setting. Make the number as small as you can without causing the icons to tromp on each other. You can click the Apply button on the Display Properties dialog to see how your changes will affect icon spacing, without having to close the dialog.

Click Apply to check icon spacing on the desktop and in a folder window.

Before you get too carried away with adjusting the spacing of icons on the desktop, understand this. The Appearance tab's Icon Spacing settings also affect the spacing of icons in disk drive and folder windows, as well as other Windows 95 container objects (like Recycle Bin). You're probably going to find that the perfect icon spacing on the desktop is less than perfect in folder windows and vice versa. So, some compromise is in order. Gee, Microsoft, I sure would like separate controls for these things.

REMEMBER: CLICK THE RIGHT BUTTON

> If you press exactly the right buttons and are also lucky, justice may show up in the answer.
>
> Raymond Chandler
> *The Long Goodbye,* 1953

Next to the desktop and icons, the most basic premise behind Win 95's user interface is the addition of extensive right-mouse-button controls. Microsoft didn't invent the idea, but they definitely got this part right—or at least, mostly right. But I'm getting ahead of myself.

The right button could be the left button if you're left handed and make the right switcheroo under Start/Settings/Control Panel/Mouse by clicking the "Left-handed" radio button. (To southpaws: My apologies for using the term "right button" throughout. You know the drill by now anyway.)

Buzzword alert: *objects* **and** *properties*

To understand what the right, or second, mouse button does, you have to start by understanding some of the thinking behind the graphical structure of Windows 95. As I said a page or two back, icons are the basic premise of this operating system. But, in a way, I misspoke because most of the icons in Windows 95 aren't just pictures, they're objects. By that, Microsoft means they aren't just disassociated pointers to files somewhere on your hard drive. They actually *are* those files or software structures on your system. So, if you trash the folder called "Program Files" that you see in Windows 95 (don't try this at home), you're actually deleting all the files contained in the actual subdirectory C:\Program Files (or it may look like C:\PROGRA~1) on your PC, as well as the subdirectory itself.

The same applies to the graphical control structures that Win 95 presents, like My Computer, Recycle Bin, and Taskbar. In most cases, these things can't be deleted. They are a safeguard added to protect us from ourselves, not just disconnected add-ons Microsoft slapped on at the last minute. They're built into the heart and soul of the OS. This point is a bit academic. The bottom line is that Win 95's graphical objects are each maintained in a hierarchical database so that they work in concert as an integral part of the operating system. And that's very definitely a good thing.

That Right Thing

Mouse

What the right button does

Here's the key point to remember about the right mouse button: Every graphical object you see on your screen has a menu of actions tailored to it (like the one shown in Figure 3.5). And you get to that menu—what Microsoft a little pompously terms a *context menu*—by clicking the object with your right mouse button. I'm going to use this term throughout the rest of this book. So, remember, "context menu" means right-mouse-button popup menu.

Figure 3.5   A right-mouse-button context menu from a disk drive icon

The big problem for most people is remembering to right-click an object to be-gin with. But in the initial stages of your Windows 95 experience, you'll save time if you remind yourself every now and again that the shortest distance between two points in this OS is nearly always to click an object with the right mouse but-ton. Chances are, if you hit a dead end in Win 95 or if you're becoming annoyed with a repetitive task, you're missing a faster way to do things because you've forgotten to right-click something.

Win 95's vaunted ease of use hinges on the user's remembering this detail—*click it with the right button.* The minute you forget that, Win 95 becomes a giant pain in the butt. So get it in your mind. And, don't blame yourself. This whole right-mouse-button deal is actually a pretty poor interface design. There's nothing blinking to remind you to right-click. You have to know it and remember it yourself.

On the other hand, once you go through the behavior-mod that retrains you to reach for a context menu, you'll really start to pick up speed. (Anyone out there recall the left-handed Ctrl-letter combinations that moved you around the Word-Star screen?) Keep in mind, behaviorists say it takes three weeks to turn a new behavior into a habit.

Properties Sheets

Every object in Windows 95, from the lowliest readme file on your hard disk right up to the most powerful and far-reaching desktop tool, such as Network Neigh-borhood, has a *properties sheet.* A Microsoft properties sheet is a popup specifica-tions page that offers status readouts informing you of basic things, such as date of creation, size, location, and attributes (as shown in Figure 3.6). Depending on

Microsoft's properties sheets are the basic configura-tion forms for Windows 95.

the nature of the object, a properties screen may also offer check-off boxes and other settings controls that let you change the behavior or configuration of the object. The properties of any plain old everyday text file let you set the file's DOS File Attributes: Read-only, Hidden, System, and Archive. You can click to turn them on or off to control the limits set on access to that file.

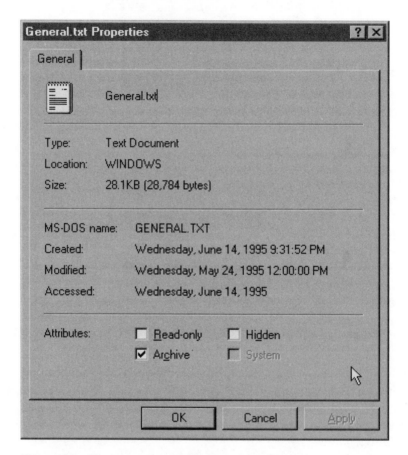

Figure 3.6   The properties of a common text file

At the upper end, properties for objects like My Computer, Network Neighborhood, Recycle Bin, and other complex objects may have several subproperties sheets and even properties within properties. Microsoft stretches this paradigm here and there to the breaking point. But once you get the hang of it, it's not a big deal.

You get to the properties sheet of any object by right-mouse-button clicking it to show its context menu. So, like I said, once you get this through your skull and into muscle memory, it can save you a lot of steps hunting around for the proper options or settings screens in the Control Panel or elsewhere. For consistency's sake, Microsoft placed the properties menu item at the bottom of (almost) every context menu, so you always know where to find it.

The design team for Microsoft's user interface (UI, for short) decided that people use the mouse pointer from the bottom up, not the top down. That's why Start and Taskbar reside at the bottom of your screen by default. Maybe you'd argue this point (and if so, read on, because you can move them both). But I tend to agree with Microsoft on this. It makes sense then, in an upside-down way, that the Properties menu item—one of the most commonly accessed elements of the Win 95 interface—is the bottom-most entry on every context menu.

Only thing is, the way context menus work, they favor top-down operation. When opened normally—meaning that a popup is opened in the middle of the screen where it isn't bumped to a different position by any edge of the screen—context menus open downward, so that the "Properties" item is farthest from the mouse pointer. The opposite should be true; they should open upward by default to maintain consistent UI.

One of my biggest peeves with Windows 95 is that there is very little facility for user customization of context menus. So, while most of us could probably conceive of much better ways to organize popups, the Microsoft Design Police haven't extended us that privilege. Boo. Hiss. But check out the next wand tip (and Chapter 5, "Customize It"). There are at least some ways to customize context menus.

Complex Properties

Perhaps the best example of when clicking a properties menu item on a context menu can get you deep into configuration settings is Network Neighborhood. (You won't find this little gem on your desktop unless you have a network client installed in Windows 95. But you can see the same screen by double-clicking the Network icon in the Control Panel [Start/Settings/Control Panel].)

The Network Properties sheet offers a scrollable list of software and hardware network components and lets you install and configure them (see Figure 3.7). Each of these components, everything from the driver for your network interface card to TCP/IP (Internet networking) services, has its own properties sheet, as well. Although the net effect is a bit daunting, it's a heckuva lot easier than trying to install and configure network layers in the old DOS and Windows.

Program files also have properties, and the controls you'll find there for DOS programs are extremely useful. Disk drives have properties that let you relabel the drive; give you information about total space, free and used; and let you control sharing and access to the drive on a network. Virtually every object in Windows 95 has popup properties.

There are properties for just about everything in Windows 95.

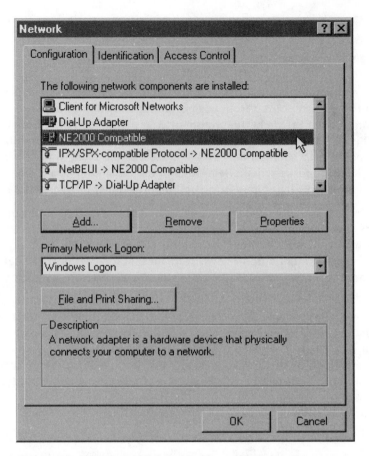

Figure 3.7 Network Neighborhood's properties

 That most primary of Win 95's controls, the Start button, is one of the very few objects in Windows 95 that does *not* have a Properties entry on its right-mouse-button context menu. Why? I don't know. So, how do you get to Start's Properties sheet? C'mon, what's the matter with you? You go to the properties sheet for Taskbar by right-clicking anywhere on Taskbar where something else isn't. You'll find a properties setting on that screen thrown in with Taskbar's settings. Then, click the tab for Start Menu Programs, where you'll finally find something that passes for a properties sheet. It's a bit cobbled together.

Otherwise Right Controls

Windows' popup menus actually change to match the context of your work.

Properties is only one of many menu items you'll find on context menus. One of the cool things about Windows 95 is that each object has a different set of menu items specially customized to its possible functions and operations. Many of the popup menus are also context-sensitive (hence the Microsoft name, context menu). This means they're very different from object type to object type and some of the menu items may appear or disappear depending on system configuration and even your current activity. For example, if you've properly installed network services, then you'll see a Sharing tab on the context menus of your disk drive objects. That menu item goes away if you're not on a network.

It pays to right-click all the desktop tools and structures you come across in Windows 95. Even after you've been using the OS for a while, you'll still come across new shortcuts now and then. For example, if you right-click the desktop itself, you'll receive a context menu that offers controls for placing and aligning desktop icons, pasting to the desktop, and creating new folders and files. It also offers a properties sheet that doubles as the Control Panel's Display program. It offers extensive controls for screen savers, wallpaper, the look and feel of graphical structures, screen resolution, the number of simultaneously displayed colors, and the display driver.

It pays to right-click everything in Win 95.

For the most part specialized context menus aren't easily user-customizable. It is possible to customize the context menus of data files specific to applications you've properly installed under Windows 95. For example, you might want to customize the popup menus of .ZIP **files created by Nico Mak Computing's WinZIP file compression utility for Windows 3.1 so that their context menus offer the option to convert them into self-extracting executable archives. (*Note:* This is unnecessary for the Win 95 version of WinZIP, which does this optionally on install.)**

To do this, WinZIP must be installed on your system. Also installed must be a utility that creates self-extracting ZIP **archives, such as PKWare's** ZIP2EXE.EXE**. From any open Win 95 folder window, choose View/Options/File Types. Scroll down the Registered File Types window until you find the WinZIP entry. Then click to select it and click the Edit button. On the next dialog, click the New button. In the New Action dialog, type the entry name you'd like to appear on the context menus of** ZIP **files; in this case, type** Make .EXE File**. In the "Application used to perform action" field, type the full pathname, including the file name of the** ZIP2EXE.EXE **utility. Depending on how you installed the program, it might look like this:**

```
C:\WINZIP\PKWARE\ZIP2EXE.EXE
```

Then click OK and close the other two open dialogs. Now you can right-click on any .ZIP **file to see your customized** .ZIP **file context menu, which will look like Figure 3.8. You can use this method to make custom popup menu entries for other programs, too, say, to add a menu item for opening Microsoft Word's WordArt utility or any other discrete program associated with any application you can localize with a single file extension.**

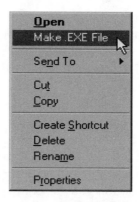

Figure 3.8   A customized right-mouse-button popup menu

GET STARTED

All things truly wicked start from an innocence.

Ernest Hemingway
A Moveable Feast, 1964

The Start button

Microsoft wants you to start with the Start button, and for good reason. There are no menus stretching across the top of the Windows 95 screen like the File, Options, Window, and Help menus of the past. Instead, there's this single Start button called "Start," in the lower-left corner of the screen. It's via Start that you access most of Win 95's settings and functions—at least in the traditional, non-right-mouse-button way of doing things. So get to know it.

The way Start's choices emerge may be a bit puzzling the first time you use it. In its infinite wisdom, Microsoft merged all the menu functions into a single menu that pops up from the Start button. Functions akin to those you find in the drop-down main menus of other operating systems open to the right and down on cascading submenus in Win 95.

Here's how it works. When you choose a menu item that has a right-pointing arrow beside it from Start's main menu, a second cascading menu pops down beside the first. It's possible to trace several layers of cascading menus on Start. When Win 95 is first installed, there's only one menu path that elicits more than two submenus: the Programs/Accessories submenu, which (depending on your installation choices) probably contains at least one Windows 95-created submenu. If, however, you customize the Programs folders with additional nested folders, it can go a lot deeper. (More on Win 95's Programs folder later in this chapter.)

Stick around; I'll help you find your way out of this interface insanity.

Are you confused yet? Yeah, I know, this is needlessly complicated. But, stick around, I'll show you how to bypass this insanity. And check out Figure 3.9. Even for a writer . . . heh, heh . . . sometimes a picture is worth a thousand words.

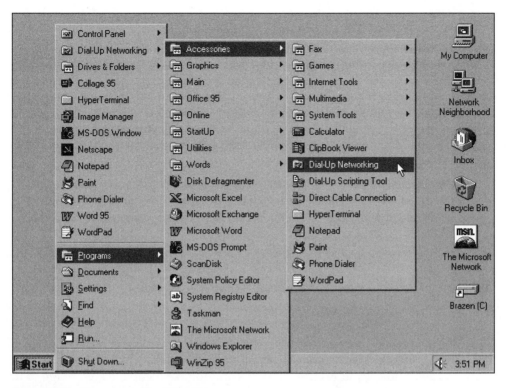

Figure 3.9 The cascading Start Menu

The fact that Microsoft makes use of cascading submenus in Win 95 is a bit of a sore point with some software developers. A few years back, Gates and crew tried to head off those developers from implementing similar structures in their applications, saying it was too confusing to users. Turnabout is a Microsoft trait.

To their credit, Bill's Boyz added a little tweak that makes using cascading menus easier. You don't have to drag (with your finger pressed on the button) the mouse along the Start Menu's entries to move the selection highlight. Instead, the highlight appears below the mouse pointer automatically, without your having to click at all. And when you move the mouse over a right-pointing arrow beside a menu entry and pause for a split second, the corresponding cascading submenu pops up automatically. So it's a lot easier to navigate Win 95's cascading menus than, for example, similar structures on the Macintosh, where you must keep your finger pressed down the whole time.

Bill's better cascading menus

Even so, you'll still find yourself swiping with the mouse and missing the corner of your intended menu selection only to wind up in East Jebib, that is, the cascading submenu for the menu item below it. This is advanced interface design?

For all those real-type folks who'd rather do it with a keyboard, you'll be pleased to learn (if you haven't already) that Microsoft didn't forget that stuff either. By pressing Ctrl-Esc, you open the Start Menu. Then, any letter you press brings you to the first menu item (top down again) starting with that letter. When you press Enter, you either launch the highlighted app or, if it's a submenu item, open the next menu. It's pretty easy. If you like this sort of thing, you might even rename all the icons on Start's launch list so that each begins with a number or letter followed by a period. That way you can just press the letter to launch or open stuff. (I explain how to add and change things on the top of the Start Menu later in this chapter.)

You can also assign keyboard shortcuts to virtually any program, including the Control Panel, which needs all the help it can get to become more accessible. To assign keyboard shortcuts, check the properties screens of any program icon.

AN ICON BY ANY OTHER NAME

We do what we must, and call it by the best names.

Ralph Waldo Emerson
"Considerations by the Way," in *The Conduct of Life,* 1860

I'm interrupting the investigation of the Start Menu to bring you this special bulletin. To fully understand how Start works and to take complete advantage of it, you're first going to have to get all caught up on what Shortcuts are. And actually, here's a place where a few explanatory words go a lot further than a picture (the Writers' Guild made me do it . . .).

Shortcuts are one of Win 95's great new little features. They're virtually the same thing as the Mac's Aliases and very similar to OS/2's Shadows. Microsoft has kept up with the Joneses in creating this feature for Windows 95 so that you and I won't have to go through some of the frustration that Mac people did when Aliases were first introduced several years back.

A shortcut is a "gopher" for the real thing.
Permit me to offer a little background. Win 95 is a far more object-based operating system than previous Microsoft OSs. That means you actually *see* your files as graphical objects. A problem with this is that there are two basic conditions warring on your computer. First, programs want to be installed with all their pieces mostly in one location. The many .DLLs, .CFGs, .DATs, and other program files that most apps use must be nearby each other, otherwise things take forever to execute—or may not work at all. The competing condition is that you don't need to see all these files. Moreover, you want to have all your programs in one place where you can find them and play with them. The big user temptation with an OS like Win 95 is to make full copies of your program files and place them in a folder or on the desktop. Doing that not only takes up a lot more disk space; it also creates problems for programs that expect to launch from the same direc-

tory, or folder, in which their support files are located. So, we needed a way to double-click a handy icon that knows where to go to find the program that's actually stored somewhere else. Microsoft calls these pointer icons *Shortcuts*. But they might just as well have called them "gophers" because that's really what they do.

The Shortcut Defined

Control Panel

To all appearances and in action, a Shortcut seems to be a full-fledged clone of a file or folder icon. But actually, it's merely a pointer to the original file. It also takes up almost no space on your hard disk. Shortcuts vary in file size, but they're usually under 300 bytes—that's less than half of 1K (at least, on most hard drives).

Say you want to launch a Word for Windows document quickly and easily from the desktop. To do that, you find the original file icon in a folder window. Then press and hold down the Control and Shift keys and drag and drop the file object onto the desktop. This creates a Shortcut icon for the file object on your desktop. Now any time you want to open the file, you can just double-click the new Shortcut icon. If you drag and drop a program icon to the desktop, Win 95 automatically creates a Shortcut, with no need for the Ctrl-Shift thing. You can also drag any closed folder out of a folder window and drop it on the desktop or into another closed folder.

In a funny way, Microsoft has been doing Shortcuts for a long time, since all icons in the old Windows represented, but were not actually, the files they were named for. So, if you deleted the Control Panel icon from a Program Manager group box under Windows 3.1, you weren't actually deleting the `CONTROL.EXE` file in your Windows subdirectory. In this one respect—Shortcut icons—the same is true under Windows 95.

Delete means sayonara!

Be warned, though. Most of the icons you see in Windows 95—and nearly all the ones you see in folders—actually *are* files on your disk. If you delete them, you'll be saying bye-bye to the actual files. That may sound scary, but once you get used to the idea it makes file management a whole lot slicker. (You'll find a more detailed explanation about the new graphical file system and deleting stuff in Chapter 4, "Files, Folders, Exploring.")

What Shortcuts Look Like

Magnified shortcut symbol

Since a Shortcut's text label does not always clearly indicate that the shortcut is literally an empty look-alike of an original file object, and since Shortcut icons look in all respects like their original namesakes, Microsoft needed a way to clue us in that a Shortcut is, well, not the real thing. If you check the properties sheet of any Shortcut, you'll see at a glance that it's a Shortcut because the sheet will have a Shortcut tab. But, you can also tell without clicking anything. Every Shortcut has a tiny, upward-curving black arrow in a white box that overlays a small portion of the lower left corner of the original icon image. This arrow signifies that, yup, this shere's a bona fide empty clone-type pointer icon. A gen-u-wine trumped up faker. Just like every icon that ever was in the old Windows.

So, because regular icons actually are the files they're named for and don't just represent them, the smart thing to do is to create Shortcuts instead of full-blown copies of program files. Using this far better alternative, you leave all the actual programs where they want to be—just as you did if you used the old Windows. You can place Shortcut icons in any folder, on the desktop, even on launch menus.

> **You can put Shortcuts in any folder, on the desktop, even on the Start Menu.**

So, Enough Theory

OK, enough of this blather. What's the best way to work with these things? First, there are several ways to make Shortcuts. The missionary position (shown in Figure 3.10) is to right-click on the object and choose the Create Shortcut(s) item from the context menu. And, boom, new object clone. The Shortcut will have the label "Shortcut to [original label to the icon]." That's because you can't have two files with the exact same filename in any folder or on the desktop. And an icon's label is actually its filename in Windows 95 because object icons—even Shortcuts—are actually files on your hard drive. Got it? It's also an extra indicator that the darn thing is a Shortcut. When you're first getting to know this stuff, it can be confusing. After a while, though, seeing "Shortcut to . . ." on everything gets real old. Hold that thought because I'll come back to it in a moment.

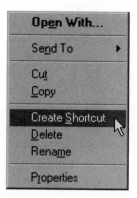

Figure 3.10 How to create a shortcut

So, once you've made a Shortcut in this manner, the next step is to drag and drop it to its new location. Once you move it out of its original folder, you can change its label to whatever you want, preferably something like the name of the original, or *target* file (as the Properties/Shortcut tab describes it). Shortening up the text label makes these guys take up less space onscreen, too.

To change a Shortcut's filename (or any icon label, for that matter), click the icon to select it, pause a second or two so as not to activate a double-click launch, and then click it a second time. The label will change so that you can see a box around the label text, and the text will be highlighted. You can just type to replace the whole name or drag-select the "Shortcut to" part and hit Delete or Backspace.

Text label ready to rename

Thankfully, everything I just described is the long way to create a Shortcut. Here's the fastest and easiest way: Right-click-drag and drop the original object to its final destination. So, for example, right-click-drag the CONTROL.EXE **file out of the Windows folder and drop it in the Start Menu folder. When you let go of the mouse button, you'll see a context menu that offers the Create Shortcut(s) Here option, as well as other types of actions like Move and Copy (see Figure 3.11). Just click the Create Shortcut(s) line, and you're done. When you do it this way, in most settings Win 95 knows better than to append the "Shortcut to" phrase in the label. (For some objects and some destinations, you may see variations on the context menu. Hey, they don't call it a context menu for nothing.)**

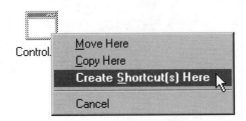

Figure 3.11 The right-click-drag and drop context menu

Shortcuts to Shortcuts

You've probably already come across Shortcuts in Windows 95 for programs or files that you don't know and haven't the vaguest notion where the original file is. Usually that doesn't much matter. But there are times when you're going to want to find the original file object, if for no other reason than to find out what other files it was installed with.

Maybe there's a readme file with the target object that could give you information on what the program does. Or maybe you want to delete the program's folder because you don't use it. (You know, like half that stuff that came pre-installed on your PC.) That's one reason why Microsoft included the Find Target function available on any Shortcut's properties sheet (as shown in Figure 3.12). When you click this button, it opens the folder of the original object and highlights that object. It's a tool that can come in very handy at times.

Another point that deserves mention is the fact that there's nothing wrong with making multiple Shortcuts to the same target file. There's also nothing wrong with doing so by making Shortcuts to Shortcuts, although copying them is easier, since that way they'll never need their labels cleaned up. Careful, though, about copying Shortcuts from one PC to another on a network. The files will point to the original PC.

Making multiple Shortcuts for the same original file may sound like overkill, but you'd be surprised. There's a lot more potential to Shortcuts that I'll talk about a bit later in this chapter. Right now, we return you to your regularly scheduled program: the Start Menu.

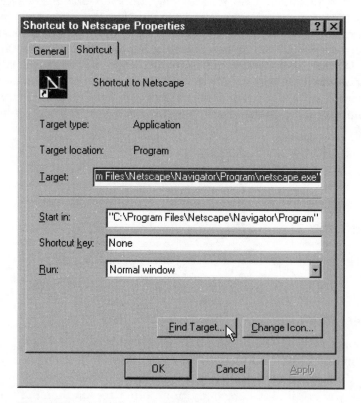

Figure 3.12 A Shortcut's Properties tab

LAUNCH A GAZILLION APPS

Was this the face that launch'd a thousand ships,
And burnt the topless towers of Ilium?

Christopher Marlowe
The Tragical History of Dr. Faustus, 16th century

How Start works One of the first things to do to make Win 95 home is to customize Start's launch lists. Launch lists? With all the computer buzzwords floating around, you'd think

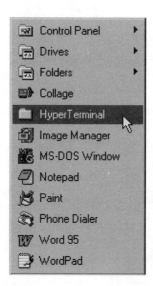

Figure 3.13 The main launch list at the top of the Start Menu

by now there'd be a standard term for this idea, which is also known as menu launching.

A launch list is a stack of program names placed on a menu for one-click launching. Start has two launch lists. One is above the top divider on its main menu (see Figures 3.13 and 3.14). The other is the area below the folders on the Programs menu. The submenus on the Programs menu are special menus (think of them as "Shortcut folders") that contain icons for applications installed on your system. But just which apps you'll find there depends on the choices you made during the Win 95 installation.

A "Shortcut folder"

If you upgraded a pre-existing Windows installation, you'll find all your Program Manager groups represented as individual folder menus with right-pointing arrows beside them. These folder submenus will be at the top of the Programs menu. Below them you'll find a second launch list of individual programs. That's Start's second launch list (see Figure 3.15).

On installation, there are no list-launch entries at the top of Start's main menu and just a few handy programs on the Programs submenu, including the Windows Explorer and the MS-DOS Prompt. You can add any programs you want to either of Start's launch lists. When they're mounted on the main Start Menu, it's a fast and easy two- or three-click launch for any of them.

One of the more annoying shortcomings of the Win 95 interface is that there's absolutely no way to single-click launch a program. Oh, you can click Start and drag up to an item and then let go. But that's actually more difficult than two quick clicks—once to open Start and once to launch the app you select.

That second launch list on the Programs submenu can come in real handy. It's a good place to set up a list of programs you don't use all the time but don't want to hunt around for in the Programs folders when you need 'em. It's also useful because, if you're anything like me, your main Start Menu launch list is either crammed to the gills with ready-to-launch programs, or it's about to be. And there's a limit to how many of those suckers you can put there.

Figures 3.14 and 3.15 Start's main launch list and Programs launch list

Understanding the Programs Folder

About your old Program Manager groups

Before I get to the meat of Start's customization, step back with me a minute and take a look at what's going on behind the Start Menu. First, Start isn't just a button on the Taskbar or a menu system that pops up on your screen. Start is also a folder inside your main Windows folder called Start Menu. The Start Menu folder is for the most part like any other folder on your hard drive. But its name is hard-wired into your system with a very specific purpose in mind. The folders in Start Menu are themselves quite different from other folders on your system.

Six of the items you see on the Start Menu aren't in the Start Menu folder. They are Shut Down, Run, Help, Find, Settings, and Documents. Everything else on the Start Menu—including the Programs menu and all the folders and program icons you see on its submenus—are actually folders and Shortcut icons visible in the Start Menu folder. As I said a few pages back, think of them as Shortcut folders. Their whole purpose is to serve as containers for the Shortcuts inside 'em. This is a bit different than anything else going on in Windows 95, and it's quite easy to get confused about it. So, listen up.

It's not that the Programs folders aren't real. They're real enough. In fact, if you open a DOS window and check out the Start Menu subdirectory (`C:\WINDOWS\STARTM~1`), you'll see that it does, indeed, contain a `\PROGRAMS` subdirectory. Each folder inside Programs also has a hardwired DOS subdirectory loosely shortened to the 8.3-character filenames and directory names that Win 95's underlying version of DOS continues to maintain. (In case you're wondering, the tilde (~) symbol in these filenames is Win 95's way of abbreviating the long filenames into DOS file system-speak.)

The difference is that these Programs folders, and the whole Programs area for that matter, were created as a bridge between the old and new Windows. Specifically, applications that get installed in Windows 95—especially the older Windows 3.1 applications that'll be around for some time to come on many users' PCs—expect to create a program group of icons. In the old Windows, these icons weren't actually the files; they were pointers to the files. And since that's exactly what Shortcuts are, Win 95 creates the Programs folders and fills 'em up with Shortcuts. Most new Win 95 apps also create Programs folders and app Shortcuts on installation as a convenience to you. Having program Shortcuts pre-made is a boon for customizing Start and the desktop.

To show that the folders in Programs are akin to the old Program Manager group boxes—in other words, that they contain nothing but Shortcuts—Microsoft gave them a different icon. It's one that evokes the look of the old Windows' Program Manager group boxes (see Figure 3.16).

A piece of the old Windows in the new

Main   Accessories   Startup

Figure 3.16   Special Program Manager–like folders within Programs

Bottom line: If you upgraded properly from a previous Windows installation, all your old Program Manager group boxes now appear as special submenus on the Programs menu. Win 95's upgrade Setup routine automatically converts Program Manager group boxes to Programs folders and Shortcuts. If you created a clean installation, which might be desirable for other reasons, you'll find the few default Windows 95 groups in Programs and none of the applications that might be installed on your system. In that case, you'll have to reinstall all your apps.

If You Performed a Clean Install . . .

To customize the Start Menu, which is what this section is all about, you must have program Shortcuts available to place on Start. If you upgraded from a previous Windows installation and were scrupulous about maintaining your old group boxes, chances are you found a whole bunch of available program Shortcuts and app folders under Programs. But if you were one of those crazed individuals (like me) who ran Symantec's Norton Desktop or PC Tools for Windows, or if you opted to install Windows 95 fresh either by buying the full fresh install floppy disk version—or by upgrading DOS only—it would seem that you're hosed at this point. But take heart, you're not.

You didn't upgrade an old Windows installation? Take heart, there are ways to get your group boxes back.

First, if you haven't installed Windows 95 yet, check out Chapter 2, "Up and Running," for stuff that could save you a lot of time. If you already performed a clean installation and saved a pre-existing Windows installation in another directory (as I advise in Chapter 2), there's an easy way to convert your old Program groups (described in the next wand tip). If you didn't save your pre-existing Windows installation and installed fresh, or if you bought a new PC with Windows 95 on it already, get out those application install disks.

You'll find a utility in your Windows folder called GRPCONV.EXE. **It's the tool Win 95's installation routine uses to convert old Windows Program Groups. It scans your Windows folder and builds or rebuilds all the** .GRP **files you tell it to. Here's how to use it on your own. Start by copying all the** .GRP **files you want to convert into Win 95's Windows folder, if they're not already there. Then, call up Start's Run command. In the Open field, type**

```
C:\WINDOWS\GRPCONV.EXE [name of group file].GRP
```

You can also use the asterisk and question mark filename variables. For the first time out, using *.GRP **for the source filenames is fast and easy. Warning: Rebuilding existing folders in Programs can be hazardous to customizations you may have already made to Programs folders of the same name.**

There's also another way that's more useful when you want to convert just one or a handful of .GRPs. **Copy them into your Windows folder and then, in the folder window, double-click each** .GRP **file icon you want to convert. That makes Win 95 convert them singly, building program Shortcuts as it goes. But it's very fast.**

It's important to understand that there may be several caveats to using programs whose icons you convert from pre-existing program installations if you did not upgrade your previous Windows installation. When your applications originally installed in the old Windows, they may have copied much-needed

files into your Windows directory. They may also have added settings lines in `WINDOWS.INI` **or** `SYSTEM.INI`**. If you run into any trouble with an application, the very best thing you can do is reinstall it from its original disks. To do that, choose Start/Settings/Control Panel and double-click Add/Remove Programs. Insert the app's first install disk in your system and click the Install button.**

Where to Customize Start

You'll find a dialog for customizing the launch lists available from Start. Or, at least, you might find it. The traditional way to get there is to choose the "Settings" menu item on Start and then choose the Taskbar item on the submenu. Yes, choose Taskbar, that bar that stretches across the bottom of the desktop. Perhaps because the Start button is housed by the Taskbar, Microsoft's Weird Names Committee decided we'd all surely intuit that Start's customizing controls are on Taskbar's properties screen. It was a bit of a stretch for me. I mean, I'm looking in Start for a way to configure it. Right-click on Start for a properties sheet? Nope, not there. So, it's gotta be on Start's Settings menu, right? But when I get there, I'm supposed to know that the Start/Settings/Taskbar menu item contains options for configuring *Start?* Microsoft moves in mysterious ways.

> **Configure Start under Taskbar?**

Anyway, on Taskbar Properties, click the Start Menu Programs tab. Or you can open this dialog by right-clicking anywhere on Taskbar and choosing Properties from the context menu.

As you become more familiar with Start configuration procedures, you'll appreciate this tip. Bypass the whole Microsoft menu structure altogether. Just right-click the Start button and choose Open from the context menu. That opens the Start Menu folder. You can then use all the standard Win 95 procedures to create, rename, and move Shortcuts around. For more on working with file objects, get into Chapter 4, "Files, Folders, Exploring." In the early going, though, I suggest sticking to the menu structure, as described in the following section. Just until you get the hang of things.

Start, As You Like It

Getting to the Start Menu Programs dialog is more than half the battle. Once you're there, the procedure for adding and removing program names on the two launch lists is pretty straightforward. You could click the Add or Remove buttons in Start Menu Programs. If you installed over a pre-existing version of Windows, click Advanced instead (as shown in Figure 3.17). You get what Microsoft terms a *rooted* Explorer window. (Explorer windows are explained in more detail in Chapter 4, "Files, Folders, Exploring.") This window focuses exclusively on the Start Menu folder and the folders it contains, including Programs (see Figure 3.18).

> **Start is pretty durn customizable.**

Once inside Microsoft's Explorer window for configuring Start, you add new program items to the Start and Programs launch lists by copying the Shortcuts of any of the Shortcuts in the Programs folders (see Figure 3.19). The fastest way to

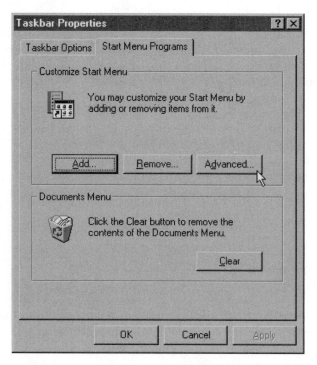

Figure 3.17 The Start Menu Programs dialog

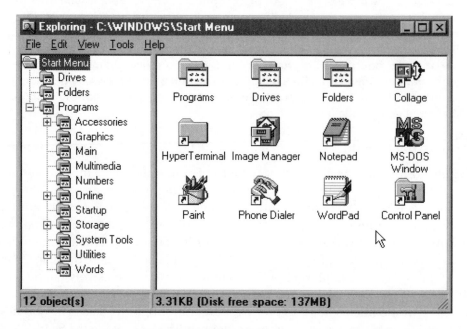

Figure 3.18 The Start Menu configuration window showing the Start Menu folder

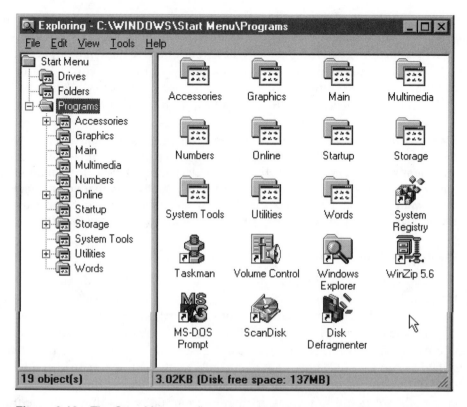

Figure 3.19 The Start Menu configuration window showing the Programs folder

do that is to right-click-drag them from the right side of the Start Menu Explorer window, and drop them onto the smaller closed folder Start Menu or Programs folder icon on the left side of the screen. You'll get a previously described context menu from which you should choose Copy. Doing this places the new Shortcuts where you want them.

Some programs you want really close at hand, so go ahead and place them in multiple locations if that suits you. When you want to delete a Shortcut, just right-click it and choose Delete from the context menu. Or, drag it to the Recycle Bin. Or click it once and press Delete.

Every program icon you see within this special Explorer window is a Shortcut, so fire away. You can add or delete Shortcuts to folders in Programs, rename Shortcuts and folders, and generally mess around with them all you like. Both Start's and Programs' launch lists instantly reflect all changes you make this way, thereby eliminating the guesswork the first few times around.

If it suits you, create multiple Shortcuts for one item, and spread 'em around for ready access.

**Be a little
careful of
Programs'
Shortcuts.**

Bear one thing in mind, though. While they're Shortcuts, the icons in the Programs folders may be somewhat difficult to recreate, since you may not know in what folder their original files reside. When in doubt, use the Find Target button on a Shortcut's properties sheet and check things out before you delete them. Accidental deletion isn't the end of the world (if this happens to you, double-click Recycle Bin because the file is in there), but it can sure chew up a lot of your time.

Want an even faster way to quickly create a program Shortcut and add it to the Start launch list? Using the *left* mouse button, drag a program or data file from any folder window, and drop it right onto the Start button. Presto, instant Shortcut on the Start Menu. The only drawback to this method is that you'll sometimes want to adjust the name of the Shortcut, since the resulting icon will use the original filename exactly, like CONTROL.EXE **instead of Control Panel.**

Manually Creating and Adding Shortcuts

**The Microsoft
"dialog way" to
configure the
Start Menu
launch list**

The way Microsoft provided for adding Shortcuts to the Start Menu is the Add button on the Start Menu Programs dialog. It gives you a browse button (see Figure 3.20) that lets you poke around your application folders to search for the main executables of your applications. It's not a bad way of doing things, but you may grow to hate it soon enough; it wasn't designed for heavy-duty use. It was designed to add a single Shortcut at a time, when you realize you need one somewhere. It also comes in handy if you inadvertently delete program Shortcuts. Even so, it's not really much easier than just manually creating a Shortcut by right-clicking it and choosing "Create Shortcut" from the context menu.

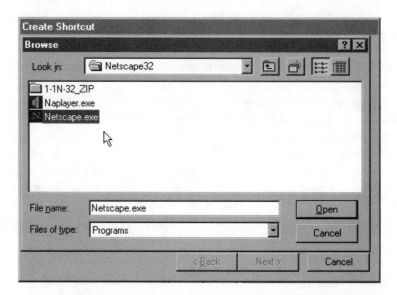

Figure 3.20   The Browse dialog from the Taskbar Properties/Start Menu Programs/Add dialog

Real Customizing

Sometimes it's just faster and easier to bypass all that dialog mumbo jumbo in favor of good old-fashioned handwork using the tips explained on the last several preceding pages. In particular, I'm talking about the last wand tip that explained how to open the Start Menu folder by right-clicking the Start button and choosing Open. If you prefer the Explorer-type window that the Start Menu Programs/Advanced button brings, choose Explore from the Start button's context menu.

How to bypass that dialog mumbo jumbo

There's another way. You can speed up the customization process by doing some customizing. (Tail wagging the dog?) Namely, make a Shortcut for the Programs folder. While you're at it, make a Shortcut for the Startup folder, too. The darn thing is three levels deep in Programs and isn't quite as easy to get to as it should be. In fact, while you're at it, make Shortcuts for all your disk drives, all the folders on your PC that you access frequently, and anything else you want to get to quickly. Create a new Shortcut folder (by right-clicking the Start button, then right-clicking the Start Menu folder's background, and choosing New/Folder from the context menu). Plop all those new Shortcuts into this folder. They'll show up on the top of Start's launch list. My brilliant name for this folder is "Drives & Folders," but call it anything you like. So next time your screen is covered up with 17 program windows, you can easily access all this stuff from the ever-present Start button.

Make a cascading folder of Shortcuts to drives and folders you open frequently and put it on Start.

While you're at it, get to the Control Panel a lot faster, too. Since there's no way to access the Control Panel from any context menu, mount a special cascading folder version of it on Start's launch list. It'll show up as a folder on Start that cascades to show each of the Control Panel programs. In fact, it lets you bypass the Control Panel window altogether and just open the specific control panel you need.

To create the Control Panel special folder, right-click the Start button and choose Open from the context menu. Right-click the Start Menu folder background and choose New/Folder. Then rename the icon text label with this line exactly as it appears and press Enter.

```
Control Panel.{21EC2020-3AEA-1069-A2DD-08002B30309D}
```

Check out Figure 3.21 to see what this'll look like when you're done. Then close the folders and give the Start button a click to admire your handiwork. You'll see a Control Panel folder at the top of the menu. When you pause the mouse pointer over it, a convenient cascading menu opens showing all your Control Panel programs. Just click any of them to launch the program directly. Hey, you're not only saving time, you're saving system resources, since you never have to open the Control Panel folder itself.

Figure 3.21   Start Menu folder window showing the special
Control Panel folder

**Steal this tip. I change my mind a lot about the Shortcuts I want on the Start
Menu. To make shuffling things around a bit easier, I've borrowed an old trick
from the Mac desktop and created a folder in Programs called "Launch List
(disabled)." I place Shortcuts in it I don't need right now, but might want to re-
add later. This way I can get them off the launch list for now.**

Start's Screen Limits

Some of Start's workings are a bit flaky. It's possible to wig it out by adding too
many launch list entries. This is especially true when you're working at 640×480-
pixel VGA resolution. If you run into this deal, the Start Menu literally runs off
the top of your screen and doesn't scroll. When that happens, some program
names will be inaccessible because they're hanging out in a virtual netherworld
somewhere.

**Why the Start
Menu could
hang ten off
your screen . . .**

Depending on the video resolution you're running, you're limited by the vertical size of your screen for the total number of programs you can successfully
add to the launch list. Windows doesn't warn you about this deal though. It will
let you add as many icons to the Start Menu folder as you want. As a point of
reference, on a standard 14-inch, 640×480-pixel resolution, VGA screen, you're
limited to about 17 program names on Start's launch list (presuming you've
checked "Show small icons on Start menu" on the Taskbar Properties screen). At
higher resolutions, there are many more slots. But I'm always running out of
room, even at 1024×768 pixels on a 17-inch display, where the magic number is
27 program names. It's one of those Murphy's Law things: The launch list always
expands to fill the space available on your screen.

It's not exactly an elegant solution, but here's a quick fix: Right-click the Start button and choose Open from the context menu. Now right-click the Start Menu folder's background and choose New/Folder. Now move some of the objects from Start into the new folder. Choose the icons for stuff you use less frequently and name the folder appropriately. My stellar name? Um, "More." Next check to make sure Start has stopped hanging ten off your display. If you still can't see all the menu items, keep moving Shortcuts to the More folder until the problem is fixed. From now on, you'll see the new folder at the top of your Start Menu, and it'll show a cascading submenu containing the program icons you moved. You can also get fancy and create multiple folders grouping by task or by any organizational scheme that strikes you. But keep in mind, every folder you add to Start is one less two-click launch you can make on its launch list.

. . . and how to fix it

For some additional tips and tricks on working with Start and the desktop in a cramped screen space, see Chapter 6, "The Mobile Win 95." There's some good stuff there.

Order, please! Seems like the MS folks should have worked a bit harder on some aspects of Start. Didn't all those usability tests show that people like to arrange the order in which programs are displayed on a launch list? Maybe group them with dividers? You might think that you could reorder them by opening the Start Menu, Programs, or Programs subfolders and rearranging the icons there. But you'd be wrong. Are you listening, Redmond? Microsoft mounts your programs as menu entries in alphabetical order, and while that's as good a default as any, defaults are meant to be customized to a user's liking. I've been hunting around for a better workaround than the renaming with letters or numbers tip on page 98 for quite some time, and haven't found one. (I've also put some third-party companies on the trail.) But, if you figure out a better way to do it, email me at sfinnie@tiac.net. **I'll owe you one.**

RANT ABOUT DOCUMENT LAUNCHING

> Poor fellow, he suffers from files.
>
> Aneurin Bevan
> *Aneurin Bevan,* Vol. 1, 1962

Document-centricity (to use that horrible buzzword) was one of the chief design goals of Windows 95 (and is perhaps the main design concept behind the someday-maybe, next-generation Microsoft operating system code-named Cairo). It is this business about being able to all but ignore the tools with which you work on data files and to focus instead on the information they contain.

I've already railed a bit about this earlier in this chapter, so I'll spare you the sales pitch. But when you sum it up, the main advantage of such a document-oriented environment (if the computer industry can ever create one that really works) is that you can open and close files instead of opening and closing applications with which you then open and close files. If nothing else, the idea would save some steps.

I know Windows 95, and believe me, Windows 95 is no document-oriented environment. But the germ of the idea is there, and you can help it along marginally. Microsoft's chief nods to document-orientation are: File icons are objects, Shortcuts can be made for them, they can be placed on the desktop or on either of Start's launch lists, and there's this thing on the Start Menu called "Documents."

The Documents menu: Some docs that you can't customize

Unfortunately, Start's Documents menu isn't all that aptly named. It should be called "Some Documents You Can't Customize." What you get when you tarry the mouse pointer on Start's Documents menu item is a cascading submenu that shows *some* recently accessed documents and files. The files on the Documents menu correspond to the Recent folder you'll find in the Windows folder. Every time you open a data file with an application that has the right pedigree, Win 95 places a Shortcut for that file in the Documents folder.

So, what's the problem? The creation of Documents Shortcuts relies on a simple programming construct called *MRU* (Most Recently Used). Some 16-bit Windows apps kept these MRU lists to support usability features like the list of recently opened files at the bottom of their File menus. Only problem is, software developers didn't all do this the same way. Now, Microsoft is advocating the one true way (its way, of course).

Bottom line: If your apps aren't Win 95 apps, or if they didn't do it the Microsoft way before, then very few if any files you've opened with that application will appear on the Documents submenu.

I'm willing to give Microsoft the benefit of the doubt on this one, but . . .

You know, I'm willing to give Microsoft the benefit of the doubt on this one. Standards are great. And they're trying to promote one. What really peeves me is this little factoid: They've made it all but impossible for us to customize the Documents submenu with documents we'd like to place there, say, more or less permanently. I mean, you can drag and drop Shortcuts for data files or folders you access frequently into the Recent folder, but they don't show up on the Documents submenu. And, while you can muck around with the System Registry to add individual items or try to make the files pertaining to specific apps show up automatically, it's not worth the trouble. Microsoft missed an amazing opportunity to give us a document-oriented feature, probably for no other reason than to force third-party software developers in line. It's pretty pathetic.

There's one control for the Documents menu. It's on Taskbar Properties at the bottom of the Start Menu Programs screen. All it does is clear out all the current documents listed on the Documents Menu. Big deal.

Happily, someone else realized right away that something was very wrong with Documents. Michel Forget and Electric Storm Software have created a $15 shareware program called the Document List Management System (DLMS) for

Windows 95. It's a separate executable that keeps track of all documents you open. You can get DLMS by downloading it from ZD Net / CompuServe, ZD Net / Web (`http://www.zdnet.com`)**, and probably several other online services.**

Document Scraps

There's one document-oriented Win 95 feature that might not occur to you to try. Called a Document Scrap, it lets you create icon objects for pieces of documents. To test it, try highlighting a block of text in any data file (this works only in apps built specifically for Win 95). Then right-mouse drag and drop it on your desktop. The result is a Document Scrap, that is, a new file that consists solely of your highlighted block of text. So, now you won't have to open a new file in an app in order to save out a piece of a previous file as a separate file.

Document Scrap 'What's wrong with....'
A Document Scrap

You can do something like this with non–Win 95 apps. Highlight the data. Right-click the desktop or a folder background. Choose New and then the application type closest to the file format of your data. Double-click the new icon. Paste the data into the new file and then save it.

When you let go of the right mouse button to drop the Scrap, you'll get the familiar context menu with options to move, copy, or create a Shortcut. Creating a Shortcut is a second useful function of the Document Scrap, especially for long documents or large spreadsheets. When you double-click a Scrap Shortcut, it opens the original file and scrolls it directly to the area you highlighted when you created the Scrap. This could be a useful attachment in an email message where you're sending your boss a long file and just want him or her to take a quick peek at one part in particular of, say, a giant spreadsheet.

If you're really interested in working with your files instead of fooling with your apps before you get to your files, check out Symantec's Norton Navigator for Win 95. Some of the more esoteric features of this Windows 95 interface enhancement product (including an extension to the Documents list) can make a big difference. Maybe Microsoft will get around to this in a couple of years.

TASKBAR NONE

> Our task is not to rediscover nature but to remake it.
>
> Raoul Vaneigem
> *The Revolution of Everyday Life,* 1967

It goes against my better curmudgeonly nature, but I've got to say that Microsoft did very well in creating the Taskbar. The ability to minimize apps, close them down to a semidormant state while you work in another program and yet keep them ready at hand when you want to reopen them is probably Win 95's single

Taskbar is pretty darn c-o-o-l

best interface feature. If you have enough RAM to feel comfortable with it, task-switching (running multiple apps and switching back and forth between them) lets you work more productively because you don't have to keep loading and exiting applications. You just leave 'em running in the background (minimized as the task buttons shown in Figure 3.22) and tug their leashes to call them back.

Figure 3.22   The default bottom-mounted Taskbar with two apps minimized

Did you ever minimize before Win 95?

Sure, if you left too many apps running in the old Windows, you might encounter the old Redmond two-step, in which a two-left-footed application stepped on the memory address of another running program. The result was the infamous Windows GPF, or at the very least the crash of one or more applications, which for all intents and purposes necessitated a Windows 3.*x* exit and reload. The truth is, this was much less the fault of the applications under the old Windows than the operating environment, which could not load Windows apps into a truly protected area of memory. Of course, the apps themselves wouldn't know what to do in a better OS like Win 95. The whole thing was a mess.

In practice, Windows 95 doesn't improve much on the situation because 16-bit apps—the ones designed for the old Windows—receive no better protection than they did in the past. Even the many 32-bit Windows 95 apps that have shown up since, which get their own memory space in Win 95, won't run as flawlessly as we'd all like them to. That's because Microsoft, to ensure 16-bit app compatibility under Windows 95, gave the older apps quite a bit of operating system priority.

When problems arise, you're far less likely to see Win 95 come crashing down altogether.

What is quite different is the behavior of applications when they do crash and the way Win 95 works when a problem crops up. You're far less likely to see Win 95 come down altogether. And when apps do crash, you can almost always just relaunch them without having to restart. (For more on handling problem situations, see Chapter 9, "Living with It.")

What Was Wrong with Minimizing

Reliability and interface design were the two biggest reasons why very few of us bothered to run multiple applications at the same time under Windows of yore, task-switching between apps like a New York City cabbie changing lanes on the Long Island Expressway.

The old interface was so befuddling that the average Windows user never figured it out. What some did figure out was Alt-Tab "Cool Switching" (so named for the line in WIN.INI that turned the function on or off). Alt-Tab let us call up a little program switcher that toggled the opening of any running apps. It was crude, but it got the job done.

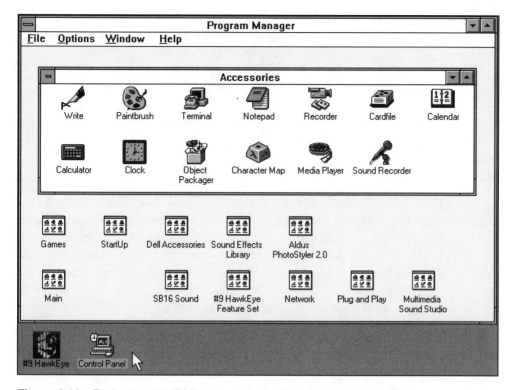

Figure 3.23 Remember this? Minimized apps at lower left of the old Windows

We were supposed to be minimizing applications to the desktop, where they showed up as, well, icons. But the method Microsoft offered for that was more a stake in the ground than a mature, useful interface design. That's because minimized app icons appeared in the lower left corner of the desktop (that colored stuff behind Program Manager), where they took up valuable screen real estate. Worse, minimized icons looked almost exactly like regular program icons. This confused the heck out of newbies because there was nothing to give them an indication that a minimized icon would open an app far quicker than launching a new instance of the program from a Program Group. (See Figure 3.23.) Besides, half the time minimized icons were covered up by some window or another, if not by Program Manager itself.

Alt-Tab fans, you'll be happy to know that Cool Switching is alive and well in Windows 95. Try it if you haven't already. You'll notice some differences right away. For one thing, you'll see all the running apps at a glance. The current app (the one that'll open if you let go of Alt) is indicated by an enclosing colored square, and the name of the current program or window appears in the status bar along the bottom. For another, like Taskbar, the new Cool Switch keeps track of open folders as well as running apps. Check out Figure 3.24.

Figure 3.24　Alt-Tab Cool-Switching in Windows 95

Bill's Better Taskbar

Enter Windows 95's Taskbar. Microsoft finally figured this all out. Its first step was to mount the Start button on the Taskbar and make minimized apps appear not as icons, but as rectangular buttons I call "task buttons" that take up far less vertical space. Taskbar is a thin status bar–like structure that stretches across the bottom of the desktop, taking up less than half the vertical space required by the minimizing area of the old Windows. You just click one of the task buttons to revive a minimized program or to bring it front and center if its window is behind a bunch of other stuff. It took 'em long enough, but I feel like cheering anyway.

Minimize, Maximize, and Close buttons

To minimize an app, you click the Underbar icon. That's the one on the left in that cluster of three icons in the upper right corner of every single window in Win 95. As explained earlier, the Maximize button in the middle is actually a toggle that goes back and forth between "maximized" and "normal" window sizes.

> **Clear the decks. Want a fast way to minimize app windows down to Taskbar so that you can hear yourself think over the cacophony of open windows on your desktop? It's easy. Right-click the Taskbar and click Minimize All Windows on the context menu. All your apps and folder windows will stay running, but they'll have disappeared from your screen, ready to open again with a single click of their task buttons. Later, for some unknown reason, you might want to reopen all those windows simultaneously (you wacko). Open Taskbar's context menu again and choose Undo Minimize All. You can also close individual apps by right-clicking their task buttons and choosing Close. For a way to get around having to close all your apps to get to the desktop, check out the wand tip on page 251 in Chapter 6, "The Mobile Win 95."**

Next, MS made it possible to relocate the Taskbar. Click and drag any gray area of the Taskbar and move it to take up new residence along any of the four sides of your screen. MS pilfered this idea from themselves to some degree. It comes from the toolbar getup in Microsoft Word 6.0 for Windows and the Microsoft Office toolbar. Anyway, depending on how you work, configuring Taskbar as a vertical column on either side of the desktop takes it out of your vertical space and, if your screen is wide enough, out of the way of your applications. Score two, Redmond.

Best of all, you can make the Taskbar disappear entirely—and yet still retrieve it in a flash. By setting it to hide itself automatically (right-click on the Taskbar, choose Properties, and then click Auto hide, as shown in Figure 3.25), you can make it vanish until you summon it back by bumping the mouse pointer against the edge of the screen. This is especially useful on a small notebook display, where sometimes even Win 95's dialogs tend to creep off the top and bottom of the screen. When Taskbar reappears with the Auto-hide feature, it smartly comes up over any open windows that might be in its way (if "Always on top" is turned on). And when you're done with it, it smartly disappears again. The darn thing also knows enough to reappear as a status check whenever you minimize something.

Check out Taskbar. You'll find its settings by right-clicking the Taskbar and choosing Properties. In addition to Auto hide, you'll find the Always on top setting, which controls whether the Taskbar goes over or under the windows it overlaps. For nitty-gritty detail on configuring Taskbar to save screen real estate on smaller screens, check out Chapter 6, "The Mobile Win 95."

Power minimizing

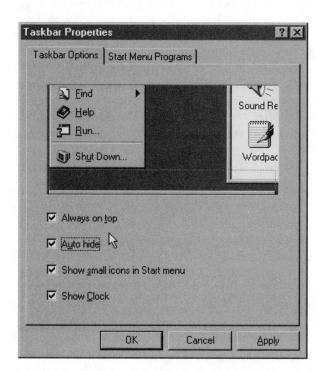

Figure 3.25   Configure Auto hide on the Taskbar Options tab

Best ever window controls

There's a big difference that's worth noting about the way Taskbar works as compared to most other task-switching schemes. The task buttons don't just show up on Taskbar whenever you minimize a program; they appear just as soon as you launch one. And it's not just programs that register task buttons on Taskbar. Each and every folder window and many program modules you open or launch—such as Help—place their footprint on Taskbar. That's both a curse and a blessing. But mostly it's a blessing.

When you've got a lot of stuff going on, things can get pretty cluttered down on Taskbar. On the other hand, how many times have you wished for a quick and easy way to bring forward an open window that's stuck somewhere behind a bunch of other open windows? I mean, time was when you had to close all those suckers down, use Task Manager, or use Alt-Tab. And half the time the thing of it was, you forgot you already had that program running or that instance of a directory open under File Manager. Sometimes you'd even launch the thing again; this might even have prompted an error message. With Taskbar, you can always see that something is open just by glancing down. You can then bring it front and center just by clicking its task button.

There's something pretty cool about Taskbar that may not be immediately clear. Since you can drag and drop most any object onto most any closed *container* object (such as a folder) in Windows 95, wouldn't it be natural to drag and drop stuff onto folder task buttons on the Taskbar? Or, shouldn't you be able to open a document file by dragging and dropping it on its application's task button? Well, you can, sort of. You can't just drag and drop a file from a folder window onto a Taskbar task button representing another folder to move the file. But, if you drag the file object and pause the mouse pointer over the folder task button, Win 95 will open that folder for you, and then you can drop it in the open folder window.

The same is true of an application window. Even if you have another file opened in an application, as along as it's a well-behaved app you can just drop a new file anywhere in the open program window and the file will be opened in the application.

Shrunk in the Wash

Taskbar is a lot like a toolbar.

Something else that's kinda nifty—but sometimes frustrating—about the horizontally configured Taskbar is its ability to shrink the length of minimized app buttons equally to make room for additional buttons. By default, each app's minimized task button shows the corresponding program icon, that program's name, and at least part of the name of any document the program might have open. On a 640 × 480-pixel VGA screen, Taskbar can display only three minimized buttons stretched out to their full lengths, showing the full breadth of this text information.

Figure 3.26 Taskbar's shrink-to-fit minimized icons

When you minimize a fourth app, Taskbar evenly shrinks the lengths of the task buttons to accommodate the fourth. The more apps or windows you open, the smaller the buttons get. When you get to six or seven task buttons on a 640 × 480 VGA display, suddenly the whole thing gets a little useless (as demonstrated by Figure 3.26). It becomes nearly impossible to figure out what the buttons represent because really all you can see are the program icons.

This whole squashed task button deal is the big criticism leveled at Taskbar. And Microsoft would do well to add a control that lets you set the maximum number of buttons on a single Taskbar row.

What makes this worse is that Taskbar has a little refresh bug that sometimes keeps it from automatically expanding contracted task buttons to fill the space vacated by a button that disappears when you close a window or exit a program. There's no one-click fix for this, but either dragging the Taskbar to another edge of the screen and back or dragging its inside edge a notch toward the center of the screen and back forces a refresh, which expands the buttons.

Unsquishing Squashed Task Buttons

Despite its shortcomings, Microsoft clearly spent some time working on Taskbar. They've provided four ways to make adjusting to Taskbar's idiosyncrasies a good bet. For me at least—and I'm a veritable app-minimizing, task-switching maniac—a certain combination of these helpful doodads turns the trick.

1. Popup labels. What, you don't have all your program icons memorized? In this graphical day and age? Shame on you (grin). Well, if you pause the mouse pointer over any minimized app button on the Taskbar whose text information isn't completely visible, a text label pops up (as shown in Figure 3.27), giving you the button's program and the names of any data files it has open. If you're fast with the mouse pointer, you may have missed this one.

Forget-me-not labels

2. Go vertical. The vertical Taskbar orientation crams many more buttons onscreen and lets you tailor the length of the buttons, looking something like

Out on the edge

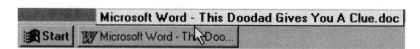

Figure 3.27 A Taskbar popup task button label

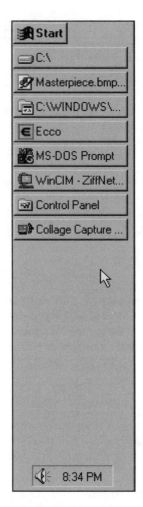

Figure 3.28   Taskbar gone vertical

Figure 3.28. The whole auto-squeeze deal is out of the picture. The vertical positioning isn't so hot on smaller displays, though, since it gets in the way of app windows.

Add a row at will. **3. *Make it bigger.***   Or, you can drag the inside edge of the Taskbar (the top edge if you've got it configured along the bottom of the screen) to extend the Taskbar to two or more rows of task buttons. If you use this in conjunction with the Auto hide setting, you probably won't mind the additional space the Taskbar takes up.

Maybe you don't care what time it is. **4. *Turn off the clock.***   The setting for turning off the clock is under Taskbar Properties. It gets you an additional full-sized button on a 640 × 480 display. Although turning it off is not a huge help, it might be enough to be useful on small displays.

Like Taskbar, but find shrinking to fit annoying? No, there's no magic solution, but here's a little tip. The problem isn't so much the size of the task button as the size of the text label. There's a folder option that can help you out. Check to see whether you've got your folders configured to "Display the full MS-DOS path in the title bar." It's a setting on any folder's View/Options/View dialog. Turning this guy off improves the at-a-glance legibility and usefulness of the Taskbar by grinding the text labels displayed on folder window task buttons down to a nub.

Time Wasn't

Speaking of Taskbar's clock, time was when you didn't know what time it was under Windows. The clock that came with earlier Windows was *absolutely, positively* useless. So the Taskbar-mounted clock in Windows 95 isn't some great leap forward; it's just Microsoft playing catch-up with itself. It deserves no special praise for allowing you to change the date and time just by double-clicking the clock face. Microsoft isn't the seventh coming just because you get a popup text label showing today's date when you pause the mouse pointer over the clock face. This stuff is just the way it should always have been.

Taskbar volume control and clock

The Notification Area, that square of indented gray matter in which the clock rests, is a pretty nifty Taskbar doohickey. This little window is a status area. It reads out information in the form of numerous color icons that appear and disappear depending on your hardware configuration, software settings, setup options, and the specific operations you launch. So, for example, when you print, a little printer icon appears in the Notification Area. Double-click that printer icon, and you get what was called Printer Manager under the old Windows. In most cases, you can click or double-click Notification Area icons to gain access to useful settings and read-out screens, like the popup volume control shown in Figure 3.29 that's keyed to the speaker icon. There's even a mute button for those embarrassing situations, like when everyone on the plane can hear those lame Beavis and Butthead system sounds on your notebook, butt munch.

Use muting on the plane, butt munch.

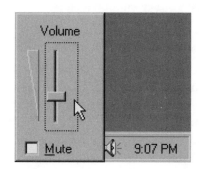

Figure 3.29 The Notification Area's popup volume control

Notebook users, in particular, are going to like the Notification Area, since context-sensitive read-outs regarding their PCMCIA cards, power status, and battery charge are standard fare there. Most Notification Area icons are invisible most of the time. They appear only when your hardware usage or an operation you launch makes it practical for them to appear.

COOL TOOLS, HOKEY NAMES

> Proper names are poetry in the raw. Like all poetry they are untranslatable.
>
> W. H. Auden
> "Names, Proper," in *A Certain World*, 1970

My Computer was probably the first thing you found annoying about Win 95.   Last but not least—because they were probably the first things you found annoying about Windows 95—are the icons Microsoft opted to load on your desktop when you first installed Win 95. I'm talking about those blame fool tools like My Computer and Recycle Bin. If you're on a network, you'll find Network Neighborhood, too. And depending on your installation choices, you may find the Inbox icon for the Exchange mail program and an icon for Microsoft Network. The Microsoft Weird Naming Committee is at it again on stuff like My Computer, Network Neighborhood, and Recycle Bin. But what these tools do is practical and maybe even inspired.

Dump the lame names. Before I embarrass myself too much by praising these lofty desktop structures, let me get to the heart of the matter. Here's how to rename them. Click on the text labels beneath My Computer and Network Neighborhood just as you would any other object in Windows 95. Give 'em any names you want. You can rename My Computer to "Win 95 Sucks" if you want. (No, Microsoft won't know.) You can't rename some of the other Win 95 desktop objects (er, at least you're not supposed to, but I'll tell you how in later chapters), including Recycle Bin and the Microsoft Network. Inbox can be renamed, but I wouldn't advise it. It's shaky enough as it is.

My Computer

My Computer

Like most *container objects* (graphical stuff that holds other graphical stuff) in Windows 95, My Computer looks and acts a lot like a folder when you open it. That's a good thing, since once you know how to use one of these jobs, you know how to use the rest. Despite that similarity, My Computer is a bit different from other structures you find in and around the place. Maybe the name isn't *that* bad, though, since My Computer delivers on its sappy name by providing a visual representation of your local drives, printers, and settings.

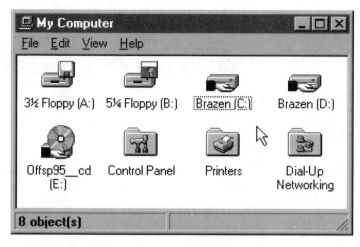

Figure 3.30 What My Computer looks like

All the stuff shown in Figure 3.30 is stuff that's physically inside this PC: two floppy drives, two hard drives, and a CD drive. In addition, My Computer gives you access to the Control Panel and the Printers folder. The latter gives access to settings for all your installed printers and offers the Add Printer Wizard for adding new ones. Dial-Up Networking contains modem connection scripts. I explain this in detail in Chapter 6, "The Mobile Win 95."

Think of My Computer as the road map to the local territories, that is, the drives, printers, and settings for other devices that are within or are directly attached to your PC. But there's also another kind of device that can show up in My Computer: any *permanently mapped* network device, such as a network volume or disk drive. By permanently mapped, I mean stuff that you've browsed in Network Neighborhood and configured to be "reconnected at logon." More on this in Chapter 8, "Connections."

Mapped network drive

The main purpose of this numero uno of desktop tools is to serve as a launch point for accessing files on any drive you work with regularly. Unlike the interface structures found in other graphical operating systems, My Computer offers a single start point to all your storage devices, printers, and control panels. So it's visually economical, lets you open up what you need, and uses the space of only a single icon on your desktop. If you'd rather not clutter up your screen with lots of icons, My Computer offers a neater, though slightly longer, route to the files, folders, and workings of your PC.

My Computer's main job: access

By contrast, Network Neighborhood's job is to show you the stuff on the local area network (LAN) that's not physically installed in your PC but that could be permanently mapped into My Computer. Network Neighborhood is also covered in more detail in Chapter 8, "Connections."

Network Neighborhood

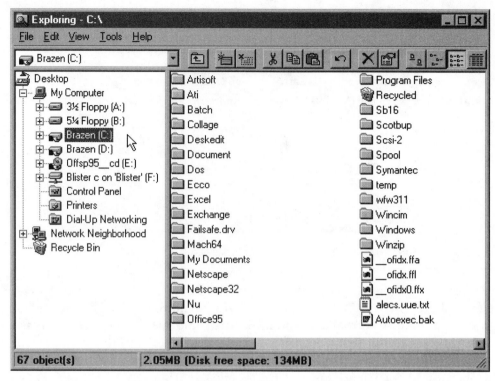

Figure 3.31   An Explorer drive window

By double-clicking any of the drive icons in My Computer, you open a folder window of that drive. To get Win 95's version of a File Manager, known as an Explorer window, right-click the drive and choose Explore from the context menu. This opens a window like the one shown in Figure 3.31. Explorer windows present a two-paned tree and file view. The tree is like an org chart of your hard drive. Entries in the left pane extend up and down and are at the top level of your hard drive. Subdirectories appear as the next level to the right. So, the left pane shows folders, or directories, only. The right pane shows the files and folders contained by the folder currently selected in the left pane.

Symbols on left pane

Like some of the better File Manager replacements designed for the old Windows—but unlike File Manager—Explorer windows show all of your PC's drives on the tree side. That can be a little confusing until you master the fine art of expanding and contracting those drives. A minus sign beside a drive or folder means it's open and showing at least the first level of subdirectories, or subfolders, it contains. A plus sign means the drive or folder is currently closed but contains subfolders. If there's no sign, there are no subfolders contained in that folder or drive.

Anyway, having all your drives available in any Explorer window is a real time saver, once you get the hang of it. It's easy to get things done without having to open several Explorer windows. (For deeper explanations of folder and Explorer windows, see Chapter 4, "Files, Folders, Exploring.")

Get around without building an entire colony of folder windows on your desktop. Windows' hierarchical folders are great, but when you want to go six directories deep to find a file, you could wind up opening all those folder windows that'll need blowing away later. Or, you can do it the fast way.

Press and hold the Shift key while you double-click My Computer. The Explorer window that pops up will have a tree pane on the left (as shown in Figure 3.31) and a folder pane on the right. In this two-paned Explorer window, clicking on a folder in the left pane opens it in the right pane. Instead of opening a second Explorer window, the contents of the new folder—the file icons and folder icons it contains—simply replace those of the previously selected folder in the right pane. So, you'll always be working with a single Explorer window. Neat, huh?

One last tip: If you do wind up with a bunch of folders open, hold down the Shift key and click the Close button (the X-button in the upper right corner) of the deepest folder. Doing that closes both it and all the folders above it in that particular folder branch.

Graphical Pecking Order

Win 95's structure of visual elements puts the Desktop in the first tier, or root level. Not surprisingly, the Desktop level contains all the tool and Shortcut objects you place on the desktop. In fact, if you copy or move a file onto the desktop, it will actually reside in this base level of this graphical hierarchy.

Win 95's hierarchical desktop tools

The second tier consists of My Computer, Network Neighborhood, and the Recycle Bin (check out Figure 3.31 again). Depending on the choices you made during installation, you may see other elements at this level, such as Briefcase. To get a gander at a tree view of the desktop tools installed on your system, right-click My Computer and choose Explore from the context menu. You'll see an Explorer window. The tree view on the left displays Win 95's graphical hierarchy.

The tree view gives an indication of how the operating system integrates the structure of your PC's hardware and your network, as well as its own components. At the third level are the top-level elements in My Computer and Network Neighborhood, such as your drives and any available workstations on a LAN. Click the plus sign to the left of each device, and you'll see the fourth tier—all the directories in a drive, for example. If any of those folders contain other folders, they'll form the fifth tier, and so on.

Recycle Bin

In addition to My Computer and Network Neighborhood, you'll very definitely find the Recycle Bin deletion tool on your desktop. The Weird Names Crew out-

Recycle Bin

I like to imagine my files are being vaporized into nothingness.

did themselves on Recycle Bin. Why would you need to "recycle" disk space? Computers, unlike most other document-producing machinery, are already environmentally correct—they've always recycled memory. Besides, this isn't much fun. I don't know about you, but when I drop my computer files in a trash can, I like to imagine they're being vaporized into nothingness. They should have called it something more satisfying, like "Incinerator Binge." (And see Chapter 4, "Files, Folders, Exploring," for exactly how to do that.)

Two quick things to know about Recycle Bin. First, you can drag and drop files to it to make them go away. Just one of the many ways that Windows 95 lets you delete on the fly. The second is that, by default, Recycle Bin keeps files you place it in, or delete in other ways, so that you can change your mind later on. You have to purge it to truly trash files and free up disk space. To purge it, right-click the Recycle Bin icon and choose Empty Recycle Bin from the context menu. To resurrect a file you deleted by accident, double-click Recycle Bin, select the file in the Recycle Bin window, and choose File/Restore. (For all about Recycle Bin's operations and how to configure it, see Chapter 4, "Files, Folders, Exploring.")

BONES FOR REACTIONARIES

A reactionary is a somnambulist walking backwards.

Franklin D. Roosevelt
Radio broadcast, 26 October 1939

I know, I know, in quiet moments some of you want to chuck all this bogus graphical popup object drag-and-drop stuff and get back to that prince of interface duos: Program Manager and File Manager. (Lurch!) Well, far be it from me to hold out on you, in case you want to know how to do it. But notice I left it until the very end of the chapter. And for a very good reason: "I'd turn back if I were you."

Unearthing File Manager

Winfile.exe
Bad old File Manager

One of the problems with doing without File Manager is that when you want to do something like rename a disk, figuring out how to do so sometimes isn't as intuitive as it should be. In fact, it might take you a while to work that one out. *Hint:* You have to do it from the properties screen of the drive object in My Computer. (There's good news for all you card-carrying reactionaries and keyboard-shortcut junkies: That good old Windows Alt-Enter keyboard shortcut still works.) The trouble is, whenever you hit a roadblock in Windows 95, the big temptation is to go back to the old way of doing things.

It'd be much easier if we could just click a disk drive's object label twice in My Computer and type to rename it, the way we do other text labels. Microsoft is busy saving us from ourselves, particularly in a networked environment, where a name change for a drive could knock others off a shared resource. But, you can't even make the change in a normal fashion if you're not on a network. It's overkill.

So, if you absolutely must, it's still possible to run dumpy old 16-bit File Manager under Windows 95. Just right-drag the `WINFILE.EXE` file out of the Windows folder and drop it somewhere to create a Shortcut. I'll warn you, though: It doesn't support long filenames, and it seems even more lame than it used to. But, heck, even I use it on rare occasions (or, at least I did until I installed Symantec's Norton Navigator, which has an excellent 32-bit File Manager with long-filename support).

Exhuming ProgMan

This is a lot harder for me to fathom, but I'm guessing that for some of us, there just may be times when we'd like to tramp back to the old way of doing things. So, while I like Windows 95 much better and will never go back, when you want ProgMan, you want ProgMan. One way to get your fix is to mount the tired old standby on Start's launch list. You'll find `PROGMAN.EXE` in your Windows folder. To do that, right-drag and drop it onto the Start button to create a Shortcut on the launch list. But you might want to tuck it in the Programs launch list, where it'll be less embarrassing. And, whatever you do, don't place it on the desktop. That's just too ironic for words.

Progman.exe
The ProgMan file

You'll notice that Program Manager looks a bit different (see Figure 3.32). It has the new look and feel of menus and graphical controls common to all applica-

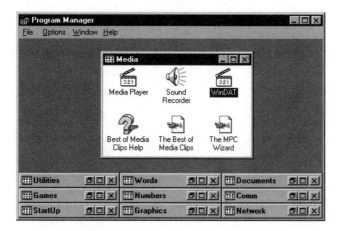

Figure 3.32   If you just plain have to: Program Manager under Windows 95

tions under Windows 95. But the most apparent difference is that closed group boxes show up as the rectangular minimized bars, quite similar to the task buttons on Taskbar. Otherwise, the Windows 95 version is a faithful, warts-and-all reproduction of the bad old original. Isn't that enough reason to drop this crutch once and for all?

*   *   *

Well, there you have it. The quintessential introduction to the Windows 95 user interface. Stick around, though, because interface tips and tricks pop up again and again around here. Check out Chapter 6, "The Mobile Win 95," for some other stuff. But if you're real serious about customizing this whole deal to your liking, crack the spine on Chapter 5, "Customize It." That's where it's really happening.

4 Files, Folders, Exploring

> His vocation was orderliness, which is the basis of creation. Accordingly, when a letter came, he would turn it over in his hands for a long time, gazing at it meditatively; then he would put it away in a file without opening it, because everything had its own time.
>
> Salvatore Satta
> *The Day of Judgment,* 1979

If you're anything like me, you're something of a car buff on the side. I'm an avid reader of auto magazines like *Automobile, AutoWeek, Car & Driver,* and *Motor Trend.* In fact, back in 1984, when I was working at my very first computer magazine (it was called *jr.,* for IBM's intentionally crippled and doomed PCjr home PC), an editor friend and I realized that a large percentage of early computer adopters were also auto nuts.

We decided, tongue firmly in cheek, to launch a new magazine to be called *Cars & Computers.* As a joke, we even submitted the idea to the publishing company we worked for. Like IBM's PCjr, *Cars & Computers* never really got off the ground. (Of course, nowadays it'd be a lot less far-fetched, but that's another story.)

Years later, working as the reviews editor of *PC Computing* magazine, I learned that parent company Ziff-Davis Publishing had commissioned studies showing that there was a huge overlap between computer magazine readers and automobile enthusiasts. It also revealed a similar overlap between computer users and musicians. I should've realized that one, since I've been dabbling with guitar most of my life.

All this is a long way to go to set up a comparison with Win 95's file-system and file-management features. But I hope you're following along with my car analogy when I say that Win 95's Explorer window and new file system make it the *Sport-Utility* of operating systems. Sport-Utes, as the auto industry calls 'em, are those expensive 4×4 family mobiles, like the Ford Explorer (get it?), Jeep Grand Cherokee, and Range Rover Discovery. They're big, safe, versatile, tough,

The *Sport-Ute* of file systems

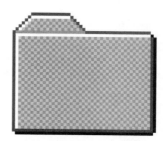

Figure 4.1 Grainy, gratuitous, giant Win 95 Folder icon

and, believe it or not, stylish—at least with the upwardly mobile family crowd. Next to that quintessential American vehicle, the pick-up truck, they're the hottest-selling things on four wheels. Even Mercedes is getting into the act.

Why am I comparing Win 95 to fad 4×4 family trucks? Well, bear with me—there's more similarity than you might think. The appeal of Sport-Utes is mostly the way they look, the 4×4 safety in bad weather, their extra storage, and the high-riding visibility they give the driver. Win 95's file system is a lot like that. No, really.

Just what *is* a file system, anyway? Nothing special. Just the heart of any operating system. In its primordial sense, a file system is the basic bits-and-bytes structure an OS uses to store data on your hard drive. In other words, it's the database format used by the computer and OS for storing and retrieving files. The workings of the file system—stuff like disk commands, directory structure, filenames, storage capacity, interface, and performance—have a big effect on the way you work with your PC.

Windows 95 offers the first truly graphical file system in a mainstream operating system for PC compatibles. The Mac has had this for years, and there have been other operating systems like IBM's OS/2 that endowed the PC with a graphical file system. But for the wide universe of mainstream DOS and Windows users, before Win 95 you were working with an ugly command-driven character-based file system.

What's a *three-toed snorty blog*? It's a lot like a *Hellifino*. Yawn. I mean, who cares? Well, you probably should. Ever look for the latest version of that all-important file on three-toed snorty blogs and just have no clue where it is or what its darn filename is? Ever try to move a directory of stuff including its three subdirectories from `C:\XYZ` to `C:\BLOGS\ABC`? Ever wish you could name a file `The Snorty Blogs.document` instead of `SNRTYBLG.DOC`—so that six months later you'd remember what the heck was in it? Ever wish you could take a quick peek inside a file's contents without having to fire up its blame-fool program? Ever wish you could quickly blow away `SNRTYBL1.DOC`, `SNRTYBL2.DOC`, and `SNRTYBLG.BAK` once you realized that it was `SNRTYBL3.DOC` that you wanted to save—without having to open up a file utility or to shell out to DOS? Ever delete a file and wish you hadn't? These are just some of the annoying file-related things that are a lot less frustrating under Windows 95.

TOOLS OF THE TRADE

> A worker may be the hammer's master, but the hammer still prevails. A tool knows exactly how it is meant to be handled, while the user of the tool can only have an approximate idea.
>
> Milan Kundera
> *The Book of Laughter and Forgetting*, 1978

Or is it the hammer's forger that prevails? Think about it.

Anyway, let's get down to the nitty-gritty about how to work with all this file and folder junk. The tools and features I'm talking about are file icons and the commands on their context menus, folders and their context-menu commands, Explorer windows, long filenames, Recycle Biddy, and a few other bits and pieces.

Files Are the Object

With only a few exceptions—like user-created Shortcuts and the Programs menu icons (detailed in Chapter 3, "The Desktop Interface")—every single file and directory icon you see in Windows 95 isn't just a pointer to the files on your disk, it actually *is* the bits and bytes on your drive. If you move a file icon from one folder to another, Win 95 actually moves the data on your disk (or truth be known, the data is re-indexed as being in a different directory, but that's splitting hairs). If you copy a file somewhere else, you're creating a second whole instance of that data on your disk. If you change its text label, you're changing the actual filename of the file stored on your drive. If you delete a file icon, you're kissing the actual file good-bye. In operating system lingo, that makes Win 95's file and folder icons *objects*.

Word Pro 95
A file object

They're called objects to impart the sense that there's something weighty about them. It was some marketing nerd's way of making 'em seem like they were things you could hold in your hand. This was very definitely not the case under the old Windows, where outside of a file manager utility, any icon you saw was literally a graphical bookmark very simply programmed to launch a program or open a file in its program. If you deleted, renamed, moved, or copied those dumb icons under the old Windows, it had absolutely no effect on the actual file the icon represented. And since the tenuous links from those icons to their actual files were controlled by character-based path statements, it was easy to inadvertently disconnect them just by moving the real file somewhere else. Suddenly, the picture on the icon went blank, and double-clicking it would elicit a vague

Documents
A folder (or directory) object

error message. The whole thing was a house of cards ready to crumple down on you at the first chance.

Some people, especially those who've spent a lot of time using DOS or Windows of yore, are a bit put off by this "objectness" of icons in Win 95. It does require a different way of thinking about how to work with icons. But it's definitely a better way. Take visualizing your hard drive, for instance. Win 95's file system and its graphical tools let you ride up high, like a Sport-Ute, where you can see your whole drive at a glance.

The DOS file system, which has been around since 1981 or so, divides up drives into user-created "directories," which may contain subdirectories. And each directory or subdirectory may contain files. On many users' PCs, there are dozens and dozens of directory branches. But from DOS, it was all but impossible to see an overview of your directories. In fact, you pretty much had to remember your directory structure, or tediously type the DIR command to summon a text listing of the subdirectories and files at each directory level.

Windows 95 doesn't change the underpinnings of any of that. What it does do is represent directories graphically as folders. When you double-click a folder, it opens as a window, and any subdirectories it contains are shown as closed folders in that window. And, of course, the file objects it contains are shown as object icons. Win 95 can also provide a graphical *tree* that depicts your entire directory structure. Now there's a handy gizmo.

Plant Trees in Your Mind

Blythe [C:]
A shared hard disk object icon

By double-clicking a hard drive object icon in My Computer, you open a window on your whole hard disk (like the one in Figure 4.2). Closed directories or subdirectories show up as manila folder icons. You can double-click any folder to open a new window to show that directory's contents. The files contained by any directory—or folder window—show up as icons that help to visually identify their functions. And since Win 95 supports long filenames, files and folders can have long descriptive text labels, which are also their actual filenames.

The upshot of all this is that you can master what many people think of as DOS—the full set of disk commands—without ever having to face the command line. And if you never used a PC before Windows became popular, chances are pretty good you never mastered DOS's cryptic disk commands. I'm talking about stuff like MD, CD, and RD (Make Directory, Change Directory, and Remove Directory, respectively), and the idiosyncrasies of the pathnames used by DOS to navigate a hard disk's directory structure. Even if you're an old PC warhorse like me, not being able to see at a glance in DOS the complex directory structure found on most experienced users' hard drives has meant having to remember exactly what names you gave to numerous branches of subdirectories, each of which could be

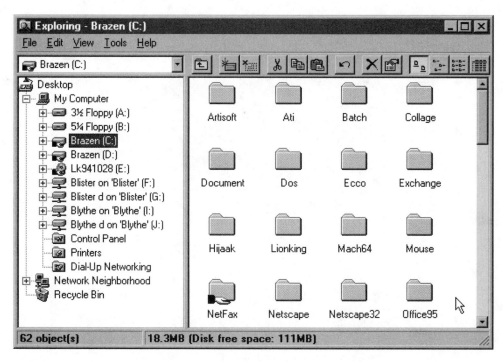

Figure 4.2 Explorer windows provide a graphical overview of your hard disk

many levels deep. Or, for most of us (because let's face it, the old memory just ain't what it used to be), it meant having to launch a separate program, like XTree Gold for DOS, the Windows File Manager, or the PC Tools for Windows 2.0 file manager, just to get a gander at your drive. What a time waster.

Just one branch, for instance, of literally hundreds on my hard drive goes like this in DOS pathname-speak:

```
C:\DOCUMENT\HOME\MONEY\MONTHLY\1995\EXPEND\BUDGETS\
```

This pathname represents a subdirectory seven levels deep on my drive. In there, by the way, I've got monthly word processor documents that project my household and personal expenditures. (Gee, maybe I should use a personal finance program, huh?) In Windows 95, I can see this graphically, and at every turn I can see all the possible sub-branches. So as I navigate the folder windows, moving ever deeper into my hard drive's folder structure, I don't have to remember the names of my subdirectories, launch a separate program, or even type anything. I can just look at the names of the folders available at each level as I go. The result of tunneling down my folder structure might look something like Figure 4.3.

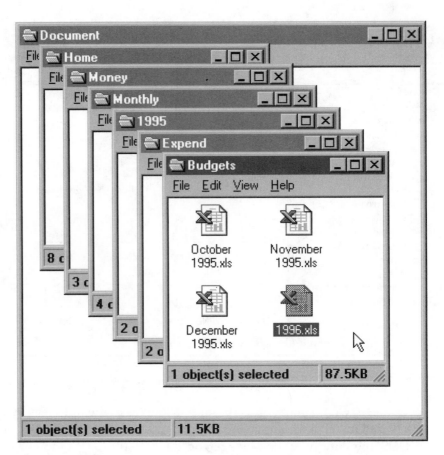

Figure 4.3   Drilling down a directory branch with regular folder windows

I might also choose another way to do this that cuts back on the number of windows I have to open. Windows 95 lets me see the directory structure on my drives all at once with the graphical tree structure that's on the left pane of every Explorer window (see Figure 4.2). Explorers are a lot like the old Windows File Mangler, only better. Their two-paned windows offer a tree view on the left side and the selected container's contents, or file view, on the right side. The best thing about the Explorer's tree view is that its top level, an Explorer window of My Computer, shows all the drives on your system—even mapped network drives. I'll come back to working with trees and the Explorer later on.

How to open Explorer windows   There are two fast ways to launch an Explorer window. The first is to right-click any drive or folder object and choose the Explore item from its context menu. Or you can click the drive or folder object once to select it, depress the Shift key, and then double-click the object. My Computer, Recycle Bin, and Network Neighborhood can also open as Explorer windows.

Watch out for an annoying gotcha when you Shift-double-click to open an Explorer window. If you press the Shift key before you click once to select the folder or container, Win 95 may think your first click means you're trying to group-select several folders in the open window. And, since it defaults to the last folder you clicked, or the upper left-most folder, your first click may select a large number of objects. Worse, with your second click, Win 95 thinks you want to open them all as Explorers. You may wind up opening umpteen Explorer windows this way by accident. I once did this in a network folder containing literally hundreds of folders. Bog!

Acting on File Objects

When you get to the subfolder you want and open it as a Win 95 folder window, you've got a whole range of actions you can perform on any given file object. You can double-click to launch it in its native program, quickly peek at its contents, delete it, check its properties sheet, rename it, move or copy it, create a Shortcut of it, and other neato file-management stuff.

Even better, although it may take some getting used to, you can access all those command options directly from any file object icon. You don't have to shell out to DOS or launch a separate program like File Manager and then choose File/Copy or sumpin' like 'at to make a copy of a file. In Win 95, most available file and disk commands are right there on a file or folder icon's right-mouse-button context menu (like the one pictured in Figure 4.4). So, to continue the example, you copy a file by right-clicking it with the mouse and choosing Copy from its context menu. Navigate to the destination folder, right-click anywhere on its background to open the context menu, and then click Paste. Voila. Instant duplicate.

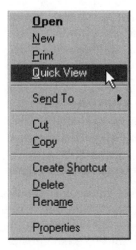

Figure 4.4 A file object's right-mouse-button context menu

Say you didn't change to a different folder window but instead pasted the copied file into the same folder window. In that case, since Win 95 doesn't allow two files in one folder with the same filename, the second instance will be labeled `Copy of [previous filename]`. Now you can rename it to something else—anything at all but the exact filename of the original file object. Or move it to another folder by dragging and dropping it with the mouse. Once it's in another folder, you could give it the exact same name as the original's.

Normal.dot

An icon label selected for renaming

To rename a file or folder object, click it (or its text label) once to select the whole object. Then pause and click its text label a second time. (Keep in mind that if you rapidly double-click the text label, Win 95 will think you want to open or launch the object, and it will comply—most probably causing you to rage your favorite four-letter word.) For anyone who likes using the keyboard more than a mouse, remember this tip: Click the object once to select it, then press the F2 key. That's the keyboard shortcut that selects an object's text label for renaming.

When an object's label is selected for renaming, a rectangular box appears around the text label and the text is highlighted. You'll also see the blinking *I-Bar*, or text-entry cursor, at the end of the label. You can just type to replace the whole name or edit the name using the usual word processor controls. Once you've made the name change, press Enter (or click anywhere else on the screen) to save the new name.

Hey, experienced mouse users, here's a simple thought that'll save you some aggravation on object icon renaming: Don't forget to adjust the double-click speed of your mouse to match the rate at which you tend to double-click.

Win 95 can interpret two successive mouse clicks in either of two ways, depending on how rapidly you make the two clicks. A rapid click-click is the "double-click" that tells Win 95 to open or launch an object. And click-pause-click activates two separate commands, which is what you're doing when you're attempting to select an object's text label for renaming. The first click selects the object, and the second tells Win 95 to prepare it to be renamed.

Since people don't all double-click at the same rate, Win 95 lets you adjust the double-click speed. Folks who are new to using a mouse tend to double-click at a slower rate than do more experienced mouse users; Win 95's default double-click rate favors this crowd. That means the more rapid click rate that experienced mouse users will try—click, click (with the briefest of pauses in between)—is apt to be interpreted as a signal to launch. Bog!

To adjust the double-click rate, launch the Mouse control panel. At the bottom of the Buttons tab dialog, you'll see the "Double-click speed" box. Click around in the Test area (shown in Figure 4.5) to get a feel for how close together two clicks must come for Win 95 to consider them a double-click. When you trip the double-click threshold, the jack-in-the-box pops up. If you're an experienced mouse user, move the slider as far in the Fast direction as you can

before your double-click trials begin to leave old jack stuck in the box. Once you fine-tune this to your liking, the whole object renaming thing stops being a nuisance and starts being convenient.

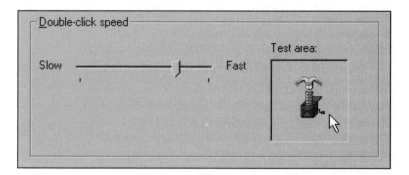

Figure 4.5 Control Panel's Mouse Properties double-click speed adjustments

Delete as You Go

Maybe it just seems like the price of doing business, but have you ever peeked inside a subdirectory on your hard disk, which was, of course, littered with document files, and thought to yourself something like, "Oh yeah, I sorta remember creating this stuff. I think it was back in 1989 before my hair turned gray. Um, do I need this stuff any more? Man, hellifino."

If this sounds familiar, maybe you'll also recall that you were faced with three basic choices:

1. You could just blow away the darn directory. (Do it! Do it! Do it!)

2. Or—knowing for sure that according to Murphy's Law, Subsection 3, you need only that useless old junk which you've just watched the trash man haul away—you could kill half an hour tripping down memory lane, looking at all those weird files with their funky old-timey fonts, trying to figure out whether you just might need any of them before you dust 'em.

3. Or you could just ignore this batch of old files and create a new directory for, say, the new files you're about to create that will, in some vague way, be related to the old ones. Usually I rename the old directory something like OLDSTUFF and hang it off the new directory, figuring I'll check into all of it someday, but never do.

Survey says!? You guessed it, number 3. I mean, do you know anyone who actually *likes* cleaning their room? Let's face it, you're no Felix Unger. And know what that means? You've probably got enough useless old doo-doo on your hard drive to be measured in multiple megabytes. I'm a horsepower guy. So, I figure:

Heck, just buy a bigger hard drive. But I'm embarrassed to admit that even though my main box has almost 1.5 gigabytes of hard disk, I'm still a bit pressed for space most of the time.

Win 95 helps you avoid the junk-it junket.

If this sounds at all familiar—and be honest, you've either faced this kind of deal some time in your computer life or you will—Win 95's file-handling tools and controls provide an environment that should subtly help you avoid the junk-it junket. I mean, it's not going to kill the whole problem. Nothing could, short of William Gibson–esque* artificial intelligence or the creation of a whole new job description: the Computer Maid. But if you take advantage of at least some of Win 95's file-management shortcuts as you work, you'll most likely find you're deleting older versions of files as you get done with them instead of waiting two or three years.

Sure, right. Sounds like I've been sucking down just a bit too much of Microsoft's marketing hype, huh? Well, I'd have thought so, too, but check it out. All those ready-to-hand visual folder navigation tools and file commands linked directly to the actual file objects on context menus makes tidying up as you go a whole lot easier.

For example, Win 95 gives you a built-in file-viewing capability. Called Quick View, it's available as a context menu item for any file object whose file format is supported by Quick View, and that's a healthy chunk of the most common file types. (Even so, there are some notable holes in Quick View's viewer list—a third-party opportunity.) When you choose the Quick View option, you see the file object's contents in a scrollable window (see Figure 4.6). Although you can't edit anything in a Quick View window, you can see the whole file. This is enough to let you make a quick-and-dirty decision about whether you can blow the file away.

Deleting a file is a satisfying two-click experience.

Instead of forgetting that you have three older versions of a file in a folder, you start to get this attitude about stuff cluttering up your folder windows. And, since burning any file is a very satisfying little two-click operation (if you configure Win 95 properly), you're a lot less likely to be lazy about it. For some of us (you know who you are), this isn't going to make much difference. But you'd be surprised how much fun it is to delete as you go. And as I said in an earlier chapter, Microsoft should reward this good housekeeping behavior with positive reinforcement. Give us cool animation-and-sound effects that combust the object in roaring flames.

For two-click deletes (right-click the object about to bite the dust and click Delete on the context menu) without being confronted with the inane delete-confirmation dialog, you make an adjustment on Recycle Bin's properties dialog (as shown in Figure 4.7). Right-click Recycle Bin and choose Properties from the context menu. On the Global tab, uncheck the "Display delete confirmation dialog" box and click OK.

*William Gibson is the author of cyber-novels like *Necromancer, COUNT ZERO,* and *Burning Chrome,* for all you sci-fi illiterates.

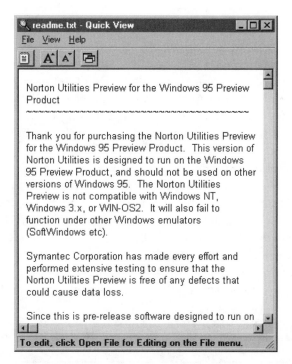

Figure 4.6 Viewing a document file's contents in a Quick View window

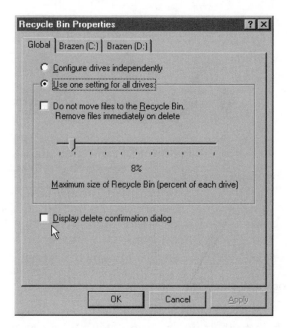

Figure 4.7 Make deletions go faster by adjusting Recycle Bin's properties

Drag Select

For those of us who've at one time or another had a passing bout of Mac envy, drag select (a.k.a. rubber-band select or, in some quarters, lasso select) is the sort of feature that tended to trigger that malady. Don't get me wrong. I like Macs a lot. But, where's the software? Anyway, for ages and ages, the Mac has let you select a bunch of files and folders by dragging a rectangle selection box around as many icons as you want in an open window or on the desktop. Win 95 mimics this operation exactly.

The way it works, you click outside any icon to be selected and drag the mouse pointer across the objects you want to select. All the icons you want to select must be adjacent to each other. The starting point for this drag deal is the corner anchor for the selection area. As you drag, an expanding rectangle—a rubber-band box—forms around the included objects, and when you let go of the mouse button, they'll be selected automatically. Trust me, it's one of those things that's a lot harder to explain than to do. Check out Figure 4.8. Bottom line: You can basically drag swipe the mouse across a bunch of adjacent objects to highlight them.

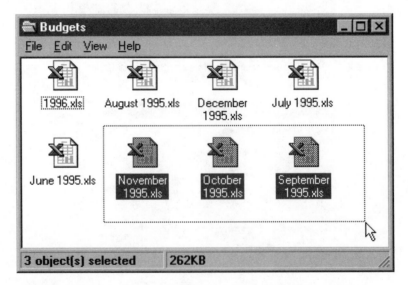

Figure 4.8   Drag selecting: the fastest way to highlight multiple adjacent objects

Once a group of files has been drag-highlighted, you can drag and drop any one of them to move them all from one folder to another. (*Note:* A drag and drop from one drive to another is a copy operation in Win 95; on the same drive, it's a move operation.) To copy a bunch of files to a different folder on the same drive, right-click drag them to their destination. (Don't forget, you can drop 'em on closed folders as well as on open ones.) When you let go of the right mouse button, you'll get a context menu that offers Move, Copy, Create Shortcut(s), and Cancel. In this case, you'd choose Copy.

Similarly, you might right-click any one of the files in a multiple selection to access the Cut and Copy commands on the context menu. Cut and Copy commands invoked this way apply to all the selected objects. If you decided to paste 'em into a different folder or something, they'd all reappear.

There are other ways to select file and folder icons. To select multiple files in a folder window that aren't adjacent to each other, click the first one and then Ctrl-click each of the rest in turn. This method is especially useful when you want to weed out a bunch of files in a directory to save disk space. Try Shift-clicking, too. It selects all the icons between the last one you selected and the one you're clicking now, in a row, column, or rectangle, depending on the folder view you're using.

Keyboard quick picks

FOLDER AND EXPLORER WINDOWS

> At the same time that we are earnest to explore and learn all things, we require that all things be mysterious and unexplorable, that land and sea be infinitely wild, unsurveyed and unfathomed by us because unfathomable.
>
> Henry David Thoreau
> *Walden,* 1854

What if you made File Manager the basis for just about everything you did in the old Windows? Excluding Start, Taskbar, and some of that other stuff I covered in Chapter 3, "The Desktop Interface," that's pretty much what Microsoft did in Windows 95. If it's an open window—and not a dialog or an application—chances are very good it's a folder window. That's sometimes true even of dialogs, such as the File/Save As dialog in the Win 95 version of Word for Windows.

Windows Explorer

So it pays to get this deal figured out. Mastering the new OS's folder windows, along with Start and Taskbar, is square one for would-be Win 95 experts. And believe me, you've read this far, so you're well on your way to being an expert.

The Many Faces of Explorer

The first thing to know is that folder windows have many faces and modes of operation. It's debatable which configuration settings constitute a truly different way of working with folders. But giving Microsoft's settings the benefit of the doubt, I count more than 20 different variations of what's generically known as the Explorer. To Microsoft's credit, though, you're not overwhelmed by the choices. They're there if you want them, but there's a default way of working that gets a lot of people by just fine. The options don't hit you over the head. In fact, if anything, they're spread out a bit too far. Table 4.1 gives you the lowdown.

Table 4.1.   The Many Faces of Explorer and the Default Folder Appearance

Settings and Controls	One-pane Folder Window	Two-pane Explorer Widow
Large Icons View	●	○
Small Icons View	○	○
List View	○	○
Details View	○	○
Sort by Name	●	○
Sort by Type	○	○
Sort by Size	○	○
Sort by Date	○	○
Auto Arrange Icons Off	●	○
Auto Arrange Icons On	○	○
Toolbar Off	●	○
Toolbar On	○	○
Browse with Multiple Windows	●	○
Browse with Single Window	○	○

● The default setting
○ An optional setting

Which Kind of Window?

As the table suggests, the fundamental decision in opening a folder window is to Explore or not to Explore. I'm sure a lot of people are happily using Win 95 right now without a clue that there is such a thing as an Explorer variation of a folder window. What they're seeing is the standard one-pane folder window, shown in Figure 4.9, which by default shows large icons for both the files and subfolders contained in the open folder directory.

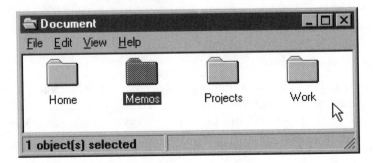

Figure 4.9   An example of the default Win 95 folder window

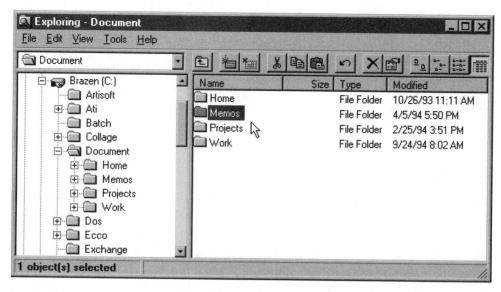

Figure 4.10 An Explorer window showing Toolbar and details view

The Explorer window is a special file manager-like version of a folder window. It's a two-paned affair. As noted earlier, the pane on the left shows a vertical tree of all the objects on the same level as the object you opened. At the top level, all the drives you see in My Computer are represented in the tree of the My Computer Explorer window (see Figure 4.2). Since you can open any drive or folder as an Explorer window, you won't always see multiple drives on the tree. Figure 4.10 shows an Explorer window opened for a C: drive. A little review: you can click the plus sign beside any of the drive letters in the My Computer Explorer window to expand the drive to the next level, that is, all the directories at the root level of the drive. Each folder directory at the root level is in turn expandable to show any subfolders it contains, and so on. When you select a folder directory in the tree pane on the left, its file and subfolder contents appear in the right pane.

The reason Microsoft calls this variant the Explorer is because of its ability to navigate your drive in the tree pane without your having to open additional windows. That's a boon for making big jumps from one part of a drive to another, from one drive to another, and even from one network volume to another. You can do all these things inside a single Explorer window in just a few clicks. It's something of a merger of the best of what the Macintosh's hierarchical folder file system has offered for years and the powerful directory-navigating tree structure of traditional DOS and Windows file managers, like XTree and the Windows 3.*x* File Manager. In fact, it's the best of both worlds.

Note that Figure 4.10 is a different look at the same directory and information shown in Figure 4.9. The tree in Figure 4.10 shows the little Document folder open and its contents are displayed in the right pane.

**Explorer win-
dows seem
complicated
but they're easy
once you un-
derstand 'em.**

Although my editor will probably have to squish the wider Explorer version to make it fit on a book page, Explorer windows take up a good deal more space on your screen. That's part of the reason the Boyz made regular one-pane folder windows the default. Another reason was probably because Explorer windows appear complicated at first blush, although they're really pretty straightforward once you understand them. Anyway, you've gotta walk before you run, and folder windows are very definitely the subsets of Explorer windows. So, let's dig into folder settings.

Folder Icon View Controls

**Folder View
Toolbar buttons**

The next several pages detail *local* folder window controls. By local I mean settings that apply only to the folder or Explorer window you're currently working with. There are also *global* folder controls—settings that affect all of Win 95's folders; I'll look at those in a couple of pages. Redmond makes little distinction between the natures of these two types of settings, but I've noticed that that's the first place people get tripped up in trying to figure this stuff out.

There are four separate folder window views, and four different ways to sort the order in which files and folders are displayed in a folder window. For good reason, perhaps, Microsoft chose to separate the controls for Views and Sorts. It's easy to become confused about these two types of controls. But, if separating them means that they're harder to get to. . . . Boo. Hiss. And, unfortunately that's what Microsoft did. But, I'm getting ahead of myself.

The four View options are Large Icons (the default setting), Small Icons, List, and Details. Their controls are shown in Figure 4.11. Each has its advantages. Here's the skinny:

Large Icons gives you a close-up view of your objects, making them large and easy to latch onto. After you've used Win 95 for a while, you'll see that the icon images are something of a subliminal guiding hand to what an object is or does. In this view, the procession of folders and files moves left to right by row. Of course, there's a disadvantage to Large Icons: You see far fewer objects in the same folder window than you do with either the Small Icons or List views.

Small Icons is probably the least useful of the views. While it shows more icons in the same window than does Large Icons, you lose much of the graphical information. Like Large Icons, it moves folders and files in a procession that moves left to right by row.

List is a lot like Small Icons, but with an important difference. It moves files and folders through your chosen sort order from top to bottom by column. It's a bit more economical with its use of most window space, so you'll potentially be able to see more icons in List than you can in Small Icons. I find it easier to scan than the Small Icons view.

Details is the view that's most closely analogous to the All File Details view of the old Windows File Manager. It shows you the least number of files in an

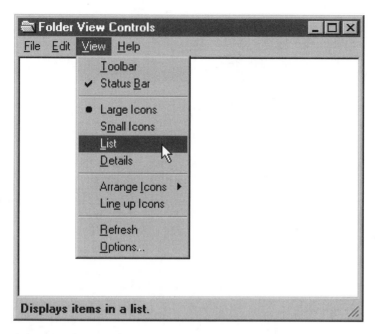

Figure 4.11 Folder window View menu controls

open folder but gives the most information about each file, including file size, file type, and (date) modified. Microsoft: It'd be nice if Attributes were displayed here, too. If you're looking for those, you'll find them on each object's individual properties sheet.

Folder Icon Sort Controls

Buried in each and every folder's View menu are its object sort controls. Views changes the way a folder displays file and folder icons; sort changes the order in which icons appear in the selected view. It's a bit confusing, but you'll get used to it pretty fast. To check out the sort orders, pull down the View menu from any open folder and click on the Arrange Icons menu item. You'll get a cascading submenu with five options.

Sorting out views and sorts

There are four sort orders on the Arrange Icons submenu (shown in Figure 4.12): by Name, by Type, by Size, and by Date. They correspond to four sort orders, respectively: alphabetically by filename, alphabetically by file type, by file size from smallest to largest, and by last-modified date from most recent to oldest. These sort orders are pretty self-explanatory, no?

With the exception of the by Type sort (see the next Bug note), the sort orders work as you might expect them to. The one thing I wish Microsoft had done was to put a check mark beside the currently selected sort as it did for Auto Arrange.

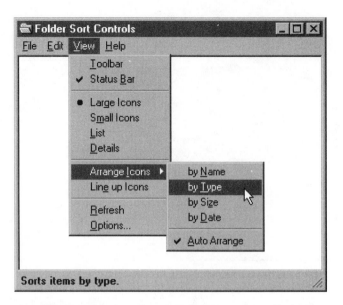

Figure 4.12   The Arrange Icons submenu for sort orders

Instead, folders default to the by Name sort, and any sort changes you make revert back to the by Name sort next time out. All Arrange Icons settings apply to the specific folder you're making changes from. So, even if you can't nail down a sort, it would be a real boon, Redmond, if we could at least see at a glance with a check mark which sort was in vogue at any given moment.

Anyone who's ever used DOS or Windows in the past is going to encounter a certain level of frustration about something Microsoft did to the Arrange Icons by Type sort. This deal doesn't sort files alphabetically in order of the letters in their file extensions. Instead, it sorts them alphabetically (with folders appearing first) by a new slice of information germane to each file object called *file type*. A file's type is a text phrase that describes it, usually as an association with a specific application. As a result, Help files with the `.HLP` **extension appear before old Program Manager group box files with the** `.GRP` **extension. That's because Win 95 types** `.GRP` **files as "Microsoft Program Group" files and** `.HLP` **files as "Help File" files.**

In Microsoft's defense, this change is one of those sow-now, reap-later deals, since the additional type information will help us all better understand what the files on our computers do. It's also indirectly a part of the general changes in filenaming, since files no longer have to be displayed showing their filename extensions. And down the road under planned Microsoft operating systems, file extensions could disappear altogether. That would be a good thing, and they're getting us ready for it.

It's possible to change these type descriptions. For example, to change the
.GRP file description, choose View/Options/File Types from any open folder.
Scroll down the Registered file types box until you find Microsoft Program
Group. Click it and choose Edit. Then, in the "Description of type" field,
change the name to something like "GRP File." That'll put .GRP files before
.HLP files. But, know what? It's not worth it. Your .INI files, for example, are
still going to come before your .GRP files because Microsoft has typed them as
"Configuration Settings" files. And you could spend the rest of your life try-
ing to stay on top of this. My advice: Get used to it.

There's a nice little feature you'll find in the Details view that lets you change
the file sort order by clicking the sort tabs that run across the top of the folder window (or across the top of the file pane in an Explorer window) as shown in Figure
4.13. So, if you click the Name tab, the sort order changes to alphabetically by
name. If you click the Size tab, the files are sorted by size, and so on. A little break
in interface consistency appears with the tab for the date column, which is labeled
"Modified." But don't let it throw you.

Modified

A one-click
sort tab in
Details view

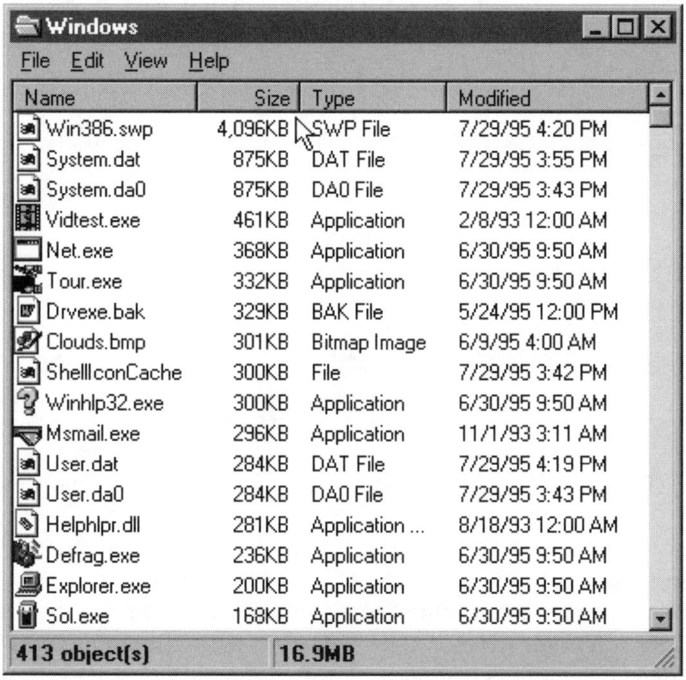

🖳 Windows			_ □ ✕
File Edit View Help			
Name	Size	Type	Modified
Win386.swp	4,096KB	SWP File	7/29/95 4:20 PM
System.dat	875KB	DAT File	7/29/95 3:55 PM
System.da0	875KB	DA0 File	7/29/95 3:43 PM
Vidtest.exe	461KB	Application	2/8/93 12:00 AM
Net.exe	368KB	Application	6/30/95 9:50 AM
Tour.exe	332KB	Application	6/30/95 9:50 AM
Drvexe.bak	329KB	BAK File	5/24/95 12:00 PM
Clouds.bmp	301KB	Bitmap Image	6/9/95 4:00 AM
ShelliconCache	300KB	File	7/29/95 3:42 PM
Winhlp32.exe	300KB	Application	6/30/95 9:50 AM
Msmail.exe	296KB	Application	11/1/93 3:11 AM
User.dat	284KB	DAT File	7/29/95 4:19 PM
User.da0	284KB	DA0 File	7/29/95 3:43 PM
Helphlpr.dll	281KB	Application ...	8/18/93 12:00 AM
Defrag.exe	236KB	Application	6/30/95 9:50 AM
Explorer.exe	200KB	Application	6/30/95 9:50 AM
Sol.exe	168KB	Application	6/30/95 9:50 AM
413 object(s)	16.9MB		

Figure 4.13   One-click sort tabs in the Details view, here
showing a size sort

Until you try these little gray sort tabs, you might not realize that they've got something a bit extra. All the sort tabs in the Details view are *toggles.* By that, I mean, click one once, and you sort alphabetically (A to Z) or numerically (0 to largest), whichever applies to the given sort type. Click the same tab a second time, and you get the reverse order: (Z to A) or (largest to 0). On the third click, the sort goes back to the original order. For serious file management, sorting by date or file size can be a big advantage. And the reverse sorting can really cut down on mindless scrolling.

The Arrange Icons Auto Arrange Setting

Auto Arrange does something very simple, and to my way of thinking, essential.

The last menu item on the View/Arrange Icons submenu is Auto Arrange. It does something very simple and, to my way of thinking, essential. The question is, do you want icons to wrap inside a folder or Explorer window automatically when you resize the window or move or delete a file? Or, would you prefer that they keep their original position, poking invisibly out of the window if you make it smaller or leaving holes wherever you delete files?

Most of the time, you'll probably want Auto Arrange on (shown in Figure 4.14). And that's what I recommend. In fact, it'd be real nice if Microsoft gave us a way to turn this on globally as a folder default. Still, if your preferences run to less auto-magic things or you're truly a Pig Pen about graphical controls, leave Auto Arrange off. Then, if you want to straighten up once every fourth year whether you need to or not, use the folder menu View/Line up Icons menu item to manually clean up.

Figure 4.14   Auto Arrange on the Arrange Icons submenu

One of the most serious and persistent bugs in Windows 95 is its tendency to intermittently lose settings you make to folder or Explorer windows. In particular, you may discover that a ghost has switched off the Auto Arrange setting the next time you open a folder. Or window sizes and positions may be mysteriously different next time out. View settings may also be visited by a poltergeist. The errant changes often occur between Win 95 sessions. So things work fine while you're working with them, but the next time you turn on the PC, your painstaking work to configure and arrange folders may be lost. It's an inconsistent problem, one that plagued the beta versions of Windows 95 but was im-

proved a lot with the shipping code. Still, it's not a fully vanquished bug. Unfortunately, I've got no real help to offer on it. It's the kind of thing that, we can only hope, will disappear with a quiet bug fix, if it hasn't already been swatted in the version you've got. And if not, we need to complain loudly because it can be truly annoying.

My last word about folder icon views and sorts is that old thing about remembering the right mouse button. It doesn't save you a ton of time or anything, but if you click anywhere on the background of any open folder (or the file pane of any Explorer window), you'll get the *de rigueur* context menu, which places cascading submenus for the icon views and sorts right next to each other. Once right-clicking becomes second nature, you'll find this is a bit faster than pulling down the View menu.

Auto Arrange isn't just for folder and Explorer windows. There's a grid under the Windows 95 desktop that is controlled by two separate areas. One of these is the Display Control Panel, whose Appearance tab offers icon vertical and horizontal spacing that applies to both folder and desktop icon spacings. The fastest route to the Display Properties screen is to right-click the desktop and choose Properties from its context menu. (This deal is detailed in Chapter 3, "The Desktop Interface."

You'll also find the Arrange Icons and Line up Icons menu items on the desktop's context menu. They can be used to organize desktop icons just as they work in folder windows. There are no View controls for the desktop, though. Large Icons is the only available desktop View.

The Folder Toolbar

It's lame, that folder toolbar you can turn on under any folder's View menu (see Figure 4.15). It takes up a lot of vertical space. It stretches too far to the right because it's chock full of spaces, and has buttons you may never use. So, if you want all the buttons fully visible, you're going to have to make your folder windows both a bit taller and pretty darn wide. And some of the most useful of the folder toolbar functions—the View controls—are all the way to the right, where they're the first things to disappear when you decide to scale back a folder's horizontal size.

The folder toolbar: Love it *and* hate it.

Figure 4.15 The folder toolbar in all its overly large, unconfigurable glory

I mean, why do we really need buttons like Map Network Drive, Disconnect Network Drive, and Properties on this toolbar? (In the case of the Properties button, why do we need a button for it at all, since it's on each object's context menu?) And why are these nearly useless buttons placed where they can help push the View buttons off the right side? I tell you, it's Microsoft hegemony at work. Or maybe they just didn't think this through.

All my folder toolbar criticisms boil down to one thing: The folder toolbar is a lot like the File Manager toolbar from Windows for Workgroups—and that was configurable. Why isn't Win 95's folder toolbar user configurable!?

*Now why didn't
Microsoft think
of this?*

Does any of us really need a separate screen-hogging toolbar at all? Ever notice that there's a whole lot of wasted space on menu bars? Every single folder or Explorer window has a bar stretching along its top that houses the File, Edit, View, and Help menus. To the right of these main menus is . . . dead air. Wasted space. *Nada.* And it stretches as far right as you've sized that particular window side to side. Even if you make a folder window exceedingly small horizontally, there's still going to be enough space left over to . . . wait a minute. Hey, I'm a genius. They should put the View buttons up there. Maybe even the Sort buttons. And maybe the Up One Level button. Now, why didn't Microsoft think of that? I mean, who cares if it's a little busier-looking. What matters is how ready to hand the controls are and how well folders get the job done.

*The toolbar
Delete button*

While they're at it, they should add one more button to the folder toolbar: a button that turns the dang thing off! The main reason I turn it on is to have one-click access to the View buttons, the drop-down drive/folder navigator at the left, the Delete button, and the Up One Level button. But it takes up vertical space, and I don't want to pull down a menu just to click it off.

GLOBAL FOLDER CONTROLS

On this narrow planet, we have only the choice between two unknown worlds. One of them tempts us—ah! what a dream, to live in that!—the other stifles us at the first breath.

Colette
"The Photographer's Wife," in *Gigi,* 1945

*Yo, Redmond:
Where are the
configurable
global settings?*

If you pull down any folder's View menu and choose Options, you've got access to the very few global folder controls that Microsoft deigned to give us. By "global," I mean once you set it, it affects every folder you open in Windows 95. Some of the stuff that should be configurable globally that isn't are user-created defaults for Explorer versus folder windows (you can do this, but it's more painful than a simple check on/off box), Auto Arrange on or off (at least make the default on, and dang the minor performance hit!), the icon view, the icon sort, toolbar on or off, and status bar on or off. If your particular preferences for folder-window settings run counter to Microsoft's prescription in this regard, you'll have to make changes to each and every folder on your system, as well as any new ones you create. Sigh. And because of the aforementioned folder bug, you might have to do this over and over again.

The short list of global settings that are there can be useful, though. And you might as well make use of them. When you open View/Options, you get a tabbed dialog with three screens.

Start with the second one, the View tab (shown in Figure 4.16). It offers three choices. The first is to make invisible in folder and Explorer windows a set of specialized program files that you're rarely if ever going to need to manipulate directly—files whose extensions are .DLL, .SYS, .VXD, .386, and .DRV, as well as DOS Attribute Hidden files. Long-time PC users may find this a bit frustrating,

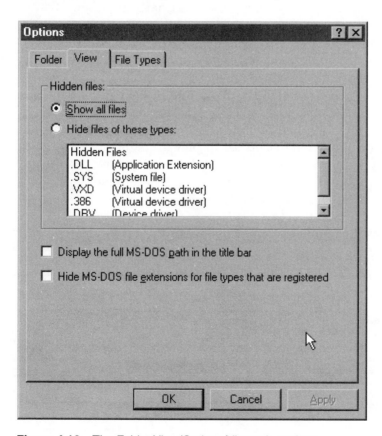

Figure 4.16   The Folder View/Options/View tab settings

since they're used to seeing these files. But the truth is, they take up a lot of extra space in folder windows. And except in very rare instances, you're not going to delete or modify them, right? Leave this with the "Hide files of these types" button clicked on. You can always change it to "Show all files" if you ever need to. Sure would be nice, though, if you could modify the list of file types directly in this dialog. I like to be able to see DOS Attribute Hidden files, for example. I could lose the rest with no sweat.

File objects without extensions? Trust me: The future isn't now.

Going along with that idea is the bottom setting, "Hide MS-DOS file extensions for the file types that are registered." (I'll get to file types in a bit.) This setting makes invisible the three-letter file extensions of all *registered* file types. Don't let the term "MS-DOS file extensions" throw you. This applies to some MS-DOS files. However, it also applies to a long list of file extensions that Win 95 installs by default, as well as the file extensions of any Windows 95 apps you install, as well as those of most 16-bit Win apps you install. Someday, file extensions will go away, and we'll all get used to looking at files this way. The idea is that you'll start recognizing a file's associated program—that is, its type or file format—by the picture on its icon. But trust me, the future isn't now. So, uncheck this one. By the way, to truly make this work, Microsoft, methinks you're going to have to put some text into the image area of the object icons. But then, I'm a word guy.

Finally, there's the "Display the full MS-DOS path in the title bar" setting. This one's really a matter of personal preference. Old-time DOS heads like me will instinctively turn this one on. But we might be mistaken in doing that. I'll tell you why in a minute. What this does is display the pathname of the folder across the title bar (as shown in Figure 4.17). It helps you know where you are in your drive's directory structure. For anyone who's new to the PC or who's never mastered paths, I recommend leaving this off.

Figure 4.17 A folder window displaying its full DOS pathname

Experienced DOS users should also consider turning it off, because when it is turned on, the task buttons for each and every open folder on Taskbar try real hard (and almost never succeed) to display those full pathnames. The result is usually a cacophony of partial pathnames littering Taskbar, rendering it practically useless. It's the very last part of a pathname—the folder name—that matters most on Taskbar, and that's the first thing to get pushed off the button on folders that have long pathnames.

Turn off this setting, and you're unlikely to miss it. Leave it on, and you'll probably never warm up to Taskbar, which is one of the best ideas in Win 95. Microsoft should have put the pathname on the status bar, where it wouldn't show up on Taskbar. Then we'd have the best of both worlds.

Reused versus Multiple Folder Windows

Here's a little tip fer ya. Microsoft thinks that we might all be very confused by the little global setting you'll find on the View/Options/Folder tab. Check it out.

Choose the setting "Browse folders by using a single window that changes as you open each folder" (shown in Figure 4.18) and something very different

Browsing multiple windows

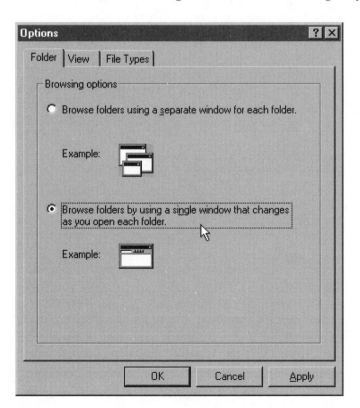

Figure 4.18　Give this setting a shot to unclutter your screen

happens. Instead of a second folder opening when you double-click a subfolder inside the open folder window, the existing folder window is reused. The contents of the window are just replaced by the contents of the subfolder. It's just like the right pane of an Explorer window.

If that sounds weird, think about it. Unless you're making a visual comparison between folders, chances are you're just tunneling down your directory structure looking for a file. When you're working this way, you could easily clutter up your screen with six or seven open folders. What's more, if you're working on a smaller screen—especially a portable PC—screen real estate comes at a steeper premium, and opening a bunch of folders doesn't help matters. And while you can achieve the same thing in an Explorer window, those guys take up a lot more screen space than regular folder windows.

There's another advantage to the single-window approach. You're going to have to manage the size of only one folder window instead of 17 or whatever. Set the size the way you like it. For instance, I make my folder window as big as I can without its slipping off the edges of the screen or overlapping my desktop tools and Shortcuts. This is by no means an absolute rule, since there'll be times when you wind up opening a second window. Any time you double-click a desktop container object—like My Computer, Network Neighborhood, or a desktop drive Shortcut icon—you'll get an additional folder. "Browse a single window" applies only to objects you open within an open folder window. So, if you wind up working with multiple open windows, Win 95 adopts the size, position, and setting information of the open window as it was last closed or changed. Or, you might create a new folder, which will use the Microsoft-prescribed defaults. (Wouldn't it be nice if Microsoft gave us a way to create user-defined defaults for all new folders?)

Give the single window a try.

I strongly recommend you try the single-window approach. I was a bit skeptical at first, but after forcing myself to work that way for a week, I've never gone back. For more on this reused window deal, check out the strategy for controlling folder windows in Chapter 5, "Customize It." There are several additional folder controls and Win 95 features sorted out there, too.

Explorer-specific Settings

Actually, there's not much to explore here. All the local controls are the same. When you open the View/Options dialog from an Explorer window, you'll find that the Folder tab with its "Browse a single window" option has disappeared. The single-window approach is the default, and only, behavior of Explorer windows. There's also one additional setting on the Views tab, whose description reads: "Include description bar for right and left panes." By default, this is turned on. Unless you're really struggling with Explorers, though, the first thing to do is turn it off. It's just a big space waster.

File Types

The View/Options/File Types dialog, accessible from any folder or Explorer window, is the direct descendant of the Associate command located on the File menu of the old Windows File Manager. But, while it does almost the same thing, what's going on underneath is so completely different that, well, it's going to take a little getting used to—to put it mildly.

The whole idea is based on the premise that applications use specific filename extensions—the last three letters of a filename—to identify them as data files owned by, or *associated with,* specific apps. So, when you double-click on a file object with, say, a .DOC extension, Windows knows to launch either WordPad or Microsoft Word to open it.

This either/or thing is part of the problem you'll encounter. File Types can't register multiple applications to the same extension. The classic example of where that can be something of a problem is on the Microsoft Network. When a user opens a text-containing file on MSN, it's usually a .DOC file. This is a good thing, because Microsoft is using a program on your local computer— which can run faster than any program running on the MSN server shared over modem lines—to open the file and show it to you. So, because of this text file display deal, when you install MSN from your Win 95 disc or disks, you're also installing the WordPad word processing applet. And, conveniently, WordPad can open and save documents in Word 6.0 for Windows format.

The problem arises when you install any version of Microsoft Word in Windows 95. Because when you do that, Word registers the .DOC extension as *its* file type. So, from now on, when you double-click an MSN document icon to open it, instead of opening the smaller, fleeter WordPad, you're going to have to wait while ponderous Word launches itself.

Now, when Word installs it claims a small set of default-associated file types. But you can go ahead and add 79 (or however many you want) additional three-letter file extensions and file-type descriptions of your own devising that Windows will also recognize as being associated with Winword (like the .AUG extension I've added in Figure 4.19). That's the whole point of the File Types dialog—to let you make custom file associations. And, for that, it works quite well most of the time.

A Word 95 file object icon

Adding a file type not only lets you double-click a data file to launch its associated application. It also lets you customize the context menus of all files with that same extension to show commands specific to the program. It's pretty neat but also more complicated than it should be. I'll get into the nitty-gritty on file types and a lot more in Chapter 5, "Customize It."

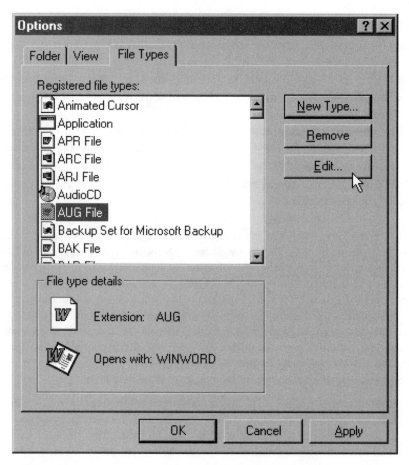

Figure 4.19   The Folder/View/Options/File Types tab dialog

Explorer Customizing

OK, so I've banged you over the head with Explorer hype. And you've gotten an introduction to, or a review of, some of the basic folder and Explorer window controls. Let's go back to that all-important point: How do you use this thing?

Here and there, I've given you some pointers on opening Explorer windows. But to recap: You can right-click any drive or folder icon (in My Computer, Network Neighborhood, on the desktop, or in a folder window) and choose Explore from the popup menu. Or hold down the Shift key and double-click a drive or folder icon. Or choose Start/Programs/Windows Explorer. This last is one of the menu items Win 95 installs on the Programs launch list. Did you take one look at Explorer windows and realize this is your kind of thing? In that case, do I have some tips for you.

First, you can create Shortcuts for specific drive or folder windows with settings that force them to open as Explorer windows. This deal works only with Shortcuts. Maybe you've made desktop drive icons, or you've placed Shortcuts to drives in a cascading folder at the top of Start's launch list (see Chapter 3, "The Desktop Interface"). Well, it's an easy process to take the next step and make those Shortcuts open Explorer windows.

Blythe (C)

A drive C: desktop icon

To create a desktop drive icon, open My Computer and right-click-drag one of your drives out onto the desktop. Choose "Create Shortcut(s) Here" from the context menu. Next, select the drive object's label and get rid of that dang "Shortcut to" text. Place the drive object Shortcut wherever you want.

It's not a bug, it's a feature. You may notice that sometimes when you drag-and-drop-create a Shortcut icon as described above, Win 95 does not insert that "Shortcut to" tag at the front of the object's label. This supposedly "cool" feature is rudimentary heuristics almost working. Say you create several Shortcuts during a Windows session, and each time you do, you delete the "Shortcut to" text. After about so many times, Win 95 gets the message and stops inserting the added tag. Wonder of wonders! Only thing is, next time you run Win 95, it's back to its old, frustrating way of doing things.

This is just another example of something that cries out for a global setting: a check box that would let you turn off the insertion of the pre-pended "Shortcut to" text. And you know what? I believe most people would eventually make use of this setting because the extra text is useful only for the first three weeks after you install the operating system. After that, the "Shortcut to" tag is a giant nuisance.

OK, back to forcing an Explorer window. By default, your newly created desktop drive Shortcut will bring up a standard folder window. To make it open a two-paned Explorer, right-click it to bring up the Shortcut's context menu and choose Properties. Click the Shortcut tab. In the Target field, type:

```
explorer /e, c:\
```

It should look like Figure 4.20. If the desktop object is for a different drive than drive C:, change the letter in the last part accordingly.

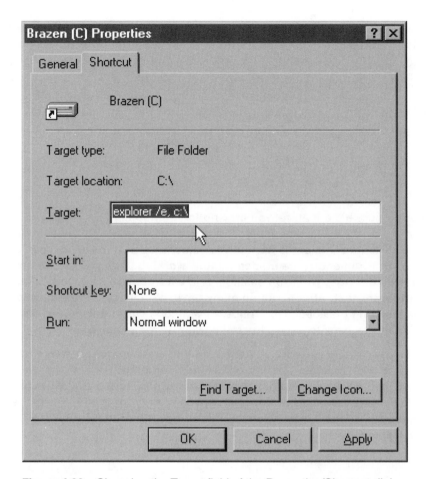

Figure 4.20 Changing the Target field of the Properties/Shortcut dialog

It's the exact same deal when you want to force a folder Shortcut to open as an Explorer window. But instead of simply typing the drive letter and specifying the root directory with the backslash, you type the full pathname to the folder on the Target line. So, a desktop icon that opens the Start Menu folder as an Explorer window would have a target line on its Properties/Shortcut tab that looks like this:

```
explorer /e, c:\windows\start menu
```

 Win 95 may automatically convert the icon images of Shortcuts you modify this way to show an image of a computer—a default association with the program file for Explorer. To change it back to the folder or drive icon, just click the Change Icon button on the object's Properties/Shortcut dialog and choose the icon image your prefer from the horizontally scrolling icon box.

With folders, you might want to refine this a little, creating a *rooted* (sorry, Microsoft's terminology) Explorer window. That means the tree pane will isolate on the specific folder you want to open, leaving out all the other folders, drives, and containers above it or at the same level. If this Shortcut has a specific purpose and you're not going to be doing a lot of Exploring elsewhere, rooting the window keeps things simple. For a better idea of what the heck I'm talking about, right-click the Taskbar and check out Properties/Start Menu Programs/Advanced. This opens a rooted Explorer window of the Start Menu folder.

To create a rooted Explorer window, add the /ROOT switch on the Shortcut's Target line. Here's how the rooted Explorer Start Menu folder setting reads:

```
explorer /e, /root, c:\windows\start menu
```

But that's not all you get. If you really like Explorer windows, why stop there? It's simple to make *all* drives and folders open as two-paned Explorer windows. To make the switch, open any folder or Explorer Window. Choose View/ Options/File Types. Scroll down the "Registered file types" box until you find the "Folder" entry (as shown in Figure 4.21). Select it and then click the Edit

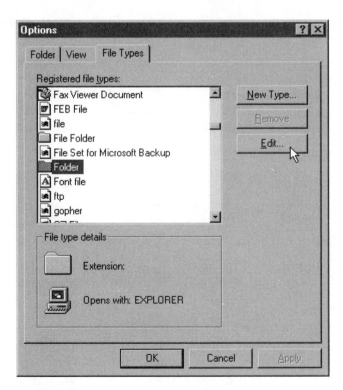

Figure 4.21   Shift into full-time Exploring—Step 1

button. In the Actions box, select the "Explore" entry. Then click the Set Default button (as shown in Figure 4.22) and close down the dialogs. From now on, even My Computer will open as an Explorer Window.

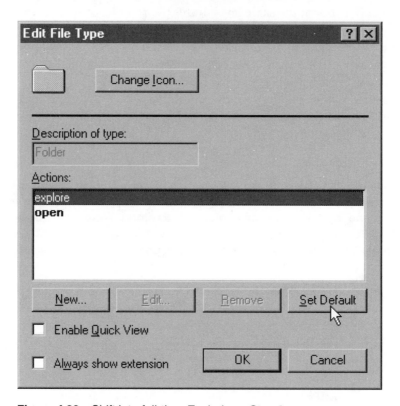

Figure 4.22 Shift into full-time Exploring—Step 2

If you opt to make the change given in the wand tip—making all folders open as Explorers by default—you can temporarily or selectively revert back to folder windows in a number of ways. First, you can right-click any drive or folder object and choose Open from the context menu. Or you can Shift-double-click to get a folder window. Or you can preset a given Shortcut to a drive or folder (but not My Computer, Recycle Bin, or Network Neighborhood) to open as a regular single-paned folder window.

To do that, you reverse the process I explained earlier. By their nature, folder windows are rooted, since they don't have tree panes. But for you to force a Shortcut to open as a regular folder window when you've set the Explore action as the default, it's back to the Shortcut's Properties/Shortcut/Target field. Make it read like this:

```
explorer [drive or folder pathname]
```

Replace the bracketed statement with the DOS drive letter or the drive and directory pathname as described previously.

A quick program note: If you've made Explore the default action for folders and you want to root a specific Explorer window, you need to add the full `explorer /e, /root, [folder pathname]` line. Win 95 needs the `/E` switch to understand the `/ROOT` switch.

THE LONG AND SHORT OF FILENAMES

Life is short, the art long, opportunity fleeting, experiment treacherous, judgment difficult.

Hippocrates
The first of his *Aphorisms* of the art of healing

Whoopee! Win 95 supports long descriptive filenames and folder names. I mean, you can name a file "I'm not sure what the heck's in here so check it out, OK.doc" if you want to. Up to 255 characters long (the actual filename limit varies because it is 256 characters minus the full DOS pathname). You might also name a folder "I don't know what any of this stuff is, so I'll delete it in 1999." And though most experienced PC users tend to turn up their noses at the whole notion of long file-naming, I think they're really just scared. Yeah, you know who you are. *What am I going to do with all that extra space? How can I come up with these names? Oh, I hate this!*

I have a hard time understanding the strong negative reactions I hear online and from many experienced PC-user colleagues and friends about long filenames. I mean, use 'em if you want to; don't if you don't. What's the big deal?

Use long filenames if you want. Don't if you don't.

To me, it's an integral part of all that file management-on-the-fly stuff I was talking about at the beginning of this chapter. I mean, if you're smart enough to give a file object a descriptive enough name so that six months hence it'll ring the bell that lets you obliterate it without even having to open it, what's wrong with that?

Well, I tell you what's wrong with it. Two main things. First, unless your file-creating apps (word processors, spreadsheets, databases, graphics programs, and the like) were designed for either Windows NT or Windows 95, they aren't going to support long filenames. So if you're already shelling out for 32-bit versions of these apps, go ahead and use long filenames . . . unless you plan to do a lot of work from the DOS command line.

Because that's the second point. The version of DOS underlying Windows 95 does NOT support long filenames. I mean, it deals with them without choking, it can even show you what the long names are, but it doesn't work with them. Instead, it works with filenames that it abbreviates on the fly. And rather than using an apostrophe to show where it made an abbreviation, it uses the tilde (~). When you see the tilde in DOS, it means there were a bunch of characters in there somewhere that DOS couldn't deal with, so it just slapped this abbreviating symbol in. And following the tilde, it usually places a number. Say you have two filenames that are similar, like these:

```
Hey Tell Your Friends About this Book.DOC
Hey Tell Your Friends About this Book, OK.DOC
```

Chances are if you booted to DOS and looked at those files, they'd look something like this: `HEYTEL~1.DOC` and `HEYTEL~2.DOC`. DOS can't handle the long filenames on its own. And Windows 95 can't handle parsing the name to figure out which words were most important, so it just starts from the beginning and does the best it can. If in the process it realizes that it's creating an abbreviation that it's already made, it just slaps a higher number at the end. One advantage to this seeming kludge is that it's pretty fast. And, fast is good. It's also pretty durn infallible. So far, in two years of using Win 95, I haven't encountered a single data integrity problem. You won't either.

One thing Win 95 can do is show you corresponding long file and directory names in the form of comments along the right side of a `DIR` (Directory) command screen (shown in Figure 4.23). Even better, the DOS prompt shows long pathnames, and you can navigate the directory structure using either the abbreviated names or the long ones. So if you don't want to, you're not stuck with that abbreviation gobbledy-gook. The big thing to remember is that this works only in a DOS window running out of Windows. If you boot to DOS, you're on your own, *compadre.*

Figure 4.23   A DOS window `DIR` command shows shortened names, but...

There's a little DOS `DIR` switch you might find useful. The `/V` switch on `DIR` commands, which stands for verbose, shows additional information in a DOS window, including both the tilde-abbreviated names and the full names of files and folders with long filenames. The two versions of the name are right next to each other, which makes reading them a bit easier. If you're a long-filename fiend, check it out.

The `/V` switch works only in DOS windows run from Windows. If you boot to DOS, `/V` has no effect. In Figure 4.24 is a directory called with `DIR` `/V`.

```
MS-DOS Prompt                                              _ □ ×

  8 x 12 ▾    ⬚ ⬚ ⬚ ⬚  ⬚ ⬚  A

File Name        Size        Allocated      Modified        Accessed

.                <DIR>                      03-15-95  9:20a  03-15-95
.
..               <DIR>                      03-15-95  9:20a  03-15-95
..
MAGLIN~1         <DIR>                      04-07-95  7:35a  04-07-95
Mag Links
HOMEPA~1         <DIR>                      04-18-95  8:43p  04-18-95
Home Page
CATEGO~1         <DIR>                      04-18-95  8:44p  04-18-95
Categories
SUE'SE~1         <DIR>                      04-18-95  8:56p  04-18-95
Sue's Edits
DONEST~1         <DIR>                      04-19-95  4:11p  04-19-95
Done Stuff
TRAILB~1 DOC      44,032       49,152       03-15-95 11:15a  07-26-95
Trailblazer Proposal.doc
          1 file(s)           44,032 bytes
          7 dir(s)            49,152 bytes allocated
                         192,602,112 bytes free
                         527,654,912 bytes total disk space,  63% in use

C:\Document\Work\WWW\Trailblazer>_
```

Figure 4.24 Same DOS window as in Figure 4.23, using `DIR` `/V` to show long filenames

So, overall, this long filename/abbreviated filename thing isn't a huge problem. Not really. In the mixed environment of 16-bit DOS and Windows apps plus 32-bit Windows 95 apps, it's a bit of a nuisance, since 16-bit Win apps see folder and filenames the same way that booted DOS does—minus any long filename support. As long as you're in Win 95's folders and Win 95 apps, you'll see the long filenames and folder names. When you run an app that doesn't fully support Windows 95, you'll see the abbreviated filenames.

There aren't two different files for every file, just two different names for it. You won't notice the difference, and frankly, you'll soon adapt to it. (Symantec's Norton Navigator includes a feature called, cryptically, Norton LFN, which adds rudimentary support for long filenames to the common dialogs of your applications.)

Don't try this
at work.

I'll tell you a story, though. Recently I upgraded my notebook PC at work from a 500MB drive to an 800MB drive. I didn't have space in my system to *add* the new drive, I had to switch them. That meant copying all my files up to a network directory, swapping the drives, and then copying all my files back down. Guess what? My company's network operating system doesn't support long filenames (for NetWare, the server needs to be running OS/2 namespace to do that). Nothing truly fatal happened. I didn't lose data. But all my long filenames, including some folders and files that Windows 95 installs with long filenames, were permanently renamed with the tilde abbreviations. And the kicker was that Win 95 wouldn't run. I tried hunting through to rename the directories to their original long filenames, but no-go. I had to re-install the operating system. Then, after that, I had to literally rename all my data files that had long filenames. You see, the abbreviated names are harder to live with than the traditional 8.3 DOS filenames.

Would that I had known about a little utility Microsoft ships on the Windows 95 CD. It's called LFN Backup, and you'll find the `LFNBK.EXE` **file in the** `\ADMIN\APPTOOLS\LFNBACK` **folder on the CD. This guy is a preemptive strike you can make when you know you're doing something like I did. Say you've decided to uninstall Windows 95 for some reason. If you do that, every single filename longer than eight characters, dot, three characters (8.3) will have been given the tilde-abbreviated names permanently. That's where LFN Backup comes in. If you run it first, it creates a little database of your long filenames with pointers to the abbreviated DOS filenames. Then, after you do whatever it is you're doing, you can run LFN Backup with its** `/R` **switch to restore the original long filenames. Before you try this, read the** `LFNBK.TXT` **file in the Lfnback folder thoroughly. Microsoft put several disclaimers in there, and the file offers good instructions on setup and usage.**

The Win 95 file
system: Hate it
or like it.

In defense of Microsoft's file system though (and it could use some defense), one reason why Win 95 is relatively easy to install, say, compared to OS/2 Warp (especially if you choose to install OS/2's excellent long-filename-supporting High Performance File System) is that the file system dovetails admirably with the pre-existing DOS file system (called FAT, for File Allocation Table). There's no need to repartition your hard drive and reformat that space as you must do to take full advantage of OS/2.

In fact, the Windows 95 file system should probably be called Super FAT, since it's an extension, rather than a replacement, of FAT. You may hate Microsoft for creating something of a kludge in providing support for long filenames in Windows 95, but you know what? They didn't name it "Windows 95" for nothing. It's not going to be around forever. And I suppose I'll be writing a book on

Windows 97 or something in the not-so-distant future. I suspect that Win 95's file system, when upgraded by some future version of Windows, will convert relatively gracefully to something like the more sincerely 32-bit NTFS file system found in Windows NT.

Long Filenames and Win 95 Apps

OK, end sermon. A couple of other points about long filenames, though. Truly Win 95 data-file producing applications have new and improved common dialogs—like File/Open, File/New, and File/Save As—that are stretched side to side to provide extra space in which to admire your long filenames. These dialogs, in all the Win 95 apps I've tried at any rate, are really miniature Win 95 folder windows. And, with only a few differences that may be specific to each app, they extend most of the same context menu services.

So, for example, when you choose File/Save As in Word 7.0 (as shown in Figure 4.25), the "dialog" presents you with a view of the default folder (the hard drive directory to which Word is currently defaulted). You'll also see all the folder and .DOC file objects in that directory. If you right-click on any of those objects or the dialog's background, you get Win 95-like context menus, like the one shown in Figure 4.26. This is a serious advantage that does away with that old problem of "I just created a file and can't do a thing with it since I don't have a directory to put it in," which used to mean cranking up a separate program just to create a directory. (Of course, WordPerfect and some other applications had Create Directory buttons, but I'll pass on that.)

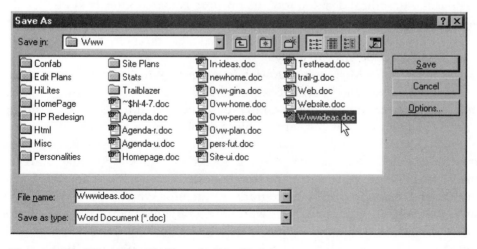

Figure 4.25 Word 7.0's File/Save As Win 95 dialog

Figure 4.26 A Word 7.0 dialog file object context menu—look familiar?

INCINERATOR BINGE

> Once something becomes discernible, or understandable, we no longer
> need to repeat it. We can destroy it.

Robert Wilson
Quoted in the *Sunday Times,* London, 17 November 1991

Ah, yes, the killer incarnate (think W. C. Fields). What is Recycle Biddy? And why should you like it?

Recycle Bin

Recycle Bin is a deletion-protection utility that's integrated into the operating system as a graphical desktop tool. Its purpose is to temporarily store files that you've earmarked for deletion until you either manually take out the trash or overload the poor thing with so much junk that it has no choice but to begin emptying itself in self-defense.

According to a Microsoft technical document, "Windows 95 supports placing deleted files in the Recycle Bin from My Computer or Windows Explorer only." That means it won't hang on to files you delete at the command prompt in a DOS window. Nor will it capture files you blow away from within Windows 3.1's File Manager. But the tech doc is a little misleading. Recycle Bin does capture files deleted from the dialogs of Microsoft's Windows 95 applications and probably those of other software companies. (But watch out for the Delete buttons in the dialogs of some programs written for Windows 3.1.) It also captures deletions from Recycle Bin-aware Win 95 file managers, like the Norton File Manager in Symantec's Norton Navigator for Windows 95. So, while Microsoft is hedging its bets a bit, chances are Recycle Bin's protection is pretty widespread.

There's really nothing revolutionary about Recycle Bin. It works much like the Mac's Trashcan and is also clearly inspired by the SmartCan utility the Norton/Symantec folks have been doing for some years. Basically, it works like this. When you delete an object anywhere in Win 95—no matter which of the many methods you choose to burn it with—the object goes into the Bin. There it sits, waiting for you to open the Recycle Bin window, open the File menu, and click Empty Recycle Bin. Or, if you're really daring, just right-click the Recycle Bin desktop object and choose the same menu item from the context menu, without even looking at the files (oh boy).

The reason deleted stuff is waiting around is because of the main feature of Recycle Bin: the ability to Restore files you've sent there. Restore moves pending-deletion files out of Recycle Bin and back to their original locations on your disk. You select a file or files in the Recycle Bin window that you decide not to delete and then choose File/Restore. The Restore command appears context-sensitively on Recycle Bin's File menu. To see it, you must have pending-deletion files in Recycle Bin and you must have highlighted at least one of them.

Cut to the chase: If you delete a file by accident, Recycle Bin is your net. And that's great because remember, "delete" means delete the actual file when it comes to everything but Shortcuts in Windows 95.

So far, so good. But bring up Recycle Bin Properties screen from its context menu, and you'll see something very interesting. Recycle Bin places a limit on itself in the form of a slider-selectable percentage of your hard drive. It does this up front and by default. And it's easy to misconstrue how that limit affects your hard disk and, as a result, Recycle Bin's functions. See Figure 4.27.

This space that Recycle Bin "reserves" on your disk isn't space that you can't use. At least, it might not be. Well, I'll put it this way. If you increase the percentage of disk space on the Recycle Bin Properties screen, the additional disk space allocated to Recycle Bin isn't suddenly unavailable to you. (Can you imagine the howls if it were?) Instead, it's the *maximum* amount of stuff in megabytes that Recycle Bin can store—pending true deletion—before it will fill up to overflowing and start taking it upon itself to kill off stuff permanently.

So, if Recycle Bin properties settings place an 8-percent limit on your 500MB C: drive, then Recycle Bin will fill up with about 40MB of stuff before it bulges to overflowing and triggers a background delete. That's why it pays to empty the trash pretty frequently. That way, you can make a final check beforehand to ensure there isn't stuff in there that maybe you really don't want to delete.

There's really nothing revolutionary or strange about Recycle Bin.

Recycle Bin's reserved space isn't completely unavailable.

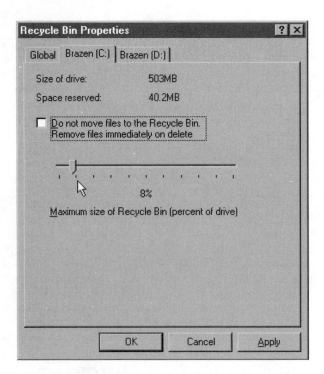

Figure 4.27 Recycle Bin Properties screen, the C: drive tab

If there's a Recycle Bin gotcha . . .

For the same reason, fight the urge to move the percentage slider down to almost nothing out of some knee-jerk instinct that it'll help you save disk space. You're using extra disk space only if you put off emptying Recycle Bin, it fills up, and you let it sit there forever without taking out the trash. When you give Recycle Bin a tight rein, it just fills up a lot and then empties stuff when you least expect it. Sometimes to your chagrin. And if there's a gotcha to Recycle Bin, this is it, because by doing that, you're defeating the whole purpose.

If defeating the whole purpose sounds like a good idea to you, open Recycle Bin Properties and click "Do not move files to Recycle Bin. Remove files immediately on delete" button. From now on, you'll be back to the old way of doing things. But you're probably making a mistake.

The first time you go to restore an entire folder you changed your mind about deleting, you may hit the frustration button. At first glance, Recycle Bin doesn't appear to store stuff hierarchically; it looks like it just plops stuff in there and doesn't even save the folders. But don't forget that the Explorer is the heart of this thing, just like it is almost everything else in Win 95. Choose the Details view from the View menu or toolbar and then click the gray "Original Location" tab to sort

Recycle Bin's collection of misfits according to the folders they came from. Then you can select and restore groups of files by folder. If a file you restore was originally contained in a folder that has also been deleted, Recycle Bin will automatically restore the folder, too.

Setting Up Recycle Bin

Back to Recycle Bin Properties screen for a second. There are two ways to set this sucker up. The obvious method, working it out solely on the Global tab, is the more difficult of the two.

Here's my recommendation. First turn off the silly "Display delete confirmation dialog" on the Global tab. How many fail-safes do we really need? Don't answer that. Some of us need 'em, and you know who you are. But for everyone else, leaving this setting on will cost you an extra click every single time you delete, unless you're using Recycle Bin as a desktop tool and you're actually dragging and dropping objects onto the Recycle Bin icon (or its open window).

Next, even if you have only one hard drive, it's easier to configure Recycle Bin optimally if you choose the top radio button on Global, the one that reads "Configure drives independently." It's easier because you get a read-out in megabytes of just how much storage space Recycle Bin has, rather than having to guess at what the percentage means as you do under Global. If you have two drives, it's clearly an advantage, since you may delete from one of them a lot less frequently. (In which case, set a smaller limit for Recycle Bin on that drive.)

Click the tab(s) for your drive(s) in turn and use the slider to adjust the setting. Give the blame fool thing enough rope so that you won't get hung—especially if you're the type who tends to go on rampaging trash binges where you toss whole directories out with the bath water and later wish you had them back. I try to keep my drives at 40MB or more—I guess I like binges. You may be just fine with Microsoft's default settings.

> **Give the blame fool thing enough rope so *you* won't get hung.**

If you're on the fence about whether to turn Recycle Bin off entirely, there's something you should know. When you're sure you want to delete something now, not later, there's a way to selectively defeat Recycle Bin's protection. Right-click on the unneeded object, press the Shift key, and click Delete from the context menu. Or, you can click the object to select it and press Shift-Delete. Or, you can Shift-drag-and-drop it to Recycle Bin. Do it any of these three ways, and it's gone posthaste.

I'm sorry, but the name Recycle Bin is too cute for words. Here's how to change it for good. Open the System Registry Editor. (It's in your Windows folder and goes by the name REGEDIT.EXE.**) Make a Shortcut for this baby and place it somewhere handy in Start because you're going to need it again and again.**

Inside the Registry Editor, choose Edit/Find, plug in the words `Recycle Bin`, and press Enter. When Find locates the first reference, it'll display an entry on its right pane that gives you a funny-shaped icon sporting the letters "ab" with a word or number highlighted beside it. To the right of that, you should see text including the words "Recycle Bin." Double-click the highlighted word or number beside the ab icon. In the Value data field, type `Incinerator Binge` **or** whatever name you like. Press the F3 key and repeat the process until Find finishes searching the Registry.

You have to restart Windows for the full effect, which includes renaming of the desktop icon (see Figure 4.28), the open folder, and the name on the drop-down navigator on the folder toolbar. There'll still be some places on bitmap menus where you'll see that sickly sweet original name. But, trust me, you'll be glad you made this change.

Incinerator Binge

Figure 4.28   You can change that sappy name—really

OTHER DISK STUFF

Electronic aids, particularly domestic computers, will help the inner migration, the opting out of reality. Reality is no longer going to be the stuff *out there,* but the stuff inside your head. It's going to be commercial and nasty at the same time.

J. G. Ballard
Interview in *Heavy Metal,* April 1971

There's a hodgepodge of other stuff that's disk- and file-system related that bears some looking at, or using, if you can find it. Sometimes finding it isn't quite as easy as you'd like.

Fer instance, mates, one of the more frustrating aspects of regular folder windows is their stark silence on such basic information as free disk space left on a drive. You can open any Explorer window and click on a drive object in the tree pane to see "Disk Free Space: 158MB" (or however many actual free MBs you've got) on the status bar. Or open My Computer and click a drive to get a similar readout, including the full capacity of the drive. Unfortunately, the readout in the status bar of a single-pane folder window tells you only about the current selection (something that's next to useless in Details view, since it gives file sizes).

Like DOS, Windows 95 does not supply *branch sizing*. This buzzword means a readout of the total size of all the objects in a folder, including the contents of any and all subfolders. Think of it as the size in MBs of everything from this point down to the end of the current folder branch.

What Explorer windows do give you is single-folder sizing. Click on any folder on the tree-pane of an Explorer window, and the status bar will show you the collective size of all the files in that folder, not including the contents of any subfolders it contains. But c'mon Microsoft, that's not very helpful. When you want to know the size of a folder, chances are you want to know the size of *everything* that folder contains, subfolders and all. The only way I know of to get branch sizing under Windows 95 is to buy Symantec's Norton Navigator for Windows 95.

Where's Format?

3½ Floppy (A:)

Well you might ask. It's actually quite easy to go looking for this basic function and not find it. To format a disk, such as a floppy, you must have it selected in My Computer and then choose the Format line on My Computer's File menu. You won't find the Format command in any Explorer or folder window (because then it would be all too easy for us to shoot ourselves in the hard drive, so to speak. After all, we're idiots). Nor does it show up on My Computer's File menu *unless you have a formattable drive selected.* So, if you're just hunting for it to know where it is, you're as apt to miss it as find it.

Of course there's a somewhat faster way: drive context menus. If, for example, you've placed a Shortcut for a floppy drive on your desktop, you can insert a floppy to be formatted and pull up the drive's context menu to get to the Format command (as shown in Figure 4.29). This also applies to the context menus of formattable drive objects inside My Computer.

Figure 4.29   Right-click a formattable drive and pick Format on the context menu

The Format dialog (see Figure 4.30) gives you what you'd expect if you've used DOS or Windows before. You can choose Quick Format (erases rather than reformats) or Full Format, and you can copy just the System files (mimicking the DOS SYS command). You can label the disk and also choose whether to copy system files to it to make it a bootable disk or leave them off to create a straight data disk that has a bit more storage space. When you opt to make a floppy system disk, it's equivalent to a DOS boot disk. Just the basic stuff needed to get to the DOS command line.

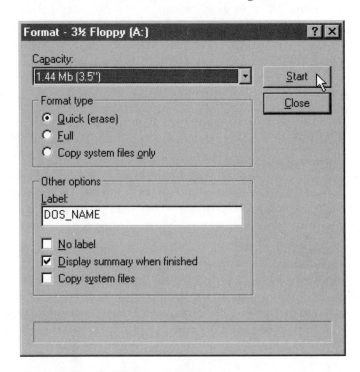

Figure 4.30   The Format dialog

How to make a startup floppy after install

OK, so that's figured out, and for the most part, it's straightforward once you know the trick. The Boyz thoughtfully added another floppy formatting feature, though. Only thing is, they placed it somewhere completely different. It's called a Win 95 Startup Disk. It's a basic DOS system disk plus several additional files added to facilitate troubleshooting in the event that you encounter a problem with your hard disk or your Win 95 installation.

In addition to the basic DOS boot files, it adds the new Win 95 versions of ATTRIB.EXE, CHKDSK.EXE, DEBUG.EXE, EBD.SYS, EDIT.COM, FDISK.EXE, FORMAT.COM, REGEDIT.EXE, SCANDISK.EXE, SYS.COM, and UNINSTAL.EXE. All of these extra utilities run from the DOS command line as DOS programs.

So where do you find the dialog that lets you create a Win 95 Startup Disk? Oh, well, c'mon now, that's just a completely different operation than Format. Why would you want to do that? Didn't you make one during installation? If you must, why, of course you have to open the Control Panel. Silly. And, quite naturally, once in the Control Panel, you'll realize in a flash that you create a Win 95 Startup Disk under Add/Remove Programs. I mean, listen buddy, this isn't rocket science. Get with the program, huh? Geez.

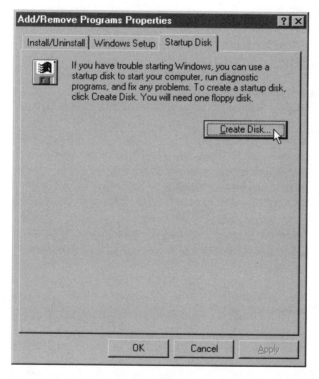

Figure 4.31   Make an official Win 95 Startup Disk under the Control Panel

If you're salting a Win 95 Startup Disk away for a rainy day, there's four additional files I suggest you add to it. From the Command folder inside your Windows folder, copy `DELTREE.EXE`, `MEM.EXE`, `MOVE.EXE`, **and** `XCOPY.EXE`. `MEM.EXE` **helps diagnose memory problems, and the other three are useful for copying, moving, renaming, and deleting directories from the DOS command line.**

Win 95's Disk Utilities

Win 95 is better prepared with disk utilities than most operating systems.

Win 95 comes with a better set of basic disk utilities than many other operating systems. I wouldn't call it a comprehensive list, but you're all set for three biggies: disk scanning and repair, disk defragmenting, and backup. Depending on the installation options you chose, you may or may not find this stuff where I tell you to look. If not, you can add utilities from the Windows Setup tab on the Add/Remove Programs control panel. Have your Win 95 CD or floppies handy.

You'll find Shortcuts for your installed disk utilities under Start's Programs/Accessories/System Tools, shown in Figure 4.32. Your principal tools are ScanDisk, Disk Defragmenter, and Backup. I've listed them in order of importance—the gospel according to Scot.

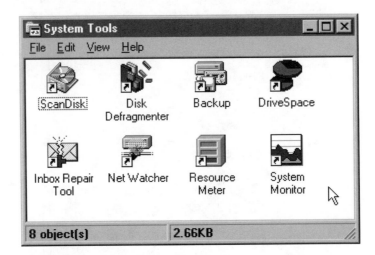

Figure 4.32   The System Tools folder

Backup

I'm one of those real-type computer users who sneers at backing up in all forms. I don't even have Backup installed on my system. But, I'm flying by wire without any redundant systems. One day that'll probably bite me.

Backup can create a backup of pretty much whatever you want it to, either to floppies or a tape-backup device. The floppy route is crazy except for, perhaps, warehousing a relatively small set of important data files. If you're as serious about this as I probably should be, consider getting a tape-backup device. They're really not that expensive, and one day it'll probably save your bacon. If you're on a LAN at work and have access to a personal network volume, you might want to configure Backup to store stuff on the network. That way if your disk ever gets hosed, you can sneer at people like me.

Disk
Defragmenter

Disk Defragmenter is the Win 95 disk tool you'll most hate to use but will appreciate the most when you do. You'll look on it as an unpleasant experience because it's another one of those "clean your room" things that's all chore and not much fun. It takes too long. No matter how long it takes, it takes too long (the duration varies widely depending on the capacity and speed of your hard drive and on how long it's been since you last defragged). And it seems no worse in this regard than other disk defrag utilities. The payoff, however, comes in the form of a noticeable performance improvement of Windows and your applications. Hard to argue with that, huh?

In a nutshell, hard drives and the DOS/Win 95 file system have the capability to store files in noncontiguous bits and pieces. If you were storing, say, the state of California on your hard drive, Sacramento might be in one place on your disk and San Francisco might be in an entirely different spot, while L.A. might be split up into bits and pieces, spread out, and speckling your whole drive like the measles (heh, heh). If drives couldn't store information that way, you'd run out of disk space fast.

L.A. might be split up into bits and pieces, spread out, and speckling your whole drive like the measles.

The problem with noncontiguous file storage is that fragmented files load more slowly into RAM, since the drive has to poke around here and there to find them. Disk Defrag moves all the files around on your disk so that they're contiguous again. It can also place the files you access more frequently at the top of the disk, where your PC can get to them a bit faster. Bottom line: Use this thing, probably on the order of once a month. It's an especially good idea to use it before you install any large application.

Of all the disk utilities that Windows 95 provides, ScanDisk is the most useful. DOS users will recognize it for what it is, a Win 95 upgrade of the DOS- and Windows-based ScanDisk available since DOS 6. And if you've been around PCs for a while, this thing is a much improved CHKDSK utility. ScanDisk looks for problems with files and directories on your hard disk. It ferrets out a range of minor and major storage disasters and fixes 'em. As with earlier versions, there's both a DOS and a Windows version of ScanDisk in Windows 95. Unlike older versions, there's no proficiency penalty about the Win ScanDisk. In fact, the Windows version is your better choice, since it fixes problems related to long filenames—something the DOS version can't do.

ScanDisk

Microsoft suggests the option of placing a Shortcut for ScanDisk in Start's Programs/Startup folder so it'll run every time you start Win 95. That's probably a good idea since ScanDisk is fast. But if you don't do this (and, you guessed it, I don't), remember to run ScanDisk about once a week or any time Windows or an application crashes. Damaged files and directory structures have a tendency over time to multiply, even to spread out or become cross-linked with other areas of your disk. It's a good idea to nip them in the bud.

Windows ScanDisk is better than the DOS version since it fixes long filename problems.

Microsoft, Bedazzle Me

Net Watcher

Depending on the installation choices you made, you may find some other tools in your System Tools folder that monitor various system functions. They include Resource Meter, System Monitor, and Net Watcher. Net Watcher can come in handy on small office peer networks, but it's not a net administrator's tool (see Figure 4.33). Basically this stuff, however, takes up room on your hard drive, assuming you installed it, unless you have a specific reason for using it. There are times when System Monitor and Resource Meter may come in handy. Check out Chapter 9, "Living With It," for some insights on them.

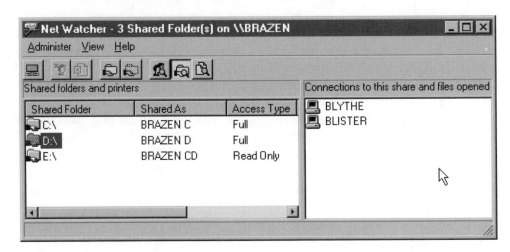

Figure 4.33 The Net Watcher utility

Another System Folder tool, the System Policy Editor, can be very useful, though. Although designed to be used by system administrators, it offers some controls that anyone might make use of, including the ability to create custom desktops by user name when more than one person is using a Win 95 PC. It might offer some solutions, for example, if you've got young kids at home using your PC. You could set up a custom desktop for them that would severely limit their access to tools that might encourage them to delete crucial stuff on your disk. System Policy Editor isn't installed automatically by Windows 95. For more on how to install and use it, check out Chapter 5, "Customize It."

DriveSpace Disk Compression

DriveSpace

One of the more powerful utilities you may find in the System Tools folder is DriveSpace. This Windows-based utility lets you set up on-the-fly compression on your drive quickly and easily. It can compress an entire drive, create a new logical compressed drive from the free space available on your system, or both of those things. The compression ratio is adjustable, and you can uncompress drives or volumes if you change your mind later. This is a very flexible, useful utility that can really improve your working conditions by giving you a chunk of additional space on a hard drive for installing new applications. In Figure 4.34, for example, I'm about to reap 235MB of extra disk space. Cool beans.

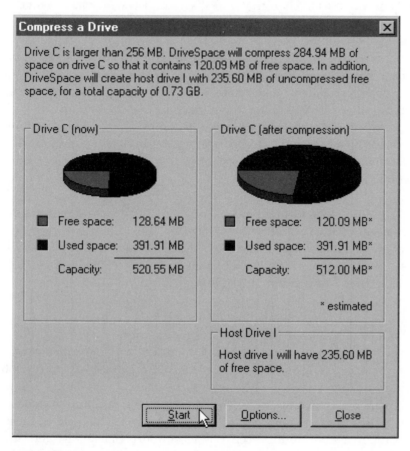

Figure 4.34   DriveSpace/File/Compress dialog

That said, though, let me flick on my curmudgeon shades and give you my negatory two cents on drive compression. First, there's nothing inherently wrong with the technology of disk compression. It's not a black art, doomed to eventual catastrophe, and there's nothing really dicey about it. It works just fine 99.8 percent of the time. What else can you say *that* about?

Know, however, that there's a small performance hit for any kind of on-the-fly disk compression. Microsoft and other disk compression utility makers tend to soft-pedal that hit, but trust me, it's there. And if you pay attention, you'll notice it. I'm just the sort of propeller head who tries to do absolutely nothing—at any time—that might take something away from the performance of my PC. I mean, who needs that? I didn't buy my Pentium 166 with a local-bus PCI drive controller only to effectively turn it into a Pentium 133 with a fast 16-bit drive controller. That's overstating the case, but you get the idea.

What's wrong with disk compression?

Still, that's not my biggest problem with drive compression. Don't you have enough hassles in your life? Aren't there enough things that can go wrong with your PC? When you take full advantage of drive compression, you've got more data on a compressed drive than can fit onto a normal drive. So, if something ever goes wrong, where are you going to put that data?

Backing out of compression gracefully can be a real headache, unless you have access to an additional hard drive or tape-backup device (and in which case, why did you need full-bore compression?). If you don't have other storage options, you're faced with having to delete stuff or buy more storage if you get into trouble.

The whole idea kind of reminds me of taking out a second mortgage on your house. It's a good idea only if you're using the cash to improve your house in a way that increases its value above the cost of the loan amount plus any upfront charges and all the interest for the life of the loan. You really don't get that sort of payoff with drive compression. It's at best a transitional solution that bridges the gap between the time when you need more drive capacity and the time when you can buy it as good, old-fashioned honest-to-goodness hardware. Yeah.

What's more, any time you make a major operating system upgrade, you've got this new compression format decision to make—a whole added complication to deal with. Folks using Stacker, an excellent DOS compression utility from STAC Electronics, are forever asking me how to back out of compression, say to upgrade to a new version, switch operating systems, switch to a different maker's compression utility, upgrade their hard drive, or whatever. The truth is, the answers aren't as tough as they sound. And Win 95 supports Stacker 4.1 and others (although, not surprisingly, there are some details to sift through). Here's the point: There are questions and concerns that hound many people using drive compression. Unless you're very confident and knowledgeable about the technology—or want to become so—who needs this extra layer of potential aggravation?

As I've stated elsewhere, I'm a horse-power guy. Hard drives are really cheap these days. Invest in a little hardware. You'll be glad you did. And if you're adding an IDE drive, while you're at it, buy an inexpensive Enhanced-IDE drive controller. You'll be glad you did that, too.

Now, there's another way to harness compression that I think is a much smarter approach. I don't know about you, but I've got a whole lot of data files and program installations that I rarely access but just can't seem to part with. It makes a ton of sense to create a compressed archive space to store this kind of stuff. As long as its just a logical drive on your system, a division of your drive hardware, you're a lot less likely to over-mortgage. And you'll incur the performance hit only when accessing the files that are compressed.

Last word on disk compression. The version of DriveSpace that comes with Win 95 is DriveSpace 2. It's good, but there's a newer version, DriveSpace 3, that's faster (according to Microsoft), has better compression algorithms, includes a compress in background feature, is easier to set up, and is more flexible. To get it, you have to purchase Microsoft Plus! for Windows 95, an approximately $40 affair that's well worth parting with your cash. I talk more about Plus in other chapters. Personally, I wouldn't attempt to compress my drive using Microsoft compression routines without getting the compression tools and the excellent interface for managing them that Plus provides.

DriveSpace

Start's Find Files or Folders

Last on the hit parade is Start's Find/Files or Folders dialog. Maybe I should have covered this under Chapter 3, "The Desktop Interface," but, hey, this chapter has the words files and folders in its name, right?

Microsoft app users, especially Winword mavens, will experience a little *deja vu* looking at the file find utility in Win 95. Microsoft has yet to really get this right, and the whole File Find deal in Word 7.0 is like the last two versions of Word—greatly changed again. It's also more complex and configurable than the Start/Find/Files or Folder feature dialog in Win 95.

There's a mostly silent minority of people using PCs who'd very much like to work with their files—perform all file management, in fact—from named, indexed filename and text searches of their hard drives. Actually, the whole idea has a lot of merit. It focuses on your data rather than on filename extensions and the hierarchy and names of your folders. Problem is, no company, Microsoft included, has figured out how to make this kind of thing foolproof. The potential for overlooking relevant files or including lots of extraneous files in a filename-based and/or text-containing search is actually quite high. In fact, one, the other, or both is pretty much a certainty. The usefulness of any file search is largely a function of the user's knowledge of the data pool and the options of the search tool. Find Files or Folders has one strike against it in that its Help information is quite weak, so even if you know what you don't know, figuring it out isn't as easy as it should be.

**It's not scintil-
lating, but it
has its uses.**

In Find Files or Folders, one of the more frustrating things is that you can name and save searches only after a fashion. The names of searches are long filenames applied by Win 95 based on the search criteria you choose. They become objects stored on the desktop, and you can rename them as you like or recall them by double-clicking. It's a bit tiresome, really. You can turn off the save feature by clicking off the check mark beside the Save Results line under Find Files or Folders' Options menu. From then on, the utility saves search criteria instead of search results. It'd be nice if you could do both things.

The true usefulness of this tool is for finding specific files or folders whose names are already known, but whose location isn't. It's also useful to experienced users for things like chasing down .DLLs and poking around for files whose names you know only part of. I find myself using Find Files or Folders all the time. It's just faster than poking around. I like it a lot. I just wish it were better.

*   *   *

It's cap and gown time, folks. You've just made it through Win 95 High School. Now it's time to do your college and post-grad work. Chapter 5, "Customize It," is a major in the System Registry—and continue on from Chapters 3 and 4. Chapter 6 is for notebook people and anyone obsessed with economical use of screen real estate. Chapter 7 gets you up on the Internet. Chapter 8 does Networks. And even if none of the rest applies to you, don't skip Chapter 9, "Living With It." Win 95: Can't live with it; can't shoot it. . . .

 # 5 Customize It

> The real world is not easy to live in. It is rough; it is slippery. Without the most clear-eyed adjustments we fall and get crushed. A man must stay sober: not always, but most of the time.
>
> Clarence Day
> "In His Baby Blue Ship," *The Crow's Nest*, 1921

After you're done with all the basic tweaks and adjustments—twiddling all the obvious knobs and punching all the apparent buttons—you're ready to bump your level of customization up a notch or two.

The point of any higher-level customization is probably very different for you than it is for me, or your colleague down the hall, or your spouse in the family room. Maybe you want to ditch all the icons on your desktop (and the ones in Figure 5.1 aren't all that easy to lose). Maybe you want different ones there than the ones Microsoft gave you. Instead of opening a bezillion folder windows all over your screen, maybe you'd like to work at adopting the single-window approach introduced in Chapter 4, "Files, Folders, Exploring." And maybe you'd like to work a little wizardry on System Registry to make things happen just a bit, or a lot, differently.

Figure 5.1 You'll find out just how to dump these guys in this chapter

The biggest advantage of Windows 95 isn't the supposed preemptive multi-tasking and multithreading, the 32 bitties under the hood, Plug and Play, or its memory management skills. The big deal is the interface and its customizability.

As operating systems go, Win 95 offers a very pretty face. But straight out of the box, it ain't just right for everyone. The trick is learning how to bend this thing to your will.

Registry's Many Faces

There are literally dozens of avenues for customizing Win 95's demeanor and operation. But 90 percent of them boil down to one thing: editing the System Registry in one way or another. The Registry is that database of all things configurational at the core of the OS. And there are lots of ways to modify it.

For example, when you make configurational changes in any of the control panels, more often than not you're also transparently adjusting settings in the Registry. When you make changes on any Folder's View/Options/File Types tab, you're invisibly editing the Registry with every change. Policy Editor (an optionally installed utility I explain later in this chapter) also makes numerous direct changes to System Registry. Virtually any properties sheet in Windows 95 writes to the Registry. And, of course, you can use the System Registry Editor (the REGEDIT.EXE file in your Windows folder) to access and edit much of the data in the Registry.

Where's the Registry Editor? I've explained this here and there, but it bears repeating. The Registry Editor is the formal name for the REGEDIT.EXE **file you'll find in your Windows folder. Windows doesn't automatically create a Shortcut for this file. To create a Shortcut, just right-click the file, drag, release, and choose Create Shortcut on the context menu, as shown in Figure 5.2. Then rename the label "Registry Editor" and put it somewhere on your Start launch lists. Elsewhere in this book, I've depicted the System Registry Editor object with an "ab" string-value icon because I like it better than the aqua-colored cubes that are the default icon for the program. So don't be fooled. They do the same thing, whatever the icon image.**

This chapter is about having it as you like it. It's about making the desktop interface do what *you* want it to, since there are several ways of thinking about this.

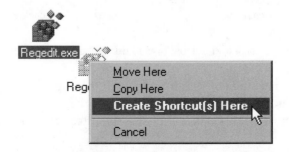

Figure 5.2   Making a Shortcut to REGEDIT.EXE

And it's about all the various tools—simple and complex—that get you there. To start out, I want to get you thinking about what you'd like to change, how you'd like to work, and what's important to you aesthetically, since most of us computer geeks are pretty visual folk. One thing's for sure: There's no way Windows 95 could be just right the way it is. Gack! It's just not in my nature to admit that.

A LITTLE DESKTOP INSPIRATION

> What Romantic terminology called genius or talent or inspiration is nothing other than finding the right road empirically, following one's nose, taking shortcuts.
>
> Italo Calvino
> *Cybernetics and Ghosts* (lecture), 1969

Now this is a strictly scientific observation. (*Don't believe him, he's lying—ed.*) In watching and talking to hundreds of computer users, I've noticed three basic strategies to customizing a desktop user interface: the Minimalist Approach, the Scattershot Approach, and the Just-So Approach. Check it out. Your taste in interfaces probably falls under one of these three headings.

The Minimalist Approach

You seek to narrow access to all operations to the fewest possible number of visible controls. It's a sort of a function-following-form strategy, or, to put it another way, it's the visually ascetic ideal. You're probably a very experienced computer user. Or it could be that you just hate messy things. I don't know. You love right-click context menus and are mindful of pruning and weeding unneeded files from your drive directories like a full-time gardener on a landed estate. Above all, you tend to be a bit religious about this; you uphold the vision of the Spartan, icon-bereft workspace as perhaps even more important than getting your work done. Some of my best friends fall into this category. Microsoft appeared to be headed in this direction during the early design phase for Windows 95, but the approach presented some very real usability dilemmas for newbies. As time went on during the product development cycle, the desktop icon thing became the Microsoft way.

It's the visually ascetic ideal.

Some of Win 95's desktop icons seem, to quote novelist John Irving out of context, "nailed down for life." I mean, just try moving or deleting My Computer, Network Neighborhood, Recycle Bin, or Inbox from the desktop. You can't! (But stick around.) Hey Microsoft, some of us don't want all this crap littering our desktops. Wouldn't it be nice if they gave us a desktop gallery configuration tool so that we could turn the appearance of these tools on or off? This is what the Department of Justice should be going after. The whole thing amounts to Redmond hegemony—something we could do with a little less of.

The Scattershot Approach

Like the minimalist folks, you're probably an experienced computer user, or becoming one. You believe that the shortest distance between two points doesn't always funnel through one portal, like Start or My Computer. You think to yourself, "Who knows where I'll be or what I'll be doing when I want to open a folder window, scat up on the Web, or open a useful program?" You're not just thinking about a single access point that you'll always be able to remember. You're wishing for 4108 points that criss-cross like spokes on a bicycle wheel. Anywhere you might be working or playing in the operating system or your apps, you want an obvious route to any one of the other 4107 points. You're also a pack rat. You buy your groceries in jumbo economy size and probably have three or four televisions. You also probably like the look of the desktop shown in Figure 5.3.

Are you with me? We're talking multiple ways to do everything and damn the aesthetics. Hmmm, I wonder what happened with your potty training . . . .

Figure 5.3   A little Scattershot action with help from Microsoft Plus!

The Just-So Approach

You're exceedingly sure of yourself. There's a part of you that finds computers a trifle annoying (and let's face it, they are). You may have tried things a dozen different ways, or you may have found the correct way to do things the first time out.

In any case, you've already decided on *The One True Way*. And that's how you do it—every time. Even if it means taking an extra step or two sometimes. Because, you know what? You don't want to think about *how* to work with your computer. You want to think about *what* you're doing with it. You also read legal documents thoroughly before signing them. You ask for friendly advice but find it rarely applies to you. And gave serious thought to whether you really wanted a PC in your home before giving in. (In short, you're saner than the rest of us propeller heads.)

You could very likely be a part of the rising silent majority of computer users. The ones to whom Microsoft and others (I hope) will be listening very carefully before building the major operating systems of the future.

What's It Mean?

My advice? Um, personally, I come down somewhere between Minimalist and Scattershot, which is a very difficult thing to do given that they're polar opposites. But a balance between these two is a good thing, and hey, if you can find some one-true-ways here and there and turn them into a Minimalist kind of thing, so much the better. Because above all else, I personally value organized, pinpoint thought on this kind of stuff.

My advice? Um, well, I like 'em all. . . .

I guess the ascetic in me (or some of my friends) must be trying to poke through the mess because I've spent a good deal of time attempting to perfect the Minimalist Approach under Windows 95, that is, trying to get to the bottom of how to clean up Microsoft's default messy desktop. There's actually more than one way to accomplish it. It can be done; witness Figure 5.4. Hold that thought, though, because I'll get serious about how to do this later.

Figure 5.4   No icons on your desktop, and nothing up your sleeve

Basic Desktop Controls

Brazen (C)
Drive icon tool

So, were you paying attention back in Chapter 3, "The Desktop Interface"? Maybe you liked the idea of placing Shortcut objects like disk drive icons, printer icons, and the like on your desktop? That way you can drag and drop stuff on to 'em, and they're close at hand. Or maybe you hated it but liked the idea of putting them in a cascading folder menu on Start?

While working with desktop icons isn't for everyone, there really isn't anything much easier to grasp the first time out. I mean, My Computer is visually economical because it jams all your drives and controls into one icon, but it's nowhere near as easy to understand as a picture of a disk drive labeled "Hard Drive." And since you can literally drag and drop stuff onto any desktop object, wouldn't it be nice to have an optional desktop printer tool that you could just drop documents on in order to print them?

To make desktop objects, just drag and drop from My Computer to the desktop.

If you're a subscriber to the Scattershot Approach or a refugee from the Macintosh, it's easy enough to do this yourself. Just open My Computer and drag and drop anything you see in there onto your desktop. The same goes for sticking Shortcuts on Start. For that, just drag and drop on the Start button.

Some review from Chapter 4: Get to know the controls that help you align and position desktop icons. If you right-click anywhere on the desktop, you'll see a context menu that offers two controls at the very top: Arrange Icons and Line up Icons. Under the Arrange Icons submenu, the biggest change comes with the setting on the bottom, Auto Arrange. With this control checked on, Windows 95 will automatically arrange all your desktop icons starting from the upper left corner, working downward in columns that march across the screen. The other controls on the Arrange Icons popup—by Name, by Type, by Size, by Date—control the order in which Win 95 sorts your desktop icons as it automatically arranges them.

The other setting on the desktop context menu, Line up Icons, comes into play when you have Auto Arrange checked off. In this mode, desktop icons can be placed anywhere on the screen, and they'll stay exactly where you put them. If you don't place them in even columns, tough turkey. Line up Icons is like your Mom straightening up your room when you were a kid. It's a quick spruce-up that creates aligned columns, while preserving the general placement you originally chose.

Finally, there's one last control you should try with respect to arranging the placement of desktop objects to your liking. The icon spacing controls will be of serious use to you only if you leave the Auto Arrange feature on. If you do, it comes in very handy. It also comes into play if you use the Line up Icons feature a lot.

Adjust desktop spacing to reduce clutter.

On Display Properties Appearance tab, click the down arrow beside the Item box and scroll down to the two Icon Spacing settings, one for horizontal and one for vertical spacing (see Figure 5.5). There's an invisible grid behind the Win 95 desktop with columns and rows like a spreadsheet. The starting point for this grid

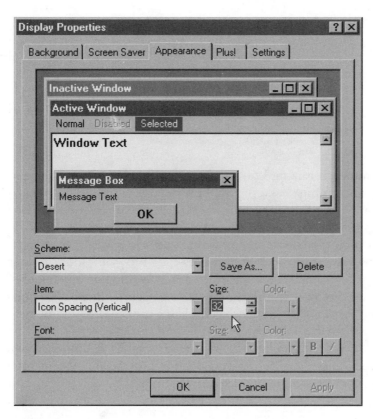

Figure 5.5 Setting Display Properties/Appearances Icon Spacing (Vertical)

is the upper left corner. When you adjust column widths (horizontal) or row heights (vertical) with the numbers in the Size box, you're actually either spreading the icons away from each other or forcing them closer together. Together, these two settings control the size of the desktop's invisible grid. The whole point is that by making judicious decisions about the size of columns and rows, you can squeeze more icons into the same space. And that, dear reader, may help you conserve desktop space, thereby relieving the feeling of desktop clutter.

If you squeeze 'em too tightly together, the text labels may start wrapping to several lines and/or the labels may overlap icons above and below. So, don't get carried away. Another thing to keep in mind about adjusting desktop icon spacing is that your changes don't apply to the desktop only. They also affect the spacing of icons in open folder windows. That's unfortunate because it can be difficult to strike a balance between the two. Would that Win 95 gave you separate controls for icon spacing on the desktop as well as folder windows. Also, it'd be very nice if Microsoft allowed us to set the grid starting point in any of the four corners of the screen so that we could control the direction and flow of icons under Auto Arrange.

But don't get carried away.

HOW TO CONTROL FOLDER WINDOWS

No one asks you to throw Mozart out of the window. Keep Mozart. Cherish him. Keep Moses too, and Buddha and Lao tse and Christ. Keep them in your heart. But make room for the others, the coming ones, the ones who are already scratching on the window-panes.

Henry Miller
The Air-Conditioned Nightmare, 1945

Digging into customizing Win 95 means approaching it from several sides. Besides focusing on the desktop, you'll find folder window controls to munch on. Customizations for the file system and objects meet in the Registry later on, so . . . first things first.

Any Folder

Microsoft added some thoughtful features to ease the transition along to a mode of working with folders that uses the "Browse folders by using a single window that changes as you open each folder" setting on any folder's View/Options/Folder dialog. (*Gasp! What's he talking about? I dunno, but I think it was in Chapter 4, "Files, Folders, Exploring."*) Using the single window setting, you'll rarely have more than one folder window open on your screen at a time. The Boyz in the Northwest have something of a vested interest in this single-window deal because each and every folder you open is a drain on system resources, and sooner or later MS is going to catch flak about that.

Navigation

Getting around with a single folder window is a lot easier than you might expect. You tunnel deeper into the directory structure by double-clicking any of the closed folders in the current window. You have several choices for backing up or teleporting elsewhere.

The Up One Level button

The easiest way to back up is probably to click the Up One Level button on the folder toolbar. Since in most situations you're going to need only one window open at a time, you can certainly afford to have it displaying a toolbar, no? Turn the toolbar on by clicking the View/Options/Toolbar menu item. The Up One Level button icon shows a folder with a left and upwards pointing arrow. A single click on this deal steps you back one pace toward the root directory of your hard drive. Handy gizmo. I use it all the time. But if the mouse seems about as useful a tool to you as using a hammer to turn a screw, forget the Up One Level button. Just hit the Backspace key. It does exactly the same thing with one key press.

If your destination is on another drive, use the folder toolbar's drop-down drive selection menu, shown in Figure 5.6. Even mapped network drives show up in this thing, which is essentially My Computer without the clutter.

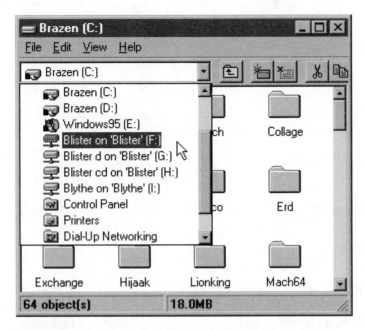

Figure 5.6 The drop-down drive selection menu on the folder toolbar

Force a Second Window

Sometimes you want a second folder window, perhaps to visually compare the contents of two directories. And for that, there's a keyboard shortcut. Win 95 defaults to multiple folder windows. In that mode, you can Ctrl-double-click any drive or folder icon to force Win 95 to reuse the existing open folder (the browse-a-single-window thing) instead of opening an additional window. Well, guess what? When you've turned on the single window setting, Ctrl-double-click gives you the reverse: a second folder window. And Shift-double-click gives you an additional Explorer window. There's also another way to open two windows at once: Use My Computer or a desktop drive or folder icon. As long as you open something outside of the current folder window, it opens a second folder instance.

Cut or Copy and Then Paste Whole Files

This is one of my favorite Win 95 tricks. You can cut objects in one location (entire files, gang-selected files, even entire folders with all their contents) and then open a different folder and paste them to the new location. See Figure 5.7 for a look-see. Copy operations work the same way, except you start with Copy instead of Cut. This feature is both powerful and fast.

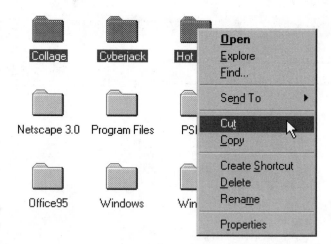

Figure 5.7   Don't drag and drop; Select, right-click, Cut or Copy, and then Paste

Try it. Right-click on any file or folder object to open its context menu. Choose Copy (for copy operations) or Cut (for move operations) on the context menu. Navigate to the new folder window and right-click anywhere on its background. Choose Paste from the context menu. Shazam! The stuff you cut or copied will reappear in the new folder.

For all of you who'd prefer to do it with a keyboard, here's the drill. Ctrl-X cuts; Ctrl-C copies; Ctrl-V pastes. Macintosh users should be right at home with this arrangement, since they've been using the default keyboard shortcuts on the Mac for years. And they're a lot better than that whole Shift-Delete, Ctrl-Insert, Shift-Insert thing from past versions of Windows and many of its applications.

It may not be readily apparent why this Cut or Copy and Paste feature has anything to do with browsing with a single folder window. Well, believe me, it's directly related. You can't drag and drop from one folder window to another when you're using a single folder window. Without this deal, we'd all give up on the single window approach the first time we needed to move or copy a file.

Send To

One of Win 95's neatest little time-savers is the Send To line available on the context menu of just about any object in Windows 95. Would you like to be able to quickly copy a file to a floppy disk? Right-click the file object, choose Send To from the popup menu, and then click the floppy drive line on the Send To submenu, as shown in Figure 5.8. You don't even have to copy the file first. Send To knows what to do.

You'll find a SendTo folder in your Windows folder. To customize it, create Shortcuts for your favorite file destinations and drop 'em in there. For example, create a Shortcut in SendTo for your main document directory or any other folder

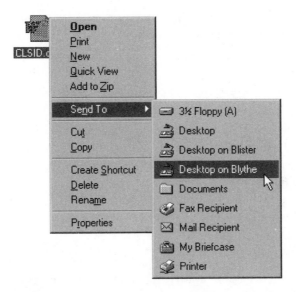

Figure 5.8 The Send To command in operation

to which you frequently move files. Try plopping Shortcuts there for Recycle Bin, drives, and so on. And don't forget to make a Shortcut of your default printer and place it in the SendTo folder. That way you can print a file without opening it just by sending it to the printer. As long as the document's file extension has been properly configured and associated (on the View/Options/File Types dialog accessible from any folder window), Send To will automatically open your application, load the document you right-clicked and sent to the printer, and then print the file. This also works with emails and faxes if you have those Win 95 services properly installed.

When you use this method to route an object to a destination that's on the same drive, Send To *moves* it there. When you route an object to a different drive, Send To *copies* it there. It's the same default behavior as for file object drag-and-drop operations.

Want to try something cool? Open your SendTo folder and use the New/Shortcut wizard to make a Shortcut whose Target, or command, line reads: `C:\WIN-DOWS\DESKTOP`. **Name it "Desktop." Click the Change Icon button on the new Shortcut's Properties/Shortcut tab and pick the Desktop icon—it's the 35th icon in the scroll box, the one with a lamp shining down on a desk. This baby will send objects directly to your desktop.**

If you're on a network, you can get even fancier by creating Desktop Send To objects for another computer on the network. Just create a Shortcut of the Desktop Send To object you made for your own PC. On its Properties/Shortcut tab, change the target line so that the drive letter specified is the letter for

another computer you have mapped in My Computer. Then type `c:\` **in the "Start in" field. Finally, rename the Shortcut** `Desktop on [name of target computer]`.

Folder Undo

**The folder
Undo button**

If you make a mistake on something like a copy, move, or delete, there's a fast way to retrieve the situation. Just click on the background of any open folder window to bring up its context menu and select the Undo menu item. Or, if you've got the toolbar switched on, just click the left and downward-pointing arrow button there. It's the Undo button. Either way, there are multiple levels of Undo for most operations, so when your brain fades and you make a lot of mistakes in a row, you're off the hook.

Single-Window Wind Up

When all is said and done, the ability to cut a file, click the Up One Level button, navigate somewhere else, and then paste the file in the new location—that's motoring. It isn't really flashy. But it gets the job done. Give the browse-a-single-window setting a shot, using some of my pointers. If you're anything like me, the light-bulb is gonna switch on over your head.

Dragging and dropping was supposed to be this wicked cool thing a couple of years back. If you have space onscreen to have two open folders on your desktop, then dragging and dropping a file or a group of files from one place to another can be the fastest way to move or copy 'em. What's more, it's a type of manipulation that closely mimics the way people think, since it's directly analogous to how we'd use our hands to move, say, apples from one basket to another.

But there's a catch: On most desktops, having space to have two folders open means you'll probably have to spend some time arranging those folders so that they don't overlap each other and so you can see all the goop inside 'em (unless you're running a 21-inch display or something). You also have to locate the folders before you decide you want to copy or move something. And that's putting the apple cart before the horse. It isn't really worth the extra effort unless you're into some serious comparison file management. And who wants to do that anyway?

Microsoft or some third party like Symantec should create a way to open a double folder window that compares two directories, automatically maximizing them on your screen side by side or top and bottom. It should be customizable for various window options, like Explorer or folder windows, icon views, and sort settings. When people get serious about file management, they often need visual comparison with detailed information about their files. This kind of work isn't much fun, so when you've got to do it—and may you never have to—there should be a better way.

There's a hidden difference of operation in the single-window approach that you might count as either a blessing or a curse, depending on your point of view. Since you're using one folder window most of the time, every folder you open will display icons according to the icon view and settings, folder size, toolbar preference, and so on, in vogue for the first folder or drive you opened. With the default "Browse folders using a *separate* window for each folder" setting, it's possible to configure some settings specific to each folder.

A last note about this. If you're grooving on this whole folder customizing thing and want a bit more, check out Chapter 6, "The Mobile Win 95." There's stuff there about how to think about the desktop, folders, Taskbar, and other settings and interface structures when you're working on a small screen. The whole browse-a-single-window thing is an integral part of that. And it's an aesthetic that kind of grows on you after a while.

Are you using Office for Windows 95? It has this little trick of creating a special user folder on your drive called My Documents. Then it tries to save stuff you create with Office apps into this directory. It's annoying. Especially for someone who, like me, has for years used a similar C:\DOCUMENT **directory for the same purpose. I don't want anything with the word "MY" preceding it on my PC. But when you try to delete this folder, you get a message saying that it's a system folder and can't be deleted. Bog!**

Fire up System Registry to fix this little problem. Run the REGEDIT.EXE **file from your Windows folder. Click on the top-most key, My Computer. Choose Edit/Find and type** my documents **in the "Find what" field and press Enter. After a minute or so, RegEdit will locate the first instance of "my document." You'll see an ab icon in the right pane. Double-click it to edit the folder pathname of your default documents directory. Or, if you don't have one and don't want one, just right click the "Personal" entry and delete it. Repeat the process by hitting the F3 key. You'll come across two other entries. When you're done, close the Registry Editor. And then go kill off that pesky folder.**

SYSTEM REGISTRY BOOT CAMP

> Nothing is *less* instructive than a machine.
>
> Simone Weil
> *Factory Journal*, 1934–35

Remember all those files with .INI extensions littering the C:\WINDOWS and application directories under the old Windows? These text files stored settings that Windows and your apps "read" to find out how things were supposed to look and act. While you'll still find some .INI files in your Windows directory, they're vestigial for the most part. All that info, and a lot more, is stored in Win 95's System Registry database.

System Registry
Editor

The Registry catalogs Plug and Play information, drivers, property sheet settings, programs, program modules, file types and extensions, multiple user profiles, and Windows performance statistics. And that's just the tip of the iceberg. Registry is complex, difficult to understand, and not something to toy with unless you already know what you're doing, you've been told what to do by someone who knows what they're doing, or you've taken some precautions I'll tell you about in a moment. Of course, where I come from, that sounds more like a challenge than a serious warning. So go ahead and switch this guy on and get a look at it. At the top level, it looks like Figure 5.9.

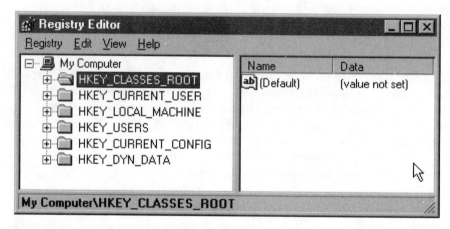

Figure 5.9   The top level of the System Registry

As noted, there are a lot of ways to make changes to System Registry. But with the sole exception of the Registry Editor, most of those peepholes into the Registry, like File Types and the Policy Editor, mask huge portions of it in the name of protecting you from yourself. That's probably a good thing, too. Until you know what this is about and how it works, it's best to proceed with caution.

Read This, OK?

Config Backup

Your number one precaution is a little utility you'll find on the Windows 95 CD in the \Other\Misc\Cfgback directory. It consists of two files, CFGBACK.EXE and CFGBACK.HLP. Copy the .EXE file to your Windows folder and put the .HLP file in the Help folder inside your Windows folder. Then make a Shortcut for CFGBACK.EXE and name it "Config Backup." Doing this is your single best defense against Registry-hacking *faux pas*. Plus, doing it regularly can get you out of other jams. (Better for getting you out of jams, perhaps, is the Emergency Recovery Utility found in the adjacent ERU folder. I talk about that in Chapter 9, "Living with It.")

What Config Backup does is create named, saved backups of the Registry. You can make up to 10 of these backups (before they start munching on each other), and I strongly advise you to make a backup before installing any application, before making any change to System Registry, and after any session when you make a lot of fine-tuning adjustments to properties sheets and the like. The most important thing, though, is to run Config Backup before you run the RegEdit program. That way, if stuff blows up, you can restore all your previous settings from your backup, as shown in Figure 5.10.

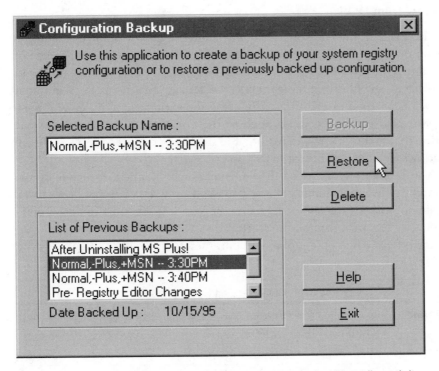

Figure 5.10   Config Backup takes a few minutes to run, but it's well worth it

Ever try choosing New on the File menu of any folder window or from the context menu of any file or folder? You get a list of objects that you can create with a click, such as a folder, Shortcut, even several app document types. Customize this thing with the Registry Editor. Start by creating a null file, or empty document, for each program for which you'd like to create new file objects. Place them in the `C:\WINDOWS\SHELLNEW` folder. Then activate RegEdit and look under the `HKEY_CLASSES_ROOT` key. This modification is made to the file extensions part of the `HKEY_CLASSES_ROOT` key (the ones that start with a period). Find the correct extension for your new document, right-click it, add a new key, and name it `ShellNew`. On the right pane, right-click the background

and add a new String entry. Label it `FileName`**. Double-click the FileName icon and type the following line in the Edit String box:**

`c:\windows\shellnew\[template filename.ext]`

In place of `[template filename.ext]`**, type the name of the file object you put in the** `C:\WINDOWS\SHELLNEW` **folder. Close RegEdit, and admire your handiwork.**

Registry from DOS

File this away in the back of your mind: There's a DOS version of the Registry Editor on the Win 95 startup disk you should have created during setup. Both the DOS and Windows Registry Editors can export, import, or recreate the Registry database to text files that have the `.REG` extension (or `.TXT` files for easy association with Notepad or WordPad). By using the export capabilities of Registry Editor, you can save a specific branch or the entire Registry in text format. After editing that text file, you can restore it to the Registry database by using either the Windows or DOS Reg Editor to import it.

You probably won't need the DOS version of RegEdit, which is there to help you out in the event things get really messed up with your Windows installation. But if you do, start the computer using the Windows 95 startup disk. Then run the `REGEDIT.EXE` program on the startup disk to import a backup `.REG` file. Check out the official Microsoft syntax and parameters for the DOS RegEdit program in Table 5.1.

Table 5.1   DOS RegEdit Syntax and Parameters

Syntax:	`regedit [/L:system] [/R:user] file1.reg, file1a.reg . . .`
	`regedit [/L:system] [/R:user]/e file3.reg [regkey]`
	`regedit [/L:system] [/R:user]/c file2.reg`

Parameter	Description
`/L:system`	Specifies the location of `SYSTEM.DAT`.
`/R:user`	Specifies the location of `USER.DAT`.
`file1.reg`	Specifies one or more `.REG` files to import into the Registry.
`/e file3.reg`	Specifies the filename to which the Registry should be exported.
`regkey`	Optionally specifies the starting Registry key from which to export a portion of the Registry. If no value is specified, regedit/e exports the entire Registry.
`/c file2.reg`	Specifies the `.REG` file to import to replace the entire contents of the Registry. Use this one only when you're sure the specified `.REG` file contains a complete image of the Registry.

The Keys to Registry

Since it stores controls for just about everything, I could devote an entire book to System Registry alone. Any casual peek at it will unearth line after line of hexadecimal ID numbers, like this tag for My Computer:

```
{20D04FE0-3AEA-1069-A2D8-08002B30309D}
```

Some of these ID numbers aren't labeled. Some Windows 95 special objects have more than one ID number. And their interrelationships with settings for other objects isn't consistently applied. Microsoft didn't create a simple environment, one where all things work in the same way. Interface structures—like the Desktop, My Computer, Network Neighborhood, Recycle Bin, and context menus—are not all created equally. Since they have special functions, they have unique settings. And in many cases, these settings are stored in .DLL files, so you can't hack into 'em.

Because System Registry is a complex topic, I'm not going to show you how to become a hexadecimal-eating programming nerd in 10 easy lessons. Instead I'm following a course of "applied hacking." Stuff you want to do to make things better, not stuff to do just for the sake of hacking.

Here's a neat trick. When you browse a directory containing `.BMP` (bitmap) image files, you'll see that they all have the same uninspired icon. With a very minor change to the Registry, you can transform the icon for each bitmapped image file into a miniature thumbnail of the picture contents. This lets you preview these image files just by looking at their icons. To make the change, **select the** `HKEY_CLASSES_ROOT` **key, or folder, in Registry Editor. Type** `Paint.Picture` **to jump down to that entry and click the adjacent plus sign to expand it. Next, click the** `DefaultIcon` **entry under** `Paint.Picture`. **Move the mouse pointer to RegEdit's right pane and double-click the ab** `Default` **icon. In the Edit String box that pops up, enter:** `%1`. **Close the box and exit the Registry Editor. Now whenever you open a folder containing** `.BMP` **files (such as your Windows folder), you'll see the actual images on the file icons. Unfortunately, this doesn't work with other picture formats—yet.**

When you open the Registry for the first time, you'll find six keys represented by mini folder icons. Surprise, this looks like an Explorer window, just like everything else in Windows 95. That doesn't quite mean you already know how to use it, however. Each of the keys is labeled with a text string that starts out with the HKEY designation. The "H" part stands for handle. Each HKEY is a named branch of configurational stuff that programmers can address at the top level.

If you were to hit every expand-this-branch plus sign you saw in the Registry Editor, not only would that take a long time, but scrolling through RegEdit afterward would take a long, long time. There's a lot of information here. But there's also

Registry has six main "keys," or branches.

a lot of repeated or only slightly altered info. The redundancy exists primarily to support multiple-user configurations, something I'll look into later in this chapter.

By the way, if you really want to expand an entire key or sub-branch in Registry Editor, select the branch and then press the Alt-* key combination. Use the asterisk on the number pad. Be prepared to hang out because even this takes a while in most HKEYs.

Here's a description of the six HKEYs. I've placed them in the order in which they appear in the Registry Editor. Note, though, that there are two main HKEY branches: HKEY_LOCAL_MACHINE and HKEY_USERS. The others are something like out-takes or modifiers of these. Don't worry about fully understanding this stuff. You don't need to. But getting the gist is a good idea.

HKEY_CLASSES_ROOT.   The first key displayed in Registry Editor points to a branch of HKEY_LOCAL_MACHINE that describes software settings. HKEY_CLASSES_ROOT focuses almost entirely on *file extensions,* which start with periods, and *file types,* which have longer names and are listed afterward. On upgrade installations over Windows 3.*x,* it displays file-extension data imported from WIN.INI. It also contains core aspects of the Windows 95 user interface, including the CLSID (Class ID) section, where all those wacky hexadecimal numbers are that refer to interface objects like My Computer and Recycle Bin.

HKEY_CURRENT_USER.   This key points to a branch of HKEY_USERS and stores settings for the user who is currently logged on to the computer. In some ways, the first three keys, including HKEY_CURRENT_USER, are the most important. This is because, in many cases, changes you make in them are automatically replicated to the related branches and values in the next three keys.

HKEY_LOCAL_MACHINE.   This key contains computer-specific information about the type of hardware installed, software settings, and other stuff. The data it contains applies to all who use the computer.

HKEY_USERS.   This key holds information about all the users who log on to the computer, including both generic and user-specific information. The generic settings are available to all users who use the PC. The information is made up of default settings for applications, desktop configurations, and so on. It also contains subkeys for each user who logs on to the PC.

HKEY_CURRENT_CONFIG.   This key points to a branch of the Config area of HKEY_LOCAL_MACHINE. That area contains information about the current configuration of hardware attached to the computer.

HKEY_DYN_DATA. This key points to a branch of HKEY_LOCAL_MACHINE that contains the dynamic status information for various devices as part of the Plug and Play information. The information for each device includes the related hardware key and the device's current status, including problems.

> **Some Registry Editor shortcuts: 1. To copy any specific field in Registry, right-click it and choose Rename from the context menu. Then right-click it again and choose Copy. 2. To move down a long list of entries (not all parts of Registry work this way), try typing the name of the entry you're trying to navigate to. 3. To jump across keys and branches to a specific item, use the Edit/Find command. 4. To hunt for instances of an interface object, type its name into the Find dialog, pressing F3 to jump to successive instances. 5. You'll unearth important references to a given object by searching for its** CLSID **name. Look in the** HKEY_CLASSES_ROOT\CLSID **branch. Click each hexadecimal entry to see the name of the object on the right pane (some are unnamed) or run Find in the branch. Win 95 program modules, options, special types, and third-party programs register their important program files in this section. (See the " 'Special Folder' Objects" section at the end of this chapter for more on CLSIDs and how to put them to work.)**

OF TYPES AND EXTENSIONS

> To put it rather bluntly, I am not the type who wants to go back to the land;
> I am the type who wants to go back to the hotel.
>
> Fran Lebowitz
> *Social Studies*, 1981

Modifying any folder's View/Options File Types dialog is like editing the HKEY_CLASSES_ROOT part of the Registry through a portal. But, because the File Types dialog masks many portions of HKEY_CLASSES_ROOT, there are times when you have to play both sides against the middle. And to do that, you need to see the full picture on adding and modifying file types.

There are actually two different types of associations between programs and their data files. Here's how to understand the difference. One is a file type, such as a Microsoft Word 7.0-format file. The other is a file extension, such as Word's .DOC extension. User-added extensions, such as .LET, .LTR, and .MEM, are those you want to associate to the Word file type. For now, follow these steps exactly. The wand tip that follows explains the ramifications and also some pretty serious advantages to fully understanding how to work this dialog.

To add a new file association, pull down the View menu on any folder window. Choose Options/File Types. Click the New Type button. Your first step—and it's an important one—should be to locate the main application file type for which you're adding a new extension in the "Registered file types" window. This is particularly true for Windows 95 apps. Sometimes it's tough to know which of several names related to a single application is the main one, but do your best. When you find it, click to select it. So, back to our Winword example, highlight the "Microsoft Word Document" type before doing anything else, like I'm doing in Figure 5.11. *Note:* Just to confuse you, this file type isn't apparent in System Registry. It corresponds to the `Word.Document.6` entry in the `HKEY_CLASSES_ROOT` key in Registry.

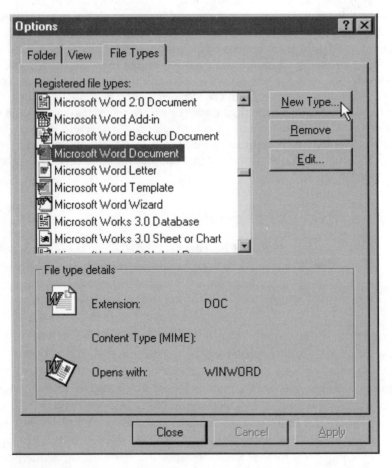

Figure 5.11   Click the main file type before adding a new type for it

See the Bug note that follows, OK? To make adding file extensions and file types for 32-bit applications, you need to follow the steps I outline in exactly the order I've outlined them.

With the application file type highlighted, click the New Type button, which brings up the Add New File Type dialog. The New Type label is a bit confusing, since you're really registering a new extension to an existing application file type. But, when you're done, it will show up as a file type. It's one of the oddities of the way Microsoft has set up this whole deal. Type the new file extension (say you're adding LTR for a new Word Letter file extension) in the "Associated extension" field, without the period. For Win 95 apps, extensions are not limited to three digits as they are in DOS and the old Windows. But I recommend you stick to the three-digit limit.

The next step is a bit of a head-scratcher at first: Click the New button on the bottom left. The new thing you're adding is an *action*, or program operation relating to a file object, such as File Open, File New, or File Print. Most actions appear as top-level items on the context menus of all files possessing a registered extension. Since, in our example, you're adding an extension to the Word 7.0 file type, you're not reinventing the wheel. You probably want your new extension to have the same default actions as Word's default .DOC extension. Those actions are: New, open, print, and PrintTo, with capitalizations exactly as they appear in this sentence.

It's a bit of a head-scratcher; click the New button.

There's definitely a screw loose in the Add New File Type dialog. There's something that's just not quite right. One problem centers around capturing the DDE information that underlies the actions of more complex programs, such as Word 7.0. This DDE code (see Figure 5.12 for an example) supports things like double-click launching a Word file into an already running instance of the program, or printing a file from the context menu without opening it. If you follow my instructions exactly in the order I give them when adding a new file extension to an existing program file type, most of the time this DDE information will be captured and stored with the new extension's System Registry information.

So don't forget, highlight the default file type for the program, click New Type, and enter the extension only for starters. For each action you're adding, click the New button, put a check in the Use DDE box, and then use the Browse feature to find the actual program file. After that, you can give the new file type a description, or just leave it blank. Sometimes this doesn't work, and the actions will be added but the DDE info is not. If you don't capture the info, you won't get the added capabilities with any file objects using the extension. Your only other alternative is to type it in manually, using the Edit button to check the code behind the actions of the program's main file type entry.

The default action for any file type or file extension is Open, which works with the associated files of almost any program that opens data files. So, type open in the Action field. *Note:* If you add custom actions, you'll need to insert an ampersand (&) before the letter in the action name that will be the command letter in its keyboard shortcut. Next, click the "Application used to perform action" field and click the Browse button. Locate the program's original .EXE file (not a Shortcut to it) in the browse box, and double-click it. Back at the Edit File Type dialog, repeat

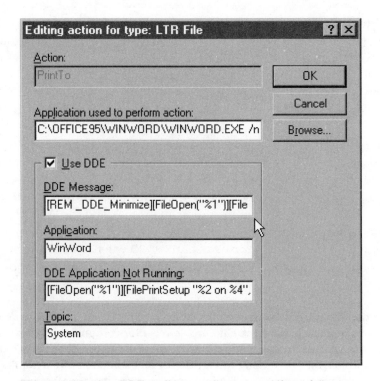

Figure 5.12   Any DDE stuff is *usually* captured if you follow directions to the letter

these steps for each additional action you found in the program's main file type. Type each action exactly as it appears originally. Back to our .LTR example for Word 7.0, the Add New File Type dialog should look something like Figure 5.13 at this point.

The Set Default button lets you preselect an action as the default action that will occur whenever you double-click any object icon that has the extension you're adding. Chances are you're going to want Open to be that default action, and probably it is already in boldface, showing that it is.

The bugs may bite ya at this point. You have three choices for the "Description of type" field. You can leave it blank, which may be the best, if not the most elegant, course. In that case, you'll find a new file type entry that, for the example, reads "LTR file." You can type something that builds on the main program file type. In this case, that might be something like "Microsoft Word Letter." Or, you can go with something that separates it from the Microsoft terminology, but that will still group all your custom extensions together, like "Winword Letter." For some reason, the bug mentioned in the previous Bug note seems to creep in at this point. I've had the best success capturing DDE info when I type nothing in the Description of type field. Leave all other fields blank, unless the main program file type uses them.

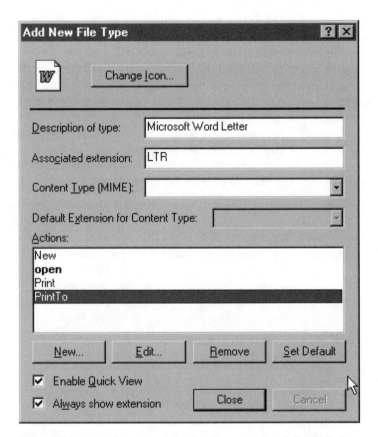

Figure 5.13 World's four default actions successfully added to a new LTR extension

Finally, for Winword files, you'll probably want to place a check mark in the Enable Quick View box since Quick View supports Winword files. The "Always show extension" check box controls whether the extension of files with this extension will be visible even with the "Hide MS-DOS file extensions for file types that are registered" setting is turned on. (Quick View and "Hide MS-DOS file extensions" are described in Chapter 4, "Files, Folders, Exploring.")

Want to bypass this rather laborious process for associating a file extension with an application? I mean, I thought editing `.INI` **files was a pain. The file types settings aren't much easier than FileMan's "Associate" command in the old Windows.**

Microsoft gave us a little keyboard shortcut that lets you perform quick and dirty file associations. Say you try double-clicking a text file to open it in Notepad. But the file has a unique extension (like `.ME`**) that means something**

to whoever created it, but not to Win 95 and Notepad. When you double-click the file, you should get the Open With dialog (take a look at Figure 5.14) because the extension isn't associated with anything. It shows a long list of all the registered programs installed on your PC with which you might want to open the file. And, at the bottom of the dialog, you'll see a little "Always use this program to open this file" check-off box. When you check that box and then double-click Notepad in the scroll box, Win 95 launches the file into Notepad while simultaneously creating an automatic file type association (defaulting to "Open"). If your new association is with an app that is a bit more complex than Notepad, you can later edit that extension association to flesh it out with multiple commands and add the DDE info, if any.

A related shortcut is to direct Windows to insert the Open With menu item on any data file's context menu by holding down the Shift key while you right-click the file object. That's especially handy if the file's extension is already associated with one program and you want to open it with another.

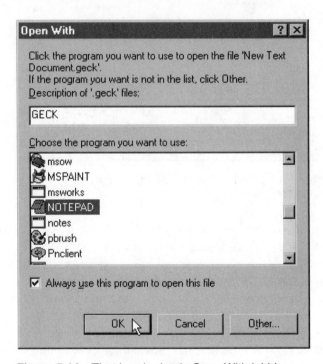

Figure 5.14   That handy-dandy Open With jobbie

Editing existing file types   Once you've mastered adding new file type extensions, editing an existing one is easy. Select the type you want to edit in the "Registered file types" box. Then instead of clicking New Type, click the Edit button. You can add actions and change the icon, but unfortunately, you can't change the extension name. Follow the same steps as you did for adding. But to get serious about cleaning up Windows 3.*x* extensions turned into file types by the Win 95 upgrade process, you'll have to resort to some System Registry Editor tricks, like the one in the wand tip that follows. It's one of the messier aspects of file types, and there's no really good solution.

Some day, you're going to be really glad you read this tip. Neither the File Types dialog nor the Registry Editor offers a search and replace function (although you can download shareware RegEdit replacements that do have this feature). So what do you do when you realize you've got 47 document file types that are all pointing to the wrong program directory on your drive (something that actually happened to me)? Here's what. You use the Registry Editor's export function to export the portion of the Registry that applies to file types and extensions, use a text editor like WordPad to perform search and replace on specific errant pathnames, and then import the data back into the Registry. It's easy.

Open Registry Editor. Click on HKEY_CLASSES_ROOT**. Choose Registry/Export. Give the file a name with a** .TXT **extension and click the Save button. Now open the file with your text editor and make the changes. Hey, this is just like editing an** .INI **file. Be careful to select search and replace strings that won't inadvertently replace correct information. And don't monkey with too much stuff in this file. When you're done, choose Registry/Import back in RegEdit. Click the down arrow beside the "File of type" field and select "All Files." Then just double-click the filename you exported to. Your modifications will be loaded back into the Registry in a flash.**

Rant about File Types and the Registry

The File Types dialog we've been chewing on is probably the main user interface to the System Registry. As a result, the dialog absorbs some of the complexity of the Registry database that's behind it. The File Types tab can be a confusing place to make decisions. I'll give you an example. Suppose you install an application that, unknown to you, wants to *own* the file extension .ZIP (originally coined by the PKWare PKZip shareware file-compression utilities and licensed for use by Nico Mak Computing in its WinZIP program). But you have WinZIP installed on your system already, and you'd like to keep the association between .ZIP and the WinZIP utility. Does this other installing application ask you whether it's OK to grab that extension name beforehand? Uh, probably not.

How Registry can bite you

This is one of the inherent problems with putting file associations in a database format that can't be text-edited by the average person who hasn't read this book. On the other hand, editing .INI files is no picnic either. For every possible switch or line entered in some .INI file for a given program under the old Windows, there should be a graphical control in the Win 95 version of the program. Microsoft has come darn close to keeping that promise in Windows 95 itself. But in applications, the premise might mean a lot of extra work and overhead for application developers. The advent of System Registry—and it *is* mostly a good thing—is going to create some tough situations for Microsoft, application developers, and, most of all, us users.

How Registry hides things from you

Back to the .ZIP file example. One problem with the File Types dialog is that it shows file types but not their extension entries—which you *can* see in System Registry. It also hides some file types, such as the Folders file type, because Microsoft wants to protect us from ourselves. Don't ask me why. And trying to reverse what an installing app did to an association it basically stole can be tricky. In trying to change an association by creating a new one for the same file extension, you may run into an error message that tells you that the extension is already associated with a file type that has a similar name. So, while you might be trying to add a New Type for .ZIP, Win 95 is telling you that an association to that particular extension is already made in a file type called ZIPFile. OK, so you can edit the ZIPFile type, right? Nope. ZIPFile isn't *on* the File Types dialog. Most of the time this doesn't happen, but every now and then, it might. And when it does, there are two things you can do. The first is go into the HKEY_CLASSES_ROOT area of the Registry and edit these things directly. That's what I do most of the time. But there's also a way to make invisible file types visible, and that's explained in the following wand tip.

To make a file type or file extension visible in the File Types dialog, open the Registry Editor and click the plus sign beside the HKEY_CLASSES_ROOT **key. Scroll through the list of file extensions and types until you find the one you can't see in the File Types dialog. (The very first entry, the *, which stands for "any file," is one of the invisibles.) The one you're looking for may be named something a little different than you might expect. When you find it, highlight it. Then move the pointer to RegEdit's right pane and right-click the window background. The popup menu item will just be "New." Click it and then opt for the Binary Value item. You'll see "New Value #1" highlighted and ready to rock and roll. Replace that placeholder name with:** EditFlags. **Then double-click the** EditFlags **icon and type this string of numbers in the Edit Binary Value box:**

```
02 00 00 00
```

Don't worry about the spaces; they pop in automatically. Close down RegEdit. You'll then be able to see the file entry in File Types.

SET A LITTLE POLICY

You do the policy, I'll do the politics.

Dan Quayle
International Herald Tribune, Paris, January 13, 1992

This part is about User Profiles and the System Policy Editor. There are two completely separate cool things you can do with this Win 95 utility. The first is to set up user profiles in the Passwords control panel. That comes in real handy when people are sharing a Windows 95 PC, say, for example, family members. That's because it lets each person using a PC customize the Start Menu, Desktop, screen saver, wallpaper, sounds, even program installations, uniquely to their taste. When Mom logs on by typing her name and password in a dialog on system startup, she gets Windows the way she wants it. When Dad logs on, he gets it his way. And to set this up, you don't even need Policy Editor.

Passwords

The second cool thing is something Policy Editor does that comes under the general heading of restrictions. In other words, you can use the utility to turn off a long list of Windows 95 functions. The average power user probably doesn't want to turn stuff off. But you'd be surprised. Turning things off can be an excellent way to customize your desktop. Folks who subscribe to the Minimalist Approach, for example, are going to be pleasantly surprised.

Peace of mind was never this easy.

If you're sharing your home PC with your kids or you have inexperienced PC users sharing a PC in an office setting, you can merge the two capabilities—customized user configurations and Policy Editor restrictions to user configurations—to create a less complex, more controlled environment for some users, while permitting others to either pick and choose or have access to everything.

A word about security: There really isn't any. Security can be set up in a client/server network environment. But in a home or small office setting, there's no real way. You can, however, make it pretty tough for someone to change restrictions. And you can set things up so younger kids really can't get into trouble. But savvy, determined older kids will almost certainly be able to work their way out of any restrictions you set for them. Especially if they're reading this book. (Hey, more power to 'em.)

Configuring User Profiles

This step is necessary only if you've got more than one person sharing a single PC. But before you skip this part, consider something. One person using one PC can use User Profiles to customize his or her desktop for different purposes. In fact, one tip that I couldn't find room for in Chapter 6, "The Mobile Win 95," is the idea of creating one desktop configuration for a notebook when it's in the office (or at home) and another while it's on the road. Instead of naming user profiles after people in that case, you'd name them after uses, like "Office" and "Road." And it would come in especially handy if you use a larger display at a desk and, of course, the internal LCD while travelling.

There's a neat notebook PC tip here.

To get User Profiles happening, open the Passwords control panel and click the User Profiles tab, as shown in Figure 5.15. Click the radio button beside the

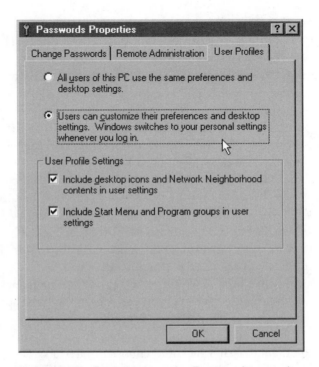

Figure 5.15 Set it this way: the Passwords control panel's User Profiles tab

"Users can customize their preferences . . ." description. Place checks beside both options in the User Profile Settings box. Then click OK.

Don't restart until you're all done. Windows wants to restart things at that point, but don't you let it. It's best to set up configurations for each and every user right away. You do that by choosing Shut Down's "Close all programs and log on as a different user" option. When you do that, Windows will show you, after only a couple of seconds, the "Welcome to Windows" dialog familiar to network users. Enter the name for your first user or custom desktop in the field beside the "User name" label and click OK. You'll be prompted about whether you want the computer to save individual settings for this user. Click the Yes button. You'll get the wait cursor while Windows churns around, creating your new user configuration. Choose Shut Down again and repeat the process for every user or custom desktop you want to create. When you're done, choose Shut Down one more time and opt for the normal Restart.

Let everyone do his or her own customizing. When you've finished creating all the users or desktops you want, you're ready to work with Policy Editor. But note, you don't *have* to use Policy Editor. Unless you want to restrict access to things in some of your profiles, each person using the PC can do his or her own customizing after logging in. Policy Editor is useful for two things: Limiting access to functions and one or two power settings that might be described as "less is more."

Using Policy Editor

System Policy
Editor

The broad swath of features supported by the System Policy Editor, with its templates and user and group policies, isn't something you're likely to make use of unless you're a network administrator at some large corporation running a NetWare or Windows NT network. If you are a net administrator, check with Microsoft for how to make it work. For all the rest of us (and I figure that's probably about 90 percent), there are nevertheless some very useful things this little utility can provide. But it's easy to miss them in the shroud of networkese. So I'll cut to the chase.

If there is more than one person using your PC, follow the steps under "Configuring User Profiles" back a couple of pages before you wreak any havoc with System Policy Editor, OK? You're asking for trouble and confusion if you don't.

**How to install
Policy Editor**

The next step is to install this sucker. Policy Editor (PolEdit for short) is an optional utility you add from the Win 95 CD. To install it, open the Add/Remove Programs control panel. Click the Windows Setup tab and press the Have Disk button. Then click Browse and navigate to the `\Admin\Apptools\Poledit` folder. Open the folder and click OK and OK again. (Don't worry about what's selected under "File name.") You should be looking at the Have Disk dialog now, showing the same stuff you see in Figure 5.16. Place a check mark beside the second line, System Policy Editor, and click the Install button. You'll find the

Figure 5.16 After some rigmarole, this is what you get
to install Policy Editor

new System Policy Editor icon on the Start/Programs/Accessories/System Tools submenu.

USING PROFILES AND POLICIES

> There is something tragic about the enormous number of young men there are in England at the present moment who start life with perfect profiles, and end by adopting some useful profession.

> Oscar Wilde
> "Phrases and Philosophies for the Use of the Young," in *Chameleon*,
> December 1894

The first thing to know about this techie little thing is that you should forget all about creating Policy (.POL) files. As far as I can tell, there's no way to use them on a local machine. They were designed to be used on a network. And, while it may be possible to make them load on a local machine, it's not worth the trouble. I spent most of a rainy Saturday trying to make it happen—so you don't have to bother.

Cutting through the layers, this means you can't set policies for a given user while you're logged on as another user. And if you can disable something while logged on as someone else, then it follows that they should be able to re-enable it themselves if they can figure out how. Like I said, though, if you're prudent, User Profiles is more than good enough for young kids—if for no other reason than it's tough to figure out how to set things up. Besides, if your under-10-year-old child figures this out, you're going to have bigger worries, like saving up for MIT.

To get PolEdit ready to set restrictions, follow the instructions under "Configuring User Profiles" above. Log on as the user whose settings you want to modify. Run Policy Editor from the System Tools submenu. Choose File/Open Registry. You'll see two icons, Local User and Local Computer. About 99 percent of any changes you might want to make will be in Local User, which when opened looks like Figure 5.17. In fact, I recommend leaving Local Computer alone. Check out Table 5.2 for the Local User settings beside which I recommend you place a check mark for kids.

Safeguard your PC from the inappropriate attentions of your curious kids. The table presumes your home PC isn't networked. If it is (I'm sorry and . . .) you'll want to disable networking stuff for kids, too. (Look under both Network and Shell: Restrictions for network restrictions.) Also, don't forget to delete the Shortcut to Policy Editor in your Start/Programs/Accessories/System Tools folder, as well as anything you may have added to the desktop, the Start Menu, and the Programs menu and submenus—anything that might get little ones in trouble. Finally, do not mess with the Shell: Custom Folders part of Local User unless you're really getting into it. Windows modifies this section automatically.

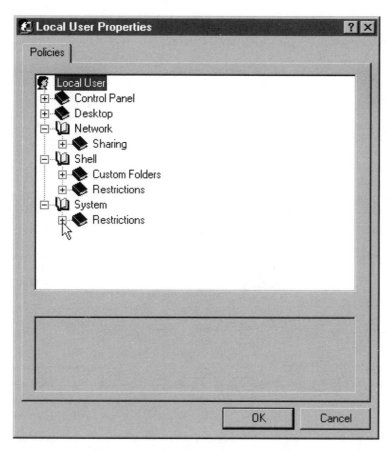

Figure 5.17 Local User Registry settings in Policy Editor

Profile and Policy Management

What if you decide you want to get rid of this stuff after you set it up? There's a certain amount of overhead in maintaining User Profiles in terms of disk space (although not much, really), extra guck in System Registry, and having to face the Welcome to Windows dialog every time you turn on your PC.

You can turn off User Profiles by reversing the steps you took in turning it on in the Passwords control panel. After Windows restarts, you'll be back to your default profile, which you'll find in the `.Default` branch of the HKEY_USERS key in the Registry. (By the way, it's repeated in the HKEY_CURRENT_USER branch.) That's why it's a very smart idea *not* to modify Local User before you add User Profiles, unless there are modifications you'd like to make globally to all profiles.

Only thing is, when you turn off User Profiles, that's all you're doing. You're not actually deleting the profiles directories that Windows set up for you. Nor are you removing your profiles settings in System Registry. I guess Microsoft figures

Table 5.2 Recommended Policy Editor "Local User" Restrictions for Kids

Top-level Checks	Sublevel Checks	Description
Control Panel: Display	• Hide Settings Page	Disables access to display drivers and controls.
Control Panel: Passwords	• Disable Passwords	Fully disables the Passwords control panel.
Control Panel: Printers	• Hide General and Details • Disable Deletion of Printers • Disable Addition of Printers	Prevents your child from accidentally disabling your printer.
Control Panel: System	• Hide Device Manager • Hide Hardware Profiles • Hide File System • Hide Virtual Memory	Fully restricts all system settings except Graphics.
Shell: Restrictions	• Remove Run Command • Remove Taskbar from Settings • Remove Find command • Hide Drives in My Computer	Reduces the likelihood that your child will delete files on your computer or run programs that shouldn't be run from the command line.
System: Restrictions	• Disable Registry editing tools	Disables the System Registry Editor. Don't forget this one.

you might want to turn User Profiles back on later (and I'll buy that). But you might want to know how to get rid of this fully after turning off User Profiles. Here's how. Run the Registry Editor and work your way down this branch:

```
HKEY_LOCAL_MACHINE\SOFTWARE\Microsoft\Windows
\CurrentVersion\ProfileList
```

When you click the plus sign beside the ProfileList folder, you'll see entries for each of your profile names that look something like Figure 5.18. Right-click each in turn and delete it. Then close RegEdit and open the Profiles folder inside your Windows folder. Trash everything you find in there. As a final check, I suggest running Policy Editor and checking to make sure your restrictions are set the way you want them.

Got your Policies settings all screwed up, and you're not sure how to get back to square one? By default, the only check mark you should see in Local User is the one beside Wallpaper in Control Panel: Desktop. Things vary a tad in Local Computer, especially if you're on a network. But here are the entries that are likely to have check marks: Network: Passwords, "Hide share passwords with

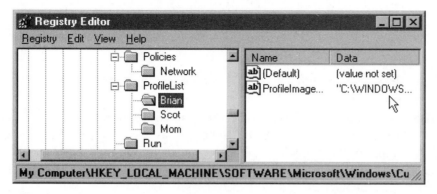

Figure 5.18 The keys to individual Policy Editor profiles in Registry

asterisks"; Network: Update, "Remote Update"; System, "Network path for Windows Setup" (the field beside Path: should contain the pathname to the drive and directory you installed Windows 95 from, such as `E:\WIN95\`); and System, "Run" (the entry inside should be Value Name: "SystemTray" and Value: "SysTray.Exe").

"SPECIAL FOLDER" OBJECTS

> Specialized meaninglessness has come to be regarded, in certain circles, as a kind of hall-mark of true science.
>
> Aldous Huxley
> *Ends and Means*, 1937

Phew! Everything in this chapter has been leading up to this section and the next one—the good parts. So I hope you stick around. I've got a little pile of secrets to tell you. Some are just the ticket for making Win 95 as you like it, and some are just cool.

Ok, we're getting to the good parts now.

I've talked about them here and there. Microsoft calls them by that brilliantly inventive name: *special folders*. What are special folders? Keep in mind that virtually every desktop or interface object in Windows 95 is some type of *container* object. That's Microsoftese for a graphical something that holds other somethings. And the quintessential container in Win 95 is the Explorer folder. Many things that don't really look like folders, like the MSN screens, are really a variant of an Explorer folder. So special folders are new folders created in the image of various Win 95 structures that mimic the functions of the originals—to a greater or lesser degree. And you can use them to customize your desktop, folders, and Start.

Microsoft cleaned up the acts of three of the functional objects in My Computer for the express purpose of helping people customize Win 95. They are the Control Panel, Printers, and Dial-Up Networking folders. To make these special folders, you create a new folder inside any folder or on the desktop (right-click

Control Panel

the background and choose New/Folder). Then you type the name you want to give the new object, followed by a period, followed by the Class ID (CLSID) number for that object in curly brackets, like this:

```
Control Panel.{21EC2020-3AEA-1069-A2DD-08002B30309D}
```

The name before the period can be anything you want it to be. It's the period and the CLSID number that identify the object as a special folder of a specific type. You'll find instructions for how to do this, including the CLSID numbers, in the `TIPS.TXT` file in your Windows folder. But so that you don't have to go hunting around for them, check out Table 5.3.

Table 5.3   Some Interface Object CLSID Numbers

Interface Object	CLSID Number
Control Panel	{21EC2020-3AEA-1069-A2DD-08002B30309D}
Dial-Up Networking	{992CFFA0-F557-101A-88EC-00DD010CCC48}
Printers	{2227A280-3AEA-1069-A2DE-08002B30309D}
Recycle Bin	{645FF040-5081-101B-9F08-00AA002F954E}
Desktop Folder	{00021400-0000-0000-C000-000000000046}
My Computer	{20D04FE0-3AEA-1069-A2D8-08002B30309D}
The Microsoft Network	{00028B00-0000-0000-C000-000000000046}
Inbox	{00020D75-0000-0000-C000-000000000046}
Network Neighborhood	{208D2C60-3AEA-1069-A2D7-08002B30309D}
Briefcase	{85BBD920-42A0-1069-A2E4-08002B30309D}

Dial-Up
Networking

The cool thing about these three special folders is that when you place them on the Start Menu, they cascade off Start as a submenu, where you can click to directly launch subobjects, like individual control panels. The Control Panel is the most useful special folder. But if you have multiple printers connected to your PC, the Printers special folder will definitely come in handy. For me, the cascading Dial-Up Networking folder is better, since I have multiple Internet access providers.

This is a very simple tip, but one worth mentioning if you're a customizing maniac like I am. Copy all the object names and CLSIDs down in a Notepad text file. Put a period between the object name and its CLSID number with no spaces. That way you can call up the text file, copy the `[Object Name].{CLSID Number}` **in one pass, and then paste it into the highlighted folder name of a special folder object you're creating.**

OK, here's the stuff that Microsoft didn't tell you. You can also create special folders for all the rest of the objects listed in Table 5.3. These objects haven't been cleaned up for this purpose, so depending on what you want to do with them, they may or may not work as you'd like. For one thing, with one exception—Recycle Bin—they do not, unfortunately, cascade off Start, so they don't give you a submenu of the objects they contain. In the case of Inbox and MSN, there'd be no advantage to that anyway, since they don't really contain objects.

Methinks, though I'm not sure, that this ability to cascade was implemented in a .DLL file. Because I've tried and tried. If you figure out some way to make these other special folder objects cascade, please send me an email (sfinnie@tiac.net). A similar imperfection exists with the menu items displayed on context menus of these "clone" objects. (I'll give you specifics in a bit.) Finally, with two of the objects, the Desktop Folder and My Computer, there's a bit of Registry hacking needed to make them serious special folder objects. But since they are *Underground Guide* creations and are basically command-line driven, you can get 99 percent of their functionality just by creating Shortcuts. And let me tell you, making a Desktop Folder object that opens its own folder containing all the objects on your desktop takes some doing, and can come in way handy.

Drop me a line with your own tips and ideas: sfinnie@tiac .net.

Recycle Bin

I said there was one exception to the negatory on cascading these unofficial special folder objects off Start. When you create a special folder of the Recycle Bin, you get the Portable Recycle Bin. It's exactly like Recycle Bin in every regard, except it's a superset because it merges Recycle Bin's context menu with the fuller context menu of any folder. The Properties item leads to the full-blown properties for Recycle Bin. This will happen even if you kill the original desktop-anchored Recycle Bin using either of the two ways I'll show you under "Desktop Makeovers" later in the chapter.

Recycle Binge

What's great about the Recycle Bin special folder object is that you can re-name it at will, just like you can any other folder. Moreover, you can move or copy it to any folder at all, including the desktop. That's kind of handy because you could put a copy of Recycle Bin in, say, a folder containing a big pile of file icons, maximize the folder window, and perform drag-and-drop deletions without having to find your way back to the desktop.

Yet another way to rename Recycle Bin

The Start Menu cascading deal is semi-useful. The special folder version of "Recycle Binge" (as I name it so that I don't get confused with the original Recycle Bin) cascades all of the pending-deletion files currently in the Bin (see Figure 5.19). If you click one of those files, you get its properties sheet.

Desktop Folder

Now this is cool, and it has lots of uses. I point out one use in a tip in Chapter 6, "The Mobile Win 95," which loads a minimized folder containing all your desktop icons onto the Taskbar. Because notebook screens are notoriously small, you often can't see your desktop icons. So this little feller moves the desktop to you.

Desktop

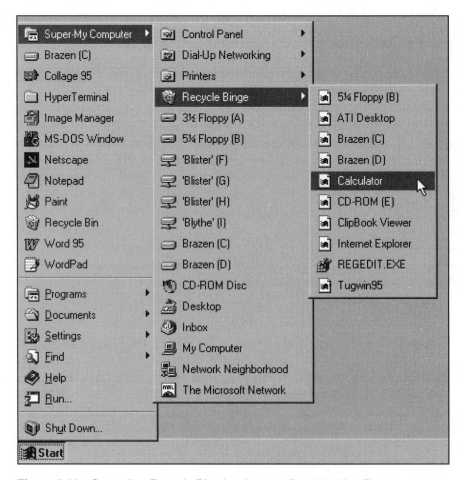

Figure 5.19 Cascading Recycle Bin showing pending-detection files

This tip is one of the most useful in the whole book.   It takes all of three seconds to create a Desktop Folder *Shortcut* with the New/Shortcut wizard, which is available from the context menu for any folder background or the desktop. In the "Command line" field on the first screen of the wizard, type

```
explorer /root,
```

On the next screen, type the name you want to give to the Desktop Folder Shortcut. I call it Desktop. Then get properties for the new Shortcut, click the Change Icon button, and scroll to the right until you see the desktop icon. It's the 35th one in the icon set, and it shows a lamp shining down on a desktop. Then click OK and OK again, and you're done. Double-click the new icon, and a folder opens showing all the icons on your desktop. This isn't the same as making a Shortcut to your \Windows\Desktop folder by the way, since that folder shows only Shortcuts you've *added* to your desktop, not Win 95's official desktop tool objects, like My Computer and Recycle Bin.

Making a special folder object of this Desktop Folder puppy requires a bit of Registry tweaking (shown in Figure 5.20). Open RegEdit and look in the `HKEY_CLASSES_ROOT\CLSID` **branch for the** `{00021400-0000-0000-C000-000000000046}` **entry. Click the plus sign beside this entry, right-click its folder, and choose New/Key. Name the new key** `DefaultIcon`. **With the new key highlighted, double-click the ab** `Default` **icon on RegEdit's right pane. In the Edit String Value box, type this line:**

```
c:\windows\system\shell32.dll,34
```

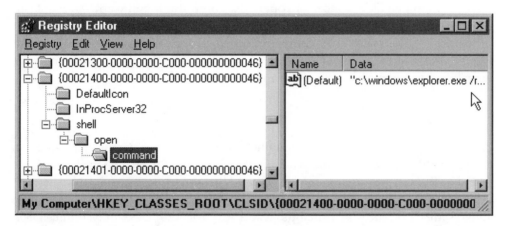

Figure 5.20   Close-up of the "Desktop" CLSID area in the Registry

Next, right-click the folder beside `{00021400 . . .` **again. Choose New/Key and name the key** `shell`. **Add a new key beneath the** `shell` **key called** `open`. **Double-click** `open`**'s ab** `Default` **icon and type** `&Open` **in the Edit String Value field. Back under at the** `open` **key on the left pane, add a new key to** `open` **and call it** `command`. **In the Edit String Value field for its ab** `Default` **entry, type this line exactly as it appears:**

```
c:\windows\explorer.exe /root,
```

Leave the `InProcServer32` **key as is. Close Registry Editor and make your new Desktop Folder object by right-clicking the desktop and choosing New/Folder. Then type this line to rename the folder:**

```
Desktop.{00021400-0000-0000-C000-000000000046}
```

and press Enter.

The caveats: Unfortunately, the Desktop Folder object won't cascade from Start. It also will have two Open commands on its context menu. But it works perfectly when you double-click it. The biggest annoyance is that the Properties context-menu item doesn't call up Display Properties, but instead it opens the standard folder properties sheet. On the other hand, you can place copies of it in any folder anywhere in Win 95. Not much point in putting it on the desktop. Yuck.

My Computer

My Sharona

Truth is, there's not much advantage to making a special folder object for My Computer—better known in some circles as "My Sharona." I mean, it's easier just to make a Shortcut for My Computer if that's what you want. But it's kinda nice to know, for example, that you can run my little undocumented Explorer command line tip in a DOS window to open My Computer if you want. And you can use it to create a half-way useful My Computer special folder object.

So here's the poop. The command string works similarly to the Desktop Folder trick but takes fewer steps to set up. To make the Shortcut, launch the New/Shortcut wizard and type this on the command line:

```
explorer /select,c:
```

Call the Shortcut whatever you want (just anything but "My Computer" because, as I've established, that's a dumb name). You don't need to change the icon on this one; it's all set to go.

To make a special folder version of My Computer, follow the same steps I describe in the previous wand tip for the Desktop Folder. Look for the {20D04FE0-3AEA-1069-A2D8-08002B30309D} entry in the HKEY_CLASSES_ROOT\CLSID branch. Skip the DefaultIcon step entirely. Follow the other steps exactly, but behind the ab Default icon on the command key, type this line instead:

```
c:\windows\explorer.exe /select,c:
```

Then create a new folder and name it like this:

```
My Sharona.{20D04FE0-3AEA-1069-A2D8-08002B30309D}
```

The exact same pluses and minuses that apply to the Desktop Folder apply to the special folder version of My Computer. I'm still working on perfecting these do-it-yourself Win 95 objects, and so far Microsoft isn't helping. For another way of attaching My Computer, see the next wand tip.

I'm not going to give specific instructions for making special folders for the rest of the objects listed in Table 5.3. The steps are identical to those for My Computer; just swap in the object's CLSID key entry listed in the table.

Inbox

The usefulness of this special folder object is doubtful. Things work OK with it, and, like Recycle Bin, you can make copies of it, put it in any folder, and so on. But since Inbox properties are available in the Control Panel (as "Mail and Fax"), there's no huge advantage to a special folder object over a Shortcut to Inbox. Yes, the special folder object's properties item works on the context menu, but as I said, that isn't a huge advantage.

InBox

Like all these special folder objects, it's possible to customize Inbox's operation in the Registry. And if it's something you really need—that is, to have Inbox elsewhere, existing as a true container instead of as a pointer—it might be worth the work.

The Inbox and MSN special folder objects share the same type of context-menu duality. Both have customized commands originally in the CLSID section of the Registry's HKEY_CLASSES_ROOT key. And both sprout double Open and Explore commands on their context menus. Not my idea of an elegant solution. But, hey, it can be done, so I'm telling you about it. Maybe you'll find a use for it.

The Microsoft Network

Creating a special folder for this one is questionable for a lot of reasons unless you go into its HKEY_CLASSES_ROOT\CSLID entry and do some serious customizing. It's among the least well-behaved of the unofficial special folder objects. It has a couple of pluses, though. First, thanks to the U.S. Department of Justice, there's a Delete item on MSN's context menu. So blowing the original one away is a breeze. Second, the Connections context-menu item—effectively MSN's Properties sheet—is available no matter where you place the special folder object. That's not entirely true of the others. (It's possible, for example, to add desktop tools and special folder objects into My Computer, but when you do, they lose their context-menu Properties menu items.) Like the others, MSN can be renamed and moved wherever you want. But then, so can its normal Shortcut.

The Microsoft
Network

There's also a serious problem with the special folder object. When you opt for its Properties menu item, you'll get a weird dialog that has two "General" tabs: the first for the standard folder object and the second for MSN. And if you click the MSN General tab and then click the Cancel button—look out. A serious Windows GPF ensues. One of the worst crashes I've seen Win 95 perform. It's kind of a kick at parties, though. Tell people, "Hey, want to see me make Windows 95 crash on command?"

**How to crash
Win 95 at will**

Like Inbox, the as-is context menu of the MSN special folder is schizophrenic in that it has two Open items and two Explore items. Worse, the default MSN "Open" doesn't work. So when you double-click the icon, it doesn't launch. I give up on this one. If you're clearing away your desktop or just want to clear the MSN icon off of it, make a Shortcut. You can always get to MSN's Connections screen by clicking the Settings button after you launch the program.

Why has Microsoft seen fit to make it so difficult to create full copies of important tool objects like My Computer, Network Neighborhood, and Recycle Bin? Or, to put it another way, why can't Shortcuts call the properties sheets of the original objects they point to?

Briefcase

Briefcase

The last two CLSIDs in Table 5.3—Briefcase and Network Neighborhood—are there only for show. No, I'm kidding. They're there so you know they exist. It's possible to make special folders for these (and other) objects, but there's absolutely no point to doing so for Briefcase. It's not really an interface object; it's just a pre-customized folder container. Each instance of the Briefcase that you make from any folder's or the desktop's context menu (New/Briefcase) is all set to go.

Network Neighborhood

Network Nanny

It would be great to have this baby tucked away as a full-blown container object inside any folder where it could give you its properties as well as access to PCs from some place other than the desktop. Of course, you can still just make a Shortcut of Network Neighborhood and rely on the "Network" control panel for the properties.

Or try this. You say you want a cascading My Computer and/or Network Neighborhood? Just make my "Super-My Computer" with Shortcuts. In fact, unless you're on a giant network, you can merge My Computer and Network Neighborhood into one cascading Start folder. To do that, right-click the Start button and choose Open. Make a new folder in the Start Menu folder and name it something like Super-My Computer**, only better. Now open My Computer and copy all your drive icons to the** Super-My Computer **folder. Create special folder objects for the Control Panel, Printers, and Dial-Up Networking, if you want. Make decisions about other objects you might like to have there. I'd definitely place a Desktop Folder Shortcut in there. Next, open Network Neighborhood (if you're network equipped), create Shortcut icons for shared drives and the like, and plop 'em in the new folder. Turn back to Figure 5.19 for ideas. On a network,** Super-My Computer **may actually perform more quickly than the real one, since it won't have to go out and poll network drives every time you open it.**

DESKTOP MAKEOVERS

A place belongs forever to whoever claims it hardest, remembers it most obsessively, wrenches it from itself, shapes it, renders it, loves it so radically that he remakes it in his own image.

Joan Didion
The White Album, 1979

Just-So folks, you're on your own. Somewhere in this book there's that just-right deal. Hope you find what you're after. And you Scattershot people, well, take the collective whole and do it all. For our Minimalist friends, whom I've largely ignored up until now, I'm going to lay out two wholly different strategies for removing all or some of the objects on the desktop. For true Minimalists, we're talking clean slate, *tableau rasa*, no *nada*. I can show you how to clear the decks in two different ways. Neither one is perfect, but when you combine them with a trick or two, they're very usable.

**Just-So folks:
Here's hoping
you stumble
across whatever
you're after.**

WARNING: Before you start any sort of heavy customization of your desktop, build in some fail-safes. Run the Config Backup utility. Turn on User Profiles and set up an experimental desktop: Dr. Jekyll and the experimental Mr. Hide. Mr. Hide gets his name in this case because you can hide him away by restarting to your normal configuration whenever you want—and he may be a bit scary until you get things worked out. Be warned, though. Even if you create a user profile, some changes in any serious desktop makeover fall outside the Registry sections that User Profiles builds redundancies for. So don't forget to run Config Backup, no matter what.

The next fail-safe is to create Shortcuts for each and every object you're about to kill off. This varies somewhat depending on your Setup options, whether or not you're running Microsoft Plus!, how you've customized your desktop, and what programs you've installed. Make Shortcuts for everything, even any desktop Shortcuts you may have added, and put 'em all in the same folder somewhere.

Your Desktop
Shortcuts

What not to do: Don't kill off stuff on your desktop yet. It's better to leave it there for now. For one of the two methods I'm about to describe (Method One), it's much better to leave all your desktop objects where they are. I won't forget to tell you to blow them away later. (Kind of puts me in mind of that mad dog scene in *To Kill a Mockingbird*. . . .)

Wipe It Clean

There are two ways to go, and each has trade-offs. Method One is easier to set up. You also don't actually *delete* your desktop icons with it; you hide them instead. That means you can use the little Desktop Folder Shortcut trick to call up a folder of your desktop icons any time you want to. Of course, there's an annoying part, too. Not only does everything on your desktop disappear; you can't even right-click the desktop to bring up its context menu. Essentially, Method One turns the desktop into a vast wasteland whose only use is for displaying pretty pictures, if you so choose.

Method Two is a bit more complex to get going. But the desktop's context menu stays in operation, including the context-menu shortcut to Display Properties. This method also gives you double-click access to My Computer and even the System Properties available from the My Computer's context menu. On the negative side, when you do open My Computer, there's a quirk in the display of the icon on its title bar (not a problem, just less aesthetically pleasing) I tell you about in the last wand tip in this chapter. Also if you open the Desktop Folder under Method Two, you'll find nothing in there except an invisible My Computer icon. But, then, there's really nothing on your desktop. Whad'd'ya expect?

On balance, if you're into easy and you want to avoid mucking directly with System Registry, go with Method One. It works just fine. If you're a true power user, you absolutely have to go with Method Two. Otherwise, I'll have to ask you to turn in your badge. And if your aim in removing the Microsoft icons from your desktop is to make way for desktop Shortcuts and special folder objects of your own devise and choosing, then you have to use Method Two, since Method One blocks desktop icons entirely.

Method One. Simple as pie. This is all you do. Run System Policy Editor. Choose File/Open Registry and double-click Local User. Click the plus signs beside Shell and then Restrictions. Toward the bottom you'll find an entry labeled "Hide all

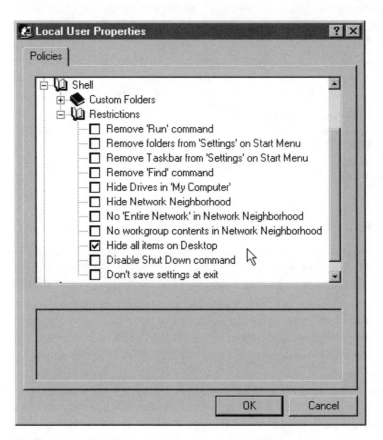

Figure 5.21 One little check mark is all it takes; wave bye-bye, desktop junk

items on Desktop," as shown in Figure 5.21. Place a check in that box, close down the Policy Editor, and restart your machine. When it comes back up, Win 95's desktop will be bare as a sheep after shearing.

> **A note about an avenue for improving on the strategies I'm presenting. System Policy Editor works from a template file called** ADMIN.ADM. **You'll find it in the** \Windows\Inf **folder. It's a text file that you can open with Notepad. Scroll down most of the way, and you'll come to the** CATEGORY !!Restrictions, **which corresponds to the Shell: Restrictions area in System Policy Editor. The path into System Registry for these settings starts with the** HKEY_CURRENT_USER **key and travels down this path:**

```
\Software\Microsoft\Windows\CurrentVersion
\Policies\Explorer
```

> **If, after hiding the desktop icons, you chase your way down that Registry branch and take a look at what Policy Editor did, you'll find several** DWORD **strings added there. What** *I'd* **like to know is, are there entries you could add there for hiding individual desktop icons? Is there a way to turn the desktop's context menu back on? If you learn anything about this, drop me an email (sfinnie@tiac.net).**

Method Two. This is the patchwork *un*quilt of desktop wiping. You'll use three very different strategies for unraveling the ties that bind the clutter. The first takes care of the Inbox, the Microsoft Network, Recycle Bin, and the Internet (if you have Plus! installed). The second is a little Registry cheat that Series Editor Woody Leonhard and I worked out. And the third takes care of Network Neighborhood.

It's the patchwork *un*quilt of desktop wiping.

Fire up the Registry Editor but don't put on the coffee. This won't take long. Drill your way down the HKEY_LOCAL_MACHINE key following this path:

```
\Software\Microsoft\Windows\CurrentVersion\explorer
\Desktop\NameSpace
```

Below the NameSpace key are CLSID numbers for some of the special tool objects (not special folders) that are glued to your desktop. There'll be at least one of them—Recycle Bin—and maybe two or three others. Check out Figure 5.22 to see what the NameSpace area looks like. (*Note:* My Computer and Network Neighborhood are more hard-wired into the Win 95 code, specifically the SHELL32.DLL file. That's why there are different strategies for them.)

If you click on each CLSID number in turn, you should see the name of the object in the right pane. You're going to delete these bad boys. Before you do, know that the process is quite reversible (aside from restoring a previous version of the Registry with Config Backup) just by re-adding the CLSIDs under

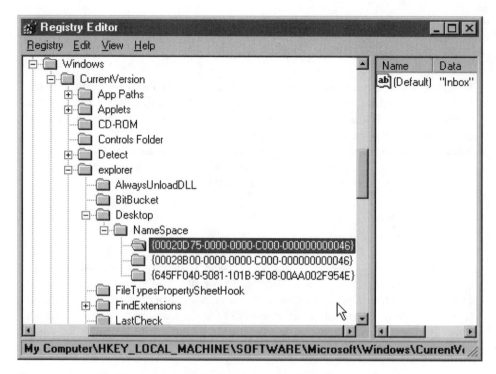

Figure 5.22 The \Desktop\NameSpace area of the Registry

Desktop\NameSpace. If you find an object in NameSpace whose CLSID number hasn't already been recorded in the little Notepad text file I suggested earlier in this chapter, record it now so it'll be easy to change your mind and reinstate it in NameSpace later.

OK, so now click each of the CLSIDs in turn and press the Delete key.

Scattershot Approachers: Notice that any CLSID number entered in a key below this Desktop\NameSpace **branch is an object that appears on your desktop. If you're heavy into desktop tools, try adding stuff here. Of course, things aren't quite as easy as you might think. If you add the Control Panel CLSID, you get something . . . that doesn't work. It appears, but you can't open it. This doesn't mean it couldn't be modified to work. Of course, the easier way is just to make a special folder object of Control Panel and plop it on your desktop. But, as I've said, not all objects are created equally in Win 95. Knowing about this might come in handy someday.**

Once those pesky CLSIDs are gone, may I please direct your attention to another area of the Registry. We've been there before. It's the HKEY_CLASSES_ROOT\CLSID\ section. In particular, locate the {20D04FE0-3AEA-1069-A2D8-08002B30309D} entry (that's My Computer's ID, pard). Click the plus sign and then the `DefaultIcon` subkey. Double-click the ab `Default` entry on the right and make a note of the line that's in there now. You should find:

```
C:\WINDOWS\Explorer.exe,0
```

Later, My Sharona.

That zero at the end is what calls the icon in the `EXPLORER.EXE` file; they're numbered from left to right, starting with zero. You're going to make an itty-bitty adjustment to which icon is being called. Change the `0` to a `4`. If, perchance, you were staring at a line that was calling the `COOL.DLL` file instead, then you've got Plus! installed, right? Just type the line `C:\WINDOWS\Explorer.exe,0` instead. Once that's done, close down RegEdit. Hmmm. My Computer has gone invisible except for its label. Neat. You won't see any other changes yet because you have to restart your computer to make stuff go away. But don't do that yet.

The last leg is handled by System Policy Editor. Choose File/Open Registry. Double-click the Local User icon and click the plus signs beside Shell and then Restrictions. Halfway down you'll see an entry labeled "Hide Network Neighborhood." Put a check mark there and close down the Policy Editor. *Note:* This way of removing Network Neighborhood is a bit more assiduous than the "Hide all desktop icons" option in Policy Editor. Unfortunately, it *really* kills off Network Neighborhood. You can still get to drives on the network, but only if you've persistently mapped them in advance.

Almost done. A few little housekeeping chores. Grab hold of your invisible My Computer icon at the top edge and drag it down so that the label is directly underneath the Start button and Taskbar. The label will disappear, but notice that if you double-click the desktop just above the Start button, My Computer appears. Not the end of the world, right? In fact, it's kinda handy.

I mentioned earlier that there was a quirk to this invisible icon with My Computer. Where Win 95 mini icons are called for—in the title bar and on the folder toolbar's drop-down navigator—you'll see this weird little printer image with a question mark (see Figure 5.23). It's the same image you see in Taskbar's Notification Area when your printer runs out of paper or something. There is, of course, a way to fix this. Using a decent Icon Editor or paint software package that can create invisible masks, create your own empty icon image and call that file instead of `EXPLORER.EXE,4` in the ab `Default` entry. If you're a Visual Basic fan, or have a friend who is, I'm told that program installs a file named `SCREEN.ICO` that you could call in the ab `Default` entry instead. I've tested it, and it works fine. The quirk vanishes.

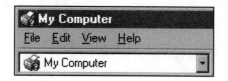

Figure 5.23   The quirk: the mini-printer with question mark icon

OK, we're getting ready to restart for the grand unveiling. If you've got any leftover desktop Shortcuts lying around, now's the time to blow them away. When Win 95 comes back up, your desktop will be clean enough to eat off of.

*   *   *

And so we come to the end of another chapter in the continuing saga of (dum, duum, duuu-um) Working on Win 95. We hope you enjoyed our program this evening and will return next week to find out: Does Abe fit Windows 95 on his notebook with that crummy little hard disk? Does Shelly get it installed without a CD drive? And what about . . . Naomi?

6 The Mobile Win 95

The world has always gone through periods of madness so as to advance a bit on the road to reason.

Hermann Broch
The doctor, in *The Spell*, 1976

Well, roadies, here we go. If you're prone to hoofing it, Windows 95 is going to be a relatively pleasant experience. A lot of the stuff that was such a pain about toting a second box around is, well, somewhat easier under this OS (you remember, that's nerdspeak for "operating system"). It's no notebook panacea, but Win 95 is the first mainstream desktop OS designed from the ground up with notebook PCs in mind.

You might be surprised to learn that some of those crystal ball gazers who predict market trends projected that about a third of 1995's personal computer sales would be portables. So if you're reading this chapter hoping to find useful nuggets that'll make life with your notebook PC easier—you're not alone. And, I won't let you down.

The interesting question, I find, is: Who's buying all these notebooks? Clearly business users are cozying up to the diminutive guys. I'm the perfect example. My current work environment—the editorial department of Ziff-Davis Interactive—made a decision a few years back to purchase notebook PCs with docking stations for most editors. It makes a lot of sense for us because we create and edit online content that needs to be updated every day. When we travel, which is pretty frequently, we don't have time to blow half a day copying our latest data files to a notebook, configuring dial-up connections, and the like. Undocking our PCs and putting 'em in the kit bag is a lot faster. Especially with Win 95.

Who the heck's buying all those notebooks?

What's more, even though notebook PCs are more expensive than desktop PCs, they're a lot less expensive than a desktop PC plus a notebook PC, which is what many business users have wound up needing in the past. The only real catch for business users is that, until recently, notebook PCs tended to have

Figure 6.1 Superfluous Microsoft "feel good" mobile computing screen art

inferior CPUs, video, and hard drive capacities. And PCMCIA (now known as PC Card) card services were a bear to set up and configure. The good news is, Win 95 completely does away with the old real-mode PCMCIA noise.

Notebooks aren't just for business folk either. Lots of home PCs are notebooks these days. Personally I think this is probably misguided. But, then, I have seven PCs and a network in my house (two of which are notebooks, I might add). I also have a kick-butt home alarm system, but that's another story. The point is, many home PC users don't want the added clutter that a full-size desktop PC entails. A notebook PC that they can tuck away out of sight or fit inside the rolltop desk is better suited to their lifestyles. And there's the added advantage that they could use it for bringing stuff back and forth from work.

However you use your notebook, Win 95 has features that'll help you take better advantage of it. The thing is, you're not going to find this stuff all in one place. It's scattered around here and there. And you could trip across a lot of it without knowing it. But once you're informed, these features can help you deal with the compromises that crop up because you have a smaller screen, run on batteries, use PC cards, have special pointing device needs, may use your PC in more than one hardware configuration, and may need to copy or access data between two PCs. And, hey, that's why you bought this book anyway, right? (Remember, don't steal this book; buy it.)

INSTALLATION STRATEGIES

> A man should ever . . . be ready booted to take his journey.
>
> Michel de Montaigne
> "That to Philosophise is to Learn How to Die," in *Essays,* 1580–88

PC Card (PCMCIA)

Installing a Win 3.1 upgrade of Windows 95 on a notebook is a somewhat different proposition than on a desktop PC. The two biggies are: How do you install from a CD if your notebook lacks a CD drive? And what's the deal with configuring support for PCMCIA? On this second point, Windows 95 is a boon in most respects. That's because it not only takes care of installing and configuring your PC card socket services (the base layer hardware support for these devices); it also loads up their drivers in protected "Windows" memory using VxD's. The point, old son: There's a lot more memory free for running DOS and Windows applications that demand low, or DOS, memory—that part of your RAM addressed as under 1MB. I'll come back to PCMCIA in a minute. First, getting the durn operating system on your notebook.

CD versus Floppy

CDs are cool. CDs are fast, and easy, and less likely to get accidentally corrupted, and fast, and just one thing to insert, and fast. Floppy disks are a royal pain in the butt. They're also multiple things to throw out, to stack in a box in the attic to be recycled somehow later maybe (hope for a lightning strike?), or to unload on some unsuspecting friend. I don't advise that anyone purchase floppy disks unless they just have absolutely no access to a CD drive. Especially if you've got a 386 machine, you want the CD; installation takes forever with floppies on a 386. But lets face it, the temptation is pretty high for owners of CD-less notebooks to go with floppies. But be aware, as I've said before in this book, the floppy version of Windows 95 is not the same as the CD version. There's more cool stuff on the CD. You may not think you want anything extra, but you might be surprised.

The question is: Do you have access to a PC that has a CD drive? If you answer "no" to that question, then go with the floppies when you buy your copy of Windows 95—if you haven't already. But if your answer was yes, read on. *Ve haf vays of gettink you koneckted to da CD in das box.*

So if you can latch onto a machine with a CD, even as a one-time gig, I recommend a somewhat unorthodox approach for installing Windows 95. It amounts to getting the CD version and either installing it from a network CD drive and/or "copying" the Win 95 files from the CD (shown in Figure 6.2) to your notebook's hard drive. Then you can install Win 95 from a directory right on your hard drive.

Before you rush off and follow my advice, there are several unfortunate trade-offs you should be aware of and requirements you have to meet. This is a little complicated, but hang in there. But since a lot of the coolest tips and tricks you can do with Windows 95 require access to the CD, I'm going to try my darnedest to get you there.

The requisite files you're going to copy onto your notebook's hard drive are going to cost you over 30MB of drive space. Of course, you could always delete them later, but I'd wait for at least a month or two. Be warned: There are times when Windows 95 may need its setup files. If you leave the files on your hard disk, that'll happen automatically. So if you have limited access to a second CD-equipped machine and little extra hard drive capacity, go with the floppies.

More than you wanted to know about Win 95 and notebooks?

I said, *ve haf vays*. In a nutshell, they involve connecting the CD-equipped PC to your notebook. Straight out of the box, there are two main ways that Windows

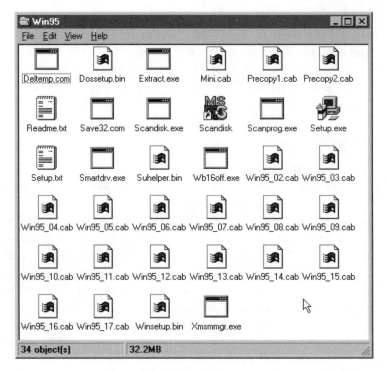

Figure 6.2   The files in the Win95 folder on the Windows 95 CD

95 enables this kind of connection. The first, and best, is to connect the PCs with a network. The second is to connect them using a Win 95 utility called Direct Cable Connection. Windows 95 has all the software you need to do this by either method. But there's a Catch-22: For Direct Cable Connection, both machines need Windows 95 installed on them already. ("Gee, Scot, that helps me a lot" . . . "Well, it'll help some folks.") To just install across a peer network of your own devising, both machines must be running Windows for Workgroups, if not Windows 95. And, of course, you'll need network adapters and cable media. Or they must be network nodes on a client/server network such as Novell's NetWare.

Do you have Internet access? If so, you can skip all this network stuff. Install Win 95 from floppies. Then surf on over to Microsoft's "Windows 95 CD-ROM Estras" page using this URL:

`http://www.microsoft.com/windows/software/cdextras.htm`

You can download all the stuff that comes on the Win 95 CD that's not available on the floppy version. It might take a little while to download, but it's the easiest way overall to get around the but-my-notebook-doesn't-have-a-CD-drive problem.

There's a third option. You could use third-party DOS or Windows-based remote control/file transfer software that connects the PCs via cable. The thing is, if you don't have this software and hardware already, it's probably cheaper to buy the Win 95 floppies. What's more, you can't use simpler file-transfer utilities. That's because you can't just copy the Windows Setup files using a simple Copy operation, since they're compressed. You need to be able to map your notebook's drive the way you would on a network and then address that drive from the DOS command line. Bog!

If your notebook can't become a node on a corporate client/server network and you don't have Windows for Workgroups on your notebook PC (it says "Windows for Workgroups" on the Windows splash screen during startup if you do), you're back to the lowly floppies, I'm afraid. At least to get started. But some people may have another option. If you work in an office, do you or others have a Win 95 CD or access to one? Even if you purchase the floppy version of Windows 95 for your notebook, you can still use the tips I'm passing along here to add the fuller features of the CD version once you've installed the floppy version. That's because once Win 95 is installed, you'll be able to set up networking or Direct Cable Connection on your notebook.

Enough caveats for you? I know, I know, it hardly seems worth it. But if you're a true computer nerd like me, you're going to want the stuff that comes on the CD. And you're not going to want to have to buy two copies of Win 95 if you can possibly avoid it. And even if you do buy two copies, you're going to want a way to get the CD options on your CD-less notebook. This whole CD and notebooks thing just plain sucks. I could have avoided explaining all this, but then the book wouldn't truly be an Underground Guide to Windows 95. So, my apologies if your eyes have glazed over.

Listen up: Does all this hardly seem worth it?

Using a Network

As noted, if you can connect your notebook to another PC with a CD drive using a network connection, you can just install Win 95 over the network (shown in Figure 6.3). It's a little slower, but overall, this is a very painless operation.

Some more things to keep in mind. First, if your network card is a PCMCIA type, you could run into some trouble later when Windows 95 attempts to configure your PCMCIA socket services. This is because more than likely Win 95 will be trying to travel across the medium via DOS real-mode PCMCIA drivers that it's trying to configure. I've personally both been successful and run into difficulties installing to notebooks over a network when using a PCMCIA network card. You'll *probably* be OK. And there's a way around it if you're not.

You'll *probably* be OK installing Win 95 across a network using a PCMCIA network adapter.

The second thing to keep in mind is that the first three or four times you start Windows 95, it may still be figuring out your hardware. Which means it may suddenly need access to its installation CD to load drivers and such. So you'd

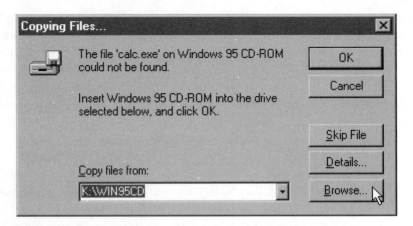

Figure 6.3   Installing from a network CD drive or volume

better be ready to hook back up to the desktop PC's CD drive (or network volume).

How do you avoid those potential pitfalls? Put Win 95's Setup files right on your notebook's hard drive right after you install. The step-by-step on how to do that is the subject of the next section.

Erecting a quick peer network isn't as tough as it

Anyway, back to networking the CD-equipped PC to your notebook. This isn't the place to tell you how to throw up a little peer-to-peer network with Windows 95; I detail that process in Chapter 8, "Connections." *Note:* Before you install Windows 95 on your Windows for Workgroups notebook via peer networking, you'll need to add Microsoft's Netbeui network protocol if the other PC is a Win 95 box. Don't worry, though; that's easy to do, and I explain it in Chapter 8.

PUT WIN 95'S SETUP FILES ON YOUR HARD DISK

> You have a row of dominoes set up; you knock over the first one, and what will happen to the last one is that it will go over very quickly.
>
> Dwight D. Eisenhower
> Address to press conference about defeat of French
> by Viet-Minh, April 7, 1954

Having your cake and eating it too with a CD-less notebook

If you use a docking station, the stuff in this section is the answer to your prayers. It's a simple solution—copying Win 95's Setup files to your hard drive from your docking station's CD drive. In fact, it may be the only way for most docking-station users to have their cake and eat it, too. Because if you install from the CD, and your notebook doesn't have a CD drive of its own, you discover early on one of the biggest pains about Windows 95: There are times when your undocked notebook really needs that darn CD. But since you're away from the dock, you're SOL. It's seriously annoying.

The Windows 95 CD contains a lot of extraneous junk that most people don't need. All the stuff that gets installed as any part of the Win 95 Setup procedure is found in the Win95 folder on the CD. Most of the optional goodies you might want to install (and that I tell you to install in various tips throughout this book) are located in the CD's \Admin\Apptools folder. You don't need any special instructions to copy that second folder to your hard drive. Just drag and drop it from the CD to your notebook. That's all there is to it. But the Win95 folder is a very different story.

You can't just copy most of the files that the CD's Win95 folder contains. Microsoft uses a proprietary file-compression format on the Win 95 floppies and the CD. The compressed files can't be copied without damaging them.

But there is a way. Windows 95 provides a special utility, called Extract, that lets you extract the files from the compressed format. More roadblocks. You can't simply use Extract to uncompress them and then copy them to your hard drive. Not if you want to be able to install Windows 95 from them. The OS expects to be installed *from* the compressed files. Besides, they'd take up a lot more space on your drive that way. Instead, you use the Extract utility with a special switch to "Extract copy" the compressed files from the CD to your hard disk; doing that leaves them in the compressed format. The compressed files in the CD's Win95 folder have the .CAB extension. And Extract's copy switch is /C.

> **Using the Extract utility could save your bacon one cold night in East Jebib.**

Get it straight (so you don't get it wrong, OK?): For the purposes of explaining this, the E:\ in the pathnames of the commands listed below refers to the CD drive of the CD-equipped PC, and the G:\ refers to the hard drive on your notebook PC connected via any network solution. Your drive letter designations will very likely be different, so change them accordingly in the commands you type. Got it? If you're lost, please check out Chapter 8, "Connections." (Or you could just blow all this off and get the floppies.)

Extraction Action

Start by connecting the two PCs. If you're using Direct Cable Connection between two machines that are running Windows 95, the notebook should be the host and the desktop PC should be the client. Step one is to create a \Win95CD folder on the notebook. You perform all the rest of the steps at the keyboard of the CD-equipped PC.

> **Put those Setup files in a \Win95CD folder you create on your hard drive.**

Insert the Windows 95 CD into the CD drive. Choose Start/Programs/MS-DOS Prompt. On the DOS window's command line, type the following lines, pressing Enter after each one. You're logging on to the directory on the CD from which you'll Extract the Win95 files:

```
E:
CD \WIN95
```

Leave the DOS window open (or minimized). Back inside Windows 95, open a folder window of your CD's \WIN95 directory. It should look like the one in Figure 6.2. Remember, all the .CAB files you see in this window are compressed. You'll use EXTRACT /C on them, and after that, you'll get to the other files in this folder. One weird step at a time.

Only real hitch is that you've got to copy each compressed file with a separate command.

There are 19 .CAB files on the Windows 95 CD. The first three have different names, and the other 16 have very similar names. I haven't been able to figure out a way to use character variables with the Extract utility. You'll have to type a separate command for each .CAB file. The only shortcut I can offer is to make liberal use of the command line's ability to remember the last command you typed and entered. So, after you've typed the command once, hold down the right arrow key at the beginning of each successive command, stop to type the slight filename changes for the next file, and then press the right arrow again to complete the command. Press Enter at the end of each full command to execute it.

Check out the first command in Figure 6.4. The first four commands are as follows:

```
EXTRACT /C MINI.CAB G:\WIN95CD
EXTRACT /C PRECOPY1.CAB G:\WIN95CD
EXTRACT /C PRECOPY2.CAB G:\WIN95CD
EXTRACT /C WIN95_02.CAB G:\WIN95CD
```

Your screen should look something like Figure 6.5 at this point. The next 15 .CAB filenames change only in the number after the underscore, from WIN95_03.CAB to WIN95_17.CAB. Here's where that right-arrow command line trick comes in especially handy.

Figure 6.4 The first Extract command ready to execute

Figure 6.5 The first of 16 similar Extract-copy commands after execution

Once that's done, close the MS-DOS Prompt window and bring up the CD's Win95 folder. Choose Arrange Icons/by Type under the folder's View menu. Ctrl-click each of the 15 files whose filename extensions are *not* `.CAB`. When they're all selected, right-click any one of them and choose Copy from the context menu. Open the Win95CD folder that you created earlier on your notebook's hard drive (you should see all the .CAB files you Extract-copied in there). Right-click anywhere on the folder's background and choose Paste from the context menu. Now all the non-`.CAB` files should appear. The optional last step is to copy the CD's `\Admin\Apptools` folder into the notebook's Win95CD folder. Unless you're short of disk space, I highly recommend this step. It's where the goodies are.

Unless you're short of hard disk space, copy the `\Admin\Apptools` folder too.

To install Windows 95 as an upgrade of your notebook's Windows installation from the new Win95CD folder, choose Program Manager's Run command and browse for the `SETUP.EXE` file in the new directory. If your notebook was already running Windows 95, the next time you need to access the install "disc," Setup will attempt to locate the disc or disks you originally installed from. Just choose the Browse button on the Setup dialog and navigate to the Win95CD folder instead. After the first time you do that, Setup will remember the new Setup path.

> **Wish I could tell you that it's easy to create floppies from your Win 95 CD. It isn't. In fact, it's pretty much impossible. Most of the `.CAB` files on the Win 95 CD are 2MB in size, so they won't fit on a 1.44MB floppy. That's why there's a lot less stuff in the floppy version of Windows 95 (see Figure 6.6). Microsoft is not-so-quietly discriminating against folks who don't have CD drives. Call me an elitist, but I have to say I agree with them. Except where notebooks are concerned. Most notebook users have little choice on this score, short of buying a whole new machine. If you have a desktop PC that doesn't have a CD drive, this might be a good time to consider the upgrade, though.**

Figure 6.6   Win 95's floppy disk 1 is very different from
the CD version

READY, SET, INSTALL

> Our friends are generally ready to do everything for us, except the very
> thing we wish them to do.
>
> William Hazlitt
> *Characteristics,* No. 87 (first published anonymously in 1823; repr. in *Complete
> Works,* Vol. 9, ed. by P. P. Howe, 1932)

Notebook users, unite. During the installation, please choose the "Portable" installation option on the Win 95 Setup screen shown in Figure 6.7. This tells
Windows to configure stuff for your type of PC, with a basic set of general options
befitting the often smaller size of notebook hard drives. Check out the Appendix
for a detailed list of the stuff Portable Setup installs—and doesn't install. You'll
also find my recommended installation choices there for notebooks and desktop PCs.

**Remember:
During Setup
you want to
customize the
list of compo-
nents to be
installed.**
If you've got drive space to spare or if it's important to you to explore some
of Win 95's optional installables (and it probably is), when you get to Setup's Windows Components screen, choose the option at the bottom: "Show me the list of
components so I can choose," shown in Figure 6.8. By doing that, Setup gives you
the chance to review what it's going to do on a point-by-point basis. If you just
follow the Typical or Portable install track, Win 95's Setup will probably neglect

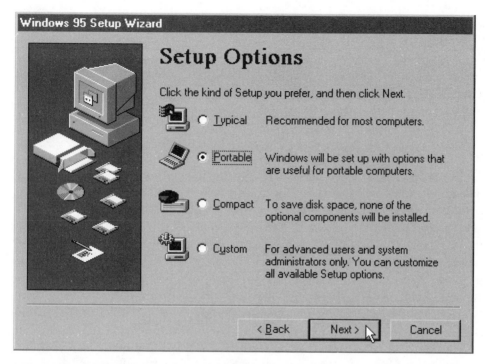

Figure 6.7   Choose the Portable Setup Option

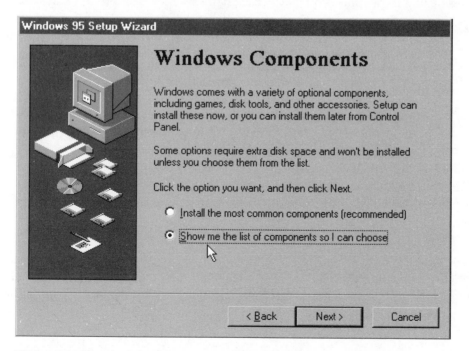

Figure 6.8   Your last chance to customize your installation—Take it!

to install stuff you might really want. It may also install stuff that you're never going to use.

Plug it all in and turn it all on.

Please take my advice. Before you install, you need to have all the hardware that you ever use with your notebook computer plugged in and ready to go. If you're performing a Windows upgrade, things will go more smoothly if all your hardware options and peripherals are correctly configured and working in both DOS and Windows prior to Win 95 installation. If you've got a docking station, you H-A-V-E to perform the install with your computer docked. Do you use PCMCIA cards? Stick 'em all in there before you install. If you've got more PCMCIA cards than slots, then choose the one or ones that are more critical to your day-to-day work with your PC, like your network card and your modem. Is your printer plugged in? Do you use an external monitor? Plug it in and turn it on.

Desktop PC users are landlubbers; we free spirits need to nail ourselves down for this install.

You can really let yourself in for some serious aggravation if you don't follow this advice. Desktop PC users don't encounter this Windows 95 bugaboo anywhere near as much because they're landlubbers, and their hardware is anchored in place. We portable free spirits need to nail ourselves down for this operating system install. If we don't, we're very likely to see prompts for the Windows 95 Setup CD or floppies at very inconvenient times—like at 35,000 feet. This prompt deal isn't a permanent fixture of notebook computing with Windows 95, but it may crop up whenever you use new hardware. So until you've used your notebook in all its various environments and have given Win 95 access to its Setup files during those times, you may occasionally see the Setup prompt and seriously lack therefore in gotta-have-it functionality.

Portable Setup installs mobile computing tools that business users are likely to need. Following is an overview of the stuff it installs by default.

Power Management

Power

Power management is a collection of functions that control its ability to shut down components of your hardware to save juice when it's running on batteries. Win 95 installs Enhanced Advanced Power Management. How's that for a marketing buzz-term? Well, tell you what this is going to deliver eventually: the Macintosh-like ability to turn the power off on your PC by choosing Shut Down from the Start Menu. (Whoopee, huh?)

Briefcase

Briefcase

Briefcase is a drag-and-drop file archive that lets you move data from a desktop PC to a portable PC, make changes to it while you're traveling, and then automatically update the same set of data on your desktop PC when you get back from your trip.

PCMCIA Support

If you're scratching your head about what PCMCIA is, the term refers to the slots (usually on the right side of your notebook) that accept usually two credit-card-sized peripheral devices. PC cards can be modems, network cards, RAM, application cards, even hard drives. Older notebook PCs don't have these guys, so if you don't have 'em, *fo-ged-abou-dit*.

PC Card
(PCMCIA)

Win 95's PCMCIA support consists of two layers: The base PC card socket services, which support the slot hardware, and the card services, which control the layer between the slot hardware and PC cards you insert into the slots. The virtualized 32-bit support that Windows 95 installs is both faster and more economical with memory.

Direct Cable Connection

This is a temporary file-transfer and resource-sharing network built right into Windows 95. If you're not on a LAN, this is a whole lot better than copying files to floppy disks to move data from one Win 95 machine to another. It uses either a special parallel cable (preferred because it's faster than a serial) or a null-modem serial cable.

Direct Cable
Connection

Dial-Up Networking

Everyone else calls this "remote access." Microsoft had to be different. Whatever you call it, it's the ability to use a modem with your notebook while traveling to dial-in directly to your office PC, a Windows 95–compatible dial-in server your company might have, or even your home PC and then operate the PC you're calling remotely with your notebook. To make this work with your home or office PC, the PC receiving the call must have the Microsoft Plus! add-on for Win 95 installed with the Personal Dial-Up Networking server configured and running.

Dial-Up
Networking

Other Stuff

There's some stuff that Portable Setup does not install unless you choose "Show me the list of components so I can choose" on the Windows Components Setup screen. This includes nearly all of the Accessories, like the WordPad basic word processor, calculator, screen savers, games, cursors, and Quick View; the Microsoft Exchange email module; Microsoft Fax; and the Microsoft Network.

Up and Running

Once you've run through the Portable Setup installation and Windows 95 has rebooted and successfully completed its first launch, restart your computer one more time. Then follow these steps, which piggyback onto stuff I talked about for PCs more generally in Chapter 2, "Up and Running."

My Computer

Right-click My Computer.

Right-click on the My Computer icon and choose Properties on the context menu. This brings up the System Properties dialog. Before you do anything else, click the Device Manager tab, shown in Figure 6.9, and look carefully at the entries you find there. If you see any yellow exclamation points or red circles with slashes though them, you've got a problem with some piece of hardware. If you pass that test, look next for what's not there. Do you have a CD drive on your notebook or its docking station (and is that drive connected now)? If so, you should see the "CD-ROM Controllers" entry in Device Manager. Do you have docking-station-based sound support, but you don't see the "Sound, video, and game controllers" entry? If you're missing something obvious in the Device Manager, and it's not sound- or PCMCIA-related, turn back to Chapter 2, "Up and Running," for tips on what to do next. Then, come back here.

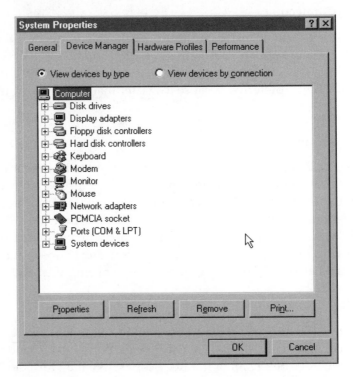

Figure 6.9 The Device Manager on the System Control Panel applet

Notebook sound can be tricky, so check the docs if you run into trouble.

Most nondocked notebooks emulate sound support with a bit of hardware and software, usually Microsoft's Windows Sound System. Check with your notebook's manufacturer or documentation first. But if you're sure that's what is needed and you didn't see the Sound entry, you can install it with the Add New Hardware control panel applet. Just answer "no" to the question "Do you want Windows to search for your new hardware?" Then look for the Windows Sound

System in the Microsoft section under "Sound, video, and game controllers." If for some reason that doesn't lick the problem, you can always remove the driver later.

One obvious thing that's apt to be missing from the Device Manager after you install is a "PCMCIA socket" entry. If you do find a PCMCIA socket line, then you should see an entry for a PCMCIA controller name when you click the plus sign. Don't fret, though, if you don't find a PCMCIA socket entry. I'm getting to that.

OK, PCMCIA

More in-depth, like. Win 95's support of PCMCIA has a lot going for it. As already mentioned, the virtualizing of the socket services is a boon, since real-mode (i.e., DOS) PC card services were real pigs about memory.

PC Card (PCMCIA)

Even better, though, Windows 95 sets this up all on its own (most of the time) in only a few minutes. If you ever tried to set up DOS and Windows PCMCIA drivers in the old days, you know how much of an advantage that is. Personally, I'd rather install a multimedia upgrade kit any day. (If you've never done either of these things, what I'm sayin' here is that before Windows 95, configuring PCMCIA card slots was one giant pain in the butt.)

> **The thing that's a little disconcerting about the way Win 95 configures your PC card slots is that it usually doesn't do this as part of Setup. If your notebook PC has a Plug and Play (PnP) BIOS, it probably will. But everybody else, and that's still the majority, has to set this in motion on their own. And the worst part about it is that you probably won't know it isn't set up if you're upgrading a Windows 3.*x* installation—unless you read this book. That's because Windows 95 will probably use your read-mode driv-ers. So your PC cards are working, but they're slower than they should be, and they're still taking up a bunch of under 1MB memory.**

> **To fix it, right-click My Computer and choose Properties. Click the Perform-ance tab. Then click the line telling you that you're using real-mode (why can't they just say "DOS"?) drivers for PCMCIA. The good news is that knowing to do this is more than half the battle, since Microsoft made the process easy from this point on. Just click the PCMCIA error message line in the window and swat the Details button (see Figure 6.10). You'll get a Help popup window. At the bottom of that is a Click Here button that installs the 32-bit PCMCIA drivers.**

So once you pass the Device Manager hurdle from the Up and Running section above, your next step is to click the System Properties' Performance tab. Check out the window about halfway down this screen. If everything's copacetic, you'll see a line that reads, "Your system is configured for optimal performance." And there'll be this big empty gray space below that. That's the hole Microsoft left to list all the stuff that can go wrong with your install. And, by the way, that's the stuff that Windows 95 *knows* went wrong. (I think we'd need something a trifle larger for all the stuff that can *possibly* go wrong. . . .)

Everyone should check the Performance tab after setup.

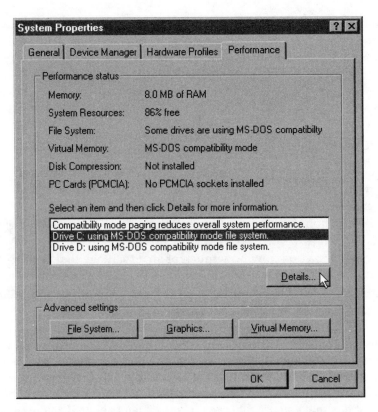

Figure 6.10 The Performance tab screen showing stuff that can go wrong

I've got one notebook PC that doesn't respond to all this special PCMCIA attention. It'll only run with its real-mode PCMCIA drivers. I don't know why yet. I've got a call into the manufacturer (who shall remain nameless until I get to the bottom of this). Nonstandard hardware is a real pain in the butt with Windows 95. Of course, it's a real pain in the butt with everything. But more than most other types of hardware, notebook PCs tend to be nonstandard.

If you run into this problem, what you want to do (besides call the manufacturer and scream holy hell) is open your `CONFIG.SYS` **file with Notepad. Then delete all the text and spaces before the** `DEVICE=` **part of all the lines that begin with this phrase:**

```
REM - by PC Card (PCMCIA) wizard -
```

If you don't find any lines like this in your `CONFIG.SYS` **file, then open the** `AUTOEXEC.DOS` **file in your root directory. Try to find all the** `DEVICE=` **lines that pertain to your PC card support and copy them into your** `CONFIG.SYS` **file. Next, delete the PCMCIA controller entry under the PCMCIA socket device**

category from the Device Manager. Your system will restart. When Win 95 comes back up, it should have reinstated your real-mode PCMCIA drivers, which will lick the problem as a temporary fix. If not, choose Shut Down and power down your PC, wait a few seconds, and turn it back on. Still not working? Scream even louder at your manufacturer. *Note:* **Even if this does work, performance with your PC card network adapter may be so bad that it's barely usable.**

Docking Station? Post-Installation

Ready for something cool? You can skip this part if you've got a PnP BIOS, that is, if your notebook PC was designed to take full advantage of Win 95's on-the-fly hardware-recognition features. Because *theoretically* you should be able to dock and undock your notebook while it's turned on. (But see the wand tip and please don't take my word for it. *Warning:* Serious motherboard damage can ensue if you do *not* have a Plug and Play BIOS.) But, more importantly, Win 95 is going to know automatically what hardware you've got available to you whether you're in the dock or not. That's what Plug and Play *is*.

Don't get carried away with Plug and Play.

This is for those lucky stiffs who have a notebook PC with a Plug and Play BIOS *and* **a docking station. Pretty rare company, indeed. But never let it be said that I discriminate against those snooty individuals who have even better hardware than I do. Anyway, you don't have to shut down your notebook to undock it if the docking station supports undocking. That's a pretty big if, by the way. You do have to do something else, though: Click the Eject PC icon you'll find in the Notification Area (that square depression where the clock sits) on the Taskbar. Doing this sends a message to Windows 95 that you're about to undock. The OS responds by changing to the lower resolution that may be needed by your notebook's LCD display. It also sends a message to all applications on the system that helps them take action (if they're so equipped) when the configuration changes. So, remember, click the Eject PC icon first.**

But all the rest of us aren't in such tough shape, either. If PnP works in real time—auto-recognizing PnP hardware on the fly—Windows 95 does something very smart, essentially Plug and Tell. It's the batch mode version of the same thing for less high-falutin' hardware.

The basic idea: With a docking station, you have two configurations (a.k.a. Hardware Profiles) for your notebook PC: "Docked" and "Undocked." If you took my advice, you created the docked version when you installed. And the first time you undocked your notebook and turned it on, Win 95 created the undocked configuration automatically. Chances are, your undocked hardware configuration is a subset with some minor tweaks, like the switch to your LCD display and perhaps the added reliance on a PCMCIA card for network or modem support.

Before You Undock!

No CD in your notebook? Pay attention.

Does your notebook have its own CD drive? If your answer is no, there's two things you have to pay attention to before you turn your notebook on for the first time outside of its dock:

1. Make sure all hardware you use when undocked is plugged in and working. Why? The first time you turn on your computer outside of its dock, Windows 95 runs the intensive hardware-detection sequence that it must undertake with non-Plug and Play hardware. This takes some time, and it's not suitable for everyday working with a PC. But it's the same "Analyzing Your Computer" routine that Setup performs during install, shown in Figure 6.11. Then, it stores what it finds in what Microsoft calls a Hardware Profile. *Note:* Even if you have a PnP BIOS, that doesn't mean all your hardware supports Plug and Play. So this pretty much applies to everyone.

2. This is where docking station folks who install from the Windows 95 CD get into a lot of trouble with Windows 95. Please take my advice. Follow the steps under the "Put Win 95's Setup Files on Your Hard Disk" section earlier in the chapter after you install Windows 95 and *before* you start your notebook undocked. To reiterate, this doesn't apply to those whose notebooks have their own CD drives (and if that's you, I'm green with envy and don't want to hear about any of your paltry problems).

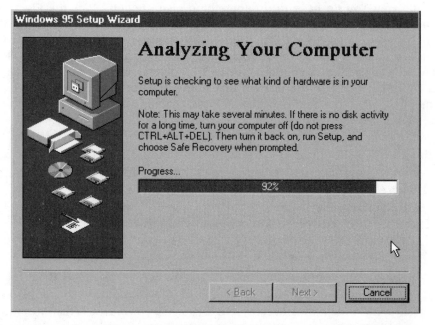

Figure 6.11 Undocked detection looks different, but it's the same as Setup's

After everything is configured, the best part of all is that Windows 95 does its level best to make your notebook work like a PnP device. Microsoft did real good here. Since Windows 95 can detect your docking station, it knows to load the docked hardware profile. And, if it doesn't detect your docking station, it loads your undocked profile. Pretty cool. While it's possible to create more than two Hardware Profiles, you mess up Microsoft's little trickery when you do. With three or more profiles, Windows 95 is no longer faced with a simple either/or proposition. So it's going to prompt you to make the choice from a real ugly DOS prompt. If you have, say, two different undocked hardware configurations, for example—one for when you're home and another for traveling—it's best to make Win 95 load all the drivers for the two variations in one undocked Hardware Profile. You're not really going to miss the memory. Promise.

Check out this Microsoft trickery.

I'm not going into a long explanation about working with hardware profiles, since so few people have notebooks with docking stations (although there's a growing number of us). Suffice it to say there's a Hardware Profiles tab under System Properties where you'll see the names of your multiple configurations (and you can rename Profiles, if that matters). The more important thing to know is that back under the Device Manager, individual entries under device categories offer a "Device usage" block at the bottom of their Properties pages that lets you turn on or off the device services by hardware profile. See Figure 6.12.

Profiles let you turn hardware on and off.

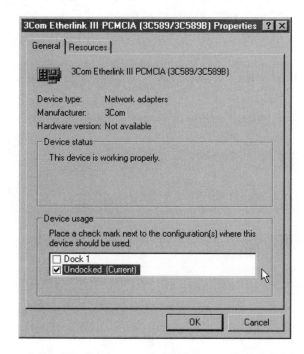

Figure 6.12   The Device usage block for my Ethernet PC card

Win 95 errs on the side of leaving everything on.

Windows 95 does a pretty good job of figuring this out on its own. But it tends to err on the side of leaving too many things switched on. This is the right approach for the uninitiated because it ensures that everything works. But you're initiated now. To save a little memory here and there, you can breeze through each of your devices and make the choices to turn a few things off in one or the other profile.

As you add new hardware to your system, you'll find that Win 95 will turn it on in all your hardware profiles automatically. Again, a precaution for the uninitiated. So, don't forget to go back and check this now and then and turn off stuff manually in the Device usage blocks.

Extra Controls for Portables

Battery and PC card Taskbar icons

A nice little segue to the Notebook Interface stuff we're about to get into are some new notebook status controls you'll see on the right side of the Taskbar in the Notification Area. The two controls are for your power source and PCMCIA cards.

The power source deal changes back and forth from an image of an AC line cord and plug to a little battery image, depending on which power source you're using. So it just got a lot harder to run down your battery by accident because the line cord fell off. If you pause the mouse pointer over either version of this icon, you get a little popup text label that tells you how much juice is left in your battery charge, expressed as a percentage. Double-click the icon and you get an OK box (shown in Figure 6.13) with the same info and the option to enable or disable the low battery warning.

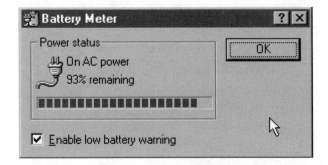

Figure 6.13   Click the Battery or Plug icon, and you get this handy dandy dialog

The Power control panel (pretty much a clone of the one you may have had in the old Windows) offers only a little bit more info. It opens Power Properties (shown in Figure 6.14), which lets you choose between various types of power-management support. If your system supports Advanced Power Management (a.k.a. APM), then definitely choose that. If you don't find a Power control panel, you either had something funky going on in your previous Windows installation or your system lacks true support for power management. You may need to check your BIOS setup screens (review your notebook's documentation) to enable power-management features. Power Properties also gives you the choice to show an option to Suspend your computer on the Start Menu. But, while being able to Suspend is nice and all, I find it very annoying that Microsoft chose to put this on the Start Menu, where it robs another launch list slot from the top of Start. Unless you use this feature a lot, I say uh-uh.

Look for the Power control panel, and if it's not there check your notebook's docs.

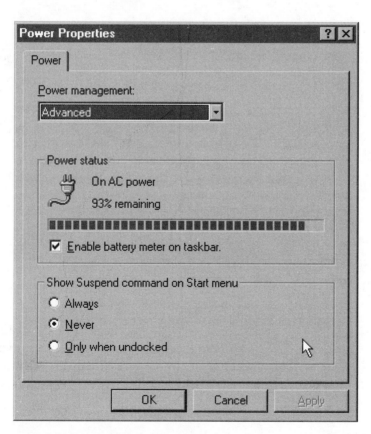

Figure 6.14 Power Properties: Choose Never or Only when undocked for Show Suspend

The PCMCIA Notification Area doohickey, when double-clicked, brings up the PCMCIA Properties, which doubles as the PCMCIA control panel. This thing, shown in Figure 6.15, is a bit of a kludge, though. PCMCIA is supposed to be Plug and Play, but I guess all the notebooks I've tried this with don't have PnP BIOSes because pretty much all the PCMCIA icon on Taskbar is good for is "stopping" a PC card before you remove it. You're supposed to be able to hot swap PC cards. But on my IBM ThinkPad, at any rate, it would seem that you're not supposed to. You can turn off the warning you'll get if you remove a card with the machine on, but what's the point?

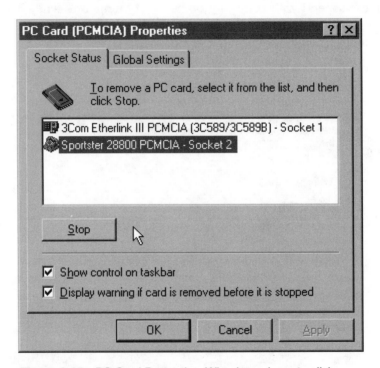

Figure 6.15   PC Card Properties: Why do we have to click Stop to remove a PC card?

This is all the more surprising, since when you insert a PC card in one of the slots, Win 95 not only detects it automatically, but also installs the driver for it, if it's needed. So are they Plug and Play or aren't they, Microsoft? Why do we need to "stop" them first before removing them?

TAKE CONTROL OF THE INTERFACE

> A journey is like marriage. The certain way to be wrong is to think you control it.
>
> John Steinbeck
> *Travels with Charley: In Search of America*, pt. 1, 1961

Face it, notebook screens are way too small. In a graphical environment such as Win 95, there's just not enough room to spread out and see what's going on. And the same applies to anyone using Win 95 with a 14-inch display on a desktop PC, since most of us have a hard time working in resolutions higher than 640×480 on monitors of that size. You can suffer through it—kicking and screaming—or you can give yourself an interface attitude adjustment that'll make it easier to work in the cramped space. Trust me—choose the second one. And try on some of this stuff for size.

Start for Notebooks

On a small screen, most of the apps you run are going to need to be maximized, that is, opened to their largest size, covering the entire desktop. Also, the number of launch-list items on the Start Menu is severely limited at 640×480 resolution (and only the latest, most expensive notebooks support higher resolutions on their integral screens). These two factors conspire to make working with a notebook screen kind of like staring through that pinhole in a piece of paper to see an eclipse.

The Start button

Here's the underlying problem. Since your apps cover everything, you can forget about desktop icons. There's not much point to them. (Wish Microsoft had realized this and done something about it.) Sure, you can minimize stuff to the Taskbar, but what a pain it is to do that manually every time you run Windows.

So why not put your desktop on the Taskbar automatically? The simplest tips are the best ones. And I'm borrowing this one from Chapter 5, "Customize It," because it fits so well here. Open your Startup folder. Right-click Start and select Open from the context menu. Double-click Programs to open it and then double-click Startup. Now right-click the Startup folder's background and choose New/Shortcut from the context menu. That launches a Shortcut-creating mini Wizard. In the Command line field, type

```
explorer/root,
```

That comma at the end is very important, so don't miss it. Press the Next button, type the word `Desktop` **to name the Shortcut, and press Finish. Next, right-click your new Shortcut, choose Properties, and then click the Shortcut tab. Press the down arrow at the end of the "Run" field and select Minimized. Last**

Desktop

step: Click the Change Icon button and scroll to the right until you find the desktop icon (it looks like the one in the margin art). Pick that icon and click OK a couple of times.

OK, so what d'ya got? Well, if you double-click the new Shortcut, you'll see a new Desktop task button on Taskbar. Click that button, and you've got a folder window showing *all* the desktop tools and Shortcuts on your desktop, something like Figure 6.16. So next time you find yourself minimizing a whole bunch of apps to get to your desktop icons, just click the Desktop task button instead. It's like having a miniature version of the desktop one click away, with no need to close anything.

Figure 6.16   Put your desktop on Taskbar

The way we've got it cranked up here, it'll load onto Taskbar every time you run Windows. Don't like it taking up space on Taskbar? Change the Run properties back to "Normal window" and plop the Shortcut on the Start Menu.

Drives & Folders

A lesser variation on the Desktop wand tip is to create a Shortcut for My Computer and put it on the Start Menu. I shave off a few steps on that one by placing Shortcuts for all the drives I access regularly in a newly created folder in \Windows\Start Menu called "Drives & Folders." That way I can open drives from Start, which is always visible as long as Taskbar is showing. And the tip looks like Figure 6.17 on my notebook. When you click on the Drives & Folders Start Menu item, you get a cascading submenu that lets you open any of its drives or folders just by highlighting and clicking. For a lot more stuff like this, including a variation on the "Drives & Folders" deal that I call "Super–My Computer," check out Chapter 5, "Customize It."

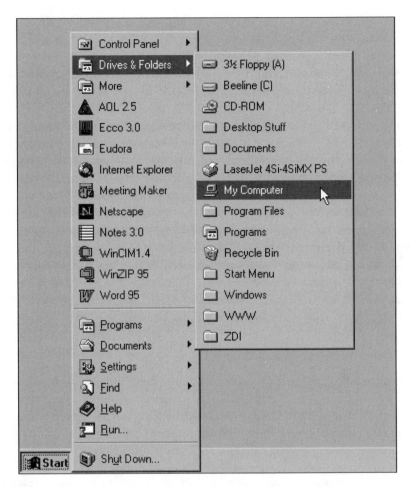

Figure 6.17 Strategies for small screens: Put drives in Start

Avoiding Start Menu Misery

Do you use a bigger external monitor at a higher resolution when you're not on the road? I do. The first thing that hits me over the head when I turn on the PC in my hotel room is that the Start Menu runs off the top of the screen, along with half my important launch-list items, including all my folders containing Shortcuts to drives and folders.

For some unknown reason, Microsoft chose to make folders default to the top of Start. Guess it's because folders default to the top left of a folder window (a good thing) when they're sorted. Anyway, I can't help you a lot with this. But what I've done is create a folder on Start's launch list called "More." When I travel, I stuff all the Shortcuts I'm less likely to use while I'm on the road in this folder. They're still available as a cascading submenu while I'm traveling, and when I get back to my blessed bigger screen, I can just pluck 'em back out onto Start.

See the User Profiles discussion in Chapter 5 (page 209) for a more elegant solution to this problem.

My Programs
folders are a
snake pit of
submenus.

Next thing to do is free up some vertical space that Start needs in order for you to add stuff. I don't know about you, but my Programs folders are a snake pit of tangled, multiple cascading submenus. It's already messy in there as it is. So, that's pretty much no-man's land for me. Maybe one day I'll clean it all out, but I'm not holding my breath. For me, it's better to customize the Start launch list. Fewer clicks, too.

So, take a usability study. What stuff have you added to the top of Start that you rarely launch? Be honest, is it really there just because you like the way the colors on the icons go together? Or is it an app you used a lot in the past, but that you really don't need any more? It struck me one day that I had three separate text editors mounted on Start. When I got to thinking about it, I realized that under Window 95, I rarely use any of them. The upshot was, I blew the directory for one of them away and removed another from the Start Menu (to somewhere I can't remember under Programs). That netted two more available entries on Start's launch list and some disk space. Other launch items, I realized, only go for a ride every fifth Sunday of the month. It's just that when I need 'em, I need 'em. And I don't want to go hunting. For stuff like that, you could create folders that hang off Start. But I move 'em to the Programs launch list.

Taskbar Too

Make Taskbar
behave or just
go away.

Of course, the single best thing you can do to give Start some headroom is to right-click the Taskbar, pull up its Properties page, and place a check mark beside "Show small icons in Start menu." With this setting happening, you have room for 14 top-of-Start launch list menu entries on most notebooks. If you're staring at the larger icons, you're seeing only seven launch entries before they move up off the top of the screen. No serious notebook user can afford the luxury of the large Start icons (unless he or she is visually impaired). Heck, I use small Start icons on my desktop PC, which has a very large display.

While you're in that Taskbar Properties screen, turn on the "Auto hide" and "Always on top" settings, too. I talked about this stuff in Chapter 3, "The Desktop Interface," but it bears a second look in light of your notebook needs. Auto hide makes Taskbar retract off the screen when you're not using it—out of the way of your application windows. When you need the Start button or a task button of a program or folder, just prod the lower edge of the screen with your mouse pointer. Taskbar will pop up to give you access. And, if you select Always on top, it'll do so *over* any and all open windows that may be in its space. If you open Start and launch something, or whenever you move the pointer away from Taskbar, it'll recede out of your way again. Microsoft really got this right. It won't bring back a huge wad of screen real estate or anything, but it's about the same amount you'd get by turning off your average business app's status bar—something I'm forever clicking on and off when I'm on the road. Now I don't have to think about it.

Say Bye-Bye, Taskbar

I think I've made it quite clear that I like Taskbar a lot. But I've run into some people who find it annoying for one reason or another. If you're one of those, there are several things you can do. Microsoft didn't provide an easy way for you to dump Taskbar altogether. And, for once, I think their OverLord mentality about such things is probably well placed. Why? Because there are times when the accessibility of Taskbar can save your bacon. But I'm getting off track. Here's how to lose Taskbar.

The simplest, though least elegant, solution is to just drag the top edge of the Taskbar down off the screen. I'm not kidding. You can effectively just move it out of the way by doing this. A very thin ribbon of it will still show along the bottom edge of your screen; that's so you can get it back. But for all intents and purposes, it's out of your face.

To lose Taskbar, just drag it off the screen.

The next best thing to dragging the Taskbar off the screen if you're trying to lose it, though, is a specific Taskbar settings configuration I call Option 1. Bring up the Taskbar's Properties (right-click the Taskbar and choose Properties from the context menu). Then, turn Always on top off and Auto hide on (see Figure 6.18). This really puts a crimp in its style. When you maximize an app or folder window to full-screen size, Taskbar will just be gone. In this mode, though, you'll have to both minimize full-screen apps *and* move your mouse pointer to the bottom edge of the screen in order to resurrect Taskbar.

Click this button to minimize an app.

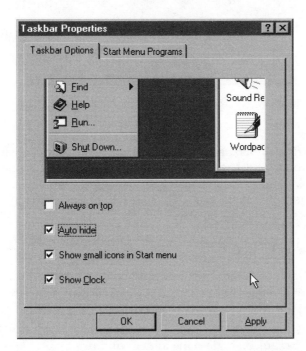

Figure 6.18   Taskbar Properties for notebooks: Option 1

Microsoft . . .
um, well . . .
deserves,
um . . . praise
on Taskbar.

That's why I prefer Taskbar settings Option 2, shown in Figure 6.19. I turn off both Always on top and Auto hide. It's the best way to work with maximized application windows because whenever you minimize them, Taskbar is right there waiting for your next move; you don't have to prod the bottom edge and wait for it to lazily reappear. Microsoft deserves praise for giving us a wide variety of options with a very simple set of interface controls.

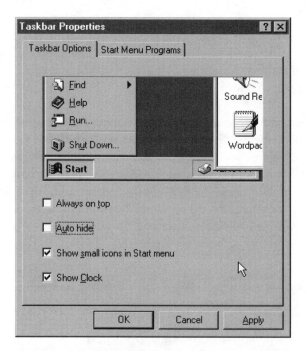

Figure 6.19   Taskbar Properties for notebooks: Option 2

When you work with Taskbar settings Option 2 and your open windows aren't maximized, you'll find that dialogs and folder windows sometimes cover Taskbar's task buttons. Rather than your moving the windows around, if you can see any part of Taskbar at all, just click it to bring Taskbar forward so that you have access to the task buttons.

Put the Squeeze on Folders

Squeeze folder
windows

Know what? Microsoft's Explorer is highly configurable. And you can make it work much better on a notebook screen if you keep an open mind. First thing to do is to forget all about two-paned Explorer windows (this stuff is explained in Chapter 4, "Files, Folders, Exploring"). They're cool, but they're big. And you can do just fine in the regular, single-pane folder windows.

I've already covered this in depth in Chapter 5, "Customize It," so I won't go into a big thing here. The main point is to work with folders as a single window whose frame remains in place when you double-click on a subfolder it contains. The contents of the subfolder just replace the contents of the first folder. You make this change from the View menu on any open folder window. Choose Options and, on the Folder tab, turn on the button next to "Browse folders by using a single window that changes as you open each folder" (see Figure 6.20). This setting affects all folder windows and takes effect immediately. To navigate upwards to the previous folder, turn on the folder toolbar under the View menu and click the Up One Level button. Or just hit the Backspace key. Double-click to open any folder you see to drill down your directory structure.

The main point to remember about working this way is that when you want to copy or move a file from one folder to another, you right-click it to bring up its context menu and then choose either Copy or Cut. Then navigate to the destination folder, right-click its background, and choose Paste from the context menu. This ability to copy or cut and paste whole files, multiple files, or even folders is one of the more powerful features of Windows 95.

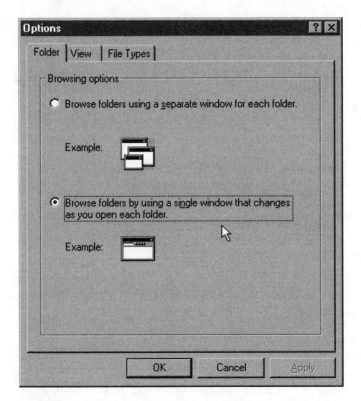

Figure 6.20 The browse a single window setting (Folder/View/Options)

See More Icons (and the Ones That Matter)

When it comes to notebook screens, smaller onscreen objects are better. So, another thing to do is stop displaying your folder icons in their default Large Icons view. It's another luxury you can't afford on a 10-inch or smaller diagonal screen. Chapter 4, "Files, Folders, Exploring" explains how to adjust icon views and sorts in folder windows. Check it out if you haven't tumbled to this yet and change your folders so that you're using Small Icons or List view. You'll be able to see a lot more file and folder objects on one screen.

There's more than one way to skin Microsoft, too. You can reduce the number of objects displayed in many folders (so that you can see more of the ones you need to see) by turning on the View/Options/View "Hide files of these types" option. This setting affects all your folders and takes effect immediately. And it makes invisible all the files with the extensions shown in the box (see Figure 6.21).

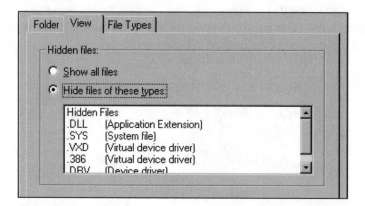

Figure 6.21   Click View/Options/View "Hide files of these types" in any folder

PACK UP YOUR KIT BAG

> The road to hell is paved with works-in-progress.
>
> Philip Roth
> *New York Times Book Review*, July 15, 1979

You're all dressed up, and you've got somewhere to go. So where's all that cool mobile computing stuff Win 95 is supposed to deliver?

Well, Casey Jones, here's the poop. There are six main mobile computing-type services this here OS has to offer. But you're not likely to trip over them or instantly intuit how to put 'em to work. I'm talking about Direct Cable Connection, Briefcase, Deferred Printing, Offline and Remote Mail, Microsoft Fax, and Dial-Up Networking (a.k.a. remote access).

The first two of these mobile computing features, Direct Cable Connection and Briefcase, are really aimed more at stuff you do *before* you leave the office, home, or wherever with your notebook. And, in particular, they're aimed at folks who have more than one PC in their lives. They focus on making it easier to keep data up to date between two PCs.

Direct Cable Connection

There's a company called Traveling Software that has made a venerable utility called LapLink for years and years. The darn thing works. Which is why a lot of long-time users have made it an essential part of their computer tool kits. Well, good old Microsoft decided that this was something that Win 95 needed, and, despite my affinity for the nice Traveling Software folk, I think MS was right. Windows 95 wouldn't really be an OS for notebook users if it didn't have the innate ability to connect to PCs quickly and inexpensively so that you could move files back and forth. It'd be like an auto mechanic who drove around without jumper cables in his or her car.

Direct Cable Connection lets you quickly and easily establish a direct serial or parallel cable link between two computers so they can share their resources. That's actually a leg up from the original LapLink utility, which offered basic file transfer only. (These days, LapLink does file transfer and a whole lot more.)

Direct Cable Connection

If one of the two computers in a Direct Cable Connection link is on a LAN, the other can direct connect and then access the LAN via the first PC. So you could, for example, link your notebook to the LAN via a simple parallel cable connected to your office desktop computer.

To establish a local connection between two computers, you need a serial null-modem standard (RS-232) cable or a special parallel cable. The serial connection is slower, but it can go down the hall, around the corner, get coffee, and then come back taking a detour through the basement. Parallel connections are faster but are limited in length to about 10 feet. For most people's purposes, the parallel route is the way to go. Unfortunately, latching onto a parallel cable that's designed to handle this isn't as easy as it should be. But, just give Inmac or your favorite computer hardware catalog company a call. They'll get you the right thing.

Serial is slower, but it can go down the hall and back.

Anyway, here are brief descriptions of the three types of parallel cables that Direct Cable Connection supports—pretty much as they appeared in the Microsoft tech doc I cribbed them from. The Microsoftese is in italics:

1. *A Standard, or Basic, 4-bit cable, including all LapLink and InterLink cables.* InterLink was an MS-DOS file transfer utility. A cable of this sort, "25-pin DIN male-to-male," is probably what you should tell the Inmac rep you want. Or you might be able to get one at Radio Shack. I use an old yellow-type LapLink cable.

ECP offers serious performance and other advantages over lesser parallel port technologies.

2. *An Extended Capabilities Port (ECP) cable. This type of cable works on a computer with an ECP-enabled parallel port (a.k.a. a high-speed parallel port). Of the three kinds of parallel cables, this type allows the fastest data transfer rate.* ECP is a high-speed bi-directional parallel port spec. Both PCs must support this, and the likelihood of both supporting it isn't great unless both were purchased recently. Of course, you can purchase a high-speed parallel port card for your desktop PC at any good computer store.

3. *Universal Cable Module (UCM) cable. This cable supports connecting different types of parallel ports.* You should also be able to find this device, which bridges the gap if your notebook has an older, slower parallel port.

Putting It Together

Before you set Direct Cable Connection in motion, you've gotta figure out a few things. This utility doesn't create equals among the two connected PCs. One of them is the *host PC*. In the old days, it would have been called the "slave." The other is called the *guest PC* (a.k.a. "client" or "master"). While Direct Cable Connection is working, you can't access shared resources on the guest PC from the host PC's keyboard. You can share resources on the host PC from the guest PC's keyboard.

For basic file transfer, you start by configuring the Dial-Up Adapter (see Figure 6.22) on both PCs. What the heck's that? Well, it's Microsoft's virtual interface card for network communications. This isn't really hardware on your system. But if you think of it as hardware, things will come a bit easier.

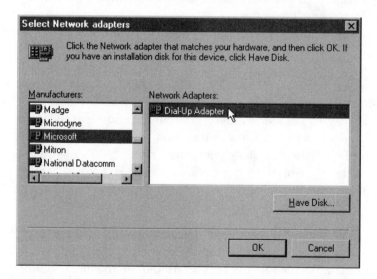

Figure 6.22 Add a Dial-Up Adapter under Network Properties

The Dial-Up Adapters on both machines also need to be running the same network protocols. And if you're connecting to an office PC, you'll want to set up the notebook with the same network stuff your office PC already has running. Among the more commonly used is IPX/SPX. But you may also find TCP/IP and Netbeui. If you don't find one of those on your office PC, install Microsoft's IPX/SPX on both machines.

You add both adapters and protocols on Network Properties. The fastest way to get there is to right-click Network Neighborhood and then choose Properties from the context menu. If you don't see Network Neighborhood on your desktop, open the Control Panel (Start/Settings/Control Panel) and double-click the Network icon. The dialog is exactly the same whichever route you choose.

To add a Dial-Up Adapter, click the Add button on Network Properties. Then choose the Adapter button on the Select Network Component Type dialog. Scroll to and click the Microsoft folder and *voila*, "Dial-Up Adapter" will appear as an installable option in the window on the right. Double-click it. Repeat the steps to install a network protocol, opting for Protocol on the Select Network Component Screen (see Figure 6.23), looking again in the Microsoft folder. This stuff configures automatically most of the time. For more information about configuring stuff on Network Properties, see Chapter 8, "Connections."

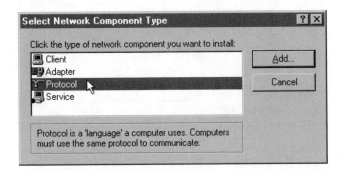

Figure 6.23   Install a network protocol under Network Properties

You also have to turn on sharing on the host PC to make Direct Cable Connection work. Look for either the Microsoft or Novell File and Print Sharing line at the bottom of the Network Properties scroll box (the manufacturer name has to match the manufacturer of your network protocol on both machines). If it's not there, click the File and Print Sharing button on Network Properties. Your next step is to close Network Properties. Win 95 will ask if it's OK to restart, but tell it to hold off.

Your last step is to enable sharing of specific devices on the host PC. To do that, open My Computer and right-click on the drive or drives in turn that you'd like to

Sharing drives with yourself

give your notebook access to. Click the Sharing item on the context menu. Each shared device gets a name you supply in the top field. You can share a specific file or folder or an entire drive on your host PC. And you'll be able to specify password protection and a level of access: Read-Only with or without a password, Full access with or without a password, or both options with two different passwords.

Since you're sharing with yourself, you'll probably want to choose Full access. And it probably makes sense to do this at the root level of the drive (see Figure 6.24). But be warned: If your office PC is on a network, you may also be turning on share rights to others on that network. It definitely makes sense to use a password in that setting, and to change it every so often.

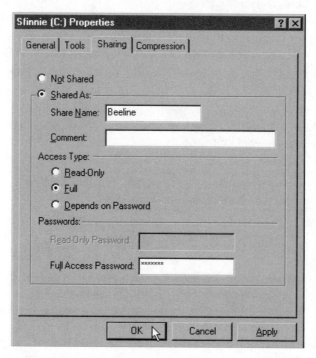

Figure 6.24   Sharing a hard drive with full access and password protection

That's everything you need to do to enable file transfer between the cable-connected PCs. If you're looking to give the guest PC full network access through the host PC, there's an extra step. Back on the Network Properties screen, you'll need to add another network protocol: Microsoft's Netbeui (shown in Figure 6.25). Do this on both machines in addition to whatever protocols you may have already added or found installed on the networked PC. If you run into trouble, double-check to make sure Netbeui is bound to the Dial-Up Adapter on both machines. When it is, you'll see a check mark beside the Netbeui line on the Bindings tab of the Dial-Up Adapter.

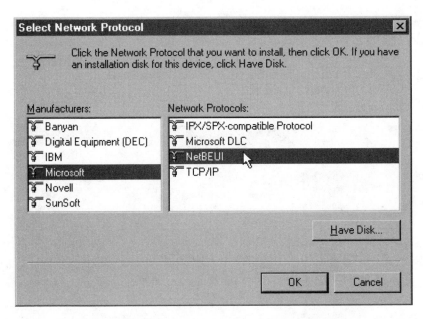

Figure 6.25   Installing Microsoft's Netbeui network protocol

Go Direct

Here are the basic steps to set this deal in motion:

1. Connect both computers with the proper parallel or serial cable.

2. Start with the host PC. Launch the Direct Cable Connection Wizard under Start/Programs/Accessories.

   Can't find Direct Cable Connection? Maybe you didn't install it? Double-click Add/Remove Programs in the Control Panel, click the Windows Setup tab, and insert your Win 95 disc. Click the communications line in the "Components" list and then hit the Details button. Place a check mark beside the Direct Cable Connection entry and then click OK. See Figure 6.26.

3. Click the Host option.

4. Specify the port to which the cable is connected on the host computer.

5. The Wizard asks if you want to use password protection. A password effectively blocks someone else from using Direct Cable Connection on your PC once you've set it up. Using one is advisable if your host PC is on a company network. Once that's done, the host gives you a status box saying it's waiting for the guest to connect.

6. Repeat the procedure on the guest PC, choosing Guest instead of Host. After you finish the guest's configuration process, the two machines will attempt to connect. If things aren't working at this point, choose Help from the Start

Repeat the steps for the guest PC, choosing "Guest" instead.

menu, click the Index tab, and type "Troubleshooting Direct Cable Connection." That'll bring up the useful Direct Cable Connection Troubleshooter. I'll tell you right now that there's an equal likelihood that your problem is with the cable you're using as with your network protocols.

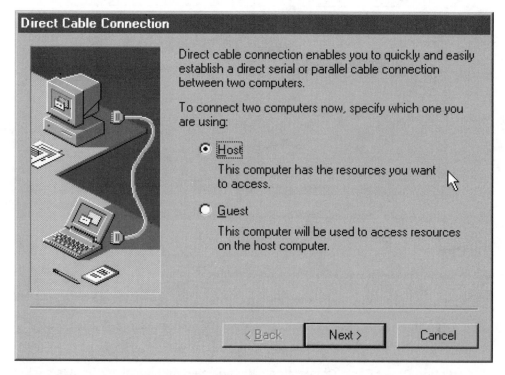

Figure 6.26   Running the Direct Cable Connection Wizard on the Host PC

If you get an error message informing you that the port is in use by another device while you are trying to configure parallel Direct Cable Connection, check the Printers folder in My Computer. If your system is on a network, you may be capturing a network printer to a local port.

Check the Properties of each printer icon you find in the Printers folder in My Computer. Under their details tabs, make sure they're capturing an LPT port number that does *not* actually exist on your PC. Most PCs have an LPT1 port. Many also have an LPT2. It's a rare PC indeed that has an LPT3 port. Network printers should be captured to ports that aren't actually present on the PC. *Note:* Under Windows 95, printers don't even have to be captured to a port unless your app software requires it.

Using It

Once you've successfully set up Direct Cable Connection, the next time you run the Wizard to connect your computer in this fashion, it will default to your last connection settings. If you want to change from host to guest on a particular computer or change ports, just make those changes in the Wizard.

The Direct Cable Connection status box isn't your average dumb message box (see Figure 6.27). In the early going, when you're first setting up Direct Cable Connection, this box tells you what's going on. And if you run into trouble, it's about the only thing you've got to help you figure out why. It's also the key in the ignition that tells you that Direct Cable Connection is working, once it is. It'll show up on both machines the whole time the connection is working, although you can minimize it to Taskbar to get it out of the way.

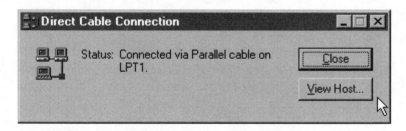

Figure 6.27   The Direct Cable Connection guest status box

Note the View Host button in Figure 6.27. If you close the Host folder on your guest PC but haven't shut down the Direct Cable Connection, you can re-open the folder by clicking the View Host button. This is particularly useful if you're working in file-transfer mode without Netbeui installed, since it's the only way to re-open a closed host-folder window.

I've found Direct Cable Connection to be a bit temperamental to get going. Sometimes you have to fidget with it a bit. But once it's running, it's a real joy. It's faster than it has a right to be, even with a standard parallel cable. Moreover, the interface is almost completely consistent with standard network access under Windows 95 when you've got full network protocols in motion. Here's how to find your way around.

Direct Cable Connection is a bit temperamental.

Once the PCs are connected, a folder will open on the guest PC that is effectively a window on the host PC (see Figure 6.28). By default, it shows all the host's *local* shared devices and resources for which you specifically enabled sharing. If you're not seeing something you expect to see, it's probably because you forgot to turn on sharing from the object's context menu. You can even access a shared printer connected to the host PC this way. If you don't have full network access

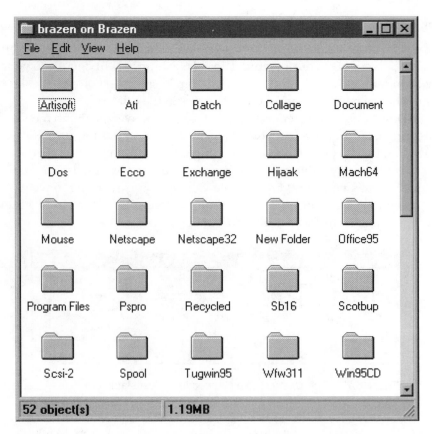

Figure 6.28 The shared local resources on host PC "Brazen" as seen on a guest

or there's no network involved with your Direct Cable Connection, this is pretty much the end of the story.

With full network access in place, you get, well, what looks for all the world like normal Windows 95 network access (when it's working right). Open the guest's Network Neighborhood (a good thing to do right off in order to force the necessary connections), and you'll see all the available network resources that the host PC sees. In Figure 6.29, SFinnie is the guest PC; Brazen is the host PC; and Blister and Entire Network are resources that the guest is accessing through the host via Direct Cable Connection. Pretty cool.

Briefcase

Briefcase

If ever there was a thing that needed explaining, it's Briefcase. But before I start on it, back to my favorite annoyance with Windows 95: The Cute Name Squad had at it again with the default desktop Briefcase, which automatically receives

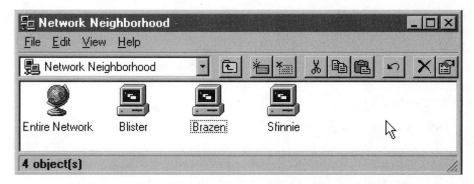

Figure 6.29   Look Ma, no network card; network-wide access via parallel cable

the name "My Briefcase." You'll find that this one, like My Computer, is easily re-named. I think that's Microsoft's point, by the way. Give it such a sappy name that it'll almost certainly occur to you to rename it.

Anyway, add a name change to your list of early things to do after installing this sucker, since it starts out living on your desktop. Or just delete it if you're not ready to use it; it's easy to add a new Briefcase later. Just choose New/Briefcase from the context menu for the background of any open folder or the desktop. But, at the very least, change its label to "Briefcase." And just because it appears first on your desktop doesn't mean it has to live there. The Briefcase is one object that can be safely and easily tucked away into any old folder.

I move it into a folder I create in my Windows folder called "Desktop Stuff." Some applications needlessly plop Shortcuts to readme files on your desktop (which is Win 95 *déclassé*, by the way). Any old thing I might want to look at later goes into Desktop Stuff, along with the Briefcase. Or you can create multiple Briefcases, if you want. This deal is pretty flexible.

> **Can't find Briefcase anywhere? Maybe you didn't install it. Guess what: On its own, Briefcase requires no extra space on your hard drive. Double-click Add/Remove Programs in the Control Panel, choose Windows Setup, and in-sert your disc or disk. You'll find Briefcase under Accessories.**

In most of the pre-release versions of Win 95, the Briefcase gewgaw was so painfully slow and so buggy that most of us twice-bitten press folk didn't even bother with it. In the later betas, things improved dramatically. And by the time Win 95 shipped, we were beginning to see Briefcase's possibilities.

What's it do? Briefcase simplifies the process of synchronizing updates to data files made by folks who use more than one PC. And, basically, it's a drag-and-drop file and folder storage (but not compression) archive with some built-in smarts that leverage Win 95's ability to keep track of changes to files by date and

Briefcase synchronizes files with the same name on two PCs.

time stamp. Because Windows 95 always knows the exact last-revision time of any file, the Briefcase always knows which of two files with the same filename is the newer version. So it can sort through a big wad of files and then report back to you requesting a plan of action about files that differ.

How to Use Briefcase

This tool was designed primarily to let you pass files from a desktop PC to your notebook's Briefcase folder in order to let you work with them while on the road—directly out of the Briefcase. Once back from your trip, you reconnect the two computers and direct Briefcase to run a comparison between the files it contains and the originals on your desktop PC.

Once you get it going, the process is ongoing. So next time you leave the office, you take the same step as when you came back: Tell Briefcase to update the files in your portable's Briefcase, which may now be out of date with the more current versions on your desktop PC. As long as you work with only one PC at a time, Briefcase's operations are simple, straightforward, and very effective.

Creating synchronized files and folders is pretty easy, too. Either the two PCs must be connected by a network or you can use Direct Cable Connection. In fact, Direct Cable Connection and the Briefcase were designed to work together. Here's how to get started:

1. Say you're moving from your desktop PC to your notebook first. It's best, if you can, to localize files being "briefcased" (what a goof) into one folder on your desktop PC. Sometimes that isn't possible though, and it's OK. Choose a copy method (drag and drop, cut and paste) for copying the files from your desktop PC into the Briefcase on your notebook PC via the network or Direct Cable Connection.

2. Disconnect your notebook and hit the road. Work on the synchronized files all you want, using your apps to load them from the Briefcase. Don't move them out of the Briefcase.

3. When you return, reconnect the two computers and then double-click the Briefcase icon (or whatever you've named it) on your notebook. From the Briefcase menu, click Update All. Or click the files and/or folders you want to update and choose Update Selection instead.

4. When Briefcase compares files, it does exception processing. On some file comparisons, it will ask for your input. On others, it can make decisions on its own. When it asks for your input, you get a dialog that shows exception files. When you click on one of them (they're always on the left side of the Update Briefcase screen, as shown in Figure 6.30), you have context-sensitive options, such as replace in one direction, or another, or skip the file.

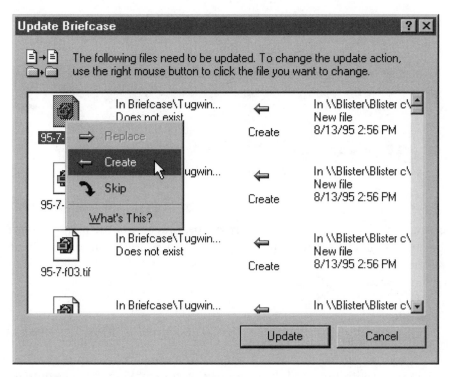

Figure 6.30 The Update Briefcase exception-processing screen

**That last step is one of the more annoying aspects of Briefcase, in part be-
cause the information it provides about the two versions of each file isn't easy
to scan and it isn't very complete. It's easy to become confused, too, about
which direction the replace is going in, since the only good identifier about
which drive the files are on is a popup label that's obscured when you call
up the context menu to make your action selection. There are no good
workarounds that I can see. I guess we'll just have to wait for Windows 97 (or
whatever) for an interface improvement.**

After you're done with the exception-processing phase, click the Update button. Briefcase will process the exceptions. When you're working on the files with
only one PC at a time and updating Briefcase whenever you switch to the other
PC, this is very straightforward. And in that case, you don't have to give much
thought to the Updating Briefcase screen (shown in Figure 6.31). When you click
Update, Briefcase just makes all the replaces and copies needed to synchronize
the files on two machines. (Can you hear the "but" coming?)

A quick summary of things Briefcase can do. You can add files to a Briefcase
at any time. You can have multiple synched sets in any one Briefcase. It lets you

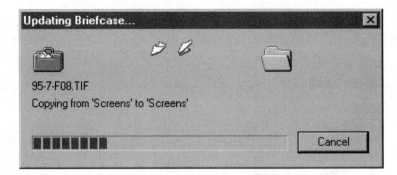

Figure 6.31 Briefcase making the final replaces and copies

check the synchronization status of any file or folder from the properties screen on the object's context menu. You can update files and folders individually or update everything in a Briefcase. You can split files away from the Briefcase to maintain them as separate entities.

A Few Kinks

This isn't Microsoft's fault (for once, yuck). It's been the bane of all file-synchronization utilities since the category first appeared. Things are fine and dandy working with time and date stamps if you're making changes only to one set of files at a time—working with your PCs one at a time and updating your files before you switch to working with them on the other PC. But what if you forget this step? What if you forget to bring your notebook to work one day? If you make changes to two instances of a file, one set of those changes is going to have a newer time and date stamp than the other. And you're going to wind up losing the changes with the older stamp, even though they might be more important revisions. In other words, what if you want this change here *and* that change there?

Ready for some hype? Here's a quote from a Microsoft technical document:

> Windows 95 provides a set of OLE interfaces that allow applications to bind reconciliation handlers to it, track the contents of Briefcase, and define the outcome of any reconciliation on a class-by-class basis. For example, when both the file in Briefcase and its synchronized copy outside have changed, Windows 95 calls the appropriate reconciliation handler to merge the two files. This could be handy when several users are simultaneously updating one large document.

Um, whaa? Translation, please.

Translation, please: When Briefcase detects that files on both sides of a comparison have changed, Windows calls the application that created them to merge their differences. But let's face it, no two applications work the same way to resolve these kinds of differences, so your mileage may vary—like, a lot. Moreover, your apps will have to be Windows 95 apps for this to work properly. I caution strongly against purposely taking advantage of the "reconciliation handler." It might get you in trouble. The better course is to religiously work with one set of Briefcase files at a time.

For the record, OLE stands for Object Linking and Embedding. A lot of the more-cool features working underneath Windows 95 are accomplished with this fairly complex and still-evolving specification. It allows programs and the operating system to talk to one another and even pass data back and forth following an established set of rules. It's also the stuff that enables things like Document Scraps and other neat functions. From my basic testing of this Briefcase feature: Good try, Microsoft. Good thinking. I'm glad you're on the case, but please don't rest on your laurels.

> **It's really easy to mess up Briefcase. Just change the share name of one of the PCs. Even if you change the share name from "Blister_C" to "Blister," for example, there's no way I've been able to find to alter the association Briefcase makes with the path of the original file. (Server names start with a double backslash: \\.) Only thing you can do is change the share name back to the way it was when you originally created the synchronization. Then Update All and split and kill the files in the Briefcase. Change the share name back and recopy the files to create a new synchronization link. There should be a better way! This one can really throw you, too.**

Win 95's support of OLE 2.0 enables a long list of cool functions in both the OS and apps.

What If You Can't Network the Two PCs?

If you can't network the two PCs, do it with a floppy. Since Briefcase does not compress files, you'll run out of room fast, but you can make more than one pass. Insert a floppy disk in the computer you're using. Copy any files or folders you want to work on to Briefcase. Move Briefcase to the floppy disk. Take the floppy disk to a portable or other computer. Move the Briefcase to that PC's hard drive and work on the files from the Briefcase.

When you return to the office, insert the floppy disk containing Briefcase in the computer that has the original files. Double-click the Briefcase icon. Click the files you want to update and click the Briefcase menu. From the menu, click Update All or Update Selection.

> **Plug and Play BIOS People Rejoice: If you are using a PnP BIOS docking station, Briefcase will automatically update files when you dock your portable computer.**

PRINT, MAIL, AND FAX—OUT AND ABOUT

Travel is glamorous only in retrospect.

Paul Theroux
Quoted in *The Observer*, London, October 7, 1979

The mobile computing features—Deferred Printing, Offline and Remote Mail, and Microsoft Fax—are aimed at making your life a lot easier on the plane, in the taxi, in your hotel room, at the branch office, or at the cottage by the lake. Wherever you are that doesn't have stuff you normally have access to when you are in your office.

Deferred Printing effectively curtails the direct connection of your printer services without disabling print functionality. So you can continue to print documents just as you would back in the office. But instead of your actually trying to send the documents out of the port at 35,000 feet (trust me, infrared isn't going to help), Win 95's Deferred Printing feature prepares the document so that it will print properly to your default printer (when you get back at the office) and spools off the print job to await your return and blessed reconnection.

The idea is to print to a printer that's usually connected but just isn't connected now. If you try to set this up for a printer that actually is connected, Win 95's context-sensitive popup menus will take over and the proper setting option won't be available; so wait until you're on the plane to set it up. Just open My Computer and double-click the Printers folder. Locate your default printer. If there's more than one printer icon showing and you're not sure which is the default, right-click on each in turn, looking for the one whose context menu has a check mark beside the "Set as Default" line. When you find it, click its Work Offline menu item (shown in Figure 6.32). Until you change this back, you'll be printing into the virtual void of your hard drive, rather than to your printer port. And printing doesn't get any faster than that.

If you use a docking station, Deferred Printing is already set up. Win 95 automatically resets printers connected to the dock, or via the network through the dock, to work off- line whenever you remove the computer. Pretty neat.

If Deferred Printing doesn't work, chances are spooling is turned off on your default printer's properties screen. To turn it back on, choose Properties from the printer's context menu, click the Details tab, and then click the Spool Settings button. Make sure the "Spool print jobs so program finishes printing faster" button is clicked on (shown in Figure 6.33). If that's not the problem, make sure your application is aimed at the default printer and try running ScanDisk, which you'll find on the Start/Programs/Accessories/System Tools menu.

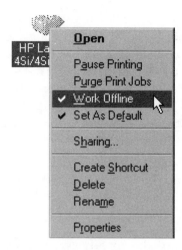

Figure 6.32   Printer icon context menu showing Work Offline selected

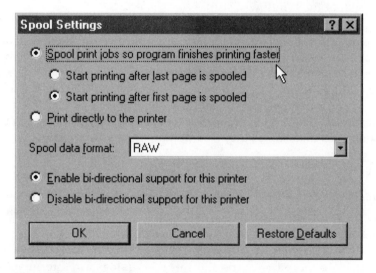

Figure 6.33   Checking to ensure print-job spooling is
switched on

Offline and Remote Mail

The mail program behind the Inbox, Microsoft Exchange, also works offline by
letting you compose and "send" mail offline, that is, while you're not connected
to a network or dialed into an online service. So, when you're on the go, you can,
for example, create new Microsoft Network email messages and then have your
messages sent automatically when you dial in later on. In the meantime, Exchange queues your messages in its Outbox.

Inbox

Unless your company has either an MS Mail or Win 95 Dial-Up Server, skip Remote Mail in all forms.

There's a whole separate deal, called Remote Mail, that I really don't advise you do. This is the idea that you could dial up your Exchange mailbox while on the road to access mail on your office network from the road. If your company uses Microsoft Mail as its internal mail package or if it sets up a Windows 95 Dial-Up Server, well then, it's worth taking a close look at. But for all the rest of us, the requirement that we install a Microsoft Workgroup Post Office on our PCs to facilitate Remote Mail is just too steep a price to pay. Microsoft does a lot of things well. More things than most companies have a right to claim. But, while I haven't had the chance to test the latest Microsoft Mail in a company-wide environment, I do have enough experience with this product line to personally believe that you should steer clear of managing your own MS Mail Post Office, even if it is designed for small workgroup use. Some things are best left to administrators. This is one of them. Besides, it takes up disk space.

In case you decide not to take my advice, I'll at least give you the starting point: You need to add the Microsoft Mail Services option under the Microsoft Exchange portion of the Windows Setup.

Need a print of something for later reference, but you're nowhere near a printer since you're stuck in a hotel room after business hours? Or maybe you're on an airplane (equipped with airphones that have data line receptacles)? Use Win 95's fax features to fax a print to yourself at your hotel's fax machine. It'll be handed to you when you get to the desk—and on plain paper if the hotel is worth its salt. Or fax-print hardcopies of email or other documents to your office or home fax machine so they'll be waiting when you get back.

Fax Attacks

Mail and Fax

As long as we're getting into a fax groove, let's check out Microsoft Fax. Some of the fax features I'm taking a peek at aren't strictly for the road, but you'll forgive me that digression, right?

Setup for this puppy is hardly what I'd call a breeze. There're bits and pieces of it here, there, everywhere. And the settings dialogs are intermixed with the Mail dialogs, that giant bundle of interface joy Microsoft coded and recoded and streamlined and nearly killed off and then resurrected in an ongoing battle throughout the beta cycle. The Mail features—known as Exchange, Mail, and In-box (depending on the humidity level that day in Redmond and what kind of moon rose the preceding evening) are convoluted to say the least. All I gotta say is, you should have seen it before they "fixed" it.

Anyway, here's how to jump-start Microsoft Fax. And, give this a shot *before* you hit the road, please, because you may need your Win 95 Setup disc or disks. If you didn't install Microsoft Fax, do that. Open the Control Panel, double-click the Add/Remove Programs icon, and click the Windows Setup tab. You'll find

Microsoft Fax in there. You also need to install Microsoft Exchange to support the fax services (but you don't need, and shouldn't install, the MS Mail Services option under Microsoft Exchange).

Sometimes you just have to gun it. And with Fax, if it's not set up right, you'll find out soon enough. The Compose New Fax icon on the Start/Programs/Accessories/Fax menu. Go this route. But know that at the end, this Wizard pretty much tries to send a fax, without giving you any option to cancel (although you can back out of it). Don't ask me why. So, you'll need a destination fax number to send to. And if you run into problems, you can go ahead and send it. Then open Inbox and delete the message from the Outbox folder.

Compose New Fax

Compose New Fax sets up your Fax Properties, if they haven't been set up previously. It also takes you by the hand and leads you through the process of creating a recipient address, creating a cover page, and addressing and writing your message. Next to Compose New Fax on the Start/Programs/ Accessories/ Fax menu, you'll find a menu item for Cover Page Editor and Request a Fax. There are four available cover page templates; you can edit them or create new ones with Cover Page Editor. Request a Fax is nifty for accessing fax documents that companies provide as a service to customers.

Cover Page Editor

Request a Fax

If you get error messages (and there are several possible ones), what usually solves the problem is removing and recreating Personal Folders (shown in Figure 6.34). Don't do this if you've been using the Inbox for other things, like email on

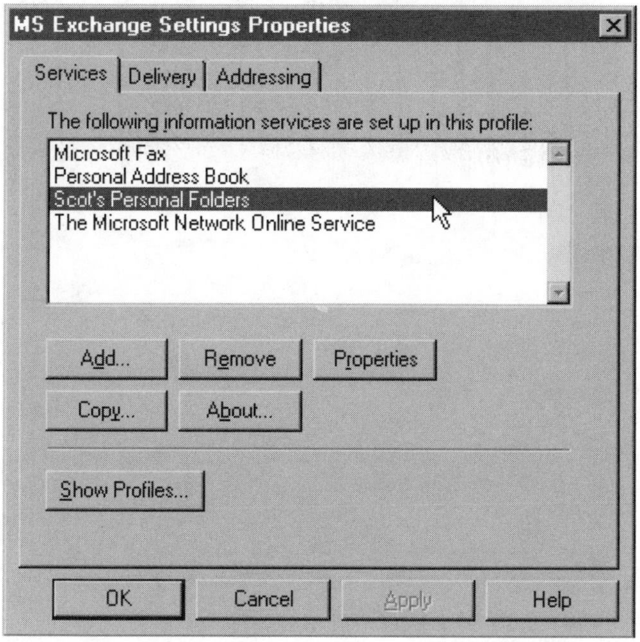

Figure 6.34 Inbox Properties, where the deed is done

the Microsoft Network. You'll lose stuff you probably wanted to save. But chances are, Windows 95 lost track of your Personal Folders, which stores messages and settings. You'll know this file by its extension: .PST. Instead of deleting your existing Personal Folders in that case, just add a new one. And if that gets you out of difficulty, you can then decide whether to delete the pre-existing Personal Folders.

To delete and/or create Personal Folders, either right-click the Inbox icon on your desktop and choose Properties or open Control Panel and double-click the Mail and Fax icon. You get the same screen either way. And either way, you're bringing up the Exchange or Inbox Properties. Since fax really is a form of email, this makes sense. It's just that these controls are somewhat complicated, and there are some circuitous settings screens buried inside that you should avoid.

To delete your Personal Folders, click on the line item that probably reads "Personal Folders" and then click the Remove button. To add Personal Folders, click the Add button, choose Personal Folders, and follow the directions. Give your Personal Folders file (the one ending in .PST) a name you can remember. Then give it a long name that'll show up in the dialogs. It's very simple. About the only option to ponder is whether you want encryption. The default is Compressable Encryption (see Figure 6.35). If this is a home PC, you probably don't need encryption. But it can't hurt. I recommend choosing this option if you're in doubt.

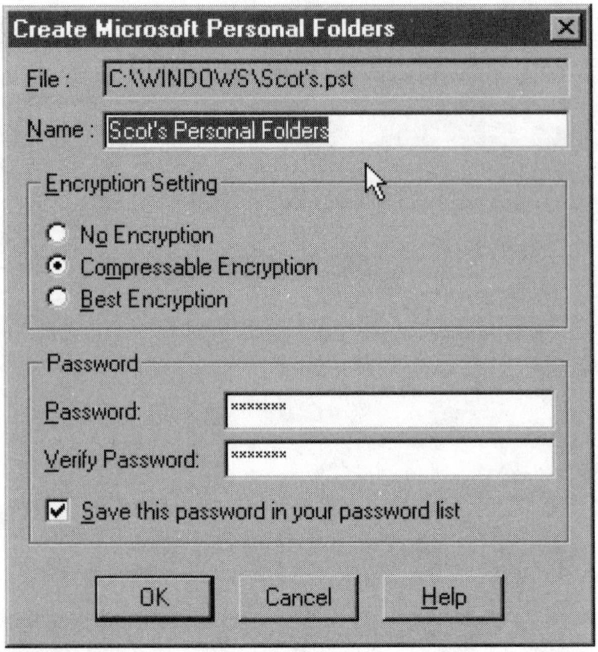

Figure 6.35   Adding new personal folders; Compressable Encryption is the default

Want the Internet mail component for Exchange but don't want to shell out for Microsoft Plus? Go here on the World Wide Web to get the Internet Jumpstart Kit:

```
http://www.windows.microsoft.com/windows/software
/iexplorer.htm
```

By downloading the Internet Jumpstart Kit, which the Microsoft site also lumps together under the name of the Internet Explorer, you'll get Microsoft's Internet Setup Wizard and its excellent 32-bit Web browser. For free. (By the way, you also get this Internet stuff and other things in Microsoft Plus!, the roughly $40 add-on for Windows 95.) To install the CompuServe mail module, get it from the `\Drivers\Other\Exchange\Compusrv` **folder on your Win 95 CD. America Online is also reportedly working on an Exchange mail driver, as are a long list of other online services.**

If you run into a problem, the properties for Microsoft Fax aren't really likely to be the culprit. To find out, open them by clicking "Microsoft Fax" on Inbox Properties and then clicking the Properties button (see Figure 6.36). If you

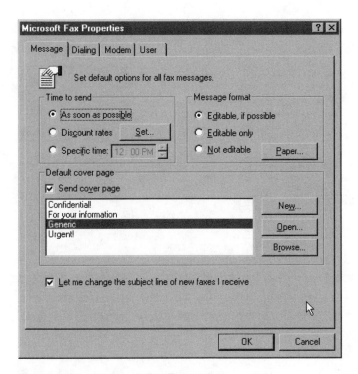

Figure 6.36 Microsoft Fax Properties

haven't found anything wrong so far, I suggest the Fax Troubleshooters. To get to them, open the Inbox, open the Help menu, choose Microsoft Fax Help Topics, and double-click the "Troubleshooting" booklet. Start with the "I can't send or receive faxes" troubleshooter.

Get the Fax

Microsoft Fax can send and receive email attachments.

One of the better features of Microsoft Fax, besides its integration into the OS, is its ability to fax email attachments. This works only if both the sender and recipient are PCs running Win 95's Microsoft Fax or similar software that supports Microsoft Fax. But, it's way cool if you do, and pretty fast.

To receive a fax via your Win 95 PC, open Inbox. Choose Tools/Microsoft Fax Tools/Options. Then click the Modem tab followed by the Properties button. On this page (see Figure 6.37), you'll find the "Answer mode" square in the upper left. Choose the "Answer after [selector for number of] rings" button and choose a number of rings. If this is a voice line, too, keep in mind that Fax commandeers incoming calls, so setting the number of rings higher might be helpful. Anyway, click OK a coupla times, and your PC will be ready to receive a fax and will pick up automatically on the next call (fax or not) unless you pick up first.

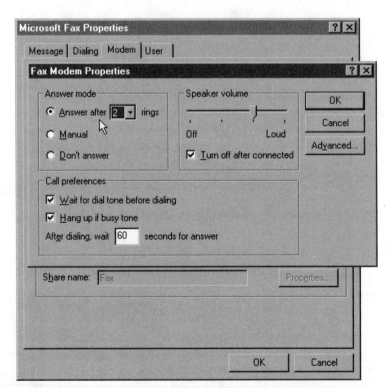

Figure 6.37 Turning on automatic fax answering to receive faxes

By turning on the "Answer after . . . rings" deal, you activate your modem as a fax modem. To deactivate it, just exit Inbox. Or, you can go back to the Modem tab and its Properties button and change the Answer mode to "Don't answer." There's also a third option in the Answer mode square: "Manual." In this mode, you leave Inbox loaded and ready to receive messages, but you're primarily using your phone as a voice line. Whenever there's an incoming call, a message box pops up giving you the option to answer it as a fax. It's sorta the best of both worlds.

Notification Area Fax Mode icon

Whenever Inbox is open and Fax is ready to send or receive, you'll see a small icon of a fax machine in Taskbar's Notification Area. By clicking the pretty little picture, you'll call up a status box that indicates the answer mode. It's the same box that pops up in Manual answer mode whenever there's an incoming call.

Win 95 can automatically receive faxes in background, if you have it set to do so. Exchange must be running, and "Answer after" must be turned on. When it receives a message, the Notification Area lets you know you've got mail by displaying a shining postal letter icon. Click it to open your Inbox and receive the message.

Received Mail icon (on right)

Using Fax with Apps

You can use Microsoft Fax to send pages directly from documents inside applications, such as a word processor or spreadsheet. Of course, this ability of Fax isn't going to hit you over the head with its obviousness. Microsoft is supposed to do all these things right, since it sits on both sides of the fence, so Winword 7.0 has a File/Send email module. If your apps don't have a Send command, then you'll have to make do by switching your default printer to the "Fax" printer that Microsoft Fax installs in order to get the same job done. That's less convenient by a lot because you're going to be switching your default printer back and forth. But, hey, I'm the King of Lazy.

To send a fax from a program using its Send command, follow these steps. Open the document you want to send. On the File menu, click Send. Older apps have a Fax Addressing tool that you use at that point. Word 7.0 opens a special full-featured message editor. Your document will appear as an attachment, though. If you want to print to yourself at your hotel, like I was talking about earlier, or if your recipient has a conventional fax machine, just click the Word document attachment icon to select it and press the Delete key. The fastest route to print the file is to have selected and copied the text before you choose the Send command. Then you can just paste it into the new message and hit the Send button on the toolbar. When you work this way, your formatting will by and large be preserved. Win 95 will even send colors.

To send a fax from a program by using the Print command, which also preserves most of your formatting (depending on the recipient's fax capabilities), open the document you want to send. On the program's File menu, click Print. Set up your printer for Microsoft Fax and then print the document.

ROAD CALL

We know what happens to people who stay in the middle of the road. They get run over.

Aneurin Bevan
Quoted in *The Observer*, London, December 9, 1935

Dial-Up
Networking

More power to you if you (and your network administrator) can make Dial-Up Networking work a *lot* better than I've been able to using the personal Dial-Up Server feature installed by the Microsoft Plus! add-on for Windows 95. From my perspective, after only limited testing (since I don't currently have access to a dedicated, company-wide Dial-Up Networking server), this feature is a bit of a boondoggle.

If they worked well, Win 95's remote-access client connected to Plus's Personal Server software would be cool.

If it did work well, and at decent speeds, Win 95's built-in Dial-Up Networking (a.k.a. remote access) client features would let you dial in to your Microsoft Plus-enhanced office PC from a notebook PC in your hotel room and access not only its local resources, but also your office network. Take it a step further, and you would be dialing in not to your personal office machine but to your company's dedicated Dial-Up Networking server. My recommendation: Get your company to either go that latter route, skip the idea, or use someone else's technology. Microsoft Plus's Personal Server host feature is a bear to configure, and once you get it going properly, it's slow as molasses.

Worse, Plus's Personal Server connection gets slower and slower. I found that while I could dial-up network two PCs via a phone line at 28.8 kbps, after a few minutes the connection rate began to step down, eventually to 14.4 and sometimes even slower. Now, that could be my particular connection, modems, and lots of other things. But I encountered the same problem over and over again. Except for experiencing the slow down, you wouldn't know it was happening by looking at the Dial-Up Networking status box on the client PC. It continuously reports the first connection rate the two PCs negotiated. Often as not I was staring at a Windows 95 status box that said 28.8, but the actual connection rate, as reported by my LCD-equipped modem, had stepped down through 19.2 to 14.4.

To make Dial-Up Networking work (personal or enterprise-wide) you have to use a complicated set of networking and connection protocols. According to a Microsoft technical document, Windows 95 supports Dial-Up Networking *connections* only via SLIP (Serial Line Internet Protocol). Microsoft Plus installs that for you, but if you're setting up only the client end of this without Plus, you can install SLIP support from the Windows 95 CD. (Use the Control Panel's Add/Remove Programs tool, click Windows Setup, and click Have Disk. Then use the Browse button to navigate the folders on your installation CD to the `\Admin\Apptools\Dscript` folder. (There's a readme file in the `\Admin\Apptools\Slip` folder.)

It's supposedly possible to use Novell NetWare networking protocols for Dial-Up Networking (though you can't be using real-mode DOS drivers for NetWare), but I found that the only way I could get it to work was to install Microsoft's IPX/SPX and Netbeui protocols. You set these up as described in the Direct Cable Connection stuff I covered earlier in this chapter. If you install Microsoft Plus on both machines, it takes care of all this for you.

Microsoft Plus takes care of a lot of Dial-Up Networking configuration automatically.

Some tips when you encounter problems. File and printer sharing for the protocols you're using must be installed, turned on, and bound to the IPX/SPX and Netbeui protocols on the Dial-Up Adapter entries on the host PC. Dial-Up Networking prefers TCP/IP. If your host PC is on network TCP/IP, you'll want to configure this protocol on the client, too. User names, password protection, and software compression are all areas that can trip you up. Be sure you've got matching settings for these things on both PCs. (If you're dialing in to an enterprise-wide Dial-Up Networking server, your network administrator should give you this information and possibly also a specific Server Type setting.)

Finally, the same thing that might trip up Direct Cable Connection applies here. Not only do you need to have sharing enabled in Network Properties; you must also physically share the resources on your host PC (the one probably in the office). You do that by right-clicking the drives and other devices on that PC and choosing "Sharing" from their context menus. The same caveat applies, too. That is, if your host PC is on a network, you'll certainly want to give these shared devices individual password protection. Access to the server end of the remote access connection may also be password protected.

> **Stop right here for a second. Are you thinking about setting up a Microsoft Plus Personal Server connection between your office PC and your notebook PC from home or on the road? Before you spend a lot of time on this, check something out at work. If you have a dedicated data line connected to the modem on your office PC, it may well be a lower-cost phone line that can only dial out. This type of line doesn't have a phone number! So, there's no way you can call into it. Check with the appropriate folks at your company to find out about this before you waste your time.**

Configuring the Client

The machine you're dialing from—probably your notebook—uses a different procedure for configuring a named, saved set of connection settings than does Direct Cable Connection. In the Dial-Up Networking folder (in My Computer), you'll find an icon called Make New Connection. It's a little Wizard that's a lot like the Add Printer Wizard in the Printers folder (see Figure 6.38). It steps you through

Make New Connection

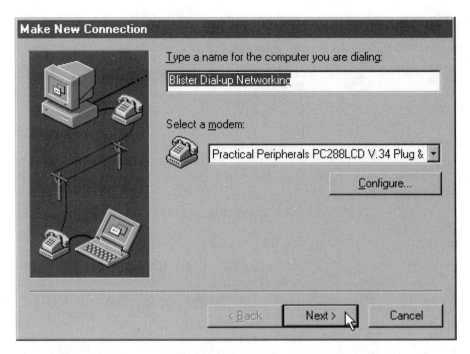

Figure 6.38   The Dial-Up Networking Make New Connection Wizard

the process of naming, plugging in phone numbers, and configuring your modem for a Dial-Up Networking connection.

It's not just for remote-access, either. You can build new connection icons in the Dial-Up Networking folder for dialing online services, a local-access Internet provider, and other types of telephone-based computer connections.

After you're done with the Wizard, you'll see a new icon in your Dial-Up Networking folder labeled with the name you gave it on the first screen of the Wizard. You can make changes to all the connection's settings after the fact by right-clicking its icon and choosing Properties from the context menu, which gives you the properties sheet in Figure 6.39. To initiate a connection, just double-click its icon.

Setting Up the Personal Server

The software you need for a PC to be on the receiving end of a remote-access telephone connection is strictly an option. It doesn't come on the Windows 95 install disc or disks. Microsoft Plus offers a simple one-PC-to-one-PC Personal Server. Microsoft was working out the kinks on a full-blown network server version of the Dial-Up Networking host software as this book went to press. The stuff I'm passing along here applies to the Microsoft Plus Personal Server only. From reading

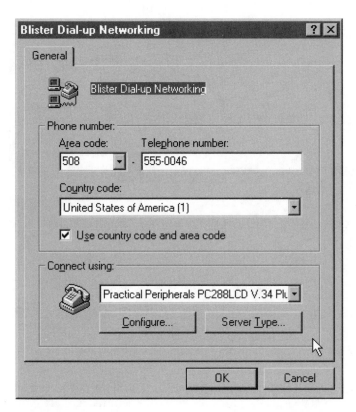

Figure 6.39   Properties for a Dial-up Networking connection

Microsoft's technical materials, though, the user interface for Microsoft's enterprise-wide Dial-Up Networking server package is very similar.

So, after you've installed Plus, open the Dial-Up Networking folder, which you'll find in My Computer. Click the Connections menu and choose the "Dial-Up Server" menu item. Click the "Allow caller access" radio button and then click Apply. The status area readout should change from Idle to Monitoring (check out Figure 6.40). If you're going Windows 95 PC to Windows 95 PC, you're all set, and you can click OK. Dial-Up Networking supports Windows NT and Windows for Workgroups, too. For connections with PCs running those operating systems, you'll need to make adjustments you'll find behind the Server Type button.

Launching a Remote Connection

After everything has been configured and the host PC has been left in Monitoring mode as described in the previous section, you launch a Dial-Up Networking session by double-clicking the appropriate connection icon from the Dial-Up

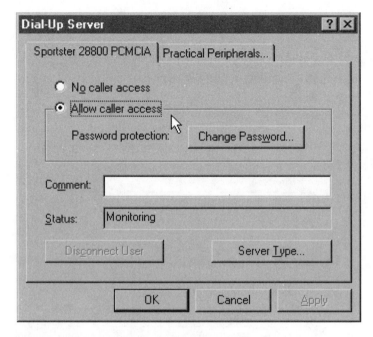

Figure 6.40 The Microsoft Plus! Dial-Up Server settings screen

Networking folder of the client PC. Once the initial connection is made, use the standard Windows 95 interface for network connections, namely Network Neighborhood. If everything is working properly, you'll find an icon representing the host PC in Network Neighborhood. You'll also find icons for all the network resources available to your host PC. (For the full dope on how to use Win 95's networking features, check out Chapter 8, "Connections.")

You can make connecting to the host PC even easier by mapping it to the My Computer folder of your traveling client PC. With a remote connection running, open the client PC's Network Neighborhood folder. Double-click the icon that represents the name of the host PC. You'll see all the devices that are physically shared on the host PC. You can right-click any of these devices, choose Map Network Connection (see Figure 6.41), select a drive letter, and click "Reconnect at startup" to place it in My Computer permanently. Repeat for any other devices you'd like to permanently map. The next time you want to launch a Dial-Up Networking connection from your notebook, just double-click the host PC's network drive icon in My Computer. Windows 95 will ask you before dialing out if that's what you want to do and after you agree, will launch the appropriate connection.

Figure 6.41 Popup menu that lets you map a network drive

Parting Shot

Microsoft's Dial-Up Networking remote access is just that—access. Unlike some other remote-accessing programs, this tool does not let you "drive" the host PC as if you were sitting at its keyboard. And, while this is definitely a bit awkward, it's a far more powerful solution than just giving you access to devices.

So, when you use Dial-Up Networking, it's not like you're back at your desk. It's more like you're another node on your office network, accessing your office PC via the network. What Dial-Up Networking is especially good for is grabbing that file you left behind, dropping a document you just finished working on in a shared network volume for someone else's review, and, if your network is properly equipped, checking your mail.

Cat got your modem? When you use Microsoft Plus's "Dial-Up Server . . ." screen to "Allow caller access" to your PC for Dial-Up Networking, you're effectively dedicating your modem and COM port to this task. If the status box on this screen reads Monitoring, you won't be able to dial out with other communications programs that would try to use the same port. So, when you return from a trip and go back to using the host machine, don't forget to open the Dial-Up Networking folder in My Computer, choose Connections/Dial-Up Server, and click the button beside the "No caller access" line.

*   *   *

It's on the Internet, boys and girls. Don't believe all the hype about problems with Win 95 and Internet connections. The next chapter makes it all clear. Heck, nothing could be worse than TCP/IP connections under pre-Win 95 PC operating systems.

7 Get on the 'Net

> . . . You got ghost stories, sure, and hotdoggers who swore they'd seen things in cyberspace, but he had them figured for wilsons who jacked in dusted; you could hallucinate in the matrix as easily as anywhere else . . .*
>
> William Gibson
> *COUNT ZERO,* 1986

So, you want to get on the Internet, and you think Windows 95 can help get you there? Well, it can. But think of this as a less negative experience than it would be under most other operating systems, rather than as a truly positive one.

With a little help from your Internet Service Provider (ISP, a.k.a. "local access provider") if you're dialing up, or from your network administrator if you'll be cruising at T1 speeds, I gar-*ron*-tee to get you there. Since my day job is as an editor for Ziff-Davis Interactive, the folks who do ZD Net on the Web (`http://www.zdnet.com`), I'm really going to have to live up to those words. Truth is, though, Microsoft has done most of my work for me.

Internet Reality

The Internet is neither easy nor cheap. Especially for the uninitiated. On the other hand, more than half the warnings you may have heard about the World-Wide Web are bogus. Things like: *People will flame you.* Nah, that's only in the usenets and newsgroups. The Web is much more civilized. *It's awash in pornography, and you have to be careful.* Well, maybe, but you really have to go looking for it. *It's so complicated to get set up, you'll never figure it out.* I might have agreed before operating systems like OS/2 Warp and Windows 95. *It'll cost you 40 bucks a month.* Not any more. Local access is getting a lot cheaper. Something like $15 to $25 is much more likely. *For dial-up access you need at least a 28.8 modem.* Oops, this one's true. If

---

*Reprinted from *COUNT ZERO* by William Gibson, copyright 1986. Published by arrangement with the Berkley Publishing Group.

Figure 7.1 Needless global Internet art from the Internet Setup Wizard

you're after surfing the graphical Web, get a V.34 28.8-kbps or faster modem. You're really not going to enjoy it with anything less.

The Internet
Microsoft's Internet Explorer

Given the costs in time, money, and aggravation to get going, take my advice: Find a way to get Microsoft's Internet Jumpstart Kit. Now you could pay about $40 to get the Jumpstart Kit as part of the Microsoft Plus! add-on for Windows 95, available at most any computer store. And, frankly, that's what I recommend. But there's another way. Microsoft has made the Internet Jumpstart Kit available for download on a wide variety of online platforms. There's two places I'm absolutely sure you'll find it. The first is at Microsoft's Web site at this URL (uniform resource locator) address:

```
http://www.windows.microsoft.com/windows/software
/iexplorer.htm
```

The second is in ZD Net's Software Library on CompuServe and the Web. It will probably be available in the ZD Net Software Libraries on most other online services, too. Microsoft circulated this list of download locations for the Internet Jumpstart Kit before the download was actually available:

On the Internet: `ftp.microsoft.com/PerOpSys/Win_News`

On the Microsoft Network: `Edit/Go To "Windows"`

On CompuServe: `GO "WINNEWS"`

On Prodigy: `JUMP "WINNEWS"`

On America Online: `Keyword "WINNEWS"`

Internet Setup
Wizard

I'll come back to Microsoft Plus's features in more detail later in this chapter. Here's what's in the Internet Jumpstart Kit, whether you get it by buying Plus or downloading the Kit: a first-rate 32-bit Web browser (see Figure 7.2) with built-in

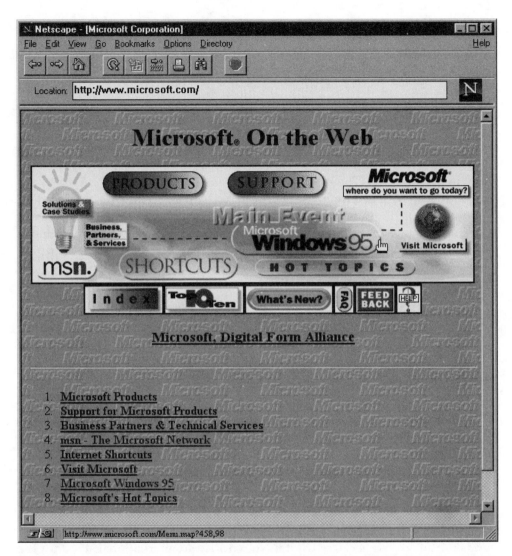

Figure 7.2   Get the latest version of this Win 95 Web browser for free on the Microsoft site

RealAudio sound support from Progressive Networks, the Internet Setup Wizard for Windows 95, and an Internet mail driver for Win 95's Exchange mailbox. In other words, you get all the basics and essentials. The Internet Setup Wizard most definitely should have been included in the OS. At least it's available for free on the Web and elsewhere.

One of the biggest advantages of using Windows 95 over the old Windows for accessing the Internet is invisible: 32-bit TCP/IP networking code that's loaded in protected memory. TCP/IP stands for Transmission Control Protocol/Internet Protocol; it's the networking language of the Internet. In addition to the conventional memory savings, the Win 95's TCP/IP stack provides a small performance boost that's also extended to Microsoft's Internet Explorer browser. Note, though, your mileage may vary, since the biggest performance limitation is your physical connection to the Internet. In other words, are you dialing up? If so, at what connection rate?

The second big advantage is that support for PPP access is built in to Windows 95. PPP stands for Point-to-Point Protocol. It is considered to be the best, by a nose, of the various types of Internet protocols. Others include SLIP (Serial Line Internet Protocol), which I talked about some in Chapter 6, "The Mobile Win 95," and TIA (The Internet Adapter, an emulation of SLIP). TIA is very often the cheapest of connection services offered by Internet access providers. I've been told conflicting things about TIA: 1. That Windows 95 doesn't support it. 2. That people (including my tech editor) are accessing the Internet via TIA under Windows 95. Making TIA work involves special scripting, which the Microsoft Plus version of the Internet Jumpstart Kit facilitates.

Although SLIP doesn't install automatically, it is possible to configure the CD version of Windows 95 to run it. I'll give you a head start on that a bit later in the chapter. PPP is better because it supports password authentication and includes built-in compression capabilities (which helps slightly with performance).

INTERNET ACCESS CHECKLIST

> Why can't somebody give us a list of things that everybody thinks and nobody says, and another list of things that everybody says and nobody thinks.
>
> Oliver Wendell Holmes, Sr.
> *The Professor at the Breakfast-Table,* 1859

Internet Local Access

Most of this chapter focuses on configuring a dial-up connection to the Internet, primarily the Web. If you've got ISDN access, more power to you. ISDN, which stands for Integrated Services Digital Network, is an international standard for digital communication over the public phone network. Bottom line—depending on your digital modem hardware, ISP's server configuration, and the ISDN service supplied by your local phone company—this more expensive means of accessing the 'Net can deliver connection rates ranging from 56 kbps to 128 kbps. In other words, anywhere from two to almost five times faster than the fastest analog modems.

A lot of what follows in this section applies to ISDN access, but since ISDN services vary widely, there are too many variables to cover it properly. Check with your local phone company and ISP. (For answers to ISDN questions, Dan Kegel's ISDN Page on the Web is your best starting point; it's at `http://alumni.caltech.edu:80/~dank/isdn/`.) If you're driving onto the Web with your company's T1 LAN-based connection to the 'Net, I'll digress here and there to give you the stuff that differs.

These are the three most difficult aspects of getting onto the 'Net with Windows 95:

1. How do you find an Internet service provider?   I get this question every day from lots of people. My Mom lives in a rural area, and she's having a tough time. My best advice is to ask a 'Net-savvy friend who lives nearby. Failing that, check the local paper for small local service company ads. Check the yellow pages, too, although you're not likely to find much there. Many Internet access companies just got into business yesterday, or the day before.

Online services like America Online, CompuServe, the Microsoft Network, and Prodigy, all offer Web access in one form or another. See Figure 7.3 for a look at AOL's browser. The caveat is that, as of this writing, their browsers aren't 100-percent Netscape Navigator–compatible and their performance leaves a lot to be desired. Netscape is the Microsoft of the Internet. Its browser technology is far and away the most popular. Many Web sites are designing their pages to take specific advantage of proprietary Netscape's capabilities. Netscape is also fast. The number two browser is Microsoft's Internet Explorer (the one that comes in the Internet Jumpstart Kit).

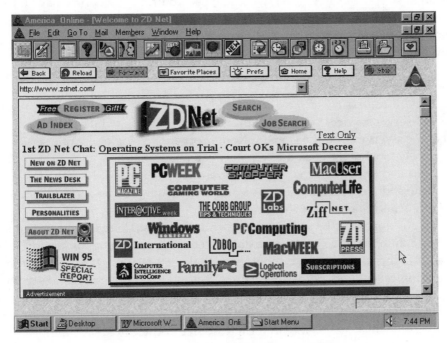

Figure 7.3   America Online's Web browser pointed at ZD Net

Using an online service is a good way to get started.

The fine point on the Internet-access and Web browsers offered by the major online services is that every single one of them has big plans up its sleeve for major improvements. And it could happen fast, so don't take my criticisms as gospel until you check out what the online services have to offer. If you're already on one of these services, using its Web-browsing features is the best way to get your feet wet because you don't need to set anything up at all.

2. What information must your ISP provide for you to configure Windows 95 properly?   Actually, this is the biggie. Many local-access providers are still figuring out Windows 95, so the info they give you may be less than perfect. Here's the stuff you need to get from them:

a. The *host and domain name* of your provider's DNS (Domain Name Server). Windows 95 expects this in two parts; for example, USER (host name) and COMPANYNAME.COM (domain name). This can be the hardest piece of information to get from your provider.

You don't absolutely need a dedicated IP address, but I recommend it.

b. Your *dedicated IP address* (if you opt for this type of service). Having your own dedicated IP number is usually a bit more expensive. If you have one, which might look something like 999.888.777.666, you'll also need the *Subnet Mask* IP address, which looks something like 255.255.255.0.

c. If you're not opting for a dedicated IP address then your local-access provider must support DHCP (the Dynamic Host Control Protocol) or have a PPP Dial-up Router. This means that each time you dial up, your access provider's server will assign you a temporary IP address from a pool of shared addresses.

d. The *IP address of the Domain Name Server*. If there's more than one IP address, you'll need them all. This is a very important piece of information. No one can do without it.

e. The *IP address(es) of the Gateway, News, and Mail servers* and any other dedicated-server services your access provider extends. Many ISPs combine some or all of these services on the Domain Name Server or a single separate server, so listen closely to what the customer rep tells you about this.

f. Your access provider will probably assign you, or will let you choose, a login name and password. Make sure you get that squared away in advance and have both items handy when you're setting up.

g. Finally you need the *phone number for dial-in access*. There may be more than one phone number, and one may be optimized for a particular connection rate, such as 28.8-kbps. It pays to ask about that. While you're at it, get the phone number for technical support. Some access providers also offer bulletin board services, which will probably have yet another phone number. Your ISP may also have a Web site that could offer useful information and downloadable software. So, get the site's URL which stands for Uniform Resource Locator (just say "Earl").

Ask these questions before you sign on the dotted line. If your access provider balks at any of them, get someone else. Customer service isn't exactly the middle name of many of these companies.

If your ISP balks at any of my questions, switch providers.

If you're connecting via LAN access to the 'Net at work, you'll need all the stuff except for the (f) and (g) parts. And instead of asking a local-access provider these questions, you'll be asking your IS personnel.

3. Where do you get a Web browser?   Once you've got access to the 'Net and have Win 95 properly configured to get there, you need something to drive with! The Internet has several ways to present information. The Web, or as it's formally known, HTTP (for HyperText Transport Protocol), is just one. It's the most visual and graphical, but you may want to try news, FTP (File Transport Protocol), Gopher, Telnet, ListServ, and many other useful services, too. If you're new to the 'Net, start with the Web. It's what the term "surfing" was coined for.

Netscape
Navigator

So, the question is, how do you get a Web browser? There's a bit of a Catch-22 about this. It's easy to get excellent Web browsers you can try out for free by downloading them from various sites on the Web. You'll also find most of them downloadable from CompuServe, America Online, the Microsoft Network, and Prodigy. If you already subscribe to an online service, poke around there. If not, ask a friend with an online subscription or Web access to help. Start by downloading Microsoft's Internet Jumpstart Kit if you haven't opted to buy MS Plus. But once you're tooling around out there, stop by Netscape's site (`http://www.netscape.com`) and download the 32-bit version of the company's latest full-blown Netscape Navigator product. You can also purchase the less full-featured Netscape Navigator Personal Edition for under $45 at many computer stores. If you go this route, be sure to go to Netscape's site and download the full version of Navigator later.

You can download excellent Web browsers and try them for free.

BUILDING THE WIN 95 ON-RAMP

> The medium is the message. This is merely to say that the personal
> and social consequences of any medium—that is, of any extension of
> ourselves—result from the new scale that is introduced into our affairs
> by each extension of ourselves, or by any new technology.
>
> Marshall McLuhan
> *Understanding Media*, 1964

If you're at this point, you've got an active (though perhaps untested) account with an access provider, all the information I spelled out in the previous section, a modem connected to a phone line you can dial out on (or network access to the

Internet), a Web browser, and your Windows 95 Setup disc or disks on the desk beside your PC.

What's more, you've decided to do this without Microsoft's Internet Jumpstart Kit because you're a real computer nerd. If you've got the Internet Jumpstart Kit, skim this section (check out the wand tips) and pick up again with the next section, "The Easier Way."

Still here? OK, turn your modem on, close down any running apps, and set aside half an hour when you won't be interrupted.

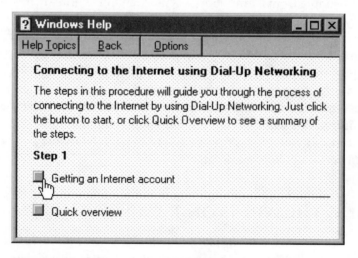 Dial-Up Adapter

A word to the wise: Windows 95's Help system provides simple step-by-step instructions for some of the stuff explained in this chapter. If you get lost, or if you'd like an onscreen guide to help you while you set up your connection, check it out. To open the Help file, click Start/Help and select the Index tab. Type `Internet, connecting to` and press Enter. There are two options listed there; pick "Connecting to the Internet." Then click the gray button beside the item at the bottom that reads "How to connect to the Internet using Dial-Up Networking." That'll give you the screen in Figure 7.4. The Help screens are a useful prompter, and they're well written.

Figure 7.4 The beginning of Win 95's connecting to the Internet help screens

Doing It

The first thing you gotta do is check your Network Properties to see if you've got a Dial-Up Adapter installed. Right-click Network Neighborhood. If you don't have a Network Neighborhood icon on your desktop, open Control Panel and double-click the Network icon. Figure 7.5 shows what Network Properties looks like with the simplest of Internet networking configurations.

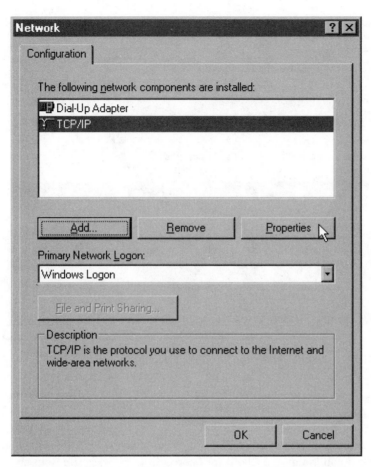

Figure 7.5   The Network Properties screen, TCP/IP configuration central

Win 95's Dial-Up Adapter is a virtual device that acts like a hardware interface for phone lines. To make dial-up to the Internet go, start by installing this guy under Network Properties. Click this stuff in succession: Add/Adapter/Add/Microsoft/Dial-Up Adapter. Then click OK to back up through the mess, stopping at the Network Properties screen. Once you make a change anywhere inside Network Properties, and click its OK button, Windows 95 will ask you to restart the computer. Hold off on that until all the configuring is done. If you're on a LAN, skip the Dial-Up Adapter step, but work through the rest (until I let you know you're done).

The Dial-Up Adapter isn't actually hardware; it's a virtual device.

Next, add the TCP/IP networking protocol. From Network Properties, do this trip: Add/Protocol/Add/Microsoft/TCP-IP, OK, OK, OKAY! Figure 7.6 shows the most important part of this step.

📡 TCP/IP -›

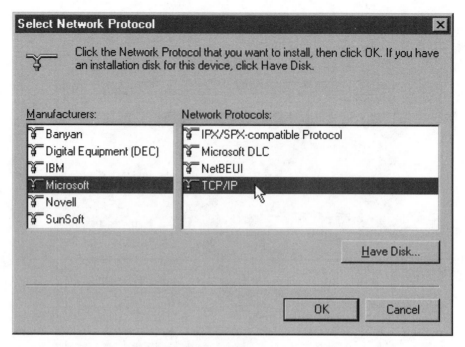

Figure 7.6 Adding TCP/IP from the Select Network Protocol screen

When you're done with that, click OK, and let Windows 95 restart your computer now.

Having trouble with TCP/IP? If your machine is on a non-Microsoft network, it may help if you install the Client for Microsoft Networks. The Help stuff is kind of silent on this point. By the way, if your PC is not on a network of any sort, adding the Microsoft Network Client *isn't* going to help. Another thing to try is re-adding TCP/IP services. Click the Network Properties Add button and then do the Add two-step: Protocol/Add/Microsoft/TCPIP and the OKs to repeat its installation.

This completes the network software installation part of our show. When Win 95 comes back up, you're ready to enter all that nifty information you got from your ISP (or MIS person). Where else? Network Properties.

Back in there, you'll find the Dial-Up Adapter toward the top. Double-click it to see its Properties and click the Bindings tab. Make sure there's a TCP/IP entry in there with a check mark beside it (as shown in Figure 7.7).

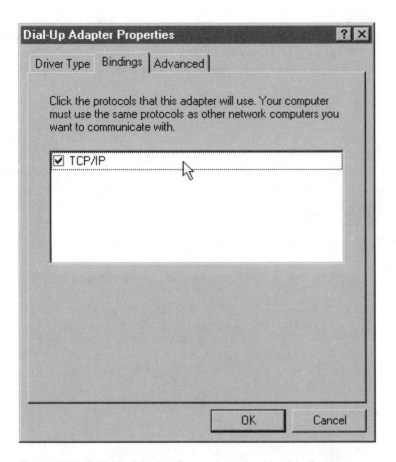

Figure 7.7   Dial-Up Adapter Properties, checking bindings

Having modem problems with Win 95? The operating system has a tendency to assume that your system's internal modem or serial ports have 16550 UARTs. A UART is a serial communications chip, and the 16550 is among the newer, faster versions. Older PCs almost certainly don't have 16550s (unless they have a newer internal model). So, if you're having problems getting your PC to recognize your modem, it might help to change the settings for your ports.

Open Control Panel and double-click the System icon. Then click the Device Manager tab. Scroll down to the Ports section and click the plus sign beside it. Click on your Communication port (or ports, in turn) and click the Properties button. Then click the Port Settings tab and the Advanced button. You can try adjusting the sliders, but if you don't have a 16550 chip, uncheck the box beside "Use FIFO buffers (requires 16550-compatible UART)." If this helps, you might want to consider getting a high-speed serial port card for your PC. You'll find them in computer stores for under $50.

To find out what type of UART your PC has, open the Modems control panel. Turn on your modem if it's the external type. Click the Diagnostics tab. Select the Com port your modem uses. Then click the More Info button. After a minute or so, you'll see the More Info screen, which lists your UART version number.

Sometimes the Host name is just your user login name.

Go configure. Right-click Network Neighborhood (which will now have appeared on your desktop, if it wasn't there before) and click Properties. Then click the TCP/IP component line and click Properties again. This brings up a fairly complex six-tab dialog (shown in Figure 7.8) that controls most of Win 95's available TCP/IP configuration screens. Start with the DNS Configuration tab. Click the Enable DNS button. The next line is where you enter the Host and Domain Name Server names for your ISP's server. (If your ISP or net administrator gave you something with an @ symbol in it, the host is the name before the symbol, and the domain name follows. Don't enter the @ symbol in this dialog.)

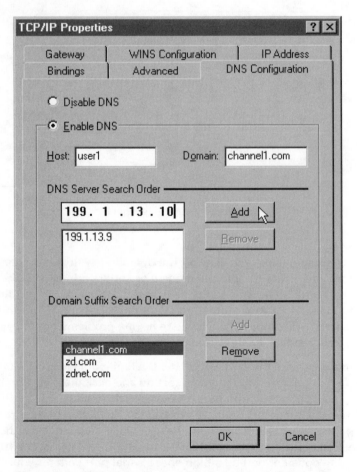

Figure 7.8 TCP/IP Properties' Configuration six tabs, open to DNS

Type the Domain Name Server IP address in the DNS Server Search Order field. If there's more than one, enter the primary one first. IP addresses are four sets of one- to three-digit numbers separated by periods. There should be at least one number in each set (if not, enter a 0). When you're done, click the Add button.

Sometimes it's the little things that get you. The DNS Server Search Order field jumps from set to set of IP numbers automatically when you enter three digits. The easiest way to get to the next field when a set has only one or two numbers is to press the period key.

If you received multiple domain name suffixes (the phrases after the @ symbol), enter them in the Domain Suffix Search order. Enter them in order of your likely usage of them, from most often to least often, if you know that. If you don't know, just guess. In fact, it's not absolutely essential that you enter domain names here.

When you're done with the DNS Configuration screen, click the IP Address tab. If your access provider will be dynamically assigning you a temporary IP address each time you dial in, click the "Obtain an IP address automatically" button and you're done with this tab. If you received a dedicated IP address, click the "Specify an IP address" button and enter the correct numbers for your personal IP address and the Subnet Mask (see Figure 7.9).

If your ISP gave you a dedicated IP address, you should have also gotten a Subnet Mask IP number.

The last part of the TCP/IP configuration is to enter the IP address for your provider's gateway. To do that, click the Gateway tab. Enter the Gateway IP address as you did on the previous screens.

Unless you were specifically instructed to enter something on the WINS Configuration and Advanced tabs, probably by your network administrator, skip them. When you're done entering this stuff, click the OK button at the bottom of the TCP/IP Properties screen.

I don't suppose you want to be infiltrated by some net geek, like Sandra Bullock and friends Telneting and otherwise worming their way in through the Internet portals of about half a dozen commercial, governmental, and institutional sites in that somewhat paranoid movie, *The Net*. Well, that's very unlikely. But to be on the safe side, double-check that File and Printer Sharing for the TCP/IP Dial-Up Adapter is turned off. From Network Properties, bring up the properties for the TCP/IP Dial-up Adapter and then click the Bindings tab. There should be no check mark beside "File and printer sharing for Microsoft Networks." Either that, or you shouldn't see this line at all. If it's there, and there's a check mark beside it, click the check mark off.

You're all done with the network configuration portion of this deal. Click the OK button on the Network Properties screen and let Win 95 restart again. Network folks are all done. Dial-up folks have one additional chore.

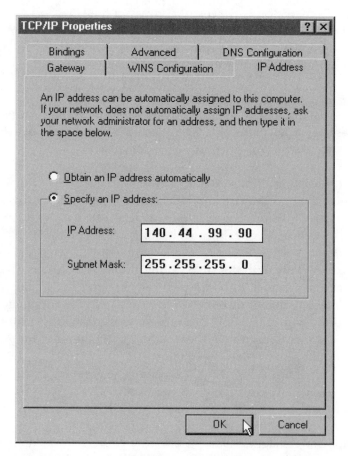

Figure 7.9 Entering IP numbers for a dedicated personal IP address

Create a Dial-Up Connection

Make New Connection

This is the easy part. But it's also where the rubber meets the road when it comes to finding out if you've done things right. The Dial-Up Networking folder is buried in the Accessories submenu, which dangles off Programs on the Start Menu. (Real handy, huh? We'll fix that in a bit.) Open the Dial-Up Networking folder and find the Make New Connection icon (shown in Figure 7.10). This deal creates a named, saved set of modem, port, and dialing properties for accessing an online destination. You can use it for any kind of network-oriented dial-up connection. You'll be using it to create a connection icon for dialing your Internet access provider.

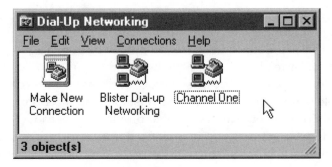

Figure 7.10   The Dial-up Connection folder

Spool up the Make New Connection Wizard (shown in Figure 7.11) and enter the name of your ISP—or call it "Get on the 'Net" if you want. You should see the name of your modem in the "Select a modem" field. And if you've used your modem before, you shouldn't need to click the Configure button to make changes at this point. Windows 95 does these sorts of things on its own—one of its better features. You have a lot less to configure than you would under other operating systems.

If your modem isn't configured properly, don't worry. Windows 95 will notice that and automatically launch the Install New Modem Wizard from the Make New Connection Wizard. Geez, Wizards within Wizards. Anyway, before you click the Next button in the Install New Modem Wizard, make sure your modem is turned on and the serial cable is properly attached. Windows 95 will search both Com (serial) ports, so don't worry about which one it's plugged into.

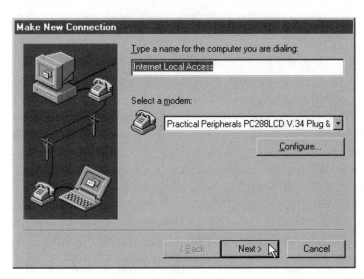

Figure 7.11   Starting the Make New Connection Wizard

On Make New Connection's next screen, enter the dial-in phone number your ISP gave you for getting on the Web. After that, click Next and you're done. When you open the Dial-Up Connection folder again, it'll be in there.

Annie get your browser, because it's getting to be that time.

Is your browser ready? It's getting to be that time. You should install it now if you haven't done so already because in order to test your new connection, you'll need to be able to do something more than just dial your access provider.

Windows 95 offers some mini-apps that provide news reader, Telnet, and FTP services, but they're lame. If you're interested in other types of pursuits on the Internet besides Web surfing, some of the most popular tools for this stuff are shareware programs you can download at many sites around the Web with your browser. To get plugged in and find stuff, search for them at Yahoo (`http://www.yahoo.com`) and ZD Net.

Party Time

Cross your fingers. Let's find out if all this configuring paid off. Double-click the Internet connection icon you just made in the Dial-Up Networking folder. When you do that, you'll see fields for entering your user name and password (shown in Figure 7.12). Enter those and then click the Connect button. (*Note:* Since most ISPs use UNIX servers, which support case sensitivity, the convention is to use lowercase for both your login name and password.) It may take a minute or two for your ISP's server to answer, negotiate, and validate your user name and password. Keep an eye on the "Connecting to" box that'll open up on your screen as dialing begins. It should look something like Figure 7.13 once you're properly connected to your ISP's server.

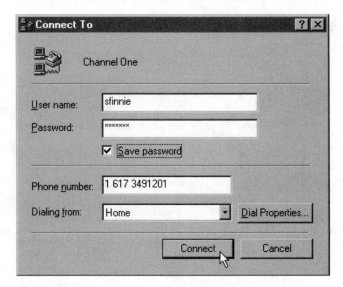

Figure 7.12 About to launch an Internet connection

Figure 7.13 When you're properly connected, the connection box looks like this

It worked? Eureka. If not, go back through all the steps. Be detail-minded. The problem could be just an errant key press or a dropped number in an IP address. If everything checks out, chances are your ISP gave you the wrong information or didn't give you enough information. Give 'em a call. Did they correctly enter the user name and password you gave them? Also, I hate to ask these "Do you have gas in your tank" questions, but is the phone line plugged in? Is the modem on? Is the serial cable connected to both your PC and your modem? (Folks with internal modems can ignore those last two questions.)

If you followed all the steps as I wrote 'em, though, by rights you should be cruising the 'Net right now. (Yeah, go ahead and fire up that browser if you haven't already.) See you on the I-way.

See you on the I-way.

Microsoft buried the Dial-Up Networking folder deep in Start's Programs submenus. That's a pain. When you want on the 'Net, you don't want to go poking around. Here are four tips for getting on the 'Net faster:

1. **When you install Microsoft Plus, it automatically configures the Internet Explorer and any pre-installed newer versions of Netscape to launch your Dial-Up Networking Internet access connection automatically whenever you launch either browser. (Other newer browsers should work this way, too.)**

2. **Mount a Shortcut of the Connection icon on Start's launch list or the desktop.**

3. **Mount a Shortcut of the Dial-up Networking folder on Start's launch list or the desktop.**

4. **Check this. If you've got multiple Dial-Up Networking connections, it might make sense to place a special version of the Dial-Up Networking folder on Start's launch list that will cascade to show a one-click-launch submenu of all your connections. To do that, right-click the Start button and choose Open from the context menu. Right-click the background of the open Start Menu folder and choose New/Folder. Select the New Folder label name for renaming and type this exactly as it appears:**

Put a cascading Dial-Up Networking folder right on Start.

```
Dial-Up Networking.{992CFFA0-F557-101A-88EC-00DD010CCC48}
```

Then press Enter. (*Note:* There are no letter Os in this string; they're all zeroes.) if you've typed the line correctly, the name of the new folder will change to just "Dial-Up Networking." Next time you open Start, you'll see the cascading version of the Dial-Up Networking folder showing a right-pointing triangle that means there's a submenu. And you'll be able to choose and launch a connection directly.

A Head Start on SLIP and Other Connections

The version of the Internet Jumpstart Kit you download can't configure SLIP connections.

The addition of basic support for SLIP connections was like a Microsoft afterthought. Even so, if they had only enough bandwidth to focus on one type of connection, PPP was the right one. It's the power-user's choice.

If your Internet access connection is SLIP and not PPP and you want help configuring it, it's almost mandatory that you buy the Microsoft Plus version of the Internet Jumpstart Kit and that you have the Windows 95 CD, since there are files on both CDs you need to add to your Win 95 installation. (If you don't have the Win 95 CD, you can get the SLIP files in the Windows 95 section on the Microsoft Network. And Microsoft Plus is also available on floppies.) The Internet Jumpstart Kit *that you download* from the Internet or an online service is mostly the same as the version that comes in Microsoft Plus. It differs in that it can't configure SLIP and other Internet connection types for you.

To install support for SLIP and other types of connections without Microsoft Plus, open Control Panel and double-click Add/Remove Programs. Click the Windows Setup tab and then the Have Disk button. Insert the Win 95 CD in your machine and click the Browse button. Then open the `\Admin\Apptools \Dscript` folder on the CD. The filename `RNAPLUS.INF` will be highlighted on the left. Click the OK button and then click it again on the Install From Disk box. The Have Disk screen will reappear at that point (shown in Figure 7.14), and you'll see an entry inside it that reads "SLIP and Scripting for Dial-Up Networking." Place a check mark beside it, and click OK.

That places a useful scripting tool in your Start/Programs/Accessories folder. It also installs SLIP and other connection types in a dialog where you can select them as an option. To get to that dialog, right-click your Internet access Dial-Up Connection icon, press the Server Type button, and then click the TCP/IP Settings button. For more on how to set up SLIP connections, double-click the Microsoft Windows 95 Resource Kit Help file (it's the `WIN95RK.HLP` file in the `\Admin\Reskit\Helpfile` folder on the Win 95 CD). Click the Find tab and type `Connecting to a SLIP Server` in the "Type the word(s) you want to find" field. If you don't have the Win 95 CD, you're SOL on this help file.

Figure 7.14 Adding SLIP and dial-up scripting without MS Plus from the Win 95 CD

THE EASIER WAY

> . . . Whatever he does to the web, he does to himself.
>
> > Chief of the Seattle-based Duwamish, Suquamish, and allied Indian tribes
> > Letter to President Franklin Pierce, 1854

For about 40 bucks spent on Microsoft Plus—you can forget all about that Network Properties mumbo jumbo. The Jumpstart Kit configures your Dial-Up Networking connection almost automatically. Plus can also install SLIP support for you. And it takes care of that *Where do I get a Web browser?* problem by delivering the 32-bit Internet Explorer. Throw in Internet mail, and latching onto Plus starts to look mighty good indeed.

CD-ROM

Microsoft Plus

If you decide to go the Plus route, you get a whole lot more than the downloadable Internet Jumpstart Kit in the bargain. Plus also offers excellent on-the-fly disk compression; spruces up the look and sound of Windows 95 in a big way; and installs

At $40, Plus is a true bargain, but it ain't perfect.

something called the System Agent, which automates system tasks like scanning your disk for errors and defragging your hard drive (see Chapter 4, "Files, Folders, Exploring"). Microsoft Plus is chock full of interface tweaks and little visual and audible extras that make customizing and using Windows 95 a lot more fun. See Figure 7.15 for a quick sense of what Plus gives you.

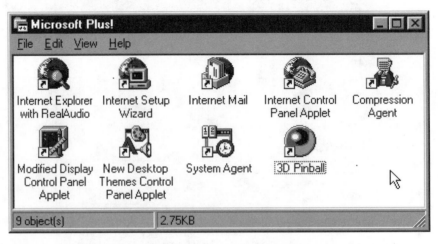

Figure 7.15   The main stuff that comes in Microsoft Plus

Plus's system requirements are a 486 with at least 8MB of RAM and a fast video card that supports at least 256 simultaneous colors. Most video cards on newer, and many older, PCs make the grade unless you also have a giant monitor and are running hi-res. And for the record, none of the three Internet Jumpstart Kit features requires more than a 386DX with 4MB of RAM (although Microsoft says the Internet Explorer browser requires 256 colors).

But, ahem, let's pause for a moment and let me go back on what I just said for different reasons: You need at least 8MB of RAM for Windows 95. I said this in an earlier chapter, but it bears repeating. Some of my colleagues in the press advocate 12MB or even 16MB, so I'm not being elitist about this. What's more, I wouldn't recommend installing Windows 95 on any PC whose CPU isn't a 486DX2/50 or better. If you've got a 486SX/ or DX/33, for example, hop on down to the computer store and pick up a 486DX4/100 or Pentium 83 upgrade chip.

Plus is cool, but it does funky things with object icons.

I like Plus a lot. But, it's not without its faults. For one thing, it changes all your desktop icons—you know, like for drives, printers, Recycle Bin, Network Neighborhood, and My Computer—to new and improved icons that look slightly different but to my way of thinking *aren't* improved. It's easy to remove 'em though. You'll find a new Plus tab on the Display Properties dialog (right-click the desktop and choose Properties). On the Plus tab, remove the check mark beside the line that reads "Show icons using all possible colors." (See Figure 7.16.) Then restart Windows, and poof, those ugly icons are gone.

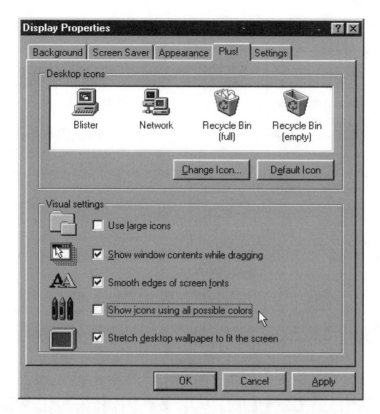

Figure 7.16 Make those wonky high-color icons hit the road

Desktop Themes is an interesting if overly complex dialog that controls sounds, wallpaper, mouse pointers, animated cursors, desktop, and other colors, fonts, icons, and a whole bunch of other stuff. A specific collection of settings for all the above is called a *theme.* Plus comes with more than 10 prepackaged themes that you can select and apply in a second or two. And it includes a long list of new sounds, wallpaper, cursors, and mouse pointers. Desktop Themes is a great idea that I have a feeling was rushed in execution. Sometimes things don't take, or you can't turn off things you should be able to. This deal makes changes to System Registry and other control structures that support Windows 95, and I'm not sure it's doing so perfectly. Nevertheless, it's tough to argue with the results. Schemes or themes, whatever Microsoft calls them—the idea of being able to save and name batches of configurations—is a home run. I only wonder what took 'em so long.

Desktop Themes

My considered advice is to use Plus's redecoration tools sparingly at first. Save your pre-existing setup as a theme before you apply one of the many interesting themes that come with the product. Other things in Plus, however, work as they should. And the Internet stuff, in particular, is first rate.

Use Desktop Themes sparingly or not at all, if you can resist them.

The Internet Jumpstart Kit

Internet Setup
Wizard

The stuff we're interested in for this chapter is what's collectively known by Plus Setup as the Internet Jumpstart Kit. That's all that Internet stuff I keep harping on. The Internet Setup Wizard launches and runs as part of Plus's standard setup. It automates the entire Internet setup process I described back there under the "Building the Win 95 On-ramp" heading. The Setup Wizard can't answer these IP address number questions for you, but anything that could be automated has been. And, instead of your having to fiddle with a bunch of properties dialogs, you just answer the questions. When you're done, your TCP/IP stack will be fully configured, you'll have a Dial-Up Networking connection icon, your Internet mail settings will have been entered in Exchange, and the Internet Explorer browser will be ready to go.

The Internet Setup Wizard isn't just for dial-up users. The very first question asks whether you connect by phone or LAN (as shown in Figure 7.17). The next asks whether you want to connect with Microsoft's dial-up service to the 'Net (more on this coming up) or via your Internet access provider.

My biggest beef with Plus's Internet Jump-start Kit is that it wasn't in-cluded in Win 95 to begin with.

If you realize halfway through that you don't have some bit of info, no sweat. You can cancel at any time, no obligation. And when you get that snippet, you can

Figure 7.17   The Internet Setup Wizard's second screen

relaunch and finish the Wizard later. In fact, you can relaunch the Wizard later to add a second, or even a third, type of connection to the Internet if you want. The truth is, there's not a lot of clarifying, tip giving, or hammering I can do on the Internet Setup Wizard. It's the next best thing to having an expert do it for you. I'll say it again. My biggest beef is that this thing wasn't included in Windows 95 to begin with.

I mentioned in passing that the Jumpstart Kit installs the Internet mail driver, too, something I didn't give you instructions for separately, since this chapter focuses on Web access. It's a nice little bene. Once you've configured it properly—always a pleasure with Exchange (that's sarcasm, son)—it lets you gather Internet mail by launching Exchange while you're dialed up to your access provider. Or you can launch Exchange and choose Tools/Deliver Mail Now (not exactly intuitive when you're looking to *receive* mail . . .) to both send and receive mail. Only catch is, when you work this way, Exchange hangs up on your Internet connection as soon as it's done sending and receiving. That's a good default action, I suppose, but kind of annoying when you want to surf afterward. See Figure 7.18.

Anyway, once it's working, you can also have Exchange go out and poll all your mail sources automatically. That's the whole idea behind Exchange as a "universal mailbox." Microsoft didn't get this right, though, since it's by no means universal. It's actually downright difficult to use. Worst of all, it's slow—not so much in getting your mail, but just in loading and exiting.

Exchange is slow to load and slow to exit.

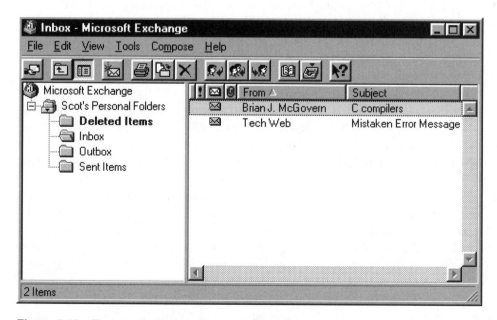

Figure 7.18 Exchange after bringing me new mail

Exchange is slated to get a raft of mail drivers.

By the time they ship Windows 97, though, maybe things will be looking up. For one thing, several companies are working on drivers for Exchange, including America Online, Apple, AT&T, Banyan, DEC, Hewlett-Packard, Novell, Octel, RAM Mobile Data, and Skytel. The real list is actually a lot longer, and I hope it includes Interchange, MCI, and Prodigy. The CompuServe driver is available on the Win 95 CD. Double-click the `SETUP.EXE` file you'll find in the Win 95 CD's `\Drivers\Other\Exchange\Compusrv` folder to install the driver in Exchange.

The Internet Explorer

This guy is pretty neat. The Internet Explorer is a Mosaic-type browser (like Netscape) Microsoft licensed from Spyglass and then modified pretty heavily for 32-bitness and integration with the Win 95 environment. It has built-in RealAudio support (that hear-it-right-on-the-Web stuff from Progressive Networks). That's a nice little benefit, although you can download the RealAudio player for free from the RealAudio site (`http://www.realaudio.com`) and add it to most any browser. So, it's not *that* impressive a feature.

Internet
Explorer

One of the nicest things about the Internet Explorer is that it makes liberal use of the Shortcut idea. When you save a Web site's URL to Internet Explorer's Favorites (so you can just hop back there next time without having to futz around remembering the URL), you're actually creating a URL Shortcut to the Web site (see Figure 7.19). You can place an Internet Explorer URL Shortcut on your desktop or on the Start Menu and then later launch the browser, connect to the 'Net, and bring up the site just by double-clicking the URL Shortcut. Netscape's Bookmarks system of storing visited Web sites is downright lame by comparison.

You can even send URL Shortcuts as email attachments.

Since URL Shortcuts are discrete files, you can also send them as attachments in email messages to friends and colleagues. As long as your friends are also using the Internet Explorer, they can launch a connection to the site right out of the email message (if their email packages or services support that sort of thing).

Another major advantage of the Internet Explorer is the way it presents dialogs and controls. Netscape is pretty easy to use, once you understand it. But the Internet Explorer's controls are far easier to grasp if you're using a browser for the first time.

The biggest drawback to the Internet Explorer, even the newer 2.0 version, is that it's not 100 percent compatible with Netscape's HTML extensions. (HTML stands for HyperText Markup Language, and it is the text-encoding language of the Web.) And since Netscape Navigator is the Toyota Corolla of Web browsers—you know, most ubiquitous—many Web sites are designed specifically with Netscape capabilities in mind. Some of the stuff the Internet Explorer has trouble with are vertical spacing and tables. It comes close—probably as close as any non-Netscape browser out there—but close isn't good enough in my book.

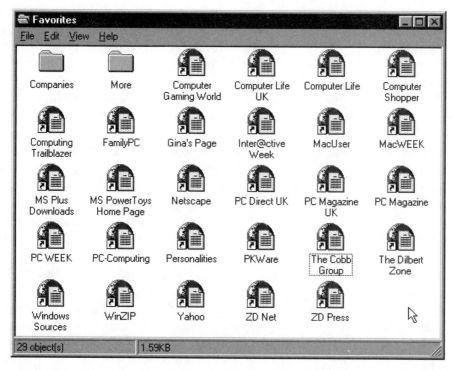

Figure 7.19 The Internet Explorer's Favorites folder displaying URL Shortcuts

Microsoft recognizes this compatibility issue, though, and is working on refining the Internet Explorer. I'm told that as soon as an update for Internet Explorer that fixes these incompatibilities is completed, you'll be able to surf on over to Microsoft's Web site and download it.

If you're reading along and you come to a heading that says "the Microsoft Network," don't think to yourself "What's this have to do with the Internet?" "Why should I care?" and "I'm skipping to the next part," OK? There's probably Internet stuff in there, too. I'm not that whacked out.

THE MICROSOFT NETWORK

> The web of domination has become the web of Reason itself, and this society is fatally entangled in it.
>
> Herbert Marcuse
> *One-Dimensional Man*, 1964

It might seem like a digression, but when it comes to Windows 95 and the Internet, the Microsoft Network (MSN) is very definitely center stage. It's confusing, though. People are wigged out enough about the difference between online

The Microsoft
Network

services and the Internet without Microsoft's blurring the edges for the sake of a marketing schpiel. But you can't fault 'em, I guess, for taking something as hot as the Internet and draping their name all over it. Or can you? First things first. I'm going to tell you how to get onto MSN. Then I'll tell you about all the devious ways Microsoft has dreamed up to get you on the Internet via MSN.

In future, the online services will be enclaves on the Internet, as opposed to being entry points to it.

I like to think of the online services as private communities dotting the vast open road of the Internet like ritzy enclaves. Rather than being front doors to the 'Net as they are now, the roles will reverse at some point in the future. The Internet will become the interconnecting interstate leading up to the driveways of the online services. For that to happen, Internet access has to get cheaper, easier, and faster. But it's in the cards. And companies like America Online, Microsoft, and CompuServe are preparing for it. When you look at things that way, you'll get a new perspective. You pay extra to belong to an online service like America Online, but you get a far more ordered and assured experience. Some day, the online services will each be a part of the vast whole—with a cover charge.

With so many online services competing for members, it's unclear whether new kid on the block MSN (see Figure 7.20) has a viable chance to play in this market. Increasingly, Microsoft is focusing on the Internet instead of its fledgling online service. In fact, it seems likely that Microsoft will shift its focus almost entirely away from the proprietary MSN online service in favor of an Internet-based content area with a membership *firewall,* or boundary. Although some pieces of

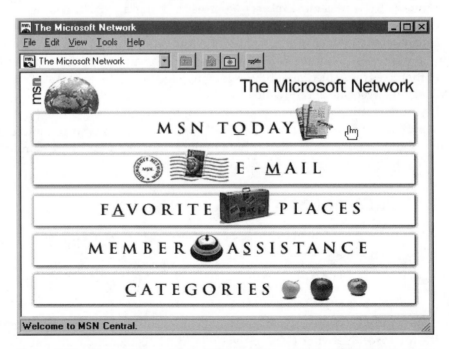

Figure 7.20 The opening screen of Microsoft's proprietary MSN online service

the proprietary MSN online service may continue for quite some time to come, MSN on the Web is going to be the real service. Given the fact that Microsoft owns a nationwide Internet access provider, and that anyone with Win 95 can sign up for its 28.8-kbps access to the 'Net via MSN or Plus, all this makes good sense for the company.

What's unclear at this writing is whether and how this Microsoft change of direction might affect MSN's setup, sign-up, and configuration procedures as provided in the initial shipping version of Windows 95. It's possible that the first Windows 95 update release, rumored to be out around the time this book hits store shelves, could incorporate a version of the Internet Setup Wizard that focuses more specifically on signing up users to Microsoft's nationwide Internet access service. Or perhaps any such changes would be made in an upgrade to Microsoft Plus and the Internet Jumpstart Kit. As you'll see later in this chapter, the initial shipping versions of Win 95, Plus, and the Internet Jumpstart Kit make signing up for the Internet-access services an intrinsic part of the setup for the proprietary MSN online service. Microsoft may well decide to leave things as they are for the foreseeable future because offering unaffiliated access to the Internet would force it to construct a semipermeable membership firewall. The Internet technologies needed for that kind of restriction are still in their infancy, and the interrelationship of the current Internet access sign-up procedures with the proprietary MSN service ensures that Microsoft can bill for Internet MSN membership. They still have to figure out whether and how to restrict folks who surf up to the Internet portion of MSN from the Web, though.

Are updates in the offing that may alter MSN procedures detailed here?

What's it all mean? Bottom line: All the stuff that follows about configuring MSN and the Internet applies to the software that shipped on the original Windows 95 and Plus disc or disks. I don't know for sure that things will change, but I wanted to give you the inside dope in case they do.

Getting On

Subscribing to MSN is a relatively easy affair. Start by installing the MSN option from your Windows 95 disc or disks. When you do, you'll also be installing Microsoft Exchange, if you haven't done so already. To install it, open Control Panel and double-click the Add/Remove Programs button. Click the Windows Setup tab. Then scroll down to the bottom of the Components window, put a check mark beside the Microsoft Network line, and click OK.

The MSN setup places the Microsoft Network icon on your desktop. To subscribe, double-click the icon. A screen will open that gives you a sales job aimed at getting you to click OK. Since you'll have many other opportunities to back out, go ahead and do so. You'll be asked some questions about the area code and exchange of your local phone number. Eventually you'll dial out to a special MSN new-subscriber number that updates the list of local phone numbers in your area and launches you into the sign-up process. You'll pick access numbers; give them your name, rank, and credit card number; and pick a user name and password. It's fairly painless, except for the money part.

Once you get it going, MSN is a breeze to log on to.

Once you get through this the first time, getting online to MSN is a cakewalk. The dial-up icon is on your desktop, and it can even remember your logon name and password for you. You just double-click, and a few minutes later you're there.

You'll find that you already know how to use this shindig. It's based—oh, what a surprise—on the Explorer folders concept. In fact, it's so straightforward for Win 95 users, there's really not much to tell. For a look at one of MSN's top levels, see Figure 7.21.

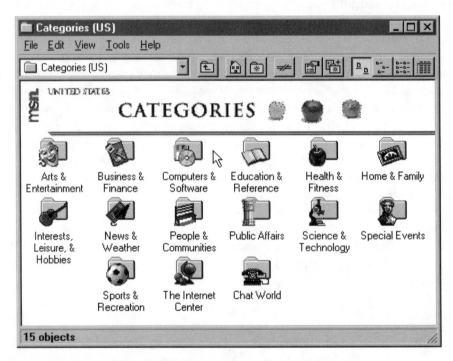

Figure 7.21   The MSN categories—that means the interest areas

The Internet and the Microsoft Network

There's a major service Redmond brewed up that isn't exactly an online service. Although it comes under the heading of the Microsoft Network, it's nationwide Internet access. And, it's a great idea. The good news is, the Internet access numbers mostly go at rates up to 28.8 kbps. Also if you subscribe to it (it's called "Internet and The Microsoft Network"), you also get access to the MSN online service at 28.8 (if you didn't have this already). This is very definitely a good thing, since MSN is kind of pokey.

How does MSN's Internet access differ from MSN itself, which also offers Internet and Web access from its Internet Center and other places? Yeah, it's confusing, isn't it? Well, there's actually some important differences between the Microsoft's Internet access and the browser services you'll find on the Microsoft Network. (Stick with me, I'm going to get this all straight in your mind.) Two things really: performance and convenience. You can either subscribe primarily to MSN the online service and occasionally nip off into cyberspace by choosing Edit/Go To "WWW" from any MSN window. Or you can subscribe to *both* MSN and its Internet access service for which you need your own browser. With this second method, you get faster dial-in numbers and you can go direct to the 'Net if you want. In fact, you can go direct to MSN, or the 'Net, and then back to the first if you want.

Sorting out Microsoft's MSN and Internet services

When you install it, this option is labeled "Internet and The Microsoft Network." So, how do you do that? Ah, grasshopper, very good question. We've come full circle, and there are two ways to do it. The first is to download Microsoft's Internet Jumpstart Kit (or purchase it as part of Plus). Dial back to the second page in this chapter for where to download. The second way is infinitely more obscure, but it amounts to the same thing.

First, the Jumpstart Kit. The second screen of the Internet Setup Wizard (Figure 7.17) asks whether you want to go by LAN or by phone. You answer by phone. The third screen (see Figure 7.22) asks how you want to connect to the Internet. If you choose, "The Microsoft Network," you're propelled into the MSN sign-up—with a twist.

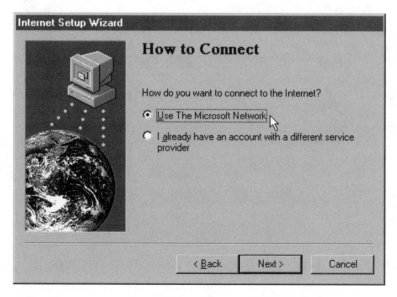

Figure 7.22   The Setup Wizard's option to use the MSN as your access provider

**Some complex
Setup wizardry
is at work here.**
At that point, MSN Setup takes over from the Internet Setup Wizard and dials out to find a local phone number for MSN. The twist is, it's not looking at the same access number database that the standard MSN sign-up routine checks. Instead it's looking at a wholly separate list of "Internet and The Microsoft Network" access numbers. And when you're all done setting this up, something additional will have been added on one of MSN's Sign In settings screens.

To get a gander at what I'm talking about, check out Figure 7.23. The new item is a drop-down selection box that gives you a choice between dialing the regular MSN number and dialing the new Internet and MSN number. Different numbers, different types of access. If you follow these steps, here's how to find the change: Double-click your Microsoft Network icon, click the Settings button on the Sign In screen, and then click the Access Numbers button. It's the Service type drop-down I'm talking about. It lets you choose between:

1. "The Microsoft Network" only

2. "The Internet and Microsoft Network," which provides both straight-through Internet access as well as MSN access.

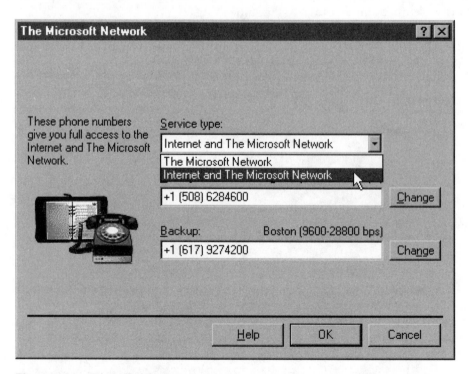

Figure 7.23 The MSN "Service type" drop-down modified by the Internet and MSN setups

OK, grasshopper, back to that other way of getting there I was talking about. If you're already an MSN subscriber, you can sign on to MSN, choose Edit/Go To, and type `Internet`. Double-click the "Getting on the Internet" icon. Then click the Upgrade Instructions button. Follow the steps you read there. Surprise, surprise. You'll be downloading something or other. And a program will launch and find you a new phone number. And . . . hey, isn't this the same thing as running the Internet Setup Wizard locally? Pretty much.

The other way to set this up is pretty much the same thing.

For you multiple-Internet-access-method folks: OK, several pages back I said that there wasn't much to bang on about the Internet Setup Wizard. I lied. There is one thing about the Internet Setup Wizard that'll drive you buggy. The problem crops up only if you choose the MSN Internet access option and you're installing on a PC that already has a different TCP/IP Dial-up Adapter connection set up. In that case, you're probably going to see one very ugly and cryptic dialog box, which I've captured in all its glory in Figure 7.24.

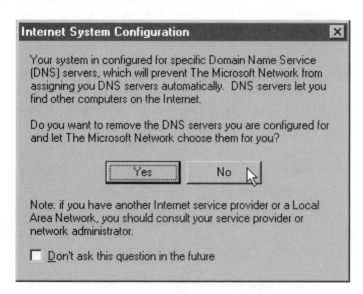

Figure 7.24   Lame-o Internet Setup Wizard message

The problem is that the six-tab TCP/IP setup screen in Network Properties can't walk and chew bubble gum at the same time. It wasn't designed to handle multiple Internet access connection settings. When you click Yes on the ugly dialog, the Internet Setup Wizard strips out pre-existing IP addresses, host names, domain names, and the like from any previous TCP/IP settings. In other words, you can kiss your previous setup good-bye. If you really want to be able to connect to the 'Net under both your previous dial-up configuration and via MSN I can get you there.

Now the odd part is, this will sometimes trip up a LAN connection, too. The first thing to try is ripping out the host and domain names on the DNS Configuration tab of the affected LAN settings. For previous dial-up settings, though, there's a real fix:

1. Open your Dial-up Networking folder (Start/Programs/Accessories/Dial-up Networking).

2. Right-click the connection setting for your previous access provider and choose Properties. Click the Server Type button.

3. Click the TCP/IP Settings button. In there you'll find settings fields that duplicate the most important settings from the DNS Configuration tab of the TCP/IP Dial-Up Adapter Properties screen under Network Properties. The only things missing are the Host and Domain names.

4. Plug your dedicated IP address (if you have one) and your first two DNS (you may have only one) IP addresses on this screen. It should work fine now, even without the Host and Domain names.

The AutoDial Controls

Internet

The Internet control panel

There's one last piece that could use a bit of amplification, and it's kind of nifty. I mentioned in passing earlier that by installing the Internet Jumpstart Kit, you get automatic activation of your Internet access dial-up connection. It's a nice little tweak and just another reason why the Jumpstart Kit should've been included in the OS.

Anyway, something you might not come across right away is the settings screen for this feature, which Microsoft calls "AutoDial." After you install the Jumpstart Kit, the Internet Explorer is planted as an icon on your desktop, labeled quite ambitiously—even for Microsoft—as "The Internet." You'll also find a new control panel called "Internet." If you right-click The Internet on your desktop and choose Properties from the context menu, you get the same screen that the Internet control panel delivers.

For those with cyber-happy kids: a way to turn off automatic connection launching.

Check it out. This screen lets you choose a default dial-up Internet access method when you've got more than one. (See Figure 7.25.) The default connection is the one that launches automatically when you launch your browser or double-click a URL Shortcut. And even if you don't have more than one means of connecting to the 'Net, it lets you turn the AutoDial feature on or off. The off part can be real useful if you've got cyber-happy kids in the house—until they figure it out. With AutoDial switched on, you launch your browser and the Dial-Up Networking connection launches a few seconds later. So you're working with your browser, instead of hunting around for the dial-up connection first.

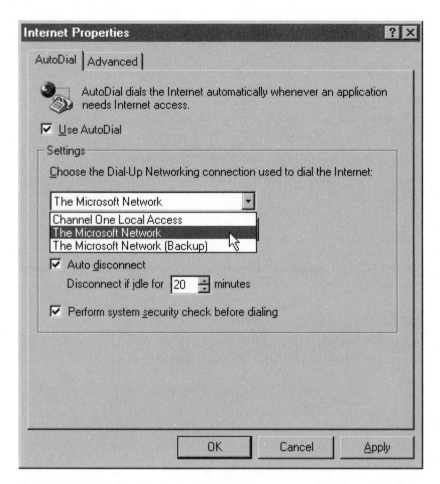

Figure 7.25 Configuring the AutoDial Internet access method selection

Even better, this deal isn't just for the Internet Explorer. Microsoft passed the simple activation hook along to Netscape and other browser makers. Starting with Netscape Navigator 1.1 (the 32-bit version for Windows 95 and NT), the Netscape browser will also launch your connection script. I've found that Netscape has to be installed before you run the Internet Setup Wizard to make this work.

*   *   *

This concludes our exercise in getting online, on the Internet, getting connected, and plugged into Cyberspace, mon. Tune in next week, when I show you how to download cold hard cash off the Web. And how to live forever by becoming a cyber-zombie. Say goodnight, Gracie. Irene, you too.

8 Connections

Madness is something rare in individuals—but in groups, parties, peoples, ages it is the rule.

Friedrich Nietzsche
"Maxims and Interludes," *Beyond Good and Evil*, 1886

If you don't use a network, never plan to use one, and couldn't care less how network stuff works under Windows 95, why, just go right ahead and skip this chapter. I probably would. Of course, if you don't at least scan this you might never know just how easy it all is. And if there's another PC within 10 yards of yours, sooner or later the two PCs are going to reach out and touch each other one night when you're not looking.

You'd also miss a few insights on some of Win 95's basic communications tools, like the Modems control panel and HyperTerminal, Win 95's comm utility. If what you're really looking for is dope on modem-based dial-up connections and non-network media cable links, check out Chapter 6, "The Mobile Win 95," and Chapter 7, "Get on the 'Net."

Mostly this chapter is about the built-in networking capabilities that Windows 95 offers right out of the box. They apply whether you've got two PCs at home or you're tired of waiting for the MIS folk to install Win 95 at work and want to do it yourself. Somewhere in between is a group of folks that the computer industry calls the "SOHO market." It's absolutely imperative that we in this business have an acronym for everything. It keeps everyone else at bay, you see. It's a sort of rite-of-passage thing. Of course, we nerds are about to be way outnumbered . . . if we aren't already.

Anyway, SOHO stands for Small Office/Home Office. In the context of networking, it refers to clusters of PCs numbering in the 2 to 15 range. Windows 95 comes with all the software stuff you need to make PCs in those kinds of numbers talk to one other, share files, share printers—stuff like that. And the hardware isn't that expensive—probably something like $150 per PC or less. In fact, it's this SOHO group that Win 95's networking features are really designed for. You see, for true macho networking, Microsoft wants you to shell out for Windows NT.

Win 95's built-in networking is aimed squarely at small-office, home-office users.

Figure 8.1   Truly useless Microsoft screen art symbolizing a network

Basic Comm Tools

Modems
**Modems
control panel**

Before I talk about the networking guts, I'll pass along a thought or two on a few basic connection tools. First is the Modems control panel (Start/Settings/Control Panel/Modems), whose whole reason for being is to let you set up newly attached modems and configure them once they're set up.

Truth is, this deal is really a hardware-detection Wizard focused on your serial ports and any modem peripherals that may be attached to them. Why did Redmond break this out as a separate part? Simple. If you forgot to turn on your modem during installation, how else would you get Device Manager (Start/Settings/Control Panel/System/Device Manager tab) clued in about what kind of problem you've got?

Configuring the modem afterward might sound more useful, but it really isn't. For the most part, Windows 95 gets things right with the detection. It configures the right serial port, it gets the connection rate down, and its default settings for things like data bits, parity, and stop bits are right for most hosts. What you're likely to need this doodad for are things like adjusting your modem's volume control and disabling call waiting. Useful nonessentials. Like almost everything else in Windows 95, Microsoft has thought out the configurational controls pretty well. There's even a place to add modifications to the modem's initialization string.

Perhaps the most useful modem configuration tool is found on the Modems Diagnostic tab (see Figure 8.2). There's a button, kind of strangely named "More Info," that when pressed sends the AT modem command set to the connected modem and then reports which commands the modem understood. The More Info dialog also reports useful info about the port and modem, such as your UART version number.

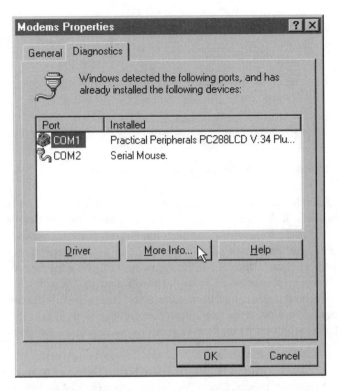

Figure 8.2 The Control Panel's Modems tool

The second communications tool is HyperTerminal, Win 95's core communications program. You'll find it on the Start/Programs/Accessories menu. Like Dial-Up Networking, HyperTerminal opens as a folder and creates named, saved, connection scripts in the form of icons stored in its folder (see Figure 8.3). Communications-wise, this tool is a lot more useful than its laughable Terminal predecessor from the old Windows. It's not real fancy or anything; it just works. Something you couldn't always say about Terminal.

HyperTerminal

But when you look in the HyperTerminal folder, you may be a little surprised to find that it looks as if Microsoft forgot to finish this part. There's no Make New Connection icon in here, the way there is in the Dial-Up Networking folder. To make a new connection, you double-click the HYPERTRM (or HYPERTRM.EXE, depending on your folder settings) icon. Real obvious, huh? On the other hand, once you know what to do, this all happens pretty easily. You'll happily create connection icons like the AT&T Mail, CompuServe, and MCI Mail connection icons that appear by default in the HyperTerminal folder without giving it much thought. It's a handy gizmo. Would, though, that it saved login names and passwords as part of the .HT connection-script files.

Hey, Hyper-Terminal is better than Terminal—even if that isn't saying much!

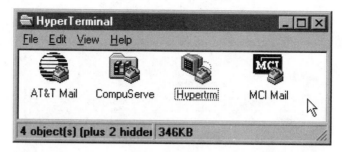

Figure 8.3 The Default HyperTerminal folder

A truly inelegant tip, but what the hey, you might not think to do this half step. You can place a cascading version of the HyperTerminal folder on Start's launch list if you want. If you do this, when you click the HyperTerminal menu item on Start, you'll see a cascading submenu of your HyperTerminal connection script icons that you can just click to launch, without having to open a folder on your screen (the default method Windows 95 offers). There's a catch, though. This tip creates a snapshot—actual copies, as opposed to Shortcuts—of your current HyperTerminal connections. New ones you might add (unless you go into this folder and add them there) won't show up in the cascading submenu automatically.

So what you do: Use the drive tool in My Computer to open the `\Program Files\Accessories` **folder. Right-click the HyperTerminal folder and choose Copy from the popup menu. Close the folder and then right-click the Start button. Choose Open from the popup. Right-click the background of the Start Menu folder and choose Paste from the popup. That's it. This tip works, but unlike others I've offered, it's not integrated into the System Registry. Doing this is a Microsoft no-no. So, I can't vouch for its reliability.**

Phone Dialer

The third communications tool is Phone Dialer, which some people probably find very useful. Shown in Figure 8.4, this little applet does just what it sounds like: It uses your modem to dial a phone number for you. It offers eight preset speed-dial settings that you can name and save. So you can launch this little deal and click a button to dial a number. After you set the dial in motion, you click the Talk button and pick up the phone. Works as advertised and might be useful. These things have been around forever, though; I think there was one in the original DOS SideKick program from Borland. It's one of those gadgets I always program and then forget to use. Besides, I've got wandering nomads for family, so I'd probably spend all my time reprogramming the darn thing.

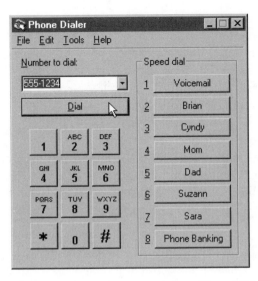

Figure 8.4   Phone Dialer ranks pretty low on the "truly useful" index, but it works

MEET THE NETWORK

> I love meetings with suits. I *live* for meetings with suits. I love them because I know they had a really boring week and I walk in there with my orange velvet leggings and drop popcorn in my cleavage and then fish it out and eat it. I like that. I know I'm entertaining them and I know that they know. Obviously, the best meetings are with suits that are intelligent, because then things are operating on a whole other level.
>
> Madonna
> Quoted in *Vanity Fair*, April 1991

At one time or another, I've tried all the popular peer-to-peer networking packages. Probably the very best of these is Artisoft's LANtastic. Its networking features are more powerful—especially the last two versions—than Win 95's. But the interface structures for using them aren't as well integrated into the operating system (although, I haven't yet seen Artisoft's Win 95 offering). Bottom line, I like what Microsoft has done on this score for Windows 95. I can't think of any significant reason to use a third-party peer network product. Like Apple's Macintosh, basic small-group networking is built into Win 95. So why look elsewhere?

Peer-to-peer networking? Um, before pushing on to other things, let me take a little white space to explain what that term means because there're really two wholly different types of network support in Windows 95. If you don't live, eat, and breathe this stuff (and believe me—that's a very good thing), it's important to get it straight up front.

Two wholly different types of networking

Most large office networks employ a separate network operating system running on a dedicated computer known as a *server.* Under this model, the server controls the interconnection between all the *client* PCs connected to the network. This architecture goes by the name *client/server.* There are several advantages to a client/server network. For one thing, it can handle very large workgroups when properly administered. For another, because there is centralized control of many networking functions, administration is easier. The fact that there's at least one other computer whose job it is to process the connections between shared peripherals and PCs (a.k.a. *nodes* on the network) means that the trafficking of network functions isn't sopping up the computing power of individual user PCs. Actually, there are several other reasons why the client/server approach is pretty much a requirement when you get into bigger numbers of PCs. But, you get the idea.

The Peer Approach

**Blythe (C:)
Shared Hard
Disk icon**

The peer network approach is very different. There's no central server that controls the traffic. Instead, some PCs are sharing out their resources—files, folders, disk drives, CD-ROM drives, printers, fax modems—while others are making use of those resources. For passing files around, this method works just fine in small groups. When you start talking about letting other people on a peer network send print jobs to a printer physically connected to your PC, however, you're talking about a noticeable degradation of performance on your PC while the print job is processing.

Win 95's architecture is a bit better in this regard than previous Microsoft desktop operating systems. In a serious small-business environment, however, you're going to want, at the very least, to set up a no-man's PC whose only function is to work as a print server. That's OK, though. It's still a whole lot cheaper than buying a powerful network server and an expensive client/server network operating system, such as Novell's NetWare. Not to mention the cost of the network administrator you'd need to hire—or become—to keep the network up to snuff.

So, keeping that background material in mind, Microsoft's soup-to-nuts peer-based networking software works quite well but is limited, as most peer networks are, for serious business use. The peer services are best suited to the small office environment. Or even just to connect any two PCs in your home. The only additional stuff you need to make a peer net fly are an Ethernet network interface card (a.k.a. NIC) for each PC and cables to connect those cards.

Client/Server Client

The second set of Windows 95 network services is a collection of software that lets you trick out the operating system as a client connected to any of several popular client/server networks. For example, everything you need to convert your office PC's DOS and Windows 3.*x* Novell NetWare client comes standard in Windows

95. Not only that, the client software that comes in Windows 95 uses none of your PC's conventional under-1MB memory. It's a bit faster; it's much easier to use; and in most network environments, it installs automatically as long as you're upgrading a properly networked Windows 3.*x* box.

Network Specs

OK, this section digs a level deeper to describe some of the basic features and functions of networked Win 95. You won't find this stuff in that pathetic manual Microsoft shipped with Windows 95. But there are readmes on the CD that talk about some of it. Anyway, here are the technical high points. And, by the way, there's no such thing as a NETWORK SPECS.TXT file. (I made it up because my editor insisted we needed some sort of art on this page.)

Network Specs.txt

Windows 95 comes with built-in support for a pretty wide range of network transport protocols (such as TCP/IP and IPX/SPX), industry-wide communications protocols (such as NetBIOS and named pipes), and existing network device standards (such as NDIS and ODI). It adds these networking protocols and services as layers controlled by a graphical, clickable dialog that makes setting things up as easy as it gets. The design also permits users to add-in software provided specifically for Windows 95 by network software providers. In short, it's easy to understand and highly flexible.

I've tested only Microsoft Windows 95 peer-to-peer services and Novell NetWare support. But, to a greater or lesser degree (as I hear tell from network administrator friends), the following network types are supported out of the box by Windows 95:

Some network types are supported better than others.

Artisoft LANtastic 5.0 and greater

Banyan VINES 5.52 and greater

Beame and Whiteside BW-NFS 3.0c and greater

DEC Pathworks 4.1 and greater (or version 5.0 and greater installed as a protocol)

Microsoft LAN Manager, Windows for Workgroups 3.*x*, and Windows NT (big surprise)

Novell NetWare 3.11 and greater

SunSelect PC-NFS 5.0 and greater

TCS 10-Net 4.1 and greater

Here are some of the networking features that come straight out of the box:

What, it's not a memory hog?   The 32-bit network software uses no conventional memory. On large block transfers over the network, Win 95's protected-mode clients are up to 200 percent faster (according to Microsoft) than real-mode clients under the old DOS and Windows.

Drivers, drivers, drivers. Win 95 includes 32-bit drivers for a long list of network interface cards. So the only disc you're going to have to scrabble around for is the Windows 95 disc. These hardware drivers are liable to be faster than the DOS-launched drivers you were probably using before.

Internet support—it's in there. There's built-in TCP/IP support (the network stuff that converses with the Internet) that's almost easy to configure. A TCP/IP stack was not part of any previous Microsoft operating system.

Forget `.INI` ***files.*** There are no `.INI` files to edit. All the settings are either configured automatically or are visible as graphical dialog check boxes, knobs, or dials you get to twiddle. As Brian, my four-year-old, says: "Cool buttons!"

One password fits all. Windows 95 offers unified user logon and password caching for logging on to Windows NT, Novell NetWare, and other networks, selectable from the Passwords control panel (see Figure 8.5). Automatic logon script processing is provided for Microsoft networks and NetWare networks. Users can access network resources using Network Neighborhood or common dialogs such as File/Open or File/Save As.

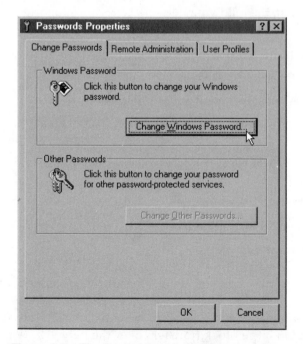

Figure 8.5   The Control Panel's Passwords program

Fewer three-finger salutes. After a server disconnects and becomes available again, Windows 95 reconnects to it automatically and updates the connection status, drive mappings, and printer connections. Bottom line: You won't have to reboot your PC when the server goes down.

Long filenames, dude. Windows 95 can recognize and use long filenames on other computers on the network running Windows 95, on Windows NT servers, and on NetWare volumes that have been configured to support long filenames using OS/2 namespace.

Yeah, work at home. Windows 95 supports several network protocols for remote access, including IPX/SPX and PPP. And the client tools for Dial-Up Networking are built into the operating system.

For network junkies. Windows 95 supports simultaneous connection to multiple networks from a single computer. The limit to the number of network connections depends on your networking software.

Sorta good security. Shared network resources can be protected with user-level security on Novell NetWare or Microsoft Windows NT networks, using existing user account databases. On Windows networks, resources can be protected with share-level security.

HOW TO MAKE NETWORKING GO

> I love to see a young girl go out and grab the world by the lapels. Life's a bitch. You've got to go out and kick ass.
>
> Maya Angelou
> "Kicking Ass," interview in *Girl About Town*, October 13, 1986

Configuring a peer-to-peer network or setting up the client portion on a client/server network doesn't get much easier than with Windows 95. Microsoft took a lot of hits on these features, and some IS departments around the world are still opting for the real-mode drivers supplied by their network operating system makers. I don't know why. There's this mysterious fear, I think, that Microsoft, the makers of the largely failed LAN Manager network operating system, doesn't know a packet from a megabit.

Truth is, the networking stuff in Windows 95 isn't absolutely perfect. I've come across the occasional bug here or there. But, heck, I've come across that with certain drivers and network layers from Novell and others. No one's perfect. I'll pick a 32-bit, out-of-my-conventional-memory network driver any day over a real-mode version of the same thing launched from AUTOEXEC.BAT. Virtualized

Network
Neighborhood

Nope, Win 95 networking's not perfect. It's just better than what was.

32-bit drivers are both faster and more frugal with conventional memory. And as long as something works, I'll stick with it. I've been using Microsoft's Novell network client and IPX/SPX protocol for well over a year now on a NetWare 3.11 network. I've found no reason to dump it in favor of a bunch of .EXEs that are going to cramp my style under 1MB. You shouldn't either. (But if you decide to make a change, try Novell's NetWare Win 95 driver.)

Real-mode Network Drivers and Win 95

Preserving real-mode drivers on Win 95 install is extra work.

If you must run the real-mode drivers on a client/server network, you need to follow a different course during installation. The following steps describe the process for setting up Windows 95 to work with a Novell-supplied real-mode NETX client (NetWare 3.*x*). Novell's NetWare drivers must be installed and working in your previous DOS and Windows 3.*x* installation before you perform the Win 95 upgrade.

1. Start the computer as usual, first making sure the Novell-supplied network software is installed and working properly. Then run Win 95's Setup and select the "Custom" Setup type.

2. When the Network Configuration dialog appears, select "Client for NetWare Networks" in the list of components and click the Remove button.

3. Click the Add button and then double-click "Client" in the Select Network Component Type dialog.

4. In the Select Network Client dialog, click Novell on the Manufacturers list and then "Novell NetWare (Workstation Shell 3.*x* [NETX])" in the Network Clients list. Then click OK.

5. Click the Next button in the Network Configuration dialog. If you want to use only the NETX client, you don't need to specify settings for your network adapter driver or protocols. Setup adds support for an ODI adapter and IPXODI, if needed, automatically by reading settings from your previous network intallation's NET.CFG file. That's it. Just continue on with the rest of the Win 95 Setup.

Your original real-mode network lines are probably still in AUTOEXEC.BAT.

If you already upgraded an older Windows installation without following these steps, then you probably have Microsoft's Client for NetWare Networks running, which is a 32-bit client. To revert to the Novell real-mode client, open AUTOEXEC.BAT and reinstate the lines that pertain to your previous network drivers. They'll be commented out with the phrase "rem — By Windows 95 Network — . . .". (The actual original lines appear where I've placed the ellipses.) Just delete the REM statement and everything up to the beginning of the path and/or filename for each driver. Then remove the Microsoft Client following steps 4 and 5 above and restart Windows. With this configuration, you'll need to set up lines in AUTOEXEC.BAT (or a CALLed batch file) that log you onto the network before Windows loads. But they were probably there before and were just REMed out.

Configuring Peer to Peer

Add New
Hardware

So, you want your own network, huh? (Hey, isn't that a pocket protector sprouting out of your shirt front?) Well, start by installing a network adapter in each PC. If possible, do this before you install Windows 95. Pick Ethernet adapters and opt for 10Base-T twisted-pair cabling. For easiest installation, buy fully Plug and Play–compatible network cards. (PnP hardware that's been officially recognized by Microsoft gets to wear a silly Windows 95 logo on the box.) I should qualify that right away by saying it makes sense to buy PnP hardware only if your PCs have PnP BIOSes. Also, PnP network interface cards will almost certainly be more expensive than non-PnP NICs, so if your budget is tight, PnP isn't a requirement. Remember: Real geeks don't need Plug and Play.

If you're adding Ethernet cards to a pile of PCs, odds are you're going to run into some Interrupt Request (IRQ) and Input/Output Range (I/O) conflicts with the default settings of those cards and other hardware in some of those PCs. (More on this in a bit.) At the very least, get NICs that are fully software configurable. I use the Artisoft NE-2000 compatible NodeRunner cards and like them a lot. But others from companies like 3COM and Intel are equally good NICs that offer software configuration. That means you can change IRQ and I/O settings with a DOS utility instead of hardware switches or jumpers on the card.

Set up all the hardware first. If your cards aren't self-terminating, they'll need terminators on the two machines at either end of the string. If you're adding the NICs to machines that already have Windows 95 installed on them, run Windows after the hardware installation and choose the Add New Hardware Wizard from the Control Panel (see Figure 8.6). Have the Windows 95 Setup disc or disks ready

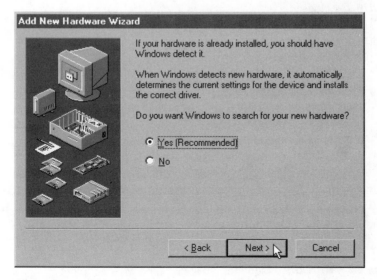

Figure 8.6   Add New Hardware—clicking Next launches the
detection routine

or the install disks that came with the cards if they specifically mention drivers for Windows 95.

If your network interface cardmaker supplied an install disk with drivers specifically for Windows 95, you should probably use them instead of any similar drivers Win 95 might already have. To install the NIC-maker's drivers, run Add New Hardware. Click Next and then No on the second screen. On the third screen, double-click Network adapters under Hardware Types. On the Select Device box, click the Have Disk button and navigate to the directory on the floppy disk that contains the Win 95 `.INF` file that'll start the setup process. Then click the Open button. You should be all set from there.

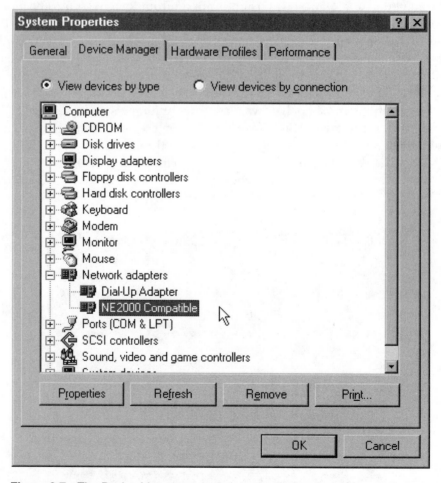

Figure 8.7 The Device Manager tab showing network adapters properly configured

System

After you install each network adapter (and install Win 95 if you haven't already), double check that it's properly configured. Right-click My Computer and choose Properties to open the System control panel. Click the Device Manager tab. You should not see any red circles with slashes through them or yellow exclamation points. These indicate conflicts or problems. You should see a "Network adapters" entry, and when you click the plus sign beside it, you should see your network card listed (see Figure 8.7). If you've got some sort of conflict, you'll probably need to change the interrupt request or input/output range settings on the card. If it's a PnP card, you can do that from Win 95. If not, start by using the NIC's software configuration to change settings. Then, back in Device Manager, make matching changes under the Resources tab of the Properties screen for your network adapter, as shown in Figure 8.8. Confused? Check out Win 95's Hardware Conflict Troubleshooter. Choose Start/Help. On the Index tab, type `hardware conflict troubleshooter` and press Enter. Follow the Windows Help instructions from there. And see the documentation for your NIC.

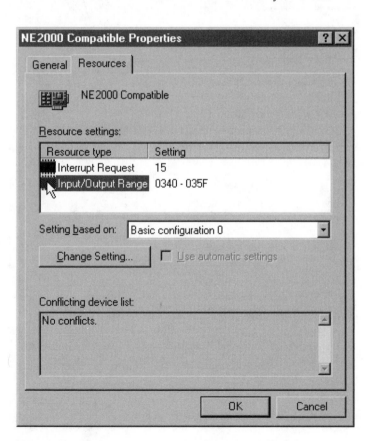

Figure 8.8   Changing a network adapter's I/O Range in Device Manager

Network

Once the hardware is going, it's time to make the network software work. Open the Control Panel and double-click the Network icon. You should find an entry for the network adapter. Each PC on your new network needs a client and a network protocol. At the minimum then, you need to add the Client for Microsoft Networks and Microsoft's IPX/SPX-compatible Protocol. If you've got some PCs on the network that are running Windows for Workgroups instead of Win 95, you'll also need to install Microsoft's Netbeui protocol on all machines. Finally, you'll need to add File and Print Sharing on any workstation that will be offering some of its resources to others on the network. Machines that will not be sharing out their stuff do not need File and Print Sharing.

Network Properties just says "Network" in the title bar; MS was probably embarrassed to call this overgrown weed a "sheet."

Add the Client for Microsoft Networks on the Network Properties screen (actually, it just says "Network" on the top) by clicking the Add button (see Figure 8.9) and then double-clicking the Client line on the next screen. When you get to

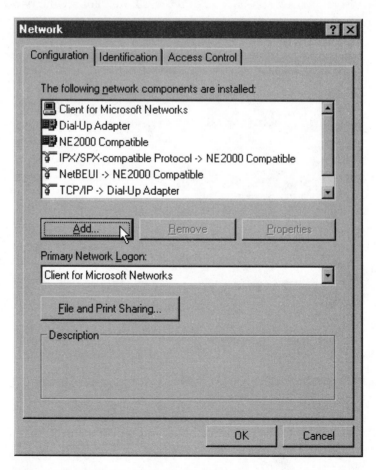

Figure 8.9   The main Network Properties screen and its Add button

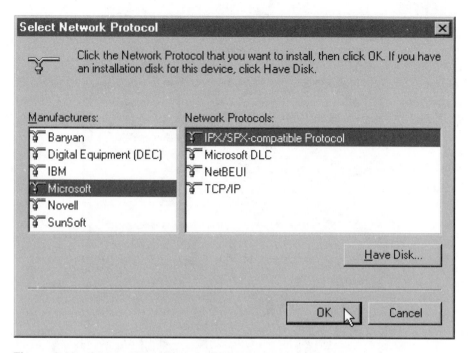

Figure 8.10   Adding Microsoft's IPX/SPX-compatible Protocol

the Select Network Client screen, click Microsoft on the left and double-click the Client for Microsoft Networks on the right.

Add the IPX/SPX-compatible Protocol by following the same routine (see Figure 8.10), choosing "Protocol" instead of "Client" on the Select Network Component Type screen. You'll find "File and printer sharing for Microsoft Networks" under "Service" on the Select Network Component screen. But the easier way is just to click the File and Printer Sharing button back on the main Network Properties screen and turn on file and/or printer sharing there.

Next, click the Identification button on Network Properties. The computer name and Workgroup fields should be filled in, as shown in Figure 8.11. The computer name could be the name of the person who uses that PC or any name the user wants.

Unless something's wrong, you're ready to rock and roll. Click the OK button on Network Properties. When Win 95 asks whether it's OK to restart, click Yes. (It will probably also request your Win 95 Setup disc or disks, so get that stuff ready.) Once back into Windows, you'll find the Network Neighborhood icon is now on the desktop. Move on to the other machines and repeat the process for each.

Finished? Well, test your home-brew network by double-clicking the Network Neighborhood icon. It may take a minute or two for the computers to begin seeing one another (in which case, you'll see Win 95's animated flashlight icon

Network Neighborhood

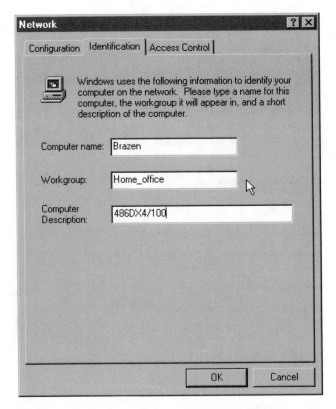

Figure 8.11 Enter a Workgroup name on Network
Properties' Identification tab

waving back and forth looking for other net denizens). If you get an error message, try restarting all the machines before you start pulling your hair out.

If you can't make it work:

1. You need to share specific devices on the network to get any real use out of it. That's explained in more detail in the "Network Explorer" section that follows.

2. Suspect your network cabling first. Double check each and every connection. Is it terminated? Are there any loose ends?

3. Suspect the configuration of your network cards second. Go back and check the Device Manager as described earlier in the chapter.

4. If the hardware checks out, try reinstalling the software. Make sure File and Print Sharing is installed. You might want to enable it on all the machines for the time being.

5. Don't forget Win 95's built-in Help. Choose Start/Help. On the Index tab, type network troubleshooter for step-by-step help in getting to the bottom of any peer-network difficulty.

Configuring a NetWare Client

I'm not promising perfection, but configuring a NetWare client is pretty darn easy. It may in fact already be done if you set up Win 95 over a pre-existing NetWare-client Windows installation. Unless there's something funky going on with your company's network, this'll probably be a pleasant experience.

Things don't go wrong much, but when they do, it can be a bear.

The downside is that when something does go wrong with the client setup, it can be difficult for the average person to figure out. There's really no such thing as a plain-vanilla NetWare network. Chances are, though, your network administrator will quite easily be able to figure out any problem you might encounter. That's because the fix will probably be found as a setting on one of the properties sheets for your client, protocol, or adapter drivers. For example, does your network run NetBIOS? If so, you can enable that by opening the properties for your IPX/SPX protocol drivers and clicking the check box beside "I want to enable NetBIOS over IPX/SPX." Figure 8.12 shows this. You might not know this is necessary, but he or she should.

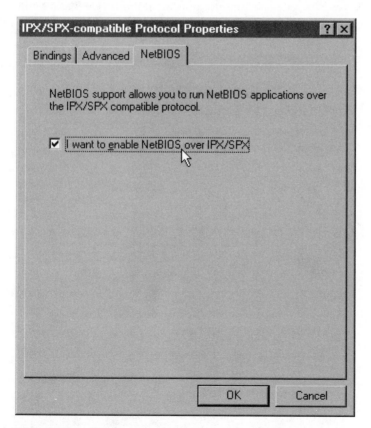

Figure 8.12   Enabling NetBIOS on Properties for IPX/SPX-compatible Protocol

When things go south, there's usually a switch on a dialog that fixes it.

So, when things go wrong, at least you don't have to go hunting around for switches and obscure DLL calls in some .INI file. Let me put it this way: I've installed Windows 95 on literally dozens of NetWare clients, and I've never been forced to give up and call the good IS folks yet. So, plunge ahead. I'll get you there.

My apologies to users of other networks, like Banyan's Vines or DEC's Pathworks. My greatest familiarity is with NetWare. It's also the most popular network in corporate America, so it's what I'm focusing on. Since I've already covered the real-mode and Novell Windows NETX options, from here on out I'm talking about Microsoft's 32-bit stuff, which starts with this junk in Network Properties:

- Client for NetWare Networks (from Microsoft)

- Network Adapter

- IPX/SPX-compatible Protocol (from Microsoft)

If you were looking at my actual Network Properties screen (see Figure 8.13), you'd also see the Client for Microsoft Networks and File and Print Sharing for Microsoft Networks. They're installed because my office PC is a notebook that I bring home and connect to my peer-net there. At home my notebook most defi-

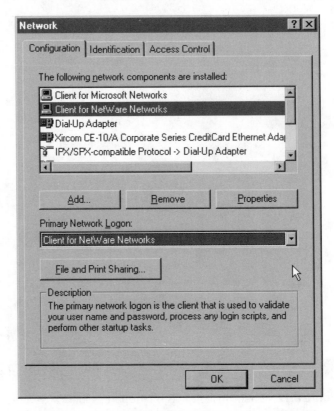

Figure 8.13 My Network Properties screen on a Novell NetWare 3.11 network

nitely needs to share its drives. In my Network Properties, you'd also find a Dial-Up Adapter and TCP/IP (for accessing the Internet, see Chapter 7, "Get on the 'Net") and the Netbeui network protocol (which aids Dial-Up Networking, Direct Cable Connection, and interfacing with Windows for Workgroups boxes on a peer network; see Chapter 6, "The Mobile Win 95").

All this stuff coexists quite nicely, thanks, without any loss of conventional memory. Try that with another PC operating system! I really like this about Windows 95. You've got the flexibility to load a lot of network services without fearing you won't be able to run any apps.

You can load up on network support without worrying about memory.

Do the Deed

To configure the Windows 95 NetWare client from scratch or to attempt to fix a problem, start by opening Control Panel and double-clicking the Network icon (or you can right-click Network Neighborhood and choose Properties from the context menu).

You're going to add the Client for NetWare Networks. Do that by clicking the Add button and double-clicking the Client line on the Select Network Component Type screen. Then, on the Select Network Client screen, click Microsoft on the left and double-click "Client for NetWare Networks" on the right, as shown in Figure 8.14. It's a lot less complicated than it sounds.

Now add the IPX/SPX protocol by following the same routine, opting for Protocol instead of Client on the Select Network Component Type screen. Odds are, you don't need to share any of your local resources on a client/server network. But

I'll get you there, step by step.

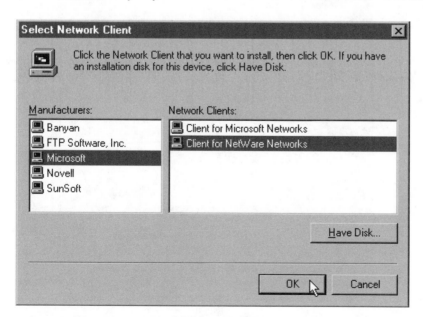

Figure 8.14   Adding the Client for NetWare Networks from the Microsoft folder

When you enable Logon Script Processing, you leave control of *some* device mappings in the hands of your IS folks.

if you do, choose Service on Select Network Component Type, click Microsoft, and then double-click "File and printer sharing for NetWare Networks."

Next, double-click the Client for NetWare Networks line on the Network Properties screen (see Figure 8.15) to bring up the client software's properties screen. You'll need to add your logon server's name and the network drive you logon to. The "Enable logon script processing" check box tells Windows 95 to read server-based NetWare scripts on startup that create permanent connections to network resources like network printers. You can also create persistent connections from within Windows 95 (see the next section, "Network Explorer," for how to do that). When you go that route, you can configure Windows 95 to start up a bit more quickly. The advantage of enabling logon-script processing is that it preserves any pre-existing network mapping. And, theoretically, at least, it gives your network administrator the ability to keep you properly connected to shared volumes and printers when there are changes on the network. (See Figure 8.15 for where to enable NetWare Logon Script Processing.)

You should be all set at this point. When you click OK at the bottom of the main Network Properties screen, Win 95 may prompt you for your Setup disc or disks. It may also prompt you to restart. Go ahead and let it do that.

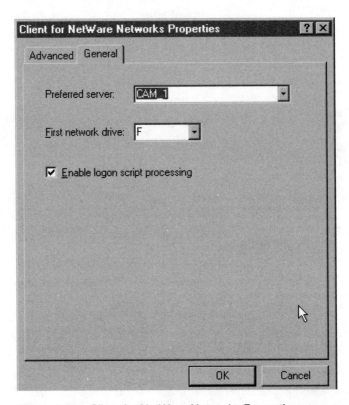

Figure 8.15 Client for NetWare Networks Properties screen

If you're running both the Client for Microsoft Networks and the Client for NetWare Networks (or another network client) for your company's client/server network, you can create a peer-to-peer network within a network. This will work with others at your company who also have the Client for Microsoft Networks installed. It can be very useful for creating quick access to file sharing among small groups of people who work closely together at a company. Best of all, you can set it up all on your own. (See the last section in this chapter, "Win 95 as Server," for an exception, though.)

All the people on such a network must have the same Workgroup named on the Network Properties Identification tab. Microsoft File and Print Sharing must be enabled. And at least one person must specifically share some local resources, such as a folder (see the "Network Explorer" section for how to do this). Remember to password-protect this shared resource.

In a complex multiple network environment, Win 95 may get confused about logon. To prevent this, enter the workgroup you named on the Network Properties' Identification tab in the Windows NT Domain field of the properties sheet for the Client for Microsoft Networks. Don't click the Logon Validation box unless you're on an NT network. Kinda weird, but, hey, it seems to work. See Figure 8.16.

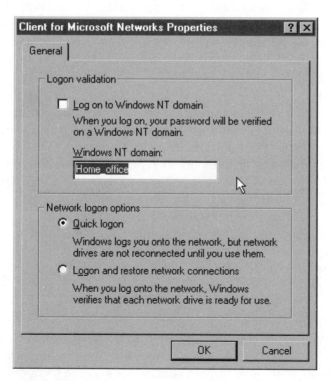

Figure 8.16 This may solve peer-net problems on NetWare networks

NETWORK EXPLORER

> I couldn't claim that I have never felt the urge to explore evil, but when
> you descend into hell you have to be very careful.
>
> Kathleen Raine
> *The Times,* London, April 18, 1992

Network
Neighborhood

You can talk about network nuts and bolts for only so long. Most people—myself included—could really care less about what's going on underneath. And we want to forget all about configuring Windows as a network client or setting it up as a peer network. We want to know how to make the darn PC print to the printer next door instead of the one down the hall. Or how to locate the shared volume that has the new version of that application we want to install. Or how to access data files via our company's wide-area network (WAN).

Ye kant git they-ah from he-ah. Um, wrong. It all starts in one place, like a lot of other stuff in Winsome 95. But it's a different place: Network Neighborhood. If My Computer is your map of known territories—that is, the drives, printers, and other devices installed in your PC—Network Neighborhood is the tool you use to explore uncharted regions.

What's known, and what isn't

Say, that's a funny thing. Since half the rest of the stuff in Win 95 is named Explorer this and Explorer that, wonder why the Micro-Boyz didn't name it Network Explorer? Think maybe some paranoid IS types were afraid their users might actually find data (albeit, maybe somebody else's) on the network? And put pressure on Microsoft? "Neighborhood" makes it sound like you know it already. But actually, Net Neighborhood is far more powerful than that.

Anyway, say you print to a printer in the next room that's connected to someone else's PC or a print server. In that case, even though that printer isn't connected directly to your PC, it'll show up in My Computer, since you or a network administrator probably made the connection permanent, meaning that Windows 95 automatically reconnects to it every time it starts. (At my company, you're on your own, son, for stuff like that.) But what if one day you get a yen to try the color printer that's down the hall and around the corner?

Network Neighborhood (shown in Figure 8.17) is the Magellan to untapped, unmapped servers, volumes, and other shared network peripherals. In other words, you use it to snoop out cool stuff on the net that you haven't already directed Windows to connect to automatically.

If you're sharing your resources, you need to set up security, unless it's a home network.

Of course, whether you're on a client/server network or a Win 95 peer network, you can't just connect to anything. As with any other network, Win 95's built-in networking functions permit each user to choose what he or she will and won't share with others on the network. And there are specific controls for letting *some* other people share *some* of your stuff, while keeping them out of things you want private. And, of course, they can do the same on their PCs.

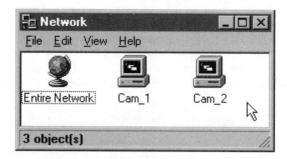

Figure 8.17 A typical Network Neighborhood window on a NetWare network

In a client/server environment, *user-level security* is usually controlled by the network administrator. So, you may be able to see a lot of things in Network Neighborhood that you can't open because you lack the privilege to do so. (But, hey, ask your network administrator.)

The other type of security, and it's sort of your first line of defense, is *share-level security*. That means that when you offer your devices—like a file, folder, printer, or fax modem—on your own PC to others on the network, you can assign them specific passwords. This is the kind of security that Win 95's peer network provides. In large corporate environments, most people aren't sharing anything with other users on the network. Companies typically set up shared volumes in which groups of people post and retrieve files. And network hardware is managed by the IS folks and doesn't belong to any one user. (I tell you *how* to enable sharing a bit later in this chapter. For more about turning on share-level password protection, see Chapter 6, "The Mobile Win 95.")

A word to the wise. Windows 95 makes configuring network stuff so easy, you may get carried away clicking around and accidentally enable file sharing. If you do this on most client/server networks, you could be leaving your PC wide open to infiltration by others in your company. Lousy snoops! The *noive*. So double check that you have File and Printer Sharing turned off under Network Neighborhood's Properties.

"My name is Scot, and I have a network in my home." Networks Anonymous. Anyway, because I do, I bring my office PC (a notebook) home a lot and then connect it to my home network. When I'm at home, I definitely want to share my office PC's stuff with my home boxes. Here's the classic example of when having share-level security comes in handy. Rather than having to turn sharing on and off each time I move back and forth from home to work, I just put in a monster password.

Windows even makes doing this easy. The first time you correctly enter the share-level password to access a password-protected shared device on another PC on the network, you get a prompt asking if you want to save the password

for future connections. If you do this, you'll be able to skip the password entry altogether in the future.

So anyway, my home machines connect to my notebook without a hitch, as if there were no password. But back at work, all my nosy colleagues would receive the password challenge if they tried to connect to my machine.

Getting Started with Network Neighborhood

Entire Network

When you open Network Neighborhood, which—you guessed it—looks like an Explorer window, you'll see two types of icons. The first is Entire Network, which has an icon depicting a globe. Double-click Entire Network, and you'll see icons for the main network servers, workgroups (or *domains*), to which you have access on the network. (On smaller networks, chances are you'll have only one workgroup. So this'll seem kind of superfluous.) When you double-click any domain or workgroup icon, you'll see icons for the individual computers currently logged onto that domain. The shared drives, folders, and printers of any of these PCs are available to you should you like to explore them.

Blister

A workstation

The second type of icon, which you'll see both in the initial Network Neighborhood window and in Entire Network, represents "servers," or workstations, that are currently logged on and sharing at least some of their resources to your primary workgroup or domain. Computer icons shown at the top level are the same as those shown when you enter Entire Network and then double-click your primary domain or workgroup. If you're a bit confused, I'm not surprised. It is a little confusing.

Think of it this way. You have a default workgroup. You choose that default workgroup by right-clicking Network Neighborhood, choosing Properties, and then clicking the Identification tab. Under the Workgroup heading on this screen, you should find the name of your primary workgroup. If it's not there, and you've got a Microsoft Windows peer network setup, you'll want to add it on the screen shown in Figure 8.11.

Folks working as clients on a Windows NT network should choose Properties for the Client for Microsoft Networks line on the Network Properties screen. At the top of the Client for Microsoft Network Properties sheet, there's a check box to enable logging onto an NT domain and a place to enter the domain name. Microsoft peer network users should find this check box disabled and leave it that way. But in some settings, it may be a good idea to enter the Workgroup name on this screen, too (see Figure 8.16).

At the bottom of the Client for Microsoft Networks Properties screen (see Figure 8.18) are settings that control the way Win 95 logs onto persistently, or permanently, mapped network resources. I've used this term *permanently mapped* here and there. If you're burning for a full explanation, skip ahead a few pages to the "What Mapping Means" heading. In a nutshell, though, a permanently mapped device—such as a network volume or printer—is one you've configured Windows (or your network logon script) to check automatically each time you turn your PC on. In the old Windows File Manager, a permanently mapped network volume showed up as a specific drive letter. In Win 95, it shows up as a volume (with a drive letter) in My Computer.

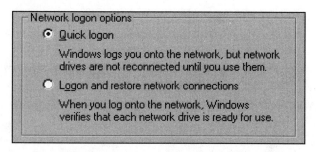

Figure 8.18   Lower portion of Client for Microsoft Networks Properties sheet

Anyway, by choosing "Quick logon" on the bottom of the Client for Microsoft Networks Properties screen, you're telling Windows to register your persistent resource mappings on startup, but to postpone testing for the availability of each of those devices to save time. Instead, it'll test such a connection only when you opt to open it. The time savings is significant (depending on how many resources you've persistently mapped and how often you use them). That's especially the case when you're not connected to the network, since with the "Logon and restore" option in vogue Windows spends a good deal of time poking around for nonexistent needles in a haystack.

Quick logon makes Win 95 startup faster.

The classic example is this: anyone using a notebook PC that's sometimes on the network, and sometimes not. In that situation, I'd advise adding the Client for Microsoft Networks and selecting the Quick logon option. Windows still tests persistent connections, but only when you actually double-click a specific network resource. In fact, I recommend the Quick logon option in most settings. Note, though, that in my traveling notebook PC example, even with Quick logon enabled, you're not going to escape drumming your fingers when you're not connected to the network. Oh, startup will remain just as quick, but the first time you open My Computer, Win 95 will automatically search for your permanent network mappings.

There is a way around this problem. Check out the "Super-My Computer" wand tip in Chapter 5, "Customize It." Essentially, it creates a Start Menu–based cascading folder of drive and folder Shortcuts that lets you avoid ever having to open the actual My Computer. Since it's a cascading menu, you can open only those devices that are actually available to you, bypassing stuff that would make Win 95 poke around for something that isn't there.

How to circumvent this whole mess when you're not on the network

Finally, if you're on a Novell NetWare network, highlight Microsoft's Client for NetWare Networks line on Network Properties and click the Properties button (see Figure 8.19). Enter the name of your primary network server and the letter of your first, or logon, drive. (*Note:* If instead of running Microsoft's NetWare client, you're running Novell's NetWare client—the one that comes on the Win 95 CD—your primary server and first drive must be specified elsewhere, such as in your AUTOEXEC.BAT file in conjunction with real-mode NetWare drivers.)

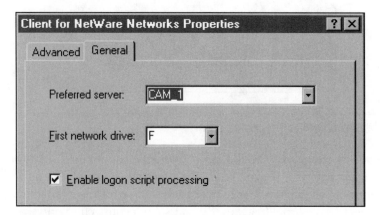

Figure 8.19   Microsoft's Client for NetWare logon server and first drive settings

Unless you're in a large corporate setting with lots of workgroups, like Marketing, Sales, Accounting, and so on, chances are your network has only one domain. In that case, you may be able to ignore the Entire Network icon in Network Neighborhood. All logged workstations in your current domain should show up beside Entire Network. The point of domains is to localize network traffic and to provide a degree of privacy and locality to groups within large networks.

Tips for Exploring

If Win 95's built-in networking sounds like it might come in handy, the stuff in this section tells you how to use its controls to set up things the way you'll like them. There are two main aspects to this: locating useful stuff on the network and making that stuff easy to get to next time. There's a third, optional aspect: sharing stuff on your PC with others on the network.

Play around and experiment with Network Neighborhood. You may be surprised by what you come across if you're in a large corporate environment. My company has a WAN, and it's pretty cool. We have major locations in New York, Boston, San Francisco, and Foster City, California. We also have smaller satellite offices in several other cities as well as other major offices in international locations. Each of those offices has its own LAN. But many of those are connected via special high-speed phone lines to each other, and that's what creates the WAN.

One of the more powerful aspects of Windows 95 networking is its ability to show the entire contents of the large LAN or WAN in a single folder window, such as the one shown in Figure 8.20. As I noted earlier in the chapter, the average person at a large corporation won't have the network privileges required to access each and every server and shared volume on a large LAN or WAN. But the cool part is that Windows 95 makes it far easier to see what's there at the top level. And knowing something is there is half the battle. Information may be the competitive advantage in business, but most of us don't know what we don't know. Running Windows 95 was a real eye opener for me, since I found all sorts of corporate resources I wasn't aware of.

On a network, knowing something is there is half the battle.

Figure 8.20   Network Neighborhood displaying a small part of the Ziff-Davis WAN

When you stumble across a server that interests you in Network Neighborhood, double-click it. If you've been extended permission to use the server, a folder window will open displaying folder icons for all the shared drives or volumes on that server. You may also see printers or other shared devices with icons that represent them. When you haven't been extended the privilege to access a server, you'll get a message to that effect, see an empty folder window, or be prompted to enter a password—depending on the type of network you're on and what kind of security it's using.

What Mapping Means

Blister on 'Blister' (F:)
Mapped network volume

If you find interesting stuff on the network that you know you'll want to access again and again, the smart thing to do is to map the resource, thereby making it a persistent connection. Network volumes and drives that you map show up in My Computer. The term *map* means you're assigning the shared device a drive letter, as if it were a new disk drive physically connected to your PC.

So, if you have one hard drive and a CD-ROM drive on your PC, chances are the CD is Drive D and any new network device you might map could become Drive E. (*Note:* On many client/server networks, Drive F is the first network drive letter, and it may already be mapped as your network logon drive. So the drive letters available to you for mapping may begin with Drive G.) Unless the other letters of the alphabet are already mapped, you should be able to map devices to drive letters all the way up to Z. To help you distinguish between local and network stuff, the icons of mapped devices look a bit different in My Computer than does similar hardware that's actually installed in your PC. The "Blister on 'Blister' (F:)" object icon shown in the margin beside the top of this paragraph is an example of what a persistently mapped network volume looks like in My Computer.

Making Permanent Connections

Windows 95 offers several ways to do most things. Right-mouse-button context menus are often the way to get something done. When it comes to network controls, you'll probably have a tough time figuring out how to do things any other way. So don't forget to use that second mouse button.

Drill down to the folder you really need; but fewer persistent connections is better.

To map something on the network, open the Network Neighborhood folder that contains the thing to be mapped. You can't map servers or workgroups, by the way. Instead, you open them and map specific devices they contain. (Under Win 95, network *drives* look like folders, so don't get confused. That's because many networks don't make any real distinction between shared drives and shared directories. The term *volume* was coined to describe something that's either a drive or a directory.) It's faster and easier in the long run to dig down into the shared volume's directory structure to map the exact folder you need regular access to rather than mapping something at the top level that you'll have to drill down from each time you access it. Balance that thought with the fact that, from a performance standpoint, the fewer persistent connections you create, the better.

When you've found the precise folder you want to map, back out of it to the previous level so that you can see it as a closed folder. Right-click on the object and choose Map Network Drive from the context menu, as shown in Figure 8.21. A small dialog called Map Network Drive will appear, shown in Figure 8.22. Check out the Drive field. It defaults to the first free drive letter in alphabetical order. If the new drive letter assignment looks fine to you, click OK to create a temporary assignment. You'll find the new icon in My Computer; it'll stay there until you shut down Windows. If you want to check around and see your other drive letter mappings, click the down arrow to the right of the Drive field. It opens a drop-down box that you can scroll to see all the letters of the alphabet.

Right-click a folder or printer on the network to map it into My Computer.

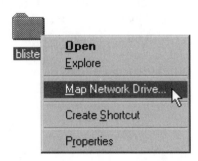

Figure 8.21 Map a drive line on the context menus of Network Neighborhood objects

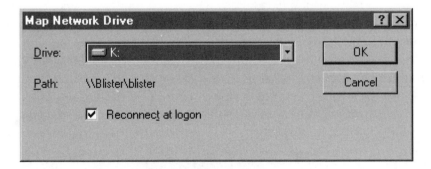

Figure 8.22 The Map Network Drive dialog

Have you found that you don't have access to any drive letters after a certain point? In other words, when you try to map, say, M through Z, you get the error message: "Invalid local device"? If you're on a peer (or some type of client/server) network, there's an easy way to fix this. Launch the System Registry Editor (open the Windows folder, drag and drop the REGEDIT.EXE file onto the Start button, and then click Start and launch RegEdit). Choose Edit/Find, type `lastdrive` in the Find What field, and click the Find Next button. Then press the F3 button to bypass the first instance. On the right side of the Registry Editor, you'll see an ab icon labeled `lastdrive`. Double-click this icon and in the Value Data field, type the letter `z`. Click OK and exit Registry Editor. That'll solve this problem.

A caveat, though: If you're on a NetWare network running real-mode Novell drivers, any change you make to the LastDrive setting must not include your logon drive, which is probably specified in `AUTOEXEC.BAT`. In other words, if your logon drive is F:, the highest letter your LastDrive setting can specify is E. That will leave F to Z for mapping resources using the completely different NetWare method. Check with your net administrator for how to do that.

Make mapping permanent.

Did you notice that "Reconnect at logon" check-off box on the Map Network Drive dialog? This is what you click to make a drive mapping permanent, or persistent. By taking this step, you'll make the new drive mapping stay in place from now on, every time you start Windows. If you don't place a check in this box, the mapping of the resource will stay in effect until the next time you restart your PC, whereupon it will be dropped.

Grab a Printer

To connect to a network printer, locate the printer in Network Neighborhood, right-click it to bring up the context menu, and choose Install (see Figure 8.23). This is the best way to map the printer permanently, make it the default Windows printer if you want, and install the driver software for it. It launches the Add Printer Wizard I talked about in Chapter 2, "Up and Running." What's cool about it is that it installs the printer driver software, if necessary, from the network printer's server. So you won't even need your Win 95 CD or floppies.

With some applications, DOS apps in particular but also some older Winapps, you may need to *capture* a printer port, too. The option to "Capture a Printer Port"

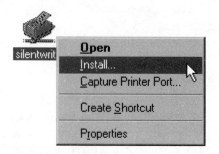

Figure 8.23   Installing a network printer

is on the same context menu (or you can access it from the Install Wizard by saying "yes" to "Do you print from DOS programs?"). Capturing a port is really the same idea as mapping a network drive to a free drive letter, but you're mapping a printer to a port instead. Only thing is, Windows doesn't automatically prevent you from capturing to an actual printer port on your system, unless you've already got a printer connected to that port and that can sometimes cause problems later. So, your best bet is to capture a network printer to a port that's *not* actually available on your system. Try LPT3, as I'm doing in Figure 8.24. That way, you'll still be able to use actual ports on your PC if you ever want to. You know, when your boss finally breaks down and buys you your own color printer.

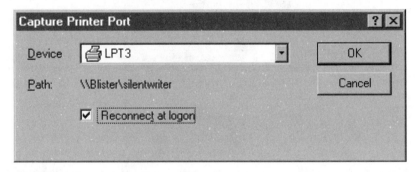

Figure 8.24 Capturing a printer port

Sharing Your Hardware

Remember, when you share your own hardware on the network, you need to think about password-protecting it. It's a good idea to enable password protection, give the password out sparingly, warn people to safeguard it, and change it frequently. Even when you absolutely trust folks around you, you never know when some practical joker might enter your system and drop a little prank utility in the right folder. The next time you start Windows 95, you could be staring at what looks like a Macintosh screen with the "Sad Mac" that indicates that there's something very wrong with your computer. (Hey, it *could* happen.)

When you're sharing your stuff on a network, don't forget security.

For a more detailed description of sharing and password protecting, there's more in Chapter 6, "The Mobile Win 95," since Direct Cable Connection and Dial-Up Networking require sharing. The one thing to know is that if you're looking to share files or folders on your drive, tunnel down in your directory structure as deeply as you can go and still provide access to all the things you want others to be able to connect to. Think about lumping things you want to share from several folders into one folder so that you're exposing less of your hard drive to the network.

How you share stuff is pretty straightforward. Use My Computer to locate the file, folder, drive, or printer that you want to share. Right-click the object to bring up its context menu. If it's sharable, you'll see the Sharing menu item on the popup menu, as shown in Figure 8.25. Click it. Give it a share name on the subsequent dialog. Then specify whether it's a read-only share or you'd like people to be able to make changes to your data. Next enter the password others will need to access your shared stuff.

If you're sharing a printer, it's even more straightforward. Give the new network resource a share name and possibly a password. Unless you're on a large network, password protection of a printer is probably unnecessary.

Figure 8.25   The Sharing line on the context menu of a folder to be shared

WIN 95 AS SERVER

> They also serve who only stand and wait.
>
> John Milton
> Sonnet 16, *On His Blindness*

Most of this chapter has been a primer to Win 95's networking features. Consider this part to be more like a heads-up about some of the more powerful things you can do with Windows 95.

Perhaps the best example of how you can turn a Win 95 PC into a server is the Personal Server feature that Microsoft Plus extends to any Win 95 installation for Dial-Up Networking. For more on that, check out Chapter 6, "The Mobile Win 95." There are also at least four other ways that a Windows 95 PC can function as a server of sorts.

On a Windows 95 peer network, any PC that's sharing its resources is a peer server. You can create a Win 95 server of sorts by dedicating a PC to the task of managing print jobs routed to a printer physically connected to it. Since that PC is not being used by someone for local computing chores, it's effectively a server. By doing this, you offload print jobs and regain control of client PCs more quickly. If your print jobs are long ones in a business setting, give the idea serious consideration.

Hey Mr. Postman

If you choose the Microsoft Mail option during Win 95's Setup or add it later using the Add/Remove Programs tool in Control Panel, you're creating a Microsoft Mail Post Office on your PC—effectively turning it into an email server. This deal is designed for workgroups using the Win 95 peer network. There are two full-blown, client/server Microsoft mail servers that the basic Win 95 Post Office can be upgraded to later on if you get carried away: the Microsoft Mail Server and the Microsoft Exchange Server, neither of which are covered in this book.

Microsoft Mail
Postoffice

The Microsoft Mail Post Office that comes with every copy of Windows 95 gives you the nuts and bolts needed to set up and manage a basic email system. Typically, one workgroup member creates a Post Office on his or her PC by using the Microsoft Mail Post Office control panel. The Post Office is simply a shared directory on the administrator's computer where email is stored. A Wizard steps the mail administrator (i.e., the sucker who has this thing on his or her PC) through the process of creating the Post Office. It is also used to add new users, delete users, and manage shared folders. After the administrator shares the Post Office directory, users can start Microsoft Exchange, enter the shared directory name, and connect to the Post Office in order to send or retrieve mail.

The second way to use Win 95 as a server: Microsoft mail

> **Maybe it's a nit, but why does the Microsoft Mail Post Office Wizard require you to create a folder manually into which the Post Office will be placed? Why can't it create this folder for you? Some Wizard.**

Too bad the client for the Win 95 MS Mail Post Office is the Microsoft Exchange client. Beware of stuff that slices and dices, that's a jack-of-all-mail trades—and master of none. Think of the Exchange client as a work in progress, and you're getting at the heart of what it's like to seriously use this thing for multiple email sources. Personally, I'd check out something else. I'd like to tell you to use ConnectSoft's Email Connection instead, but I can't do that in all good conscience because it also has problems. Your best bet for multiple mail sources is still to use multiple programs, each dedicated to a specific email service or package. That's why it's too bad Microsoft didn't ship the Windows 95 version of the Microsoft Mail client with Windows 95. Or else finish Exchange.

Here's hoping Microsoft decides to finish Exchange someday.

The Microsoft Mail Post Office included in Windows 95 is a workgroup edition, meaning it's limited to exchanging mail with users of a single Post Office in a single workgroup. A single Post Office can potentially support dozens of users, depending on the server performance of the Post Office computer. But, if you've got a peer network running, why not make that dedicated printer server your dedicated MS Mail Post Office, too? I mean, if you must use MS Mail.

You get the option to install the Microsoft Mail Services during initial setup. If you didn't install it and really want to add it later, run the Add/Remove Programs control panel, click the Windows Setup tab, scroll down to the Microsoft

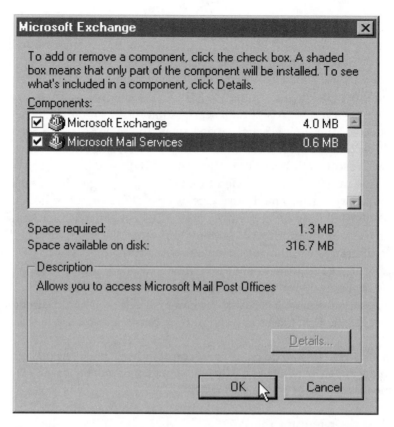

Figure 8.26 Adding the software that lets you set up an MS Mail Post Office

Exchange line, and click the Details button. And then . . . you'll be looking at the screen shown in Figure 8.26. Put the big check next to Microsoft Mail Services and click OK. Don't say I didn't warn you.

Half-faxed Server

Mail and Fax

The third type of Win 95 server is Microsoft Fax. It lets users within a Win 95 workgroup share a fax modem installed on one of the PCs in the workgroup. After the fax modem has been shared, other users can send and receive faxes through it. (This doesn't work for other types of modem communications.) The Windows 95 PC that the modem is connected to is effectively a fax server. The Boyz call it a "network fax server." How original.

The Exchange Inbox of the fax server receives all faxes for the workgroup. Received faxes appear in the Inbox identified as a fax by a folded page icon. If the icon represents a rendered fax, double-clicking it launches the Microsoft Fax viewer application. Otherwise, Exchange opens it as an email message. You can forward and reply to faxes in the same way you can an Exchange mail message.

The fax server's owner must use Microsoft Exchange to manually route faxes from the fax server to the intended recipients via email. Sounds like fun, no? Anyway, expect that kind of thing to improve for outlays of additional cash as third parties like Delrina and others ship products that build heavily on, or replace, the basic features of MS Fax in Windows 95.

Major short-coming: Received faxes have to be manually routed by the "administrator."

Microsoft recommends that any fax server PC that's also a user's PC be a 486 with at least 12MB of RAM. A dedicated fax server can get away with 8MB. I don't know what the requirements would be if it's a dedicated PC that's also a print server and an MS Mail Post Office. But, if no one's minding the Inbox, no one's going to receive faxes anyway. It also needs a 14.4-kbps fax modem. I'd pass on this whole deal unless you've found a third-party fax package that overlays Microsoft Fax.

In case you're not taking my advice, here's how you set up a fax server:

Inbox

1. Double-click the Inbox. Under the Tools menu, choose Microsoft Fax Tools/Options.

2. In the Microsoft Fax Properties dialog, click the Modem tab.

3. At the bottom of the Modem tab, check the box with the description "Let other people on the network use my modem to send faxes." On the popup dialog, choose the local drive on which you want to create the Fax share directory. This creates a folder on your PC called NetFax.

4. Click the Properties button to the right of the "Share name" field. Give the NetFax folder a sharename and make decisions about password protection. To send faxes, users need full access.

5. Click OK to enable the Microsoft Fax shared fax server.

To configure a computer as a client to the fax server, do this:

1. Double-click the Inbox. Under the Tools menu, choose Microsoft Fax Tools/Options.

2. In the Microsoft Fax Properties dialog, click the Modem tab and then click the Add button.

3. In the Add a Fax Device dialog box, double-click the "Network fax server" line.

4. In the Path field, type the network name of the Microsoft Fax shared fax server. The network name is formed by joining the server's computer name (found in the Network option in Control Panel) with the NetFax folder's sharename. For example: \\BRAZEN\WOODY'S FAX. (How come we don't get a browse button here, Redmond?) Then click OK to confirm your choice.

I'm making Woody route faxes to me—heh, heh.

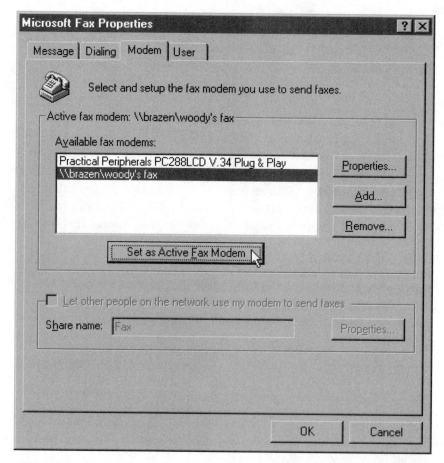

Figure 8.27   Making someone else have to deal with routing received faxes

5. In the Microsoft Fax Properties dialog, click to select the fax server pathname. Then click the Set as Active Fax Modem button, as shown in Figure 8.27.

Win 95 PC "NetWare Server" Makeover

Your IS department has the power to turn off peer network-within-a-network services.

Most of us don't want to turn our PCs into servers on a corporate client/server network. Still, there are times when doing that can be extremely useful. In some corporate settings, Win 95's peer network-within-a-network services that could be employed for this purpose will have been disabled by your net administrator. He or she might want to do that to protect corporate data, since the security that's available on a peer network is share-level security—which ain't the best kind. User-level security, the type used by NetWare servers, is a more sophisticated method of sharing resources that stores a list of specific users and groups of users, each of which is assigned a level of access.

Anyway, there's a point to this little excursion into boring network security stuff. There's a way to contort Win 95's peer network features so that they act more like a NetWare server with user-level security that can be controlled centrally by your net administrator.

For example, if Sharon wants to share a portion of hard disk with user-level security, she could ask her network administrator to specify the users and groups that have access and the type of access allowed. When Jim goes to access Sharon's hard disk, he uses the same user name and password that he uses for his NetWare file server. Sharon's computer will then ask the NetWare file server to authenticate Jim. If the password is valid, he'll be granted access to Sharon's shared volume.

If this sounds like something you need, you'll have to ask your network administrator to create a user (with no password and no trustee assignments) called WINDOWS_PASSTHROUGH on a NetWare file server. Because most Bindery information is not available without an object logged on, Windows 95 needs this logon to scan the NetWare Bindery.

Look alive, soldier, we're almost done.

The advantage to the pass-through approach for network administrators is that they can maintain security and access centrally with a utility like NetWare's Syscon. The range of access privileges allows the administrator to create a variety of access profiles. For example, the administrator could set up a group for read-only users and another for full-access users.

*   *   *

Hey, that's it. You're now a Win 95 network guru. No kidding. Nobody knows half this junk. OK, so maybe no one wants to know half this junk. But it couldn't have truly been an Underground Guide to Win 95 without the lowdown on networking. Admit it. You already know that sooner or later, this chapter is going to come in handy. Yup. Someday it'll save your bacon.

OK, so I'm full of baloney. Turn the page, smarty.

9 Living with It

> Familiarity breeds contempt. How accurate that is. The reason we hold truth in such respect is because we have so little opportunity to get familiar with it.
>
> Mark Twain
> *Notebook*, 1898

This last chapter is a bit of a catchall. It's about working with the OS—month in, month out. Installing and uninstalling applications. What to do when you have problems with apps, or they crash. What to do when Win 95 crashes. How to configure the multimedia stuff, which isn't for everyone. Most of all, though, it's about making Windows run better, faster, more efficiently. And how to make heads or tails of some of its troubleshooting controls.

Living with Windows 95 is mostly a pleasant experience. Really. No, it's not as powerful as that Sherman Tank of operating systems, Windows NT. But, for the time being at any rate, it's the most pleasant place to do business there is. That distinction includes consideration of the Macintosh, OS/2, DOS and Windows 3.*x*, and any other OS on the planet.

Microsoft claimed a 20-minute learning curve for Windows 95. And they've got market research to "prove" it. That's bogus. No OS takes only 20 minutes to learn. But all things considered, Windows 95 is easier to use than any OS except whatever one you were already using. And therein lies the rub. It takes some practice to get used to its running gear and conventions. To know your way around it. To tune it up, tweak it to perfection, and make it work for you the best way it can. It takes a little knowledge. That's what this chapter is about. Not from an interface perspective. Been there, done that. But from the perspective of mastering its general performance settings and controls, dealing with problems, and managing apps.

Figure 9.1   More uncalled-for mood art

INSTALLING APPS

> The Buddha, the Godhead, resides quite as comfortably in the circuits of a
> digital computer or the gears of a cycle transmission as he does at the top
> of a mountain or in the petals of a flower.
>
>   Robert M. Pirsig
>   *Zen and the Art of Motorcycle Maintenance*, 1974

A little truth: You don't work *with* an operating system, you work *in* it. You work
with your data and your applications. Now I can't help you with your data.
That's up to you. But I can give you some pointers for making sure that your apps
do what you want 'em to and don't do what you don't want 'em to. That starts
with their installation.

Add/Remove
Programs

The cardinal rule Microsoft wants you to remember when installing Windows
95 applications is that you should open Control Panel, launch Add/Remove
Programs (see Figure 9.2), and click the Install button. (Or, you can click the
Add/Remove Software button on AutoRun CD-ROM screen, like the Win 95 one
shown in Figure 9.3.) Then, rather than letting you choose from what disk or disc
you want to install, Windows 95 automatically searches your floppy and CD
drives. This may sound more convenient, but in practice it often takes more time.

**Not only that, there are times when Add/Remove Programs/Install is downright
frustrating. Windows 95 expects to find the file** `SETUP.EXE` **(or** `INSTALL.EXE`**)
in the root directory of the installation floppy or CD. But what if you down-
loaded the program from an online service onto your hard drive? Or what if the**
`SETUP.EXE` **file is in a subdirectory on the floppy or CD? The whole thing is
kind of a nuisance because in those instances, you'll have to wait about 30**

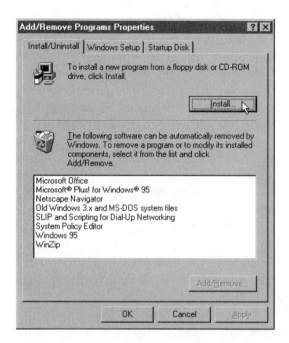

Figure 9.2　Add/Remove Programs: Click Install to install

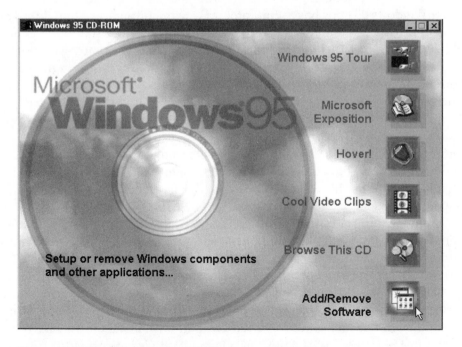

Figure 9.3　Win 95's AutoRun CD Program, with Add/Remove
Software selected

seconds for the SETUP.EXE **search to fail. Then you get to hit the Browse button, and from there it's pretty much like installing a program under the old Windows: You navigate to the correct drive and folder and double-click the** SETUP.EXE **file. Save us from random conveniences.**

So what are the consequences of just using the Start/Run command? When you use Add/Remove Programs, you're explicitly informing the System Registry that an application is being installed. Add/Remove Programs adds information about the application to the Registry, such as which parameters to use when running the app and which files to delete when uninstalling it. That's not the case with Start/Run. So, theoretically at least, you won't be able to uninstall a Windows 95 app if you use Start/Run to install it, and its configurational settings may wind up in the vestigial SYSTEM.INI or WIN.INI files in your Windows folder, instead of the Registry where they belong. In fact, Microsoft recommends that if a setup application uses a name other than SETUP.EXE or INSTALL.EXE, you should start that setup application by double-clicking its icon in a folder window, not by using Start/Run.

The better apps take care of all this for you. Guess what? Many Windows 95 app developers seem to think this whole thing is kind of lame. They expect that many people who install their Win 95 apps will just do what they've always done: Launch the setup programs from the Run command or just double-click them in a file manager or folder window. Their better Windows 95 apps have setup programs with built-in traps that directly call System Registry—no matter what method you choose to install with. Unfortunately, most of these setup programs (the ones I've sampled anyway) don't tell you they're doing that. So you may remember half-way through that you launched a program's setup file the "wrong" way and abort it needlessly. All the Microsoft programs (I've tried), for example, know enough to plug into Registry no matter how you launch their setup routines. But none of them lets you know that it's doing so. The only setup program I've seen to date that gives you some indication is Netscape's Navigator, whose setup program (which is licensed from another company) has a splash screen with the marketing term "InstallShield." That maybe doesn't hit you over the head with its obviousness, but it's a step in the right direction.

Windows95 (D:)

Another thing. I talked about the AutoRun feature for CDs in Chapter 1, "First Things First." Stick a Windows 95–compatible CD in your Win 95 PC, and after a few moments, it'll launch a program interface for the CD. These interfaces vary, but most of them have a button called "Install." In the Windows 95 CD's case, it quite logically says Add/Remove Software. You can be pretty confident that any such button will properly install a Windows 95 app from the CD (although I'm sure some bonehead company will make the mistake of offering an Install button on its AutoRun screen that does not correctly address the System Registry).

The one easy way to know for sure that a Win 95 application was properly installed and registered in System Registry is to check that its name is listed on the bottom part of the Add/Remove Programs Properties screen. All the programs shown in Figure 9.4 are Windows 95 apps that were properly installed. They're also uninstallable from this dialog.

How to find out whether it installed right

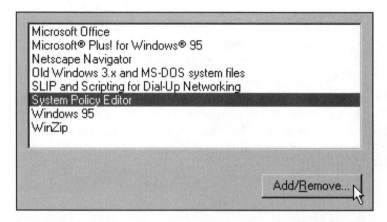

Figure 9.4   Uninstall apps by selecting them and hitting the Add/Remove button

You're still installing 16-bit Windows 3.*x* apps? (Well, OK, but why?) None of the above applies to these apps, which are second-class citizens under Win 95. You can't use Add/Remove Programs to uninstall them no matter what you do. And if they need to add settings lines to SYSTEM.INI and WIN.INI, well, that's why those two files still exist. Some programs reside in a gray area. They've been updated for Windows 95 but aren't really Windows 95 apps because they're 16-bit and aren't Registry-aware.

It's perfectly OK to use Add/Remove Programs to install any 16-bit application, if you want. There's just no real advantage to doing so. If there is an advantage, it's just that you're getting into the right habit, according to Microsoft. Personally, I think it's incumbent upon app developers to ensure that any old way we choose to install their apps will get 'em properly registered. We shouldn't have to think about this. And I think that's exactly what's going to happen.

You may be a real glutton for installation punishment, like me. You know, you never met a shareware utility you didn't download, you get software in the mail all the time that you just have to run, and you install every version of Netscape that ever was (more than 25 by last count—they've almost got more flavors than Baskin-Robbins). If so, put Add/Remove Programs right on Start by dragging it out of Control Panel and dropping it onto the Start button.

Shades of Uninstall

Add/Remove...

So once you've got apps—Windows 95 stuff, that is—installed, Add/Remove Programs starts becoming a truly useful place. Not only can you fully uninstall Windows 95 apps from there, but with many, you also can selectively install or uninstall components. The paradigm Microsoft uses for this was first introduced with Word 6.0 for Windows and spread rapidly to all their multicomponent programs. You get a stack of top-level program component headers in a list box. Click any of these headers to tunnel down to options beneath it. There's a box beside each and every item you find. If there's a check mark in the box, that item is already installed (or, it's the default setting on initial installation). If there's no check, it's not installed. If you place a check mark in an empty box, it'll be installed after you're done making choices. If you clear a check box, that item will be uninstalled when you click OK. While this isn't particularly ingenious, we're not talking rocket science here, and it works.

The bad news is that not every Windows 95 program will work this way. Moreover, not every one will have (or even need) selective install/uninstall. The good news is you already know how to launch your app's setup programs. You may still need the setup disc or disks for some applications. But many programs copy their setup routines into their installation directories, so you won't need the disks unless you want to add something. And it's empowering to be able to uninstall something whenever you want to. It makes you more willing to try new applications, and that's a very good thing.

Microsoft's motives weren't entirely altruistic.

A little subtext is in order because despite this good thing that Microsoft did, its motives weren't entirely pure. The Boyz pretty much had to add this uninstall feature. Without it, they'd be forcing us users to edit the System Registry in order to fully uninstall programs. (Or worse, asking independent software vendors to support us when we couldn't figure out how to do that.) Believe me, if you thought editing .INI files was an arcane process, you ain't seen nothing until you start hacking around with System Registry.

Rip out that crummy program lickety-split.

Anyway, so how do you do this selective install/uninstall thing? It's as easy as selecting the program's name on the Add/Remove Programs Properties screen and clicking the Add/Remove button. What you'll see next depends on the installed application, not Windows 95. And it varies quite a lot. In the simplest form, you get a warning box asking if you're sure you want to fully remove the program. Other apps pop up a box, like the one from Microsoft Plus! shown in Figure 9.5, that asks whether you want to Add/Remove components, Reinstall, or Remove All.

Figure 9.5   The Plus! Setup program launched from Add/Remove Programs

WHEN THINGS GO BUMP IN THE NIGHT

> From ghoulies and ghosties and long-leggety beasties
> And things that go bump in the night, Good Lord, deliver us!
>
> Anonymous
> Cornish prayer

It's probably no surprise that Windows 95 apps have fewer compatibility problems than Win 3.1 apps have under either Win 3.*x* or Windows 95. Even so, Microsoft has done some compatibility testing of existing Windows apps (pissing off a lot of software developers in the process). The long and short of it is, Microsoft says more than 2500 apps work OK under Windows 95. To check the list out for yourself on Microsoft's Web site, direct your browser to `http://www.microsoft.com/windows/thirdparty.htm`. There's a much shorter list of known application problems in the `PROGRAMS.TXT` file that you'll find in your Windows folder.

What goes wrong with some 16-bit Winapps

So, what can and therefore (by Murphy's Law) will go wrong with some 16-bit programs? Some DOS and Windows apps don't run well under Windows 95 because they were written to take advantage of characteristics of older operating systems. For example, certain applications use a portion of the title bar to include items other than the title, such as a Quick Help button. Because Windows 95 title bars are not formatted in the same way as Windows 3.*x* title bars, some information may be overwritten when you run these old applications. Other programs use interrupts that are not automatically supported by Windows 95. Still others don't handle long filenames well or incorrectly check for the operating system's version number.

When you maximize the windows of some apps, they overrun Taskbar, even when you have Taskbar Properties set so that it's Always on Top. That's because the app uses specific window metrics rather than what amounts to the "make me full screen size" command to control its maximum size. What happens next is that Windows 95 realizes something is wrong and politely moves the Taskbar out of the way. To get to the Start button, you may have to press Ctrl-Esc. The thing to do is to send the app window back down to custom size and resize it manually to a maximum size that leaves Taskbar be.

Some Win 3.*x* apps have trouble with long menu item names. That's because they specifically called the Win 3.*x* System Font for their own menus. To solve this problem, you'll have to revert to the Windows Standard scheme on the Appearance tab of the Display Properties control panel.

Finally, some applications, notably Notepad and WordPad, won't let you save files with a file extension other than one that they specifically support or that has been created as a File Type for them (see Chapter 5, "Customize It"). When you append a different extension, they append yet another period and their default extension (that's .TXT for Notepad and .DOC for WordPad). Annoying. You can get around this problem by enclosing in quotation marks the whole filename as you want it to appear.

Windows 95 provides a utility that helps to improve the compatibility of many 16-bit applications with Windows 95. You can use the Make Compatible utility (see Figure 9.6) to troubleshoot when, for example, you have trouble printing from an application or an application stalls or has performance problems. It can switch from Enhanced Metafile printer-spooling to Raw data; increase stack memory to an application; and emulate earlier versions of Windows. It also solves other common problems that give apps fits under Win 95. To run the Make Compatible utility, locate the MKCOMPAT.EXE **file in the System folder contained in your Windows folder. It's a little sparse on instructions, and even the Win 95 Resource Kit doesn't tell you much. But get it going by choosing File/Choose Program. Select File/Save when you're done.**

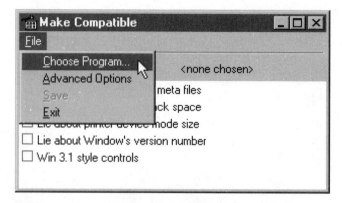

Figure 9.6   The Make Compatible program can save you app frustration

Crash without Burn

Win 95's vaunted reliability notwithstanding, you're not going to kiss application errors good-bye. What does happen far less frequently is failed applications' pulling down the whole thing. In fact, very often you can just relaunch a program that crashed. I have not noticed 32-bit Win 95 apps to be hardier in this regard than their 16-bit brethren. If anything, I've noticed that Win 95 apps have a greater tendency to crash than 16-bit apps do. This isn't the way it's supposed to be.

Overall, I'd have to say that the number of crashes is reduced and that crashes are far less nerve-wracking because Windows 95 is more graceful about handling them. For one thing, unless a program freezes, Windows 95 gives you detailed (albeit, unintelligible to all but hackers and programmers) information about what caused the crash behind a Details button. You don't have to look at this information. But if you've got a recurring problem and you're on the phone with the tech support line for either Microsoft or your app provider, it can come in handy.

Was Win 3.1's Dr. Watson your pal? You won't need him anymore.

Bottom line: Most of the time when an application crashes, you can terminate it without also killing off other applications you were running. And while that may not sound like much, it's a vast improvement over the old Windows—which seldom if ever delivered on that one. This is easy to do, once you know how. When something goes haywire, don't shut down Windows. Instead, simultaneously press and release the Ctrl, Alt, and Delete keys. What you'll see is the Close Program box in Figure 9.7. Inside Close Program, you'll see a list of all the separate programs and system functions currently running in Windows. If something has crashed, you'll see the words [not responding] beside it. That's the item that needs to go in order for you to regain control. Select that item and then click the End Task button. Sometimes it takes a minute or so for Win 95 to respond with a verification screen. If there's more than one item that's not

What to do in the event of a crash

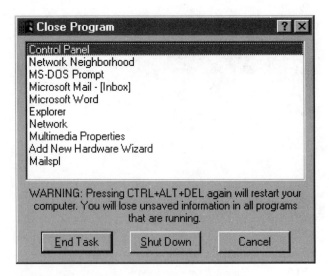

Figure 9.7   The Close Program screen can get you out of a lot of jams

responding, reopen the Close Program box and repeat the process. Leave the other apps going; more often than not, you're still in business. Get acquainted with this thing, because it's going to save your bacon someday.

If the operating system itself gets hung with the entire screen frozen, or you get one of those real serious error messages, or if your system spontaneously reboots, there's not a whole lot you can do, I'm afraid.

Pin the tail on the donkey.   But there's an opposite kind of problem you'll sometimes have to contend with. A sort of pin-the-tail-on-the-donkey thing, where you're not sure what's wrong, and you've got to track down the culprit. The classic symptoms are this. You open the Close Program box, and nothing appears to be wrong. None of the running programs has that [not responding] deal beside it. But you know something very definitely is wrong because your programs aren't working correctly.

Sometimes when Win 95's underlying Explorer shell or the Taskbar hangs, it can appear that the entire operating system is in trouble when really it isn't. And these two OS components don't always report something's wrong in Close Programs when they've gone bad. If you can find nothing else amiss, open the Close Program Box and try ending first Explorer and then Systray. Win 95 automatically relaunches new instances of these programs after the original is terminated. And a lot of times, one of these two steps turns the trick.

When in doubt, suspect everything.   If you've got a lot of programs running, it pays to suspect everything. If you can, try minimizing and maximizing program windows. The least responsive program onscreen is apt to be the one that's got the problem—even if it appears to be running just fine in the Close Programs dialog. Often, you'll find the culprit just by clicking on its program window, because things will hang at that point. But if you're patient, eventually Win 95 may be able to return control to you after a couple of minutes. If you find a program like that, attempt to save any data it may have loaded, and then terminate it in the Close Programs box. With luck, things will start working normally after that. (Restarting at this point is optional. If you're working with important data, I'd advise it. However, my experience has been that Windows 95 recovers from this sort of crashed app situation extremely well.)

If your search for the culprit comes up empty, your next strategy is to end every program in the Close Programs dialog, one at a time, checking between each one to see whether things are repaired. If nothing works or you get hung up in Close Programs, click its Shut Down button. If you can't open the Start Menu (a common malady in crash situations), Close Program's Shut Down button is a more graceful means of saying bye than your other options: pressing Ctrl-Alt-Delete twice in succession or just hitting the power button. When you close Windows in these less graceful ways, you'll not only lose any unsaved data in any of your running applications, you'll probably also lose some information that hadn't yet been saved to Windows 95's virtual memory swap file (more on this later in this chapter).

What to do when things look bleak

Win 95 can correctly close most programs you leave open and running when you choose Shut Down from the Start Menu. Some Windows 95 programs can even interrupt the shut down to allow you to save unsaved open data files when this happens. Clearly all that grace goes down the drain in many crash situations. And it's certainly the case whenever you force a reboot with double Ctrl-Alt-Delete, the reset button, or the power switch.

Graceful program shut downs

By the way, here's a little off-the-subject tip: Win 95 doesn't close folder windows that you leave running (open or minimized) on shut down. The next time you start Windows, those folders will still reappear where you left them. You can use that to your advantage with any folder you access frequently.

One last folder window tip

There's a utility buried on the CD that's designed to back up important system initialization files so that they can be reinstated in the event of a system catastrophe. You might want to check it out. It's called the Emergency Recovery Utility, or ERU, and you'll find it (the `ERU.EXE` file, that is) on the CD in the `\Other\Misc\Eru` **folder. (Real obvious, huh?) Anyway, this birdie—shown in Figure 9.8—saves** `CONFIG.SYS`, `AUTOEXEC.BAT`, `WIN.INI`, `SYSTEM.INI`, `PROTOCOL.INI`, `USER.DAT`, `SYSTEM.DAT` **(these last two are the System Registry files),** `IO.SYS`, `COMMAND.COM`, **and** `MSDOS.SYS`. **You can also create custom backups and store them on any drive, floppy, or network. To restore system configuration files (selectively, if you want), use the** `ERD.EXE` **utility, which is in the same folder. The** `ERU.TXT` **file explains all this stuff.** *Note:* **This thing can only help you if you use it. Microsoft recommends running it before you make any major hardware or software configuration update to your system. (***Program note:* **To make this guy work, you have to have** `CONFIG.SYS` **and** `AUTOEXEC.BAT` **files in your root directory, even if they're empty.)**

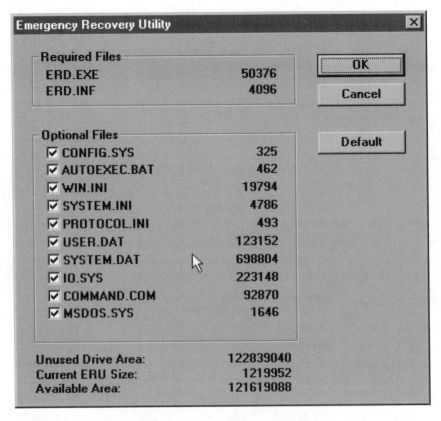

Figure 9.8   The Emergency Recovery Utility's custom screen

MEDDLIN' WITH MULTIMEDIA

You have riches and freedom here but I feel no sense of faith or direction.
You have so many computers, why don't you use them in the search for
love?

Lech Walesa
Quoted in *The Daily Telegraph*, London, December 14, 1988

Multimedia

There's room to get real technical about the Multimedia control panel and the
multimedia support provided by Windows 95. In a nutshell, it has built-in support for digital audio and video, including basic utilities for recording, playing,
and editing these media. The result is convenience, better control, and better quality multimedia presentations.

Using an architecture called Media Control Interface, Win 95 supports a wide
variety of devices out of the box, including VCRs, DAT drives, CDs, scanners, and
video disc players. But that's the good news. Understanding the specs and getting

this high-end media stuff to work isn't a whole lot easier than performing similar tasks under the old Windows. And I'm not even going to try here, since a lot of this is highly dependent on the multimedia hardware you're using.

What's vastly better is that the control interfaces offer a much deeper level of settings than you might expect. So, like other technical things in Windows 95, if you understand the technology already, you'll probably find a way to configure it to work without editing `.INI` files or running additional layers of software. Moreover, some of Win 95's 32-bitness shows up here in the quality of its multimedia capabilities.

The best part is a vastly improved and deepened interface.

So anyway, you go to the Multimedia control panel (which looks like Figure 9.9), whether you want to turn off the volume control icon on Taskbar or configure a video compression driver. There are five tabs on Multimedia Properties: Audio, Video, MIDI, CD Music, and Advanced. Most people will be able to skip Advanced. In essence, it's something like a Device Manager for multimedia software and hardware. The MIDI tab is for people working with electronic musical instruments and devices connected to the MIDI ports on their sound cards, so that lets most of us out too.

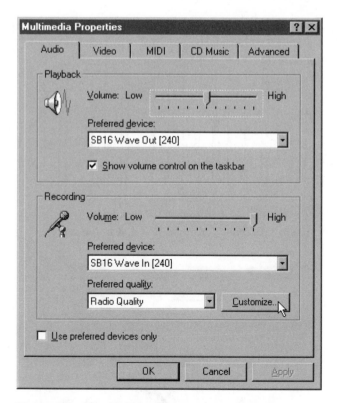

Figure 9.9 The Multimedia control panel showing the Audio tab

The other three tabs offer very simple controls that are repeated in the buried recesses of the Advanced tab (see Figure 9.10). The CD Music tab ensures Win 95 is properly oriented to the drive letter on your system that's playing an audio CD (this is only important if you've got more than one CD drive on your system) and controls the initial volume of the CD drive's headphone jack. The Video tab controls the size of video images displayed on your monitor. And the Audio tab offers basic settings for the device and volume level used for recording and playback of sound.

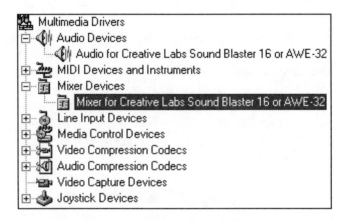

Figure 9.10 Device Manager-like Multimedia Advanced tab work area

Behind the Customize button accessed from the Recording area of the Audio tab, you'll find stuff that lets you configure recording quality, recording format, and attributes. If you're into recording sounds, like creating a RealAudio recording to post on the Web, this stuff can be very useful. For example, selecting a higher Hz (hertz) number than the default, as I'm doing in Figure 9.11, would emphasize higher sounds in your recording. Selecting a higher KB/s (kilobytes per second) setting would increase the amount of data recorded for an interval of sound, thereby boosting its quality considerably. The Customize screen is pretty cool.

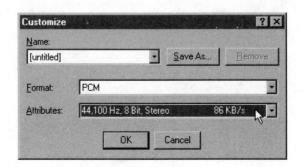

Figure 9.11 On the Customize screen, boost KB/s to gain sound recording quality

Media Applets

But that's not all you get. Although the CD Player, Media Player, Sound Recorder, and Volume Control are optional on some Setup tracks, they're all standard fare in Win 95. Media Player and Sound Recorder return from the old Windows, and they're very similar to their predecessors. Media Player supports some additional formats. But both CD Player and the Volume Control utility are new and quite useful.

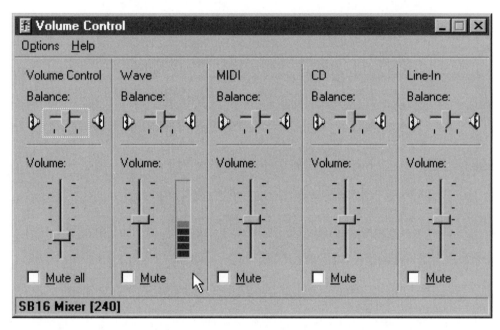

Figure 9.12   Volume Control gives you sound level controls for seven devices

Volume Control looks and acts suspiciously like a utility that ships with Creative Technologies Sound Blaster soundcards. This handy gizmo lets you turn down your PC speaker volume, adjust balance, control Wave and MIDI levels, and other stuff (see Figure 9.12). It's a nice touch. Quick tip: You can also get this guy by double-clicking the Speaker icon in Taskbar's Notification Area.

Meanwhile, the CD Player, displayed in Figure 9.13, finally brings that Mac audio CD playback feature to PCs, so you can rock out at work. There's even a little database that lets you enter the name of the artist, the album title, and the names of the tracks. Newer CDs support this, so the next time you insert the CD Win 95 will automatically identify the CD and call up your database entries. You also can select random play, continuous play, and other settings. The minimized CD Player Taskbar button even shows the current track number and playing time.

Play audio CDs in your PC's CD drive.

Figure 9.13 The CD Player applet lets you play audio CDs on your PC

You'll find the Multimedia applets buried a little deep on the Start/Programs/Accessories/Multimedia submenu. If you don't find them in that folder, you probably need to install them using the Add/Remove Programs control panel. Click the Windows Setup tab, insert your Win 95 disc or disk, and you'll find them by selecting Multimedia and clicking the Details button.

PERFORMANCE TUNING

> Speed, it seems to me, provides the one genuinely modern pleasure.
>
> Aldous Huxley
> "Wanted, a New Pleasure," in *Music at Night and Other Essays*, 1949

Remember all that talk about the Performance tab in Chapter 2, "Up and Running"? That was just to check to make sure you weren't running on a couple less cylinders than you were supposed to be. Here's where you use the System control panel's Performance tab, and a bunch of other stuff, to fine-tune your Win 95 installation to a resonant growl.

Truth in book writing a moment: Unless there's something wrong with your PC or Win 95's configuration, this section isn't going to give you a 50-horse boost or anything. Windows 95 is pretty dang good about tricking itself out for speed the first time. But if you follow all the instructions and tips on the next several pages, you can expect to squeeze the equivalent of another 20 ponies out of your machine. Grease-smeared hot-rodders would reckon that to be a very good day's work indeed, and so should you.

Performance Tab Stuff

Open the System control panel and click its Performance tab. (I explained the basics of this dialog in Chapter 2, "Up and Running," but it's worth a quick repeat.) About halfway down the main Performance tab screen, you should see a line that reads "Your system is configured for optimal performance." If instead you see a window with an error message or messages in it, turn back to Chapter 2 and get it straightened out. Like now. The good news is, you're probably going to see some type of performance improvement when you get rid of that problem. More often than not, when a window appears on the Performance tab, the problems reported pertain to Windows' having to resort to real-mode drivers instead of protected-mode VxDs. Real-mode drivers are the ones that are loaded in DOS, usually from `CONFIG.SYS`. Ninety-nine times out of 100, they're slower than Windows' 32-bit VxDs.

System

If you find error messages on the Performance tab, turn back to Chapter 2, like now.

Here's some help for figuring out real-mode driver problems. Windows 95 automatically unloads all real-mode drivers for which it already has protected-mode drivers. Real-mode drivers and TSRs that Windows 95 can safely replace with corresponding protected-mode drivers are identified in the safe driver list. You'll find this list in the `IOS.INI` file in the Windows folder.

If a real-mode driver provides better performance (a rarity) or provides some functions not present in the Windows 95 protected-mode driver, you should remove the real-mode driver from the safe driver list in the `IOS.INI` file. That'll force Windows to run it from your `CONFIG.SYS` file. More often than not, though, a real-mode driver performs more slowly and can safely be replaced by a Win 95 protected-mode driver. So, for example, if you get a new Win 95 VxD for a previously unsupported real-mode driver, you should add the real-mode driver to the safe driver list. You'll find details on how to do this on the "Real-mode Drivers and the IOS.INI Safe Driver List" page in the Win 95 Resource Kit Help file.

Finally, if you believe that a protected-mode driver should be controlling a device but the device shows up with a real-mode driver warning on the Performance tab, you can check entries in the `IOS.LOG` file in the Windows folder. This file is created whenever a protected-mode driver is not available or if the OS detects an unknown device driver controlling a device. In most cases, the first line in `IOS.LOG` states why the protected-mode driver was not loaded.

File System Tweaks

At the bottom of the Performance tab, under the heading "Advanced settings," you'll find three buttons: File System, Graphics, and Virtual Memory. A good chunk of the stuff you'll be performance tuning will center around these dialogs. Some of the things you'll find on these screens are related more to troubleshooting than performance. I'll come back to troubleshooting a bit later in the chapter.

File System...

The File System Properties screen opens to the Hard Disk tab, just the way it looks in Figure 9.14. There are two main settings: your PC's "role," which Microsoft also calls a computer "profile" (Microsoft: Way too many *profile* types in Windows 95), and Read-ahead optimization. Both settings control minor changes in the way your hard disk buffers, caches, and reads various types of data to lend a modest boost in disk performance. The Read-ahead optimization slider bar devotes up to 64K of RAM to read-ahead on large-chunk data transfers in order to increase throughput. In for a penny, in for a pound. My advice is to crank this sucker up.

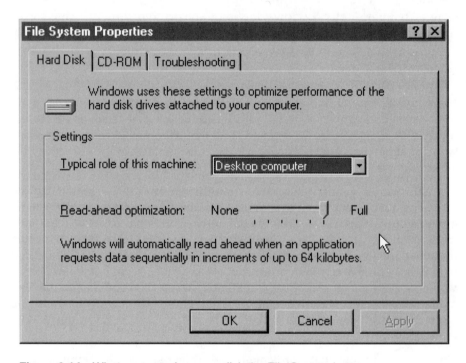

Figure 9.14   What you get when you click the File System button

Consider available RAM for "Typical role of this machine."

The "Typical role of this machine" setting offers three choices: Desktop computer, Mobile or docking system, and Network server. The easy thing is to just pick the description that applies to your PC. If, however, you've got a high-powered notebook PC with lots of RAM and well-optimized memory—and you rarely run it on battery power—switch to Desktop computer. Similarly, if you've got a desktop PC that has limited memory, I'd advise choosing Mobile or docking system. These "role" settings control the amount of RAM devoted to caching previously accessed paths and filenames. They also adjust buffer settings generally, with Desktop computer and Network server roles increasing the time before the buffers are written to disk. The longer this stuff stays in RAM, the more often it can be re-executed quickly. Once written to disk, it takes a bit longer to re-execute.

Windows 95 has a built-in feature that helps it prevent file fragmentation on your hard disk. Under the old MS-DOS, when you copied files to your hard disk, the file system allocated the very first available space it found on your hard disk, no matter how small it was. That virtually ensured pretty heavy fragmentation. (For an explanation of file fragmentation, see the "Win 95's Disk Utilities" section in the Chapter 4, "Files, Folders, Exploring.") Win 95's enhanced file system searches first for a free 512K chunk of contiguous disk space before copying. If it can't find one, it goes back to the old MS-DOS way of doing things. This one little change can help programs launch faster, since it's far more likely that the disk won't have to skip around looking for executable code in 17 locations.

You can help this along considerably—and keep Windows 95 running at top performance—by running Win 95's Disk Defragmenter utility, oh, about once a month. If you install and remove a lot of programs and copy, create, or delete a lot of data files, you might want to defrag more often. For more on Disk Defragmenter, see Chapter 4.

On to the CD-ROM button on the File System Properties screen, shown in Figure 9.15. Windows 95 doesn't really know how fast your CD-ROM drive is. So check the documentation for your CD drive and select the correct setting on the drop-down menu beside the "Optimize access pattern for:" description. Chances are your CD drive is at least a double-speed drive, unless it's an older model.

The "Supplemental cache size" slider bar controls the size of cache used for data transfers from your CD drive. This cache is paged out from RAM to your hard drive because your hard drive is faster than your CD. Nevertheless, it starts in RAM. So your decision about how large to make the supplemental cache should be based on how much RAM you've got. If you've got 8MB or less, slide the slider to Small. If you've got 12MB of RAM, pull the slider one notch back from Large (the actual size of the cache in kilobytes appears in the status statement at the bottom of the dialog). Anything more than 12MB, boost the cache size to the limit.

Make the right CD caching decision.

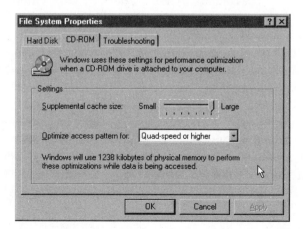

Figure 9.15 File System's CD-ROM tab on a PC with 16MB of RAM

Graphically Speaking

Graphics...

Skip the File System Properties Troubleshooting tab for now and click the OK button and then the Graphics Button. You'll get a screen that looks like Figure 9.16. From a strictly performance standpoint, the default setting on the Advanced Graphics Settings dialog's slider bar is Full. This turns on all graphics hardware acceleration (stuff that enables your display adapter) available in the display driver. So your first check is to ensure this thing is set to Full. As long as you're not having any problems with your mouse pointer or running Windows or applications, you're done.

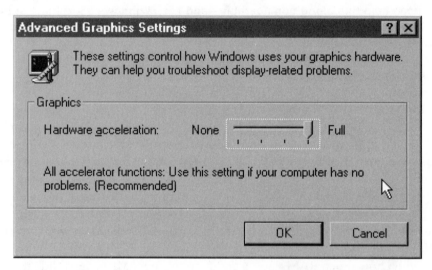

Figure 9.16   "Full" is the default setting for Advanced Graphics Settings

The Full setting presumes you have a graphics accelerator on your video card. It also presumes that the display driver loaded for your video card is the right one for your card. So if you're having problems that you suspect might be video driver-related, you can use the slider to troubleshoot and correct for them.

Advanced Graphics is really a trouble-shooting tool, not a performance improver.

The first notch from the right on the slider may correct mouse pointer display problems. It disables hardware cursor support in the display driver. The second notch from the right attempts to correct more serious display errors by preventing the video card from performing some bit-block transfers. It also disables memory-mapped input/output for some display drivers. The None setting tries to correct for even more serious problems, such as when your PC hangs. You might use it if you received an error message at system startup stating that an application caused "an invalid page fault in module <unknown>." In such cases, None may temporarily fix the problem. But check to make sure you've got the right video driver installed, and call the manufacturer to get the problem resolved.

Virtual Memory

Virtual Memory is next in the cavalcade of performance considerations. I've got what might be your number-one best performance tip: Don't mess with this thing (see Figure 9.17). I'm not kidding. About 98 percent of the time, Windows sets up virtual memory far better than you could ever do on your own. And it adjusts the size of the swap file automatically.

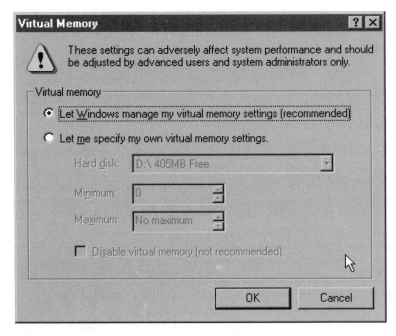

Figure 9.17 Virtual Memory settings, with the swap file on a second hard drive

What's a *swap file?* Essentially, it's a cheat. Windows fools itself and your programs into thinking that it's loading data into RAM. In actuality, it's temporarily paging some of that data out to your hard drive in a special format that it can read very quickly. Basically, it's taking notes. The use of this type of memory swapping is known generically as *virtual memory*. And Windows is by no means unusual in employing the strategy. Most graphical operating systems use virtual memory, some better than others. Win 95's use of virtual memory is superior to the old Windows' virtual memory arrangement.

According to Microsoft, the single best thing you can do to optimize your virtual memory settings is to ensure the swap file is on a drive that has lots of free disk space so that the swap file has room to expand if necessary. The more programs you run simultaneously and the more RAM you have, the larger your swap file will be. If your PC has only one hard disk, one of the biggest performance

Mom says, Clean up your hard disk for faster performance.

boosts you can give Win 95 is to make sure there's at least 100MB of free disk space on the drive. Realistically, your swap file probably isn't going to be that big most of the time. And since it's a temporary swap file (meaning it's created each time you start Windows 95 and deleted whenever you shut down or restart in MS-DOS mode), it uses only the disk space it really needs. Anyway, don't forget to use the machete on the encroaching jungle of unneeded data and program files now and then. Keep your disk safe for democracy (and virtual memory).

If you've got more than one hard disk in your PC, chances are you're missing out on a chance to give Windows a real shot in the arm. If your swap file is on the same drive that Windows and all your main applications are on, it's best to move the swap file to the other drive, so both disks can work at the same time. That makes things load and execute more swiftly. Here's how to make the switch. And, by the way, this is the one time when you *should* make adjustments on the Virtual Memory screen.

Click the button beside "Let me specify my own virtual memory settings." Then click the drop-down button to the right of the "Hard disk" field. You should see your second drive listed in the drop-down with a number in megabytes indicating how much free space is available on that drive. If the amount of free space on the second drive is both less than 100MB and less than the amount of free space on your C: drive, leave things as they are (or else clear away some space on the second drive). Otherwise, choose your second drive. Don't mess with the Minimum and Maximum settings. Click OK and let Windows restart. When Win 95 comes back up, check the Virtual Memory settings again. You should find that the "Let Windows manage my virtual memory settings" button was automatically reselected. If not, select it now and click OK.

This isn't reverse psychology.   Warning, warning, Will Robinson. Do not click the "Disable virtual memory" check box. Doing this will completely disable many computers or seriously degrade Win 95's performance on others. This setting is there only as a troubleshooting tool to correct a corrupted swap file. And that's an exceedingly rare problem under Windows 95 (unlike Windows 3.*x*). I hope you weren't one of those kids who immediately stuck their fingers to the stove burner when Mom said, "Don't do that, it'll *really* hurt."

Beat Slow-Poke Printing

HP LJ 4   Let's face it, printing has never been quite right under Windows. And Win 95 doesn't exactly ring in a new age of printer performance. Things are better, but there's still a ways to go in this department. What's needed is a brand new multi-threaded print engine with true background operation. What we got instead is some 32-bit stuff and an improved spooling file format, called *Enhanced Metafile*, or EMF for short. This deal works with all non-PostScript printers, and it does make printing go a bit faster. (*Note:* PostScript printers use the "RAW" spool file format, which is configured automatically when the driver is installed. RAW was the format used by Win 3.*x* for all spooling.) What EMF doesn't do is give you more reliable background operation. So, you'll still be stuck waiting for dialogs and windows to open and staring at the wait cursor until the print job finishes spooling.

There's no magic wand I'm going to wave over this situation. But you should definitely take a moment to make sure your spool settings are correctly configured. *Spooling* is the process of rasterizing a print job to a file in a format that can then be sent to the printer. When you send a print job to the printer, the fastest thing for the computer to do is create this spooled version of the job. Once it's done that, it can devote more cycles back to you and other things you're doing. It still has to manage interactions with the printer as hardware while the print job is running, but by spooling, you dispose of the dirty work upfront. What EMF does is make the spooling process run faster.

Unless you're truly in a hurry for most of your print jobs, the best settings configuration isn't the default one with most drivers. You definitely want spooling turned on, and you want the printer to start printing after the *last* page is spooled. The advantage to this is that you get back to the other stuff you're doing on your PC faster. The trade-offs are that it takes longer to complete the print job overall and it temporarily uses more space on your hard drive.

To open the Spool Settings screen, open the Printers folder in My Computer. Right-click your default printer and choose Properties from the context menu. Click the Details tab. The Spool Settings button is toward the bottom; clicking it delivers the box shown in Figure 9.18. Make sure the field beside the "Spool data format" line reads "EMF," unless yours is a PostScript printer. Then click the "Start printing after last page is spooled" button. That's about all you can do to ensure peak performance. *Note:* Some applications may have trouble printing to the EMF spool format. If you have trouble printing with a specific app, try switching the "Spool data format" line to "RAW."

Are you printing to a non-PostScript printer on a network print server? Unless that print server is running Windows 95, it's possible that you could regain control faster after initiating a print job by switching to the RAW spool data format. Because the EMF format requires Windows 95 to process it, that work will have to be carried out on your PC. The other alternative is to ask your network administrator to install Windows 95 on the print server. Theoretically, doing that should boost performance at both ends.

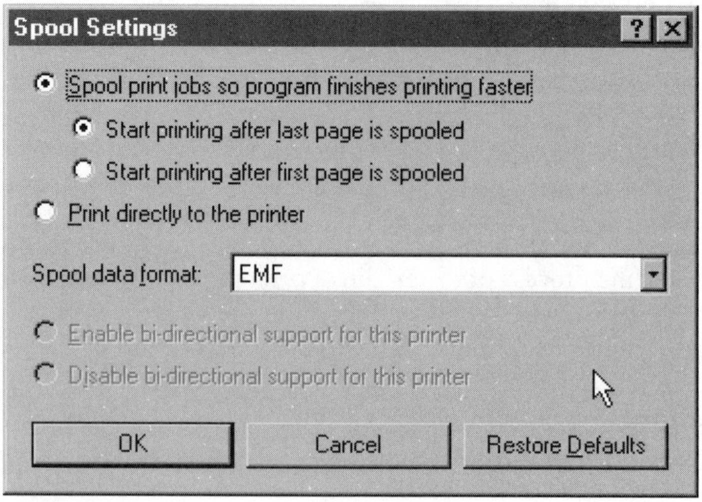

Spool Settings

○ Spool print jobs so program finishes printing faster
  ● Start printing after last page is spooled
  ○ Start printing after first page is spooled
○ Print directly to the printer

Spool data format: [EMF ▼]

○ Enable bi-directional support for this printer
○ Disable bi-directional support for this printer

[OK]   [Cancel]   [Restore Defaults]

Figure 9.18   The only way to go in setting up your printer's spooling

Memory and MS-DOS Mode Tricks

Command.com

DOS is dead, long live DOS. Yuck. One of the things that's confusing about Windows 95 to long-time Windows users is the more integrated nature of DOS and Windows 95. You've probably heard this somewhere. Heck, I've probably written it somewhere in this book: You don't need CONFIG.SYS and AUTOEXEC.BAT files at all to run Windows 95—unless your hardware requires a real-mode driver to work properly under Win 95. So, how come you don't need a memory manager? Win 95 loads its own. That's what's going on behind that shimmering blue-sky screen on startup.

Boost system resources, DOS functionality, and available memory.

Here's the catch: DOS needs these things to be working if you want to take advantage of stuff like extended or expanded memory and the like when you choose Restart in MS-DOS Mode from the Shut Down menu. For that kind of thing, it's truly a lot easier said than done to dump CONFIG.SYS and AUTOEXEC.BAT. Microsoft in its infinite wisdom gave us the DOSSTART.BAT file to load AUTOEXEC.BAT files when we choose the Restart to MS-DOS mode option on the Shut Down menu, but there's no equally convenient way to load CONFIG.SYS device drivers. Moreover, you're not really "restarting" to MS-DOS mode, you're exiting Windows to it. How to fix this? The wand tip that follows explains Method 1, the heavy duty approach. Methods 2 and 3 are detailed a bit further down.

> *Method 1.* **There's a nifty way to restart in MS-DOS mode with full** CONFIG.SYS **and** AUTOEXEC.BAT **support. The real beauty of this is that when you're running Windows 95, you're not running** HIMEM.SYS, CONFIG.SYS, **or anything else from DOS, so you're saving system resources.**

Open your CONFIG.SYS **and** AUTOEXEC.BAT **files with a text editor. Save them with the** .W95 **extension to create backups. Then reopen the originals. Find the** COMMAND.COM **file in your root directory, right-click it, and choose Properties. Click the Program tab. Then click the Advanced button to reveal the screen shown in Figure 9.19. Now check "MS-DOS mode." Copy and paste your** CON-FIG.SYS **file's contents into the "CONFIG.SYS for MS-DOS mode" window. Copy your** AUTOEXEC.BAT **file into the "AUTOEXEC.BAT for MS-DOS mode" window. Click OK and close down the** COMMAND.COM **Properties screen.**

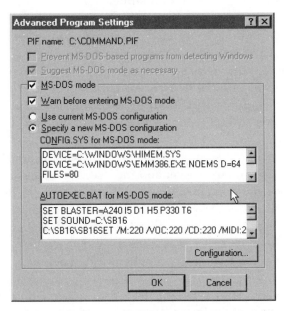

Figure 9.19 Give MS-DOS mode full device support and save system resources

Close and delete your CONFIG.SYS **file. In your** AUTOEXEC.BAT **file, delete all the lines except the ones loading stuff like** Prompt=PG, **your Path statement, and any other environment variables you might want available from a DOS window in Windows 95. Then save and close your new leaner, meaner** AUTOEXEC.BAT. **Check and note your free system resources on System's Performance tab. Restart Windows and make sure everything's working (CD, soundcard, and so on—you may need to move some additional lines from** DOSSTART.BAT **to the** AUTOEXEC.BAT **portion of** COMMAND.COM**'s Properties.) Then check the Performance tab again. You should see a noticeable increase in the percentage of free system resources.**

The last step is to understand your new way to access MS-DOS mode. Instead of choosing it from the Shut Down menu, from now on you get to it by double-clicking the COMMAND.COM **file in your root directory. The restart to MS-DOS process will act very similarly to what it's like when you choose it from the Shut Down menu. It's even error trapped to keep you from launching it**

accidentally. The one difference is that it forces a full restart of your computer. To make the whole thing more convenient, make a Shortcut to COMMAND.COM **and put it where you want it. By the way, another tip: You can restart Windows 95 from the MS-DOS mode command line by typing** exit **and pressing Enter.**

Method 2.   If you have devices that require real-mode drivers or if you're leery of monkeying around with the method given in the previous wand tip, there's a half step. Many items, like CD-ROM drives, sound cards, and other devices, load device drivers in CONFIG.SYS and then launch TSRs or other driver layers in AUTOEXEC.BAT. To save some conventional memory while you're in Windows 95 and yet still have full device support when you choose Restart to MS-DOS mode on the Shut Down menu, follow these steps. Leave CONFIG.SYS alone. But move all the lines except the environment variables you'd like supporting DOS windows in Windows 95 into the DOSSTART.BAT file, which you'll find in the Windows folder. This requires some fiddling, too; you'll need to make sure that devices like sound cards are still working properly. But it's a great half step.

Method 3.   If all of the above sounds kinda hairy, just do this. Windows 95 probably REMed out your DOS mouse driver and the MSCDEX.EXE CD-ROM driver in AUTOEXEC.BAT, since you don't need them in Windows 95. You don't need them in a DOS window either, since Window's drivers are in vogue in DOS windows. But you might need them when you choose Restart to MS-DOS mode from Shut Down. Just copy those two lines (*sans* REM statements) to the DOSSTART.BAT file. This won't save any system resources, but what the hey, at least things work.

After all this guff about MS-DOS mode, let me leave you with a last little tip about memory. If you want the best performance and the most available memory for DOS apps, do something that might be counterintuitive: Strip CONFIG.SYS **and** AUTOEXEC.BAT **as bare as you can following the steps in the previous wand tip. Then run your DOS apps from a maximized DOS window, if they'll let you. Why? Because Win 95's 32-bit disk access, protected-mode drivers, and other fast stuff are still in effect in a DOS window. What's more, with everything stripped out of** CONFIG.SYS **and** AUTOEXEC.BAT**, you'll have more free conventional memory for messing with those programs.**

Finally, if you want to get a better sense of system resources, you need more than the basic statement you'll find on the top of the Performance tab. The Resource Meter (Start/Programs/Accessories/System Tools, if you installed it) shows System, User, and GDI resources at a glance and, when launched, affixes itself to Taskbar for one-click peeks. There's not a lot to this gadget, shown in Figure 9.20, and frankly, it's not really worth placing in your Startup folder. If you want to get serious about system resource monitoring, get Symantec's Norton Utilities for Windows 95.

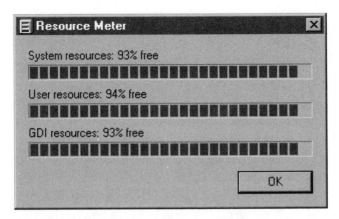

Figure 9.20 Win 95's rudimentary but better than nothing resource meter

SHOOT TROUBLE IN THE FOOT

To err is human, but to really foul things up requires a computer.

Anonymous
Quoted in "Quote Unquote," February 22, 1982, BBC Radio

This is a story about troubleshooting tools—the very cute and pretty, and the very ugly and powerful. The pretty part is System Monitor. The ugly part is the Troubleshooting tab on the File Systems Properties screen that you'll find on the Performance tab of the System control panel. (Man, what a mouthful. Think they buried this thing deep enough?)

System Monitor

I've already said that I prefer Norton Utilities for Win 95's system resource monitoring tools, and I'll stick by that statement. But you should know that System Monitor is pretty useful as a troubleshooting tool in the hands of someone who understands how PCs work. That last part's the trick. You can make lots of pretty pictures with this thing (see Figure 9.21), and it tracks some useful statistics, but when you get right down to it, it doesn't really help interpret the data you gather. Still, there might come a day when it'll be very useful indeed. It's the kind of thing you should probably install. If you don't, you'll probably need it.

Anyway, to make any real use of this thing, you have to use it over time. You use Edit/Add Item to add any of the more than 45 types of system actions (several of which are network-oriented) that System Monitor tracks. Here are some pointers for tracking various types of performance problems.

If you suspect an application might not be freeing memory when it stops using it, keep a watch on "Kernel: Threads" over time. You're watching for whether an app creates threads and doesn't reclaim them. Windows 95 automatically removes threads when the program closes, but if you identify a memory leak

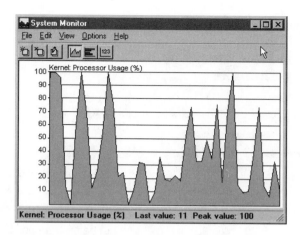

Figure 9.21 That third peak from the right was MS Word 7.0 crashing on launch

while the application is running, it's probably a good idea to exit and relaunch it periodically.

It might be time to add some RAM if the values for "Memory Manager: Discards" and "Memory Manager: Page-outs" show a lot of activity.

To check for problems with a slow-performing PC, check the values reported by "Kernel: Processor Usage," "Memory Manager: Page Faults," and "Memory Manager: Locked Memory." If the Processor Usage values are high even when the user is not working, check for applications that might be working that you weren't aware of. Do this by opening the Close Program box (Ctrl-Alt-Delete). If the values for Page Faults are high, it might mean that running apps need more memory than you've got. And if the Locked Memory statistics continually show a large portion of the Allocated Memory value, then inadequate free memory might be affecting performance. Or you might be using a program that locks memory unnecessarily.

File System Troubleshooting

LFN Backup is probably the only reason to mess with File System troubleshooting.

"It is recommended that only advanced users and system administrators change these settings." That's what is says at the top of the Troubleshooting tab on the File System Properties screen. There isn't a help button in sight. And you know what, unless you're directed by a technical document or a technical support person to adjust something on this screen (see Figure 9.22), don't mess!

Permit me a small digression. Back there in Chapter 4, "Files, Folders, Exploring," I mentioned a little utility called LFNBK.EXE, which stands for Long File Name Backup. This doohickey creates a simple database of all your long filenames and their locations, correlated with their underlying 11-character DOS

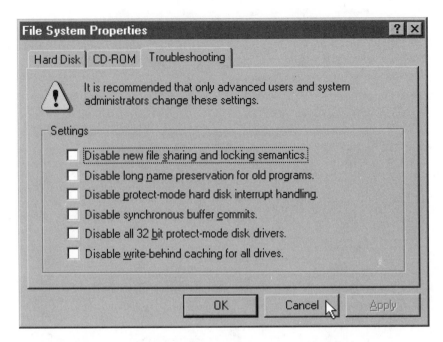

Figure 9.22 Nothing checked off here. And trust me: Keep it that way

filenames. It's a useful tool, especially if you have to move or rename your Win95 folder for some reason, since that can blow away your long filenames. Well, I've tested LFN Backup in that fashion, and it did pretty darn well. I bring it up because to use that utility, you have to place a check mark beside "Disable long name preservation for old programs." After you restore your long filenames, you have to remember to come back and clear the check box. It's the only time I've ever needed anything on this dialog on any of the dozens of PCs on which I've used Windows 95.

In fact, barring serious problems with your PC—especially if it's an older model—or running LFN Backup, I don't think you're going to see this screen much. So wave bye-bye. If you're a serious glutton for punishment, you can find explanations of these settings on the "Using File-System Troubleshooting Options" page of the System Resource Kit's Help file.

Last but not least, don't forget ScanDisk. This little disk-error diagnostic and repair tool is really quite useful. As with System Monitor, you'll find it in Start/Programs/Accessories/System Tools. Run it once a week. This thing can repair long-filename troubles, whereas its DOS counterpart cannot. And tiny disk errors—probably having to do with long filenames—seem to crop up more frequently under Windows 95 than previous Microsoft OS stuff.

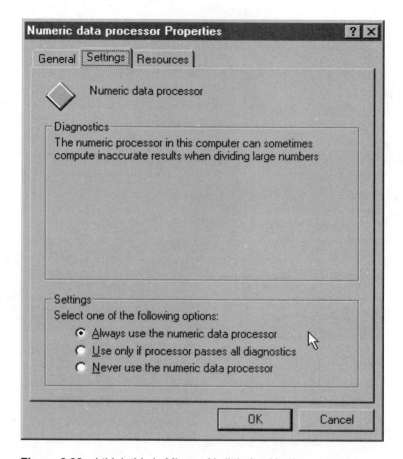

Figure 9.23   I think this is Microsoft's little Intel barb

Pentium owners: I'll leave you with this tip about a little troubleshooting tool you'll find on the Device Manager tab of the System Control Panel that looks like Figure 9.23. It tells you point-blank whether you've got the flawed Pentium chip with the numeric coprocessor bug. Click the plus sign beside the System Devices line on Device Manager. Then double-click the "Numeric data processor" entry. If you've got the bad chip, you'll see a message at the top of the Settings tab that reads "The numeric processor in this computer can sometimes compute inaccurate results when dividing large numbers." You have choices on the bottom of the screen, but unless you're doing mission-critical mathematics, leave it where you found it: "Always use the numeric data processor." If you need to turn it off with one of the other settings, contact Intel for a replacement chip and choose the second option: "Use only if processor passes all diagnostics." With that setting, it'll turn back on automatically after you install your upgrade Pentium chip.

*   *   *

That's it, folks. This concludes the regularly scheduled part of our program. It's on to the Appendix if you want more inside dope about Microsoft's current year-dated OS. What do they think—that it's like a car model or something? I don't know about you, but I don't tend to read appendices on the train, so I'll sign off here (and besides, I already wrote the Appendix).

I hope y'all will come back for the next edition, which will be on Windows 96 or whatever Microsoft decides to call the next one. Keep it in gear.

Appendix

Cheat Sheets

The only way to win is to fight on the side of your adversaries.

Francis Picabia
Who Knows: Poems and Aphorisms, 1950

It's come to this, huh? Broke down, did you? What kind of Windows geek resorts to learning all the true secrets by reading them from cheat sheets? Ah hah! My kind of reader. That's why I wrote this shindig. I mean, why plow through 400-some-odd pages of stuff when you can just turn back here and get maybe a third of the good stuff in under 20 pages? No pesky pictures. No cute margin notes. In short, no frills. Well, maybe I exaggerate a little. I mean, if this is all you read, you'll miss out on all those wand tips. And there are a lot of 'em, let me tell you. But, hey, it's your time. Without further preamble, let's have at it.

CHEATS FOR CD SETUP

My two recommended Setup tracks start with the Custom Setup option for all desktop PCs and the Portable track for notebooks. They're also based on opting for the Microsoft Network and Microsoft Fax options on the Get Connected screen.

Windows 95 CD Setup Options Guide

	Win 95's Standard Setup Options				Scot's Setup	
	Typical	Portable	Compact	Custom	Custom	Portable
Get Connected						
Microsoft Network	No	No	No	No	**Yes**	**Yes**
Microsoft Mail	No	No	No	No	No	No
Microsoft Fax	No	No	No	No	**Yes**	**Yes**
Accessibility						
Accessibility Options	Yes	Yes	No	Yes	**Optional**	**Optional**
Accessories						
Briefcase	No	Yes	No	No	**Yes**	Yes
Calculator	Yes	No	No	Yes	Yes	**Yes**
Character Map	No	No	No	No	No	No

	Win 95's Standard Setup Options				Scot's Setup	
	Typical	Portable	Compact	Custom	Custom	Portable
Desktop Wallpaper	No	No	No	No	No	No
Document Templates	Yes	No	No	Yes	Yes	**Yes**
Games	No	No	No	No	**Yes**	No
FreeCell	—	—	—	—	**Yes**	—
Hearts	—	—	—	—	**Yes**	—
Minesweeper	—	—	—	—	**Yes**	—
Solitaire	—	—	—	—	**Yes**	—
Mouse Pointers	No	No	No	No	**Yes**	No
NetWatcher	No	No	No	No	No	No
Online User's Guide	No	No	No	No	No	No
Paint	Yes	No	No	Yes	Yes	**Yes**
Quick View	No	No	No	No	**Yes**	**Yes**
Screen Savers	Yes	No	No	Yes	Yes	**Yes**
Flying Windows	Yes	—	—	Yes	**No**	**No**
Add'l Screen Savers	No	—	—	No	**Yes**	**Yes**
Resource Meter	No	No	No	No	**Yes**	**Yes**
System Monitor	No	No	No	No	**Yes**	No
Windows 95 Tour	No	No	No	No	No	No
WordPad	Yes	No	No	Yes	Yes	Yes
Communications						
Dial-Up Networking	No	Yes	No	No	**Yes**	Yes
Direct Cable Connect	No	Yes	No	No	**Yes**	Yes
Hyper Terminal	Yes	Yes	No	Yes	Yes	Yes
Phone Dialer	Yes	Yes	No	Yes	Yes	Yes
Disk Tools						
Backup	No	No	No	No	No	No
Disk Defragmenter	Yes	Yes	Yes	Yes	Yes	Yes
Disk Compression	Yes	Yes	Yes	Yes	Yes	Yes
Microsoft Exchange						
Microsoft Exchange	No	No	No	No	Yes	Yes
Microsoft Mail	No	No	No	No	No	No
Microsoft Fax						
Microsoft Fax	No	No	No	No	Yes	Yes
Microsoft Fax Viewer	No	No	No	No	Yes	Yes

Windows 95 CD Setup Options Guide (continued)

	Win 95's Standard Setup Options				Scot's Setup	
	Typical	**Portable**	**Compact**	**Custom**	**Custom**	**Portable**
Multimedia						
Audio Compression	Yes	Yes	No	Yes	Yes	Yes
CD Player	Yes	Yes	No	Yes	Yes	**No**
Jungle Scheme	No	No	No	No	**Yes**	No
Media Player	Yes	Yes	No	Yes	Yes	Yes
Musica Scheme	No	No	No	No	No	No
Robotz Scheme	No	No	No	No	No	No
Sample Sounds	No	No	No	No	No	No
Sound Recorder	Yes	Yes	No	Yes	Yes	Yes
Utopia Scheme	No	No	No	No	No	No
Video Compression	Yes	Yes	No	Yes	Yes	Yes
Volume Control	Yes	Yes	No	Yes	Yes	Yes
Microsoft Network						
Microsoft Network	No	No	No	No	Yes	Yes

Note: Boldfaced entries in Scot's Setup columns indicate settings you must enter specifically. The nonboldfaced entries in Scot's Setup that differ from the standard Setup options occur automatically as a result of the choices made under Get Connected. Scot's Setup tracks use more disk space than Windows' standard setups, but they're worth it.

DOS FILES DELETED BY SETUP

This part lists DOS and other files that are deleted by Win 95's Setup. Be aware, though, that these files are deleted from your old DOS directory only if you install Windows 95 into your existing Windows 3.*x* directory. If you install Windows 95 to its own directory, your old DOS files are all preserved so that you can optionally boot using the old DOS. Setup installs new DOS 7 files into the Command folder inside your Windows folder.

DOS Files Deleted by Setup

ANSI.SYS	ATTRIB.EXE	CHKDSK.EXE	CHOICE.EXE
COUNTRY.SYS	DBLSPACE.BIN	DBLSPACE.EXE	DBLSPACE.SYS
DEBUG.EXE	DEFRAG.EXE	DELTREE.EXE	DISKCOPY.EXE
DISPLAY.SYS	DOSKEY.COM	DRVSPACE.BIN	DRVSPACE.EXE
DRVSPACE.SYS	EDIT.COM	EDIT.HLP	EGA.CPI
EMM386.EXE	FC.EXE	FDISK.EXE	FIND.EXE
FORMAT.COM	HELP.COM	HELP.HLP	KEYB.COM
KEYBOARD.SYS	LABEL.EXE	MEM.EXE	MODE.EXE
MORE.COM	MOVE.COM	MSCDEX.EXE	MSD.EXE
NETWORKS.TXT	NLSFUNC.EXE	OS2.TXT	RAMDRIVE.SYS
README.TXT	SCANDISK.EXE	SCANDISK.INI	SETVER.EXE
SHARE.EXE	SMARTDRV.EXE	SORT.EXE	START.EXE
SUBST.EXE	SYS.COM	XCOPY.EXE	

WINDOWS 95 READMES

Readme Files Found in the Windows Folder

File	What's in It
README.TXT	Contains a wholly different summary of readmes and basic information. Meant to be read before installing.
CONFIG.TXT	Release notes on CONFIG.SYS command entries.
DISPLAY.TXT	Help for problems with monitors and display adapters, including details for specific models.
EXCHANGE.TXT	Release notes for the Exchange Mail module, including installation, compatibility, and troubleshooting tips.
EXTRA.TXT	How to access online services and the Internet to download stuff like Microsoft's free PowerToys Win 95 add-ons.
FAQ.TXT	Extremely useful information about setup, uninstalling, and other techie stuff. FAQ stands for "Frequently Asked Questions." This is among the best two readmes.
GENERAL.TXT	A listing of known problems with hardware and software.
HARDWARE.TXT	More hardware problems and solutions.
INTERNET.TXT	Basic sales pitch for using the Microsoft Network to access the Internet.
MOUSE.TXT	All about the little furry things and how to make 'em work.
MSDOSDRV.TXT	Release notes on .SYS drivers for CONFIG.SYS.

(continued)

Readme Files Found in the Windows Folder (continued)

File	What's in It
MSN.TXT	Very basic solutions for problems accessing the Microsoft Network online service.
NETWORK.TXT	Useful introduction to making Windows 95 work in a variety of network scenarios.
PRINTERS.TXT	Network printing, TrueType fonts, and tips for a variety of specific printer models.
PROGRAMS.TXT	Basic list of DOS and Windows 3.*x* programs that have problems and what to do about them.
SUPPORT.TXT	Includes the tech support number, as well as where to get support online, via other media and internationally.
TIPS.TXT	Along with FAQ.TXT, this list of tips—some of which are higher-order—is the very best readme of the lot.
WINNEWS.TXT	How to get Winnews online. Winnews is Microsoft's newsletter about Windows 95. It contains lots of useful information.

MOUSE AND KEYBOARD SHORTCUTS

This part contains the basic mouse and keyboard shortcuts circulated by Microsoft. Check it out. Most of these tips were explained somewhere back there in the main part of this book, but it's kinda nice to be able to see them all in one place.

Basic Efficiency Tips

To Do This...	Do This...
Copy a file	Press Ctrl while you drag the file to a folder or right-click-drag it.
Create a Shortcut icon	Press Ctrl+Shift while you drag the file to the desktop or a folder or right-click-drag it.
Close the current folder and all its parent folders	Press Shift and click the Close button (X) on the folder.
Tab through pages in a properties dialog	Press Ctrl+Tab or Ctrl+Shift+Tab.
Switch between opening a new window and closing an existing window	Press Ctrl and double-click a folder. If you have more than one window open, this operation closes the active window. If you have only one window open, this operation opens a new window.
Bypass AutoRun when inserting a CD	Press Shift while inserting the CD.

Shortcuts for a Selected Object

Shortcut	Action
F2	Rename.
F3	Find.
Ctrl+X	Cut.
Ctrl+C	Copy.
Ctrl+V	Paste.
Delete key	Delete.
Shift+Delete	Delete file immediately without putting it in Recycle Bin.
Alt+Enter	Display properties.
Alt+double-click	Display properties.
Ctrl+click the right mouse button	Place alternative commands on the context menu (Open With).
Shift+double-click	Explore an object. If the object does not have an Explore command, this starts the default action (usually the Open command).

Shortcuts for Managing Folders and Windows Explorer

Shortcut	Action
F4	In Windows Explorer, display the combo box and move the input focus to the list.
F5	Refresh display.
F6	In Windows Explorer, move the focus between panes.
Ctrl+G	In Windows Explorer, choose the Go To command.
Ctrl+Z	Undo.
Ctrl+A	Select All.
Backspace	Go to the parent folder.

Shortcuts in the Windows Explorer Tree

Shortcut	Action
* on numeric keypad	Expand everything under the selection.
+ on numeric keypad	Expand the selection.
− on numeric keypad	Collapse the selection.
Right arrow	Expand the current selection if it is not expanded; otherwise, go to the first child.
Left arrow	Collapse current selection if it is expanded; otherwise, go to the parent.
Ctrl+arrow key	Scroll without moving the selection.

Shortcuts in Open and Save Dialogs

Shortcut	Action
F4	Display the Look In list.
F5	Refresh the view.
Backspace	Go to the parent folder if the focus is on the View window.

General Keyboard-only Commands

Shortcut	Action
F1	Start Help.
F10	Go to menu mode.
Shift+F10	Display context menu for selected item.
Ctrl+Esc	Display Start Menu and move the focus to Taskbar.
Ctrl+Esc, Esc	Move the focus on Taskbar so that you can use Tab and then Shift+F10 for context menu, or use Tab and arrow key to change tasks, or use Tab to go to the desktop.
Alt+Tab	Switch to the next running application.
Alt+M	When the focus is on Taskbar or the desktop, minimize all windows and move the focus to the desktop.
Alt+S	When no windows are open and no items are selected on the desktop, display the Start Menu. Then use arrow keys to select menu commands.

Microsoft Natural Keyboard Commands for Win 95

Shortcut	Action
Win+R	Display Run dialog.
Win+M	Minimize all.
Shift+Win+M	Undo Minimize all.
Win+F1	Start Help.
Win+E	Start Windows Explorer.
Win+F	Find files or folders.
Ctrl+Win+F	Find computer.
Win+Tab	Cycle through Taskbar buttons.
Win+Break	Hot key to display System Properties dialog.

EXPLORER COMMAND-LINE SWITCHES

You can use the command-line switches for Windows Explorer in the Target field of Shortcut links or in batch files. You'll find the Target field on the object's Properties/Shortcut tab. These are the available documented parameters. Check Chapter 6, "The Mobile Win 95," for an undocumented parameter.

Syntax: **explorer [/n] [/e][,/root,*object*][[,/select],*subobject*]**

Explorer Switch Parameters

/n	Open a new window even if the specified folder is already open.
/e	Use Windows Explorer view. The default is Open view.
/root,	Specify the desktop as the object that will be used as the root of this single-window folder window.
/e,root,	Specify the desktop as the object that will be used as the root of this Explorer window.
/root,*object*	Microsoftese: "Specify the object in the normal namespace that will be used as the root of this Windows Explorer Folder. The default is to just use the normal namespace root (the desktop)." The syntax for stating an "object" name is hazy.
,*subobject*	Specify the folder to receive the initial focus unless /select is used. The default is the root.
,/select	Specify that the parent folder is opened and the specified object is selected.

LOCATIONS OF KEY FOLDERS AND FILES

The following tables describe Win 95's basic folder structure and locations of its key files.

Primary Windows 95 Paths

File Type	Folder Location
Core Windows 95 files	Windows
Shortcuts to applications	Windows\Start Menu and C:\Program Files
DOS commands	Windows\Command
Help files	Windows\Help
Font files	Windows\Fonts
Setup and device installation files	Windows\Inf
PIF files	Windows\Pif
Drivers	Windows\System
VxDs	Windows\System

(continued)

Primary Windows 95 Paths (continued)	
File Type	**Folder Location**
I/O Subsystem	Windows\System\Iosubsys
Viewers	Windows\System\Viewers
VxDs added after installation	Windows\System\Vmm32

Locations of Key Windows 95 Files

Description	Filename	Location / Folder
Real-mode operating system and system detection	IO.SYS	Root directory of startup drive
Command-line processor	COMMAND.COM	Root directory of startup drive
Real-mode stub to start Windows 95	WIN.COM	Windows
Protected-mode Virtual Machine Manager (VMM)	VMM32.VXD	Windows\System
Registry	SYSTEM.DAT	Windows
Registry current backup	SYSTEM.DA0	Windows
Registry when first created by Setup	SYSTEM.NEW	Windows
User Registry	USER.DAT	Windows
User Registry first created by Setup	USER.NEW	Windows
Log of the Setup process	SETUPLOG.TXT	Root directory of startup drive

ABOUT THE REAL-MODE (DOS) OPERATING SYSTEM

Windows 95 uses a new system file, IO.SYS, which replaces the old DOS system files (IO.SYS and MSDOS.SYS). The new IO.SYS is a real-mode operating system file that contains information needed to start the computer. The drivers loaded by default in IO.SYS include these:

- HIMEM.SYS
- IFSHLP.SYS
- SETVER.EXE
- DBLSPACE.BIN or DRVSPACE.BIN (if found on the hard disk)

Most of the common functionality provided by the various CONFIG.SYS file entries are now provided by default in IO.SYS. The following table lists the common entries in CONFIG.SYS that are now incorporated into IO.SYS and shows the default values for Windows 95.

Default CONFIG.SYS Settings in Windows 95 IO.SYS

Setting and Default	Description
dos=high,umb	Specifies that DOS should be loaded in the high memory area (HMA). This is the default for Windows 95.
himem.sys	Enables access to the HMA. This line loads and runs the real-mode Memory Manager. HIMEM.SYS is loaded by default in Windows 95.
ifshlp.sys	Installable File System Helper, which loads device drivers. It allows the system to make file system calls. Until it is loaded, only the minimal file system from IO.SYS is used.
setver.exe	Optional TSR-type device. It is included for compatibility reasons. Some DOS-based applications require a specific version of DOS to be running. This file responds to applications that query for the version number and sets the version number required.
files=60	Specifies the number of file handle buffers to create. This is specifically for files opened using DOS calls and is not required by Windows 95. It is included for compatibility with older applications.
lastdrive=Z	Specifies the last drive letter available for assignment. It's not required for Windows 95 but is included for compatibility with older applications.
buffers=30	Specifies the number of file buffers to create. This is specifically for applications using IO.SYS calls and is not required by Windows 95.
stacks=9,256	Specifies the number and size of stack frames. This is not required for Windows 95 but is included for compatibility with older applications.
shell=command.com /p	Indicates what command process to use. The /p switch indicates that the command process is permanent and should not be unloaded. If the /p switch is not specified, the command process can be unloaded when quitting the operating system.
fcbs=4	Specifies the number of file control blocks that DOS can have open at the same time. Use a **fcbs=** line in CONFIG.SYS only if you have an older program that requires such a setting.

MSDOS.SYS Startup Values

To override default values in Windows 95 IO.SYS, place an entry in CONFIG.SYS with the value you want. Windows 95 Setup creates a hidden, read-only system file named MSDOS.SYS in the root of the computer's boot drive. This text file contains important paths used to locate other Windows files, including the Registry. You can edit this file by setting its attributes under Properties so that it is no longer a read-only hidden system file and then open it with a text editor. MSDOS.SYS also supports an [Options] section under which you can add settings that tailor the startup process. The following table describes each entry in MSDOS.SYS.

[Paths] Section Values

Entry	Description
HostWinBootDrv=c	Defines the location of the boot drive root directory.
WinBootDir=	Defines the location of the necessary startup files. The default is the directory specified during Setup; for example, C:\Windows.
WinDir=	Defines the location of the Windows 95 directory as specified during Setup.

[Options] Section Values

Entry	Description
BootDelay=n	Sets the initial startup delay to *n* seconds. The default is 2. **BootKeys=0** disables the delay. The only purpose of the delay is to give the user sufficient time to press F8 after the Starting Windows message appears.
BootFailSafe=0	Specifies whether to use Safe Mode for system startup. When the value is 0, this setting is disabled.
BootGUI=1	Enables automatic graphical startup. 0 disables this setting.
BootKeys=1	Enables the special startup option keys (that is, F5, F6, and F8). Setting this value to 0 prevents any startup keys from functioning.
BootMenu=0	Specifies whether the Startup Menu appears by default. Setting this value to 0 eliminates the need to press F8 to see the menu.
BootMenuDefault=#	Sets the default menu item on the Windows Startup Menu. The default is 1 if the system is running correctly and 3 if the system was previously stalled.
BootMenuDelay=#	Sets the number of seconds to display the Windows Startup Menu (before running the default). The default is 30.
BootMulti=0	Specifies dual boot capabilities. Setting this value to 1 enables the ability to start DOS by pressing F4. The option is disabled by default. It is not available when you press F8 to use the Start Menu unless the value is set to 1.
BootWarn=1	Enables the Safe Mode startup warning and menu.
BootWin=1	Specifies whether Windows 95 is the default operating system. Setting this value to 0 disables Windows 95 as the default for use with DOS 5 or 6.*x*.

(continued)

[Options] Section Values (continued)

Entry	Description
DblSpace=1	Specifies automatic loading of DBLSPACE.BIN.
DoubleBuffer=0	Specifies whether a SCSI controller needs a double-buffering driver loaded. Setting this value to 1 enables double-buffering.
DrvSpace=1	Specifies automatic loading of DRVSPACE.BIN.
LoadTop=1	Specifies whether to load COMMAND.COM or DRVSPACE.BIN at the top of 640K memory. Set this value to 0 if compatibility problems occur with any software that makes assumptions about what is used in specific memory areas.
Logo=1	Specifies whether the animated logo is displayed. Setting the value to 0 also avoids hooking a variety of interrupts that can create conflicts with third-party memory managers.
Network=0	Specifies whether Windows 95 network software components are to be installed. If set to 1, enables Safe Mode with Networking as a menu option.

INITIALIZATION FILES AND THE REGISTRY

Although the Registry replaces the basic function of the initialization files used in earlier versions of Windows, the SYSTEM.INI, WIN.INI, and WINFILE.INI files and others still appear in the Windows directory. They continue for compatibility with earlier Windows-based applications and device drivers. For example, entries in WIN.INI and SYSTEM.INI created by 16-bit Windows apps are not updated in System Registry because they don't know how to access the Registry.

If you install Windows 95 as an upgrade over Windows 3.1, some .INI file settings are copied into the Registry, including settings from CONTROL.INI, PROGMAN.INI, SYSTEM.INI, and WIN.INI. Other .INI file entries are not moved to the Registry, but remain in the .INI file for compatibility purposes. Most of these entries can be changed without editing the .INI files by using the graphical tools provided with Windows 95. However, some .INI entries cannot be set using the Windows 95 user interface.

WIN.INI Settings in the Registry

Windows 95 migrates settings from configuration files into the Registry during Setup. The following table shows where WIN.INI entries migrated to the Registry. For information about specific WIN.INI entries moved during Windows 95 installation, see Setup Technical Discussion in the Windows 95 Resource Kit Help file.

Registry Paths for Migrated WIN.INI Sections

WIN.INI Section	Subkey in Hkey_Current_User
[desktop]	\Control Panel\Desktop
[Windows]	\Control Panel\Desktop
[sounds]	\AppEvents\Schemes\Apps\event\current

The following tables list entries retained in WIN.INI for compatibility with applications written for earlier versions of Windows. These values can be set using Control Panel and other tools in the Windows 95 interface.

WIN.INI Entries Kept and Supported by the User Interface

[Windows]

CursorBlinkRate	Device	DoubleClickHeight	DoubleClickWidth
DoubleClickSpeed	KeyboardDelay	KeyboardSpeed	MouseSpeed
MouseTrails	SwapMouseButtons		

[Intl]

iCountry	iCurrDigits	iCurrency	iDate
iDigits	iLZero	iMeasure	iNegCurr
iTime	iTLZero	s1159	s2359
sCountry	sCurrency	sDecimal	sLanguage
sList	sLongDate	sShortDate	sThousand
sTime			

WIN.INI Entries Kept but Not Supported by the User Interface

[fonts]: *font-name*	**[ports]:** *portname*
[PrinterPorts]: *device*	**[embedding]:** *object*
[FontSubstitute]: *font-name=font-name*	**[Mail]:** *MAPI*
[mci extensions]: *extension*	**[Windows]:** *Load and Run*

SYSTEM.INI Settings in the Registry

The following table lists SYSTEM.INI entries that migrate to the Registry when Windows 95 is installed in the same directory as a previous Windows 3.*x* installation.

Registry Paths for Migrated SYSTEM.INI Entries

SYSTEM.INI Entry	Subkey in Hkey_Local_Machine
[386Enh]	
Network	System\CurrentControlSet\Services\VxD\Vnetsetup
Transport	Software\CurrentControlSet\Services\VxD\transport entry
[network]	
Comment	System\CurrentControlSet\Services\VxD\Vnetsetup
ComputerName	System\CurrentControlSet\Control\ComputerName
EnableSharing	System\CurrentControlSet\Services\VxD\Vnetsetup
LMAnnounce	System\CurrentControlSet\Services\VxD\Vnetsetup
LogonDomain	Network
LogonValidated	Network
MaintainServerList	System\CurrentControlSet\Services\VxD\Vnetsetup
Reshare	System\CurrentControlSet\Network\LanMan\sharename
Username	Network\Logon
WorkGroup	System\CurrentControlSet\Services\VxD\Vnetsetup

The following tables list entries that are retained in SYSTEM.INI for compatibility with applications written for earlier versions of Windows.

SYSTEM.INI Entries Kept and Supported by the User Interface

[386Enh]

AllEMSLocked	AllXMSLocked	AltKeyDelay
AltPasteDelay	DMABufferSize	Display
DOSPromptExitInstructions	Keyboard	KeyPasteCRSkipCount
KeyPasteKeyDelay	PasteSkipCount	KeyPasteTimeout
MaxDMAPGAddress	MaxPagingFileSize	MinUserDiskSpace
Mouse	Paging	PagingDrive
ScrollFrequency		

SYSTEM.INI Entries Kept and Supported by the User Interface (continued)

[boot]

DISPLAY.DRV	KEYBOARD.DRV	MOUSE.DRV
NETWORK.DRV	SOUND.DRV	

[NonWindowsApps]
CommandEnvSize

SYSTEM.INI Entries Kept but Not Supported by the User Interface

---

[386Enh]

Device=filename	KeybdPasswd	Local
Local Reboot	MessageBackColor	MessageTextColor
NetAsyncTimeout	NetAsynchFallback	NetDMASize

[boot]

386grabber=filename	comm.drv=filename	drivers=filename
fixedfon.fon=filename	fonts.fon=filename	language.dll=library-name
oemfonts.font=filename	shell=filename	system.drv=filename
taskman.exe=filename		

[drivers]
alias=driver-filename

[mci]
Entries written by applications

WINDOWS 95 RESOURCES ON THE WORLD-WIDE WEB[*]

If you're on the Internet, check out the huge store of Windows 95 reference material and doodads on the Web. There's everything from useful Win 95 utilities to step-by-step instructions for things like how to set up SLIP Internet access for Windows 95. The Web is an ever-changing place. So my apologies up-front if you find that some of these URLs have changed or that a few sites no longer exist. (*Note:* In some Web browsers, you must type http: // before the rest of the URL.)

Craig's Interactive Windows 95 Experience
www.vitinc.com:80/~cbonsig/win95/win95.html

Cutter's Windows 95 Crossroads
www.io.com/~kgk/win95.html

---

[*]Links list Copyright © Ziff-Davis Interactive.

Dylan's GUI Windows 95 Page!
cville-srv.wam.umd.edu/~dylan/windows95.html

Frank's Windows 95 Page
oeonline.com/~frankc/fjcw95.html

IAC-Win95/Canary Islands/Home Page (Win 95 En Español)
www.iac.es/galeria/ronald/wingrp.htm

MarkG's Win32 Programming Page
www.epix.net:80/~markga/

Microsoft's Windows 95 Home Page
www.microsoft.com/windows

Microsoft Windows Inquirer
www.haywire.com/inquirer

Microsoft WinNews Archive
biology.queensu.ca/~jonesp/win95/winnews/winnews.html

MIT Systems Win95 Home Page
web.mit.edu/afs/athena.mit.edu/astaff/reference/win95/

Net Ex Unofficial Windows 95 Software Archive
www.netex.net/w95/windows95

Net Ex Windows 95 Archive and Discussion Forums
www.netex.net:80/w95

The NUSSU Special Interest Group
www.alumni.nus.sg/nussu/sig/win95/

The One-Stop Windows 95 Site
www.win95.com/

OS/2 Warp vs Windows 95
www.austin.ibm.com/pspinfo/os2vschg.html

Process Software's Windows 95 Page
www.process.com/win95/

Randy's Windows 95 Resource Center!
www.cris.com/~randybrg/win95.html

Win95 Dial-Up Networking White Paper
www.wwa.com/~barry/wn95slip.html

Win95-L Windows 95 FAQ
www.primenet.com/~markd/win95faq.html

Windows 95 Annoyances Page
ocf.berkeley.edu/~daaron/win95ann.html

Windows 95 Info Page
www.pcix.com/win95/win95home.html

Windows 95 Internetworking Headquarters
www.windows95.com/

The Windows 95 Page!
biology.queensu.ca/~jonesp/

Windows 95 Question-Answer-Information Database
www.whidbey.net/~mdixon/win40001.htm

The Windows 95 TCP/IP Setup How-To/FAQ
www.aa.net/~pcd/slp95faq.html

Index

X